DISCOVERIES
THAT CHANGED
THE WORLD

To the memory of Selman A. Waksman
(1888–1973, Nobel Prize in Medicine 1952),
whose discovery saved countless thousands of lives,
including mine.

DISCOVERIES
THAT CHANGED
THE WORLD

by Rodney Castleden

Futura

A *Futura* Book

First published by Futura in 2008

Copyright © Omnipress 2008

ISBN: 978-0-7088-0485-8

Produced by Omnipress Limited, UK

Printed in the EU

Futura
An imprint of Little, Brown Book Group
100 Victoria Embankment
London EC4Y 0DY

Photo credits: Getty Images

CONTENTS

3 THE AGE OF ENLIGHTENMENT

4 THE NINETEENTH-CENTURY WORLD

5 THE MODERN WORLD

INTRODUCTION

The word 'discovery' conjures up two very different but equally vivid images in my mind. One is a sea captain on the quarterdeck of his wooden sailing ship, looking intently through a telescope at a new land that has just become dimly visible on the horizon. He might be Captain Cook, Ferdinand Magellan or Christopher Columbus. The other is a white-coated scientist peering equally intently down a microscope at a prepared slide. He might be Louis Pasteur, Pierre Curie or Alexander Fleming. These two images represent two very different kinds of discovery, one using a telescope and the other using a microscope. One involves reaching out into the exterior world and exploring it; the other involves reaching inwards into an interior world, into the resources of the human intellect, in order to design scientific experiments and draw reasoned conclusions from them. We might think of them as microcosmic discoveries and macrocosmic discoveries, and they are both equally important to us.

In antiquity, much that was said about the nature of the world was the result of religious belief – faith – or the result of hypothecation. The procedure was to set up a reasonable hypothesis, for example, 'Let us suppose, given what we can see and in the absence of any evidence to the contrary, that the Earth is flat.' This is a reasonable assumption, given the way we see the world immediately around us. For some reason that has never been understood, from very early on, the Greek philosophers had the idea that the Earth was a globe; later, when astronomers studied the movements of the planets, the idea that planets had circular orbits followed, in spite of the planets' apparently erratic and jerky wanderings. With the concept of circular planetary orbits came an idea of the solar system as a kind of set of transparent globes nested inside one another. Most people intuitively think of the universe as a whole as an infinitely large globe. Perhaps the oddest thing about our evolving awareness of the universe over the course of the last 2,000 years or more is that subsequent discoveries have confirmed that these deeply embedded intuitions are absolutely correct. They are correct even though some of them are counter-intuitive.

Discoveries often lead directly to inventions. Once someone discovered that liquids expand and contract when they get warmer and colder, it was a short step to exploiting that property to make a thermometer. In 1856, William Perkin discovered mauve, the first synthetic dye. The significance of this discovery was picked up in Germany, where a synthetic chemical industry was born. From then until World War I, Germany led the way in the development of thousands of chemical products derived from coal tar, such as dyes, photographic developers, drugs and explosives. The German labs showed how much it was possible to achieve by systematic and purposeful scientific experimentation, and other western countries followed suit. A great deal of industrial progress has depended on discoveries that were made as a result of scientific experiments in laboratories. Sometimes the process works in reverse and inventions lead to discoveries. As a result, there is a fine line between discoveries that changed the world and inventions that changed the world.

Discoveries have to be made by somebody. Sometimes it is very clear who the discoverer is. Insulin was discovered – and at a truly amazing speed – by Frederick Banting. But sometimes it can be surprisingly difficult to identify who the discoverer really was. The point has often been made that although Christopher Columbus is said to have discovered North America, there were people living there already, the native North Americans, and they must have discovered it first. As far as the European discoverers were concerned, they had found a New World whose wealth could be tapped and exploited; it was a completely positive experience. But for the native North Americans and South Americans being discovered by Europeans turned out to be catastrophic, a completely negative experience. But, looking at the situation more academically, what counts in terms of the orientation of this book is that knowledge of a part of the Earth has been added to an existing perception of the whole. It is possible to approach the discovery of Eurasia, for example, by two routes, western and eastern. The Europeans started off knowing their own homelands well, and gradually expanded their knowledge of lands further afield until the geography of China was fully understood. The Chinese similarly started off by knowing China well and gradually, haltingly, reached out to take in knowledge of the lands round the Indian Ocean.

The history of exploration and geographical discovery has nearly always been presented in western literature as the history of Europeans' growing awareness of the world outside Europe. Clearly, it would be possible to write a very different narrative from the perspective of non-Europeans. In this book, I shall attempt to go a little way towards restoring the balance.

Complete objectivity in writing history is impossible to achieve, however hard we may try. This comes home most vividly when we see dramatized re-creations of historical events. They may be equally committed to an honest and authentic portrayal of the past, yet convey very different impressions. The recent TV series *Rome* (2005–07) was much darker, bloodier and more brutal than the series *I, Claudius* (1976) made thirty years before. Similarly Helen Mirren's portrayal of Elizabeth I in 2005 was very different from Glenda Jackson's in 1971, though both actresses portrayed the queen with great integrity. There are many pasts, and which of those pasts we recognise and comprehend depends very much on who we are, where we are and what we are looking for.

Discoveries are made by looking outwards or inwards. Still others are made by looking both downwards into the Earth and backwards in time, such as the classic discoveries of archaeologists like Arthur Evans and Heinrich Schliemann. And the excitement of those discoveries has always been with us. There is a tendency to see archaeology as a modern science, beginning maybe with the unearthing of the Roman cities of Pompeii and Herculaneum, but people were excited by making contact with the past in this way long, long before. Vergil was writing about the excitement of archaeological discovery 2,000 years earlier, in *Georgics I*.

Surely a time will come when a farmer on these frontiers,
Forcing through earth his curved plough,
Shall find old spears eaten away with flaky rust,
Or hit upon helmets as he wields the weight of his mattock,
And marvel at the heroic bones he has disinterred.

There is in some instances a problem in identifying discoverers, as the discovery can be a long process that involves several people. Sometimes those people are collaborators, co-workers in a research team; sometimes they are rivals, competing with each other to be the first to break new ground; sometimes they are strangers to one another, researchers who are working in different universities, different countries or even different decades, but whose papers and books become links in a long chain of reasoning.

A classic example of a discovery that is difficult to attribute to a particular discoverer is the Kuiper Belt. From 1930 onwards there was speculation that a belt of asteroids or comets might exist in the outer solar system out beyond the planet Neptune. A number of astronomers contributed to the debate: Kuiper, Leonard, Edgeworth, Whipple, Fernandez, Duncan, Tremaine and Quinn, just to name some high-profile examples. The astronomers who actually saw and knowingly identified the first objects in the Kuiper Belt were Jewitt and Luu. Tombaugh discovered Pluto, which turns out to be a Kuiper Belt object, but he thought he had discovered a planet. The Kuiper Belt was named after Gerald Kuiper who, ironically, did not think that the belt existed! The nearest I can get to unravelling this particular tangle is to say that Leonard was the first to propose the existence of a belt of objects and Jewitt and Luu were the first to identify objects within it, in 1992, *knowing* what they were. Some astronomers have tried to be fairer towards the pioneers by naming the belt the Edgeworth-Kuiper Belt. It would be fairer to call it the Leonard-Edgeworth-Whipple-Fernandez-Duncan-Tremaine-Quinn-Jewitt-Luu Belt, which is obviously unmanageable and absurd, and it may be that astronomers will eventually settle on a neutral and impersonal name, such as Trans-Neptunian Belt. That would probably be fairer to all concerned.

Maybe the Kuiper Belt sounds rather obscure and we might expect its story also to be obscure and complicated. Maybe we will find it easier to pin down the very familiar and high-profile discoveries, such as evolution, the Ice Age, Troy, Knossos, psychoanalysis. But who discovered evolution – was it Alfred Russel Wallace or Charles Darwin? And who discovered the Ice Age – was it Jean de Charpentier, Ignaz Venetz, Friedrich Schimper or Louis Agassiz? Who discovered Troy – Robert Wood, Frank Calvert, Heinrich Schliemann or Wilhelm Dörpfeld? Who discovered Knossos – Arthur Evans or Minos Kalokairinos? Who discovered the technique of psychoanalysis – Sigmund Freud or Joseph Breuer?

The truth is that as John Donne wrote; 'No man is an Island, entire of it self; every man is a piece of the Continent, a part of the main; if a clod be washed away by the sea, Europe is the less.' Discoverers talk to other people, listen to other people, read books and research papers that are bursting at the seams with other people's ideas, and inevitably ideas and fragments of ideas end up being shared among a group. It is likely that several people will contribute to any discovery. The theories of relativity and continental drift are large-scale examples of discoveries that were really group efforts, the result of several great minds each contributing important elements to the one Big Idea.

Another link between inventions and discoveries is that it is often an invention that makes discovery possible. A classic and very simple example of this is the invention of the telescope in 1608, which made it possible for Galileo to peer at the night sky and discover the moons of Jupiter in 1610.

Some discoveries, like some inventions, fail to register – or their significance or potential fails to register. A major problem, worldwide, is the threat of flooding by rivers. There have been several serious floods in Britain over the last ten years, and the people whose homes and businesses have been damaged by flooding have demanded that the authorities do more to protect them. The response is for the authorities to undertake to put in more flood defences, yet a far more effective solution is known to exist. While undertaking fieldwork for my research degree back in the 1970s, I surveyed a 32-kilometres (20-mile) length of a floodplain in the English Midlands. I mapped all the landforms, however small, that might be guiding the movement of flood water. I then spent seven years mapping the movements of flood waters each time the river overtopped its banks.

What I discovered was that there is a regular and orderly pattern of movement in the flood water, directed by a suite of previously unrecognised micro-landforms. The pattern shifts dramatically as the flood gets higher and higher, but it repeats exactly in one flood after another. In other words, floods are entirely predictable and orderly events. I also discovered that a river systematically uses the whole length of its floodplain to store small quantities of flood water at a time, so that the river can flow on, just filling its channel. The water out on the floodplain is spread out in shallow sheets, and therefore moves very slowly down valley. It trickles back into the river channel a mile down valley, four days later, by which time the flood peak has swept right down to the sea.

The discovery was that in a state of nature, the River Nene was prone to small-scale flooding along the whole length of its floodplain, which started very close to the river's source. What had happened over the last 200 years was that farmers in the upper catchment area had informally embanked the river, dug drainage ditches across the water meadows of the floodplain and in effect prevented flooding to the west of Northampton. The result was that the river was made to carry higher volumes of water through Northampton and on downstream, making it far likelier to cause serious flooding. The discovery led to the recommendation that the river in the upper catchment area, or rather the three headstreams in that area, should once again be allowed to flood the upper floodplain. It would only be for short periods, to a shallow depth, and would not prevent the use of the land for grazing. I communicated these findings and my modest solution to the relevant authority, which showed absolutely no interest in taking any action. Years later, in the 1990s, people died in basement flats near the river in Northampton as a direct result – not of natural river flooding but of negligence, of a failure by the authorities to heed warning and take advice. Those and other deaths were plainly avoidable. Serious flooding by rivers in towns such as Tewkesbury, York and Lewes are similarly avoidable. And the same applies to flooding in the lower courses of much bigger rivers such as the Rhine and the Mississippi.

Other researchers have come to the same conclusion with regard to other rivers, and made similar recommendations. They too have been ignored. It is as if we have made an unwelcome discovery. This curious unwillingness on the part of authorities to listen to a new idea is a general problem, and it has been a general barrier to human progress. There is even a name for it – the Semmelweiss Reflex, which is named after a curious episode in the history of medicine in the mid-nineteenth century. When Ignaz Semmelweiss, a Hungarian doctor, discovered the cause of childbed fever in 1847, and the way to avoid it, the medical profession did not want to know about it. His idea was rejected without consideration and Semmelweiss was literally driven insane by rejection and frustration. That unthinking rejection is what is now known as the Semmelweiss Reflex.

But to the discoverer, a discovery is always an exciting event. That process of discovering something new and the elation that it produces is what drives discoverers on. It is what drives geographers, geologists and climatologists, physicists, astronomers and research chemists alike to work long hours, endure incredible hardship and in some cases risk their lives in the chase. And that excitement spreads to the rest of us, looking on. We admire the courage and the persistence of the discoverers, and revel in the new knowledge and the new insights they give us.

Discoveries are central to human progress, a crucial part of what it means to be a human being

I
EARLY
DISCOVERIES

ASIAN MIGRATION INTO NORTH AMERICA

(35,000 BC)

Many of us tend to think of North America as having been discovered by Europeans, whether in 1492 by Christopher Columbus or a few centuries earlier by Vikings who were tentatively venturing westwards from Greenland. When we start thinking about it more seriously we realise that there were people in North America already, the native North Americans. It must have been their ancestors who originally discovered the continent, wherever they came from.

Some scientists believe that the first people may have arrived in Canada from Asia as early as 50,000 BC, with successive migrations bringing more people in at later dates. A major migration from Asia took place following 12,000 BC, a time when the ice sheets covered huge tracts of Canada and sea levels were very low. But sea level was low during earlier glacial episodes too, and there is no reason why people should not have entered Canada from Asia at those earlier times of low sea level as well. The Bering Sea that separates Asia from Alaska is a wide area of shallow water north of the Aleutian Islands, and during glacial episodes it has frequently been exposed as an expanse of lowland, known as Beringia. It was used again and again as an entry point to North America for migrants wandering eastwards from Asia. There has been a great deal of controversy about the date of the immigration into North America, but the circumstantial evidence suggests that it happened repeatedly.

Geneticists are currently exploring the possibility that the ancestral population did not leave Siberia until 35,000 BC and stayed in Beringia long enough for a significant number of specific mutations to take place. It seems that the people who later emerged from Beringia into North

America were already recognisably distinct (in DNA terms) from the Asian stock that had entered Beringia from the west. The Asian people migrating into Beringia in 35,000 BC are thought to have remained there for as much as 15,000 years before moving east into Alaska. That length of stay would have been long enough for the people to become genetically different from their Asian forebears. This is known as the Beringian incubation model. A problem with it is that it presupposes that the sea level would have remained low for a very long time, and between 35,000 and 20,000 years ago there were two warm interludes when the sea would have risen and flooded Beringia.

Once Asiatic people had safely reached the higher ground of Alaska, the movement of people further eastwards and south-eastwards would have depended on warmer conditions. When the ice covering the Rockies and central Canada started to melt back, ice-free corridors opened up along the eastern flank of the Rockies and the British Columbian coast, enabling people to move south and east. That could have happened around 30,000 BC and again around 8,000 BC. It seems that the environmental changes making this possible happened very suddenly, creating many (if brief) opportunities for people to press on into the new lands.

But the latest DNA data suggests that once the inflow of immigrants from Alaska started there was a fairly swift and uniform colonisation of North and South America, all the way to the southern tip of South America, Tierra del Fuego. The earliest archaeological site at the southern end of South America dates from only 15,000 years ago.

Startlingly, parallel genetic studies of moose reinforce this model for the human migrations and showed that the moose were behaving in the same way as the people! The scientific analysis shows that North American moose entered North America relatively recently, by way of the Bering land bridge, and in one migration along one corridor rather than in several migrations along more than one corridor.

It also seems from the DNA record that there were also some movements of people back in the opposite direction, from North America back into Siberia.

After many generations, the overland human migrants reached and settled northern Brazil some time between 18,000 and 15,000 BC. In parallel with this major land migration there were migrations by sea. People were island-hopping across the Pacific and arriving on the west coasts of North and South America by that route too.

If the earliest human colonisation of North America was as recent as the research suggests, many questions are raised. Beringia, the land bridge connecting Siberia and North America, was exposed as dry land scores of times during the Ice Age – on every occasion when the climate was cold enough to produce a really low sea level. So, why did people living in Asia not cross to North America when any of the earlier opportunities presented themselves? It is possible that they did, but the evidence of their migration did not survive. One of the problems in high latitudes is that recent episodes of glaciation have destroyed much of the evidence of what happened earlier. Indeed, a background problem in any history of 'firsts' is that the further back in time we go the less evidence there is. All sorts of things happened in the past that we know nothing about.

THE REDISCOVERY OF BRITAIN

(35,000 BC)

The English Channel and southern North Sea are very shallow sea areas. Under the present warm conditions the sea level is high and they are flooded. But during the long cold stages of the Ice Age, when the sea level was low, the Channel and the North Sea were often exposed as dry land. At those times it was possible for Stone Age people from the European mainland and the roaming herds of animals they hunted to exploit these lowland areas and wander across into Britain.

For a long time it was thought that people arrived in Britain for the first at a very late date, but a couple of spectacular recent archaeological discoveries have changed that. One was the discovery of Boxgrove Man. The shin bone of this hominid (*Homo heidelbergensis*) was found at a water hole in a raised beach deposit near Chichester in 1993, and it conclusively proved that human hunters were living in West Sussex 500,000 years ago. Then research on a hominid settlement on the East Anglian coast, along with the re-analysis of bones found in the 1980s in a quarry at Westbury-sub-Mendip in Somerset, showed that people were living in southern Britain as much as 200,000 years earlier than that. There are so far no remains of Anglia Man or Westbury Man, but clear signs of their activities. At Westbury, for instance, there were bones belonging to rhinoceros, hyena, wolf, bison and cave bear – all displaying the distinctive straight cut marks that could only be made by butchery with sharp knives. There were also deliberately shaped flints that were man-made hand axes. The implication from this new research is that people migrated to Britain as much as 700,000 years ago.

Anglia Man, Westbury Man and Boxgrove Man were all rather primitive creatures, ancestors of Neanderthal Man. Modern people, it seems, did not arrive in Britain until much later, in 35,000 BC. When the most severe cold conditions of the last glacial episode set in, around 16,000 BC, almost all of Britain was covered by ice. These hostile conditions would have been accompanied by a marked lowering of sea level that would have drained dry the whole of the English Channel to make a broad level plain – an escape route. The cooling and the ice cover would have forced people to migrate further and further south through Britain, and back across the floor of the English Channel. Probably for about three millennia, starting in 16,000 BC, Britain was virtually emptied of people. Then, when the great global warming episode of 8000 BC happened, back they came again.

We should see this cyclical coming and going of people as repeating over and over again through the last half million years. We now know, thanks to the discovery of Boxgrove Man, that there were people living in Britain in a warm phase as early as 500,000 BC. We know from indirect evidence of Westbury and Anglia Man that there were people in Britain 200,000 years before that. Britain was probably repeatedly rediscovered and recolonised in antiquity.

Phoenician and Carthaginian traders came to Britain to get tin at least as early as the fifth century BC, so they will have taken a knowledge of the geography of the West Country back to the Mediterranean. By the first century BC, Mediterranean geographers and politicians were still very much focused on the Mediterranean, though they were aware of a world beyond. Diodorus Siculus, writing in the first century BC, said: 'Opposite that part of Gaul (France) which lies on the ocean there are many islands out in the ocean of which the largest is that known as Britain. In ancient times this island remained unvisited by foreign armies. In our day, however, Gaius Caesar was the first man of whom we have record to have conquered the island . . . Britain is triangular in shape, very much as is Sicily, but its sides are not equal. This island stretches obliquely along the coast of Europe and the point where it is least distant from the mainland, we are told, is the promontory which men call Cantium (Kent), and this is about one hundred stades from the land, whereas the second promontory, known as Belerium (Land's

End), is said to be a voyage of four days from the mainland and the last, writers tell us extends out into the open sea and is named Orca (Duncansby Head, close to Orkney).' Diodorus knew quite a lot about the people who lived in Britain too. They lived life in 'the ancient manner', still using chariots for warfare, just as the Greek heroes had done way back in the Trojan War. The country was divided into many independent kingdoms generally co-existing peaceably.

The sudden interest in geographical detail in the first century BC was not purely academic. As the Roman emperors reached out to acquire new territories, they naturally became interested in the political structures they would need to subvert or conquer – and the human and physical resources they might take over. Commercial interest drove exploration and discovery, then as later.

POLYNESIANS DISCOVER FIJI, TONGA AND SAMOA

(1300 BC)

Polynesian navigators discovered and settled the Fijian Islands in about 1300 BC. The Melanesians followed them in about 300 BC. Recent research by the Fiji Museum has revealed that the skeletons excavated at Natadola in Sigatoka belonged to the first settlers on Fiji and that the ancestors of those early settlers came originally from southern China. The original migrants could have left China as far back as 5000 BC, with their descendants settling in Papua New Guinea. Their descendants in turn migrated eastwards to Fiji and other South Pacific islands.

At Bourewa near Natadola, sixteen skeletons have been uncovered, and along with other evidence they show that Bourewa was the very first human settlement in the Fiji Islands. These same people were responsible for landing on and colonising other islands in the neighbourhood too. They set up colonies on Vanuatu, New Caledonia, Tonga and Samoa. The main evidence is their distinctive elaborately decorated and well-made pottery.

A piece of black glassy stone, immediately identifiable as obsidian, was discovered near Natadola in 2005. It can only have come from the obsidian mine in New Britain, Papua New Guinea, 1,865 kilometres (3,000 miles) away. The obsidian had been worked, in other words it had been shaped into blades, and probably arrived on a voyage within a hundred years of the pioneer settlement being founded. The piece of obsidian may have been kept by the colonists as a keepsake and a good-luck charm, a reminder of where they had come from, the ancestral home.

The Fijians' oral tradition says that they are the descendants of Chief Lutunasobasoba and his companions, who arrived in the Kaunitoni canoe. The colonists are said to have landed at Vuda and then moved inland to live in the Nakauvadra Mountains. There is no evidence to substantiate any part of this oral tradition of the voyage of discovery, which we have to treat as folklore and not history.

HANNO'S VOYAGE TO WEST AFRICA

(490 BC)

In the fifth century BC, European perceptions of the nature of the world and its shape were changing. Doubtless many uneducated people went on thinking that the Earth was flat, like a tabletop, and that if you went too near the edge you would fall off, but scholars and philosophers were coming to a different conclusion. In 480 BC Parmenides stated his belief that the world was a sphere. That sphere turned on an axis. Oenopides calculated the angle at which the Earth's axis was tilted to the plane of the ecliptic, the great circle in the sky that is the apparent orbit of the Sun. This looked forward to later discoveries: that the Earth travelled in a circular orbit round the Sun, and that its axis was titled at an angle to that. In 450 BC, Anaxagoras speculated that the Moon might be shining with reflected light from the Sun, which explained lunar eclipses. In this 'thought' world, in which the Earth was emerging as a sphere floating in space, it would certainly have been possible for ambitious and well-informed navigators to think in terms of sailing round Africa in order to reach the Indian Ocean; they would have seen no danger of falling off.

The fifth century BC scholar Herodotus wrote at length about the geography of the world as it was seen in his time. There was a well-established (and as it turned out *wrong*) view that Europe was a very large continent compared with Asia or Africa. That was partly to do with chauvinism – the conviction that Europe was much more important than the other continents and therefore had to be larger. Herodotus wrote scornfully, 'I cannot help laughing at the absurdity of all the map-makers – there are plenty of them – who show Ocean running like a river round a perfectly circular earth, with Asia and Europe of the same size. Let me give a proper notion of the size and shape of the two continents.' Then, instead of explaining that Europe was much smaller, as it in fact was, than Africa (at the time called Libya) or Asia, he argued that it was *larger.* 'Europe is as long as the other two put together.' But at least the great Herodotus, the father of History and the father of Geography too, knew that Africa was 'washed on all sides by the sea except where it joins Asia' and explained how he knew this. Even though Herodotus made one or two major mistakes, his writings are still well worth reading for the comprehensively detailed view they give of the world as it was, and as it was seen, in 450 BC.

There had been a great voyage of exploration undertaken in about 600 BC by Phoenician mariners acting on the orders of the Egyptian pharaoh Necho. Necho had called off an ambitious project to join the Nile to the Red Sea by a canal in order to mount this expedition, and seems to have been looking for a trade route round Africa, an alternative route into the Indian Ocean. Herodotus was impressed by the importance of this voyage, which was nothing less than a circumnavigation of Africa. The orders were to sail clockwise, from the Red Sea and the Arabian Sea southwards through the Indian Ocean, round the Cape of Good Hope, eventually to return to the Mediterranean by way of the Straits of Gibraltar. This voyage circumnavigated Africa hundreds of years ahead of the great Vasco da Gama expedition.

Necho's fleet put ashore at some convenient spot every few months, sowed seed, gathered a crop and so generated its own food supply. Herodotus believed in a small Africa that did not extend very far south, an Africa that was wholly in the northern hemisphere. What he says about the voyage suggests that it really happened, as he reported in evident disbelief that the sailors said that when they rounded the southern coast of Africa 'they had the sun on their right, to the north of them.' That is in fact exactly what you see in southern Africa. This piece of circumstantial evidence, typical of the fine detail in Herodotus, shows that the story about the Egyptian circumnavigation was absolutely true.

Another attempt to circumnavigate Africa was made by Sataspes the Achaemenian, who was sent off on the expedition in about 480 BC as a punishment by Xerxes (the alternative was impalement). Sataspes travelled to Egypt, where he commissioned a ship and a crew to take him to the Straits of Gibraltar. His voyage, unlike Necho's, was to be an anticlockwise circumnavigation of Africa, returning by way of the 'Arabian Gulf'. Sataspes followed the African coast southwards for several months, but eventually turned round and headed for home. His report to Xerxes gives us some clues as to how far he journeyed.

At the most southerly point in the voyage, he found the coast inhabited by small men wearing clothes made of palm leaves. When he landed, the small men fled and he was able to enter their abandoned villages and take food. Sataspes was evidently describing the pygmies who inhabited central Africa, which suggests that he may have reached the mouth of the Congo. He gave as his specific reason for returning the fact that his ship came to a standstill because there was no wind. This suggests that he reached the doldrums, the belt of no wind that runs along the equator. Sataspes' description implies that he reached the equator.

It was no mean achievement. Xerxes was nevertheless a king with a long memory. He had not forgotten that he had offered Sataspes the choice between impalement and the circumnavigation of Africa. Sataspes had not circumnavigated Africa, so Xerxes had him impaled.

At about the same time, perhaps a decade later, there was another voyage round Africa. This was undertaken by the Carthaginians, and led by a commander called Hanno. Rather more is known about this voyage because Hanno recorded details of the places he visited.

Hanno's voyage began in about 490 BC. A fleet of more than sixty fifty-oared galleys set sail from the city of Carthage. Hanno claimed he had 30,000 men and women on board, although this number would have seriously overloaded the ships and a figure nearer 5,000 seems more likely. The object of the voyage was to sail west, out through the Straits of Gibraltar, the Pillars of Hercules, into the Atlantic Ocean and then head south-westwards along the coast of West Africa. Carthaginian colonies would be established along the course of the voyage.

Two days' sailing beyond Gibraltar, Hanno founded his first settlement, Thymiaterion, which has been identified as the Moroccan town of Mehidya. After founding four more settlements, Hanno stayed for some time with a friendly tribe called the Lixites. He described passing various river mouths. One of them, described as a big, wide river teeming with crocodiles and hippopotamuses was the Senegal.

Several colonies were indeed founded as planned, but frequently Hanno's attempts to land were thwarted. There was determined opposition by the African natives. These were referred to as 'Ethiopians', meaning black men. These natives were 'wild men clad in the skins of beasts who threw stones and drove us off, preventing us from landing.' Colonies were successfully set up in Madeira, the Canary Islands and in the territories that are now known as Senegal and the Gambia. From the River Sénégal, Hanno sailed south for twelve days, hugging the coast and watching the native Africans running away as they approached. Then they arrived at a coastline where the people spoke a language that none of the interpreters could understand. They had reached the coast of Sierra Leone or Liberia. On that twelfth day, he dropped anchor by a mountainous coastline covered by forest. This was possibly Cape Mesurado, near Monrovia.

Rounding the mountainous cape for two days, Hanno entered an immense expanse of sea. This was the Gulf of Guinea. Sailing along the Guinea coast at night, he saw many fires, some small and some large. After landing to take on water, Hanno sailed on for five days to reach the Horn of the West, which was possibly Achowa Point, which is just west of Takoradi in Ghana. The bay to the east of the Horn of the West had islands in it. These seem to have been the western part of the Niger Delta. Here Hanno disembarked. Exploring by day, Hanno and his followers could see nothing but forest. By night, they were aware of many campfires. They also heard the exciting sounds of flutes, cymbals and drums, and the shouting of crowds of people. The Carthaginian adventurers were alarmed and decided to embark from the island.

Hanno saw 'a huge mountain of fire' from which molten lava poured into the sea. By night the coastline seemed to be full of flames. In the middle was a big flame, taller than the others and rising to the stars. When he saw it by daylight, he saw that it was a very high mountain, which was called the Chariot of the Gods. This was evidently a volcano, and can only have been Mount Cameroon. The African name for Mount Cameroon is (still) Monga-ma Loba, 'the Seat of the Gods'. Mount Cameroon is even today capable of ejecting lava flows that can run all the way to the sea; it did so in 1922.

Three days' sailing south from this coast of fire was the Bay of the Horn of the South. The Horn of the South was probably Cape Lopez in Gabon, about 800 kilometres (500 miles) north of the mouth of the Congo. There the sailors saw fierce creatures with shaggy hair, which could have been an unusually savage tribe but are more likely to have been the gorillas of the central Africa rainforests. Three female specimens were caught, killed and skinned, so that their skins could be taken back to Carthage. Interestingly, this part of the story is corroborated by the later Roman historian, Pliny the Elder, who reported that the gorilla pelts had been on show in the Temple of Tanit in Carthage until the city was destroyed.

If the original intention had been to sail right round Africa, that was abandoned as the African coast continued inexorably southwards. At the equator, the fleet began to run out of supplies, and Hanno decided to turn back and head for home. 'We did not sail any further because our provisions were running short.'

The return voyage must have very difficult as much of it would have been against the Canaries Current, which flows from north to south along the west coast of North Africa.

One major result of the Hanno voyage was that the shape of the bulge of West Africa was established, at least for the time being. One quirk of the history of discovery is that knowledge, even hard-won knowledge gained at great cost, can be lost or forgotten. When the Portuguese retraced the path of Hanno's voyage in the fifteenth century AD, they seem to have been sailing into the unknown. But the full story of Hanno's voyage itself may never be known.

The Carthaginians were very aware of the commercial value of geographical knowledge and the short *Periplus*, the official version that Hanno inscribed and left hanging in the Temple of Ba'al Hammon in Carthage, was almost certainly a carefully edited version. It is no accident that modern scholars have great difficulty in identifying many of the places mentioned. The main purpose of the voyage was to consolidate the Carthaginians' route to the gold market of central and southern Africa, and this was not mentioned.

Some commentators argue that Hanno did not get very far, that he only reached Senegal. But his use of the word 'gorilla' supports the idea of a longer voyage. 'Gorilla' comes from a Kikonga phrase that means 'powerful animal that beats itself violently'. In Hanno's day, this language was spoken only in the lower Congo Valley. Hanno's use of the word gorilla therefore strongly suggests that he reached the equator, where the Congo reaches the Atlantic.

On the other hand, there are other commentators who believe that Hanno went much further than the *Periplus* admitted. They believe he crossed the equator, rounded the Cape of Good Hope and followed the coast of East Africa all the way north to the Red Sea. This would have established contact with the gold centres of Zimbabwe. Somehow, later generations of Arab traders knew about the location of the gold mines of Zimbabwe, and they may have been privy to the unofficial version, the secret version, of Hanno's voyage. The Arab traders too were fully aware of the commercial value of this geographical knowledge and guarded it jealously. Hanno may well for commercial and political reasons have kept silent about the most significant aspects of his voyage – the circumnavigation which gave him the location of the gold mines.

In the first century AD, at a time when variant traditions were available, Pliny the Elder wrote about Hanno's voyage. He was sceptical about some of the claims made for and by the Carthaginians, but insists that Hanno was under orders to sail right round Africa. It is also clear from a passing comment of Pliny's that the Hanno voyage was just one part of a major Carthaginian effort to establish the geography of the world. 'When the power of Carthage flourished, Hanno sailed round from Cadiz to the extremity of Arabia and published a memoir of his voyage, *as did Himilco when he was despatched at the same date to explore the outer coasts of Europe.*' [Pliny *Natural History* 2.169] Himilco's account was subsequently lost, but was evidently available in late antiquity. Pliny referred to it and so did a later writer, the Roman aristocrat Rufus Festus Avienus, who lived around AD 350. Avienus quotes Himilco's narrative three times when he wants to describe the Atlantic coastline of Europe in his poem *The Sea Shore*.

Although commissioned to explore the Atlantic coast of Europe, Himilco was by no means the first to do so, and Avienus points out that the Tartessians (the people who lived in Andalusia in southern Spain in the Iron Age) sailed those waters to visit the Oestrumnidan Islands for trade. Later, Carthaginian traders followed the same route. Avienus does not positively identify the land of the Oestrumnides tribe, but offers clues to their location. The islands were two days' sailing from Ireland and had both tin and lead mines. The trade routes were located along the hill ridges. The tribe who lived there was vigorous, spirited, skilful and energetic. It has been suggested that the land of the Oestrumnides could be Brittany, the Scilly Isles or Cornwall. Cornwall is rich in metal ores, but cannot be regarded as an island group. The Scillies are an island group, but had no mines. Brittany has several small offshore islands and is rich in metal ores. Avienus gives another clue that suggests Brittany by stating that the region beyond the Oestrumnides is the country of the Celts. At that stage the British were never described as Celts – in spite of some modern conceptions to the contrary – though the Iron Age inhabitants of France certainly were. Another possibility is that Britain itself was perceived as an archipelago, so that the islands of the Oestrumnides were the Scilly Isles, Cornwall, Wales, the rest of Britain, the Channel Islands and Brittany. The precise position of Britain in relation to mainland Europe was not understood at that time, and was (surprisingly) still being misrepresented on medieval English maps, so the Carthaginians may have seen the land of the Celts (including France) as lying somehow behind the British Isles and Brittany.

The Andalusians traded with the people of Brittany, and also with the inhabitants of Cornwall, Wales and Ireland. In the Bronze Age, tin was sent from this region to Andalusia in increasing quantities.

The Phoenicians' interest in the tin trade began as early as 1000 BC. Possibly Cadiz was a port serving this trade. Several ancient authors reckoned that Cadiz was founded as early as 1100 BC, though so far this has not been verified by archaeological evidence. There is more evidence for the early trading operation after 800 BC, which is when the Phoenicians founded Carthage as a trading station – and founded Malaga too.

All this shows that when Himilco sailed into the waters of the Atlantic fringe he was not sailing into the completely unknown. Like Hanno, he had been commissioned to find the centres of metal-working operations, and probably he was specifically told to track down the tin, lead and gold mines. The ancient historian Diodorus Siculus gave a detailed description of the tin trade as it was carried on in the first century BC, and had probably gone on for centuries before. Tin extracted from the Cornish mines was beaten into squares and then transported to harbours such as 'Ictis', which is believed to be Mounts Bay. There the tin was loaded on to ships and sailed south, some being unloaded on the coast of Brittany for transport overland, the rest being taken on by sea into the Mediterranean Sea. Transport by sea was simpler and cheaper than overland transport, and remained so for hundreds of years to come.

The longer sea route took the tin along the Atlantic coast of the Iberian peninsula, through the Straits of Gibraltar, then along the length of the Mediterranean to reach Phoenicia (modern-day Lebanon). The land route started at Morlaix in Brittany. From there, the tin was taken on pack horses right across France to Massilia (modern Marseilles), where it was loaded back onto ships bound for Phoenicia. The main advantage of the land route was that it avoided the dangerous crossing of the Bay of Biscay, where many ships must have foundered in storms.

The timing of Himilco's exploratory expedition is significant. By the end of the seventh century, the Phoenicians and the Tartessians had quarrelled, which must have disrupted their trading operation. The Phoenicians must also have been shaken by the invasion of their homeland (now Lebanon) by the Babylonian king Nebuchadnezzar in 586 BC. This led to the emergence of Carthage as the new capital of a Phoenician trading operation in exile. The loss of central control from

Lebanon meant that the colonists were able to set new agendas, reach out to new trading goals. This was the context for the great voyages of Hanno and Himilco.

In the sixth century, there were also Greek navigators and traders operating in the western Mediterranean. Marseilles is their best-known colony. The Greeks and Carthaginians were hostile towards one another. The Carthaginians regarded the western Mediterranean basin as their patch and drowned every foreigner who ventured west of Sicily.

Himilco's account described his voyage as difficult and full of problems. It had the effect of discouraging the Greeks from venturing west, which may have been the intention. To begin with, he said it took four months to reach the Oestrumnides, when it cannot have taken a quarter of that time. Along the route, like Hanno, Himilco may have founded colonies. It has been suggested that Abul and Alcacer do Sol, not far from Lisbon, may be Carthaginian colonies founded at that time. Near Tartessus, Himilco founded the port of Gadir, a Phoenician word meaning 'walled city'.

Himilco claimed that the voyage was difficult because for long stretches there was no wind, which would be very unusual in the North Atlantic. He was also impeded by masses of seaweed in the water. This is a problem today in the vicinity of Cape St Vincent in south-west Portugal. There were sea monsters too, he said, and this seems to have been part of the Carthaginian propaganda campaign to frighten off their Greek trade competitors. It was very successful propaganda, in that from then on, right up until the nineteenth century, there were regular scare stories about monsters in the Atlantic.

Avienus repeated the problem caused by the lack of wind; he mentioned fog too, which Himilco could have encountered anywhere in these waters.

Avienus did not mention any exploration of the North Sea, but it is probable that an expedition to clarify the distribution of resources on the north-west European seaboard would have included it. In fact, it is hard to see how such a voyage could have omitted a tour of the North Sea basin and a circumnavigation of the British Isles. Scholars have speculated that Himilco visited Heligoland, which is one of the places where the ancients found amber, a much-prized material in the Bronze Age, and Himilco may well have been required to locate the source of the amber. This hypothetical exploration of the amber sources could explain why Greek writers started to write about a legendary amber river, which they named Eridanus. But perhaps the most significant outcome was the establishment in the fifth century BC of regular trade between Carthage, 'the people of Ireland' and 'the island of Albion' – Britain.

DISPLACEMENT AND FLOTATION

(290 BC)

The mathematician Archimedes was born in Syracuse, Sicily in about 290 BC. He was a relative of the king of Syracuse, Hieron II, who gave him a problem to solve. The king had a gold wreath that he suspected contained some silver. He asked Archimedes to devise a method to discover how much. Because silver is less dense than gold, Archimedes decided to try to discover the density of the wreath. To do this, he needed to relate the weight of the wreath to its volume, but because the wreath was an irregular shape finding the volume was a problem.

Archimedes noticed that when he got into his bath the water level rose. His own body was displacing an equivalent volume of water. He realised that he had found a solution. It is said that Archimedes was so excited at the moment of discovery that he jumped out of the bath and ran out into the street shouting 'Eureka!' ('I've found it!').

He realised that he had found a way of measuring the volume of an irregularly shaped body. All he had to do was to fill a vessel to the brim, lower the wreath into it and then measure the volume of the water it displaced. By measuring the wreath's volume as well as weight, Archimedes was able to calculate its density, and therefore find out whether it was made of pure gold or not.

When Archimedes got into his bath he may have noticed that he felt lighter. When anything is immersed in a liquid (or a gas) it experiences an upward push that is equal to the weight of the fluid displaced. By using this phenomenon, which is now known as Archimedes' principle, Archimedes might have immersed the wreath in water and measured its immersed weight, to see how much weight it had lost. He could have used this to find out how much silver had been mixed with the gold in the wreath, though – ironically - he probably did not do this.

Objects put into water sink until their weight is exactly balanced by the weight of the water they displace. If their average density is greater than that of water, they cannot float – they sink.

Archimedes was brilliant at applying simple principles and using the simplest equipment to solve problems. He solved Hieron's problem.

THE CHINESE
DISCOVER AMERICA
(AD 458)

The works of the Chinese historian Ma Twan-lin contain an extract from ancient official records concerning a traveller's tale that was told in the year 499. The story was told by a Buddhist priest called Hwui Shin (or Hue Shen), who had just returned from a long journey he had made to the east, across the Pacific Ocean. He had somehow reached North America in 458 and lived there for several decades before making his way home. The story was given sufficient credence at the time to be included in the official records by the imperial historiographer, and it was from these records that Ma Twan-lin copied it.

The story Hwui Shin told described the geography of a land called Fu-sang, including the people who lived there, and it has caused considerable controversy among later historians. Some believe that Hwui Shin was describing Japan; others think he reached America. E. P. Vining recently reviewed the evidence and came to the conclusion that it was America that Hwui Shin discovered. The original story as told by Hwui Shin was accompanied by a commentary by the imperial historian, Li-yan-tcheou, who said that the journey began from the coast north of Beijing, reached Japan after a journey of 12,000 li. From there it was a further 7,000 li to the north to reach the country of Wen-shin and another 5,000 eastwards to reach the country of Ta-han. From Ta-han it was another 20,000 li to reach Fu-sang. The li was a variable unit of measurement, about 530 metres (580 yards). This would put Wen-shin in Kamchatka, Ta-han would be in south-west Alaska and Fu-sang would be Mexico.

Hwui Shin reported that the people of Fu-sang lived in houses made of planks, and they had no walled and gated cities. The people used the bark of the fu-sang tree to make woven cloth for dresses. They also had developed writing and used the bark of the fu-sang tree to make paper. There were no armoured warriors in Fu-sang, as there was no warfare. There was crime, though, and the country had two prisons, one for serious crimes and one for minor offences, but in both the sentences were for life.

The Chinese annals also contain accounts of a Kingdom of Women, a Great Han country and a Land of Tattooed Bodies, and all of these appear to relate to Fu-sang. But the Hwui Shin account just outlined is the most matter-of-fact of the accounts and it does appear to describe an actual country. On the other hand, the country described does not really tally with Japan or Mexico, which is where Vining believes Fu-sang was located. The ancient Chinese literature mentions that Hwui Shin and the band of Buddhist missionaries travelling to Fu-sang with him went into the hills and mountains. In the interior they encountered deserts and a huge canyon with its sides striped in different colours and a river winding among boulders at the bottom of it. This sounds very like the Grand Canyon of Colorado.

In recent years, a search has been made in Central America for artefacts of Chinese origin, objects that would prove that Chinese explorers had been there. The Chinese used stones with holes drilled through them for anchors, and anchors of this type can be found there today. On the other hand, this is a very obvious low-tech way to make a boat anchor and people of many different cultures have used them; the Minoans used them in Bronze Age Crete. The stone anchors cannot be used as proof of contact with China – or for that matter Bronze Age Crete.

There is really too little to go on. The Chinese may have reached and explored North and Central America in the period 460–500, but the archived account does not really provide positive proof. The possibility that the Chinese had discovered North America in the fifth century was raised by the French scholar Deguignes in 1761. The idea was ridiculed and shelved. Then in 1841, Hwui Shin's narrative was published by a German scholar, and translated into English by Charles Leland in 1875. One major objection to the story was the apparent improbability of a fifth century Chinese junk successfully completing not only a Pacific crossing, but returning. But that objection can easily be overcome once the pattern of ocean currents is taken into account. The route described in Hwui Shin's story would have taken him by the North Pacific Current to Alaska. Glass fishing floats from Japan are sometimes washed up on the North American coast, carried by this current. From Alaska, he could have used the California Current to take him to Mexico. To sail west and return home to China, he could have used the North Equatorial Current. The strong clockwise circulation of the waters of the North Pacific itself corroborate the story; geography is in its favour.

The story of Hwui Shin is unsettling because it runs against the conventional history of exploration that we are used to hearing. It remains a possibility, as yet unproved, that just about the time when the Roman Empire was collapsing in Europe, Chinese Buddhist missionaries were arriving in Mexico – to preach to the pre-Columbian proto-Mayan natives. The story of Hwui Shin is a kind of alternative history, a lost history, and Hwui Shin himself is a kind of lost Columbus. The history of the Americas can clearly be written in more than one way, though a hypothetical patriotic song entitled 'God bless Fu-sang' has a very disorientating ring to it.

GREENLAND, NEWFOUNDLAND AND LABRADOR

(981 and 986)

In 981, a Norse expedition led by Eric the Red, an Icelandic colonist, sighted the coast of Greenland and made landfall there. This gave Eric the idea of setting up a daughter colony, in effect the first European colony in the New World. He returned to Iceland, but five years later, in 986, the preparations for this bold scheme were complete and a substantial fleet set sail for the west. Eric the Red took twenty-five ships with him, loaded with 700 people as well as horses, cattle and provisions. It amounted to a major colonial expedition.

The colonists set up the first Viking colony on the south-eastern coast of Greenland. The name 'Greenland' was not given ironically, though it might have been. The coastline the Icelanders saw was indeed covered with verdant pastures, and the newcomers could have had no idea that behind the coastal mountain range lay a colossal ice sheet.

In the summer of 986, one of the Icelandic Norse adventurers, a man called Bjarni Herjólfsson, was heading from Iceland to Greenland to join his father, when he was blown off course in a storm. Instead of landing on the coast of Greenland, he was taken well to the south of the southern tip, Cape Farewell, and sighted the coast of Newfoundland, a second major discovery. He described the new land as 'well-forested with low hills'. Herjólfsson followed the coastline to the north, it is thought, so that he saw the coasts of Labrador and Baffin Island. This was the first European sighting of the North American mainland – and it happened 500 years before Columbus.

Herjólfsson realised that these were not the lands he was trying to reach. They did not fit the descriptions he had read of Greenland. This realisation made him turn round and head for Greenland.

It was inevitable that after hearing this tale others would be tempted across the treacherous, iceberg-strewn sea beyond Cape Farewell. In 995, Leif Ericsson, the son of Eric the Red, bought Bjarni Herjolfsson's ship in Greenland and set sail in it to try to replicate his voyage and rediscover the lands that Bjarni had seen. Leif Ericsson found them again, naming them Helluland, Markland and Vinland. Leif landed in Labrador and spent the winter there before returning to Greenland the following spring. In 996, Leif's brother Thorvald sailed south-west from the Greenland colony to revisit the Labrador coast, which had become known to the colonists as Vinland.

Thorvald Ericsson intended to set up a colony in Vinland, but he became involved in a skirmish with the natives and was killed, shot with an Amerindian arrow. Ericsson's crew decided to overwinter in Labrador, as Bjarni had done, before returning to Greenland in the spring.

In the space of a few years, the Norse colonists that had settled in Iceland had made two very significant steps to the west, landing and founding colonies in both Greenland and Labrador. The settlements may have been only temporary, but they enlarged the European view of the world, extending it to the west. Europe began to think Atlantic. Experiences such as these made the Columbus voyages, which took place later and further to the south, an inevitability. It is Bjarni Herjólfsson and Leif Ericsson rather than Columbus who should be credited with the European discovery of the New World.

MAGNETIC POLES
(1269)

The French physician Pierre de Maricourt, also known as Petrus Peregrinus de Maricourt or, in English, Peter the Pilgrim, carried out the first scientific experiments that we know about on a magnet. He wrote a groundbreaking paper about them, called *Letter about the Magnet*. According to the subtitle, he wrote it while he was encamped at the siege of Lucera, when serving in the army of Charles of Anjou.

One of his experiments involved positioning a sliver of iron at various points on the surface of a spherical lump of lodestone (magnetic rock). At each position he drew a mark to show the orientation of the sliver of iron. A pattern appeared as a result of the experiment: lines, like lines of longitude on a terrestrial globe, that converged on two points. De Maricourt called the points where the lines of force converged the magnetic poles – and the term is still used today. But he was sufficiently trapped in the medieval mindset to attribute the magnetism of the Earth to the influence of celestial magnetic poles, not to magnetic poles within the Earth itself. Pierre de Maricourt pointed out that magnets could make one another move and that this might be a method for producing perpetual motion.

Letter about the Magnet was a very popular and influential paper in the Middle Ages and later. It was quoted by de Maricourt's disciple, the English monk Roger Bacon, and by Thomas Bradwardine in 1326; it was much in use at the University of Oxford. The *Letter* was first printed at Augsburg in 1558, which gave its ideas wider currency still. The English physician William Gilbert (1544–1603) added the idea that the Earth contained a colossal bar magnet to explain the behaviour of magnetic compass needles. This turned out to be untrue; the intense heat in the Earth's interior would melt a solid iron bar, and the structure is in concentric layers. Nevertheless, the idea of the Earth as a magnet with a magnetic field continued to develop, and Gilbert's idea of the Earth's magnetic poles approximately coinciding with the poles of rotation (1600) turned out to be true.

MARCO POLO'S VISIT
TO CHINA
(1280)

Marco Polo was a Venetian merchant and explorer. He was born into a noble family in Venice in 1254, while his father Nicolo Polo and his uncle were away on an expedition to Bokhara and Cathay (China). The two brothers, Nicolo and Maffeo, had been engaged in ambitious, long-distance trading for a long time. In 1259, they were based in the Venetian quarter at Constantinople, which gave them as Venetians the advantage of tax relief and political privileges. But they sensed that the political situation was dangerous and they moved their business to Soldaia in the Crimea, for safety. They were right. In 1261, Constantinople was captured by Michael Palaeologus, the ruler of the Nicaean Empire. He burnt down the Venetian quarter and had any Venetian citizens who were caught blinded.

The Polo brothers, meanwhile, continued their business uninterrupted from the Crimea, at least for the time being. But then the Crimea too became destabilised and they decided to move their business operation east to Bokhara, in what is now Uzbekistan, and traded there for three years. In Bokhara, they met some envoys returning from Kublai Khan, the Chinese emperor, and they travelled with them further along the Silk Road into Cathay.

In 1266, Nicolo and Maffeo Polo were well-received in the capital of Cathay (now Beijing) by the great emperor, Kublai Khan, the grandson of Genghis Khan, who it seems had never seen Europeans before. He was delighted with them and commissioned them to act as his ambassadors to the Pope. He wanted them to ask the Pope to send a hundred well-educated Europeans, men who were learned in the arts and sciences. It was a marvellous opportunity, this meeting and sharing of two great civilisations. The Polo brothers were sent off with a Mongol called Koeketei, who was the khan's ambassador to the Pope. They were given a letter from the khan requesting the embassy of intellectuals and also a large gold tablet that would guarantee hospitality (food, lodging and horses) anywhere in the khan's domain. Koeketei abandoned the Polos halfway back, but the Polos still had every intention of carrying the potentially epoch-making mission, but they found when they reached the West in 1269 that the situation had changed alarmingly. When they reached Acre in the Holy Land, they heard that no new pope had been elected following the death of Clement IV the previous year. The vacant papal throne meant that no embassy could be authorised. No doubt with an acute sense of frustration and disappointment, they returned to Venice, waiting for the election of a new pope.

In 1271, after the election of Pope Gregory X, the Polo family set off again for the East with the new Pope's message for the khan. This time they took with them the young Marco, who was then seventeen. They travelled though Mosul, Baghdad, Khorassan, the Pamir Mountains, Kashgar, Yarkand, Khoton, Lob Nor, the Gobi Desert, Tangut and Shangtu, arriving at the court of Kublai Khan in 1275. The places they passed through on the second half of this journey were almost totally unknown to Europeans, though they were familiar stopping places for Asian traders. The khan was once again very pleased to see them and especially interested in the young Marco Polo, who was soon sent off as an envoy to Yunnan, Burma, Karakorum, Cochin China and Southern India. Marco was taught the languages of the khan's subjects. For three years he served as governor of Yang Chow.

The khan was reluctant to allow these useful Westerners to leave his court, but they were apprehensive about what might happen to them in the wake of the old khan's death, which was surely not far away. For their own safety, they needed to be out of Cathay before he died. Eventually an opportunity arose by chance. They were commissioned to escort a young noblewoman on a long sea voyage. After long delays on the coasts of Sumatra and India, they managed to sail to Persia. The Polos finally returned to Venice in 1295, bringing with them the great wealth they had acquired along the way. But when they arrived at their family mansion they were initially rejected and ridiculed because they were unrecognisable; the clothes they were wearing were worn and outlandish. Nobody believed them when they said they were the Polos.

In 1298, Marco Polo commanded a galley at the Battle of Curzola, in which the Venetians were defeated by the Genoese. He was taken prisoner and kept confined in Genoa for a year. He had his notes, which he had originally written for the khan, sent across from Venice and another prisoner, Rusticiano of Pisa, helped him to make a continuous prose record from them. It was written in Old French and entitled *Divisament dou Monde* (*Description of the World*). When it was translated into English, it was given the more explicit title, *The Travels of Marco Polo*. The original is now lost, and the translations contain many variations.

When Polo was released by the Genoese he returned to Venice, where between 1310 and 1320 he wrote a new version of his travels in Italian, which he called *Il Milione*. He died in 1324. The original text of *Il Milione* was lost, though not before being translated into Latin. This Latin version was then translated back into Italian. The various transformations of the text created lots of errors and misunderstandings.

Map-makers tried to incorporate Marco Polo's geographical information into their maps. This was not achieved with any accuracy, but at least hitherto empty spaces on maps were now filled in.

Marco Polo did not introduce into Europe the idea of block printing from China. Indeed he rather oddly did not mention the distinctive Chinese printing method at all. Discrepancies and omissions like this have led some modern commentators to dismiss Marco Polo's book as a traveller's tale in the worst sense of the phrase – a tall story with little truth in it. It is indeed hard to understand why the great khan would have wanted to use as envoys foreigners with little or no understanding of the languages spoken in China. Perhaps the Polos exaggerated their importance in Cathay to make a good story better, but it cannot be seriously doubted that they travelled there.

The impact of their travels in the East was profound. The Polos were not by any means the first Europeans to reach China by the overland route along the Silk Road – Giovanni da Pian del Carpine, for instance, had done it. But the fact that Marco wrote a book about it ensured that their journey was widely known. It became by far the best known and the most widely read book about the East. It was Marco Polo's description of the Far East and its wealth that inspired Christopher Columbus to attempt to reach it by sailing west. Among Columbus's belongings was a heavily annotated copy of Marco Polo's book.

Europeans had to come to terms with the fact that there was a great civilisation flourishing in eastern Asia, one that was in many ways more advanced than the great European civilisation. It encouraged a mental outreach that would bear fruit in the physical outreach of the Columbus and Magellan voyages and other major European voyages of discovery.

PTOLEMY'S
GEOGRAPHY TAKEN
TO ITALY
(1405)

Ptolemy, or Claudius Ptolemaeus, was born in a Greek colony in Egypt in about AD 90. Very little else is known about him, except that he was an astronomer, and made his astronomical observations at Alexandria during the reigns of the emperors Hadrian and Antoninus Pius. Shortly after his lifetime it was said that he had lived in the Temple of Serapis at Canopus near Alexandria.

The ancient Egyptian temples were often centres of learning, with their own museums and libraries. Plato, long before, described how his ancestor Solon had gone to Egyptian temple priests to acquire historical information about the lost empire of Atlantis. Plato's story is often dismissed as fable, but if Solon went in search of a history of the eastern Mediterranean that had been forgotten by the Greeks, the scholarly temple priests of the Nile Delta are exactly the people he would have consulted. Ptolemy lived centuries later, but it would still have been quite natural for him, as a scholar, to be attached to the Temple of Serapis, which functioned as a limb of the great Library of Alexandria.

Ptolemy's model for the motion of the heavenly bodies, known as the Ptolemaic system, assumes that the Earth is at the centre of the universe and that the heavenly bodies revolve round it. The Ptolemaic system was later to be challenged by Copernicus and Galileo, who both (correctly) put the sun at the centre of the solar system.

Ptolemy's work as a geographer had further-reaching effects. A lot of Ptolemy's work was not original. He was largely a compiler and corrector of other people's work, but no less useful for that. Ptolemy's great work was the *Guide to Geography*. This, along with a lot of other classical learning, was forgotten or even lost in Europe, and only kept alive by Arabic scholars. It was the rediscovery by Europeans of those Arabic copies that fuelled the Renaissance. The Renaissance, or Rebirth, was in large measure a rediscovery of ancient knowledge and ideas. A copy of Ptolemy arrived in south-eastern Europe in the Middle Ages, where it was discovered in a bookshop and taken to Italy for perusal in 1405. It was then that Ptolemy's book took on a new lease of life.

Before Ptolemy's time, the astronomer Hipparchus pointed out that the only way to construct a reliable and trustworthy map of the world was to use astronomical observations to fix the latitude and longitude of all the principal points on its surface. This emphasis on co-ordinates was fundamental to good cartography. It was a good idea in principle, but the means of acquiring this sort of information were lacking. Then, just before Ptolemy's time, Marinus of Tyre started to collect determinations of latitude and longitude from itineraries. It is not clear how far Marinus got, but Ptolemy evidently used Marinus's work and started where he had left off. Ptolemy divided up the equator into 360 parts and these became our modern degrees. Ptolemy drew lines through these points, connecting them to the North and South Poles to make lines of longitude. He drew another set of lines parallel to the equator to mark the latitude. Then he located his known points on this grid.

Then Ptolemy made an odd mistake. Eratosthenes had correctly calculated the circumference of the earth as 40,234 kilometres (25,000 miles). Posidonius had wrongly reduced this to 28,970 kilometres (18,000 miles), and Ptolemy unfortunately followed Posidonius instead of Eratosthenes. As a result, significant errors were built into his map from the start. Ptolemy was also working on relatively little data on longitude. All things considered, Ptolemy made an honest attempt at a world map, and Europe, Asia and Africa are all recognisable. He also produced regional maps, and in effect invented the atlas. He established regional and world maps as a new way of looking at the world – and that was a major step in changing people's perceptions.

The *Guide to Geography* contained tables of places and their locations, showing an admirable scientific rigour of approach, one that would be a model to the Renaissance world. For all their faults, Ptolemy's maps were far better than most of the maps constructed in medieval Europe. The rediscovery of Ptolemy's maps, together with the statistical tables that had led to their construction, was a turning point in the European Renaissance.

It was in 1405 that a copy of Ptolemy's *Geography* was taken to Italy. The year 1405 was a turning point in Eurasian history. It brought the death of Timur, which was good news for Asia, and the birth of modern geography in Europe, which marked the beginning of a period of outreach to the rest of the world. It was also the year when the very first major Chinese voyage of exploration was launched.

The errors in Ptolemy themselves had an effect on European history. Ptolemy extended eastern Asia a long way eastwards, shortening the distance between Europe and China by fifty degrees of longitude, and making a westward route from Europe to the Far East seem much more manageable. This in turn justified Columbus's belief that it was possible to reach China by crossing the Atlantic – which is what he had been led to believe.

Toscanelli sent Columbus a chart that showed Japan (then known as Cipangu) as lying 4,830 kilometres (3,000 miles) to the west of the Canaries, which is less than one-third of its true distance. Columbus needed to 'sell' his voyage to a sponsor, and this led him to use the most favourable figures and the shortest distances. He was deliberately choosing the largest credible extension of the Old World in order to make the estimated sailing time more attractive to a sponsor. Ptolemy calculated the length of a degree of longitude at the equator as 80 kilometres (50 miles) miles, against the reality of 95 kilometres (60 miles), but Columbus proposed an even shorter distance – 70 kilometres (45 miles). The result of these games that Columbus played with numbers was to pull Japan eastwards to the longitude of the Western Antilles and the coast of Cathay to the longitude of the west coast of Mexico. Columbus was using Ptolemy along with other geographical sources to window dress his case for a voyage of discovery across the Atlantic.

THE VOYAGES OF ZHENG HE

(1407–33)

In 1405, the Emperor Yung-lo ordered the first major Chinese voyage of exploration. It was a huge enterprise, organised on a very large scale by comparison with the voyages undertaken by European explorers during the next 200 years. The epoch-making Columbus voyage of 1492 was undertaken with just three small ships. The Chinese expedition of almost a hundred years earlier involved a huge fleet of sixty-three war-junks carrying an army of 28,000 men.

This huge fleet sailed under the command of the Muslim eunuch, Ma, who took the name Zheng He. His war junks were gigantic vessels with five or six decks, and displacing about 1,500 tons each. They were equipped with magnetic compasses to aid navigation. They were also accompanied by support vessels that included horse ships, carrying mounts for the expedition's soldiers. The fleet carried enough grain, wine, livestock and other provisions to sustain it for a whole year sailing on the high seas. Given the scale of the expedition, it is surprising that it did not go right round the world. It could easily have done so. That it did not is just one of many surprising things about Zheng He's voyage.

The expedition fleet also carried cargoes of porcelain, silk, satin, gold and silver, which were to be traded for lions, rhinos, myrrh and ambergris.

The huge fleet first sailed southwards from China to explore the islands of Indonesia. In 1407, Zheng He returned to China with the Prince of Palembang on board. Zheng He had engaged his warriors in battle, defeated them and now brought him in chains to show him off to the Chinese emperor.

The following year Zheng He was sent off on a second voyage. This time Zheng He took his invasion fleet – that is what it was – westwards into the Indian Ocean and sailed as far west as Ceylon (Sri Lanka). The native Sinhalese attacked the Chinese, rightly seeing the fleet's arrival as an invasion, but they were easily overpowered by superior forces. The Sinhalese royal family was captured, including the King of Ceylon, and taken back to China to show to the emperor.

In 1412, Zheng He set off on a third expedition, this time sailing westwards to cross the entire width of the Indian Ocean. He reached the Straits of Hormuz, the entrance to the Persian Gulf. A fourth expedition followed in 1416, which crossed the Indian Ocean to reach Aden. In 1421, a fifth voyage of the great invasion fleet, or the Star Raft as it was called, began. In the following year, Zheng He's fleet reached Malindi on the East African coast of what is now Kenya. Ten years later there was a sixth voyage, also led by Zheng He. This one visited the coastline of East Africa and the Red Sea.

There has recently been an attempt to inflate the importance of these Chinese voyage. The '1421' hypothesis was put forward in 2002 by Gavin Menzies, a retired British Royal Naval submarine commander. Menzies proposed that there was a much more ambitious programme of exploration, with voyages led by five admirals, Hong Boa, Zhou Man, Zhou Wen, Yang Qing and Zheng He. Fleets commanded by Hong Boa, Zhou Wen and Zhou Man sailed westwards across the Indian Ocean, rounded the Cape of Good Hope and sailed north through the Atlantic Ocean to reach the Cape Verde Islands. There the combined fleet split up, with Hong Boa and Zhou Man sailing south-west to South America and Zhou Wen sailing west to the Caribbean, landing on Cuba before sailing north along the east coast of North America and on to Greenland in search of the North Pole. Zhou Wen sailed right along the Arctic coast of Asia to return to China.

Meanwhile, Hong Boa and Zhou Man sailed on southwards to reach the Straits of Magellan, where they separated. Hong Boa's fleet headed southwards in search of the South Pole, landing on the Antarctic Peninsula. Hong Boa then sailed eastwards with the West Wind Drift to reach Kerguelen Island and Western Australia, making landfall near Bunbury before returning to China. Zhou Man passed through the Straits of Magellan and then travelled north along the Pacific coast of South America, taking advantage of the Peru Current. Then he used the South Equatorial Current to take him right across the Pacific. He explored the coastlines of Australia and New Zealand before heading back towards China. But then, instead of returning home, he turned north-eastwards, crossing the North Pacific to reach the Pacific coast of North America. After following this southwards with the aid of the California Current, Zhou Man sailed back to China using the North Equatorial Current.

This breathtaking hypothesis of a Chinese discovery of the whole world by 1421 won widespread popular acceptance when it was published, but it is not entirely convincing. Much depends on conspiracy theory. The knowledge acquired by the admirals is supposed to have been destroyed subsequently because the mandarins, the bureaucrats of the imperial court, were afraid that the cost of future voyages would ruin the Chinese economy. When Emperor Zhu Di died in 1424, his successor, the Hongxi Emperor, forbade any future voyages of exploration and ordered the destruction of the evidence of the earlier voyages.

One piece of evidence offered for this large-scale acquisition of geographical knowledge is a Chinese world map incorporating information alleged to date from 1418. It shows the Old World and the New World in recognisable form, Australia in the middle of the South Pacific and the coastline of Antarctica. It in effect shows the world as we know it. But the crucial map was not drawn in 1418. It was drawn in 1763. The 1421 hypothesis is intriguing in showing what the Chinese fleets *might* have achieved. A Chinese discovery of the whole world was certainly technically possible at that time, though that does not amount to proof that it was achieved.

The voyages of Zheng He were not purely voyages of exploration and discovery. They were voyages of aggression and power. As much as anything, Zheng He's voyages were intended to show the world the might and prestige of China. They amounted to a kind of travelling trade fair, a floating Crystal Palace. The Chinese were interested in conquest, domination and lucrative trade. On the final voyage, when Zheng He visited twenty countries, Zheng He exacted tribute from eleven of them, including the city of Mecca. What the Chinese wanted was the complete subservience of the outside world, and they seem to have been unimpressed by the many varied cultures they encountered. It is a pity Zheng He did not reach Europe. It would have been interesting to see whether seeing the cities of Europe would have changed the minds of the Chinese about the West – and we can only speculate about the response of European nations to the arrival of Zheng He's huge fleet.

PERSPECTIVE
(1412)

The word 'perspective' comes from the Latin word *perspicere*, meaning to see clearly. The Italian architect Filippo Brunelleschi is credited with discovering perspective at some time between 1410 and 1415.

Perspective is a systematic way of drawing objects on a flat surface in such a way as to make them appear three-dimensional. One characteristic feature of perspective drawing is that objects are drawn smaller with increasing distance from the eye. Another characteristic is that objects are distorted when viewed at an angle. The wall of a house, for example, may be exactly square, but when drawn from one side it becomes a trapezium. A ceiling, also an exact square in fact, can become a diamond. Brunelleschi noticed that when the exterior of a house is viewed from a corner the horizontal lines marking its sides – the base of the walls, the gutters, windowsills and door lintels – instead of appearing to be parallel converge on two vanishing points, both on the horizon. Using this phenomenon, it became possible to construct a drawing of a house that created a perfect illusion of solidity.

Some aspects of perspective were already understood already, as many artists had arrived at the same conclusion intuitively, but Brunelleschi turned the observations into a simple system. The Bayeux Tapestry, embroidered in 1075–80, shows three-dimensional scenes reduced to two. Soldiers are shown naturalistically, with one leg half hidden behind the other; some men stand behind horses. In the Utrecht Psalter, made in 830, there is an illustration to Psalm 44 that shows buildings in three-quarter view. A city wall with gates, bastions and towers appears, if not in strict one-point linear perspective, at least sketched freely in a way that demonstrates a working knowledge of the principles of perspective. Among the ruins of Pompeii is the House of Menander. It is a portrait fresco of a seated man. One knee of this seated figure points towards the viewer and is acutely foreshortened, giving a convincing illusion of a three-dimensional object. The fresco, engulfed in ash in the AD 79 eruption, must have been painted between 60 and 75.

It is therefore possible to push back the proven knowledge of perspective to the beginning of the Christian era. Can it be pushed back any further? Rather surprisingly, it can. In the first century BC, Alexandros of Athens executed a drawing of a group of women on a marble panel. A kneeling girl has one leg half hidden behind the other. Another girl stands behind her. Alexandros creates not only accurate proportions but an illusion of shallow space. A frieze from the famous Mausoleum at Halicarnassus shows a similar bas-relief perspective. One drape overlies another; a shield is half hidden behind a torso. This frieze was sculpted in 359–51 BC. A very similar technique was used in the frieze of the Battle of the Gods and Giants from the Treasury of the Siphnians at Delphi, carved in 530 BC.

Nor was this technique an invention of the classical civilisation. Neolithic long barrows built in southern England in 3500 BC show an interest in tricking the eye with false perspective. The business end of many long barrows, the end where the burials, mortuary buildings, facades and forecourts were placed, was usually built higher and wider than the other end. The tapering wedge shape made the long barrow appear to be much longer to visitors, and therefore more impressive, than it actually was. Even in the neolithic, people were playing conjuring tricks with space.

What Brunelleschi did was to make systematic rules that made it easier for other artists to pull off the trick of perspective drawing successfully, building up the structure of pictures from a series of flat shapes. Some twenty years afterwards, Brunelleschi's friend, Leon Alberti, wrote a book giving artists detailed instructions on the technique.

II
THE GREAT AGE
OF DISCOVERY

CAPE BOJADOR
(1433)

Cape Bojador is a West African headland just over 160 kilometres (100 miles) to the south of the Canaries. It is neither an outstanding landmark topographically nor the westernmost point of West Africa, which is Cape Verde in Senegal, but it marks an historic boundary in the history of African exploration.

The Portuguese Prince Henry the Navigator initiated and organised the series of exploratory voyages that opened up the north-west coastline of Africa to Europeans. Prince Henry was not driven by a thirst for geographical knowledge for its own sake. There was a powerful commercial reason for his great project. The Portuguese had important trading links with the East, but found it increasingly difficult to maintain them with a hostile Muslim bloc evolving in the Middle East. What the Portuguese wanted was a sea route to the East that bypassed this Muslim world entirely, a sea route right round Africa. A sea route from the Indian Ocean eastwards to Cathay (China) had been rumoured to exist for a long time. It was now a question of finding a sea route from the Atlantic Ocean to the Indian Ocean, round Africa.

The earliest voyages in the series were unpromising; the coastline south from the Strait of Gibraltar trended towards the south-south-west, taking the mariners further and further away from India.

In due course, Prince Henry's captains mapped the North African coastline as far south as the Canary Islands and Cape Bojador another 320 kilometres (200 miles) further to the south-west. Voyage after voyage reached the Canaries, and a few reached the sandy headland of Cape Bojador, but none seemed to be able to venture beyond the cape. There was a psychological barrier to overcome. Some of the ships' crews were afraid of falling off the edge of the world if they went any further. Others were more rationally afraid that the ocean current sweeping inexorably southwards along the coast, the Canaries Current, would prevent them from ever sailing home again. Still others were terrified of the Sea of Darkness, which they imagined lay beyond the headland.

As the sailors headed further and further south, nearer and nearer to the equator, it became hotter and hotter, and the people they saw occasionally on the shore were coal black, as if charred by the extreme heat. The Portuguese sailors feared that they too would be roasted coal black if they ventured any further. There was plenty for the Portuguese sailors to fear, plenty to stop them from venturing beyond Cape Bojador.

Prince Henry sent one of his squires, Eannes, with the specific order to sail round Cape Bojador in 1432, but he failed to do it. He too turned back, out of fear. Back at his base at Sagres, the prince gently chided Eannes and sent him off again the following year on the same mission. This time Eannes reached and successfully rounded Cape Bojador. The coastline he discovered beyond it was unpromising. It was barren and uninhabited, which gave no encouragement for any further southward sailing, but at least there was no specific terror lurking beyond Cape Bojador. The sinister spell of the cape had been broken; the hurdle had been overcome.

Cape Bojador was a landmark in the history of exploration and discovery in two senses. It marked the physical southern boundary of the Portuguese world until the early fifteenth century. It also marked a psychological barrier that for a long time the Portuguese navigators could not bring themselves to pass. Once it was rounded, the way south was open.

Henry the Navigator followed this up immediately by sending another ship, commanded by Afonso Baldaya, to explore the coastline to the south of the cape. The southward creep gained momentum after Cape Verde was reached. After that the coast of Africa fell away to the east for hundreds of miles and there was great optimism that the West African coast, the coastlines of what are now Ghana and Nigeria, was actually the southern coast of Africa. Could it be that there was now a clear run eastwards into the Indian Ocean? Unfortunately it turned out that beyond the delta of the River Niger the coastline swung southwards again and the huge mass of central and southern Africa lay in the way.

THE MOUTH OF THE RIVER CONGO
(1483)

The mouth of the River Congo was discovered in 1483 during the course of the Portuguese programme of exploration along the Atlantic coast of Africa. It was the Portuguese navigator Diogo Cão who made the discovery.

The river mouth is a huge expanse of open water 11 kilometres (7 miles) across. A ship on one side of the river mouth could only just make out a thin blue strip of coastline in the distance, marking the further shore. When sounded in the nineteenth century, the water turned out to be incredibly deep in places too, as much as 140 fathoms (255 metres/840 feet). Diogo Cão interpreted the mouth of the Congo as a strait that would provide access to the fabled kingdom of Prester John, the mythical Christian priest-king whose kingdom was believed to lie somewhere in the centre of Africa.

The discovery of the mouth of the Congo was the beginning of a long-running search for the river's source. Finding the source of the Congo proved to be as difficult as finding the source of the Nile – two great puzzles in unravelling the physical geography of Africa.

The Portuguese recorded that the Congo flowed with such force at its mouth that it was impossible to sail into it against the current, except close to the shore on each side. The volume of fresh water flowing out was enormous: in fact, so great that the Atlantic was still fresh water 95 or even 130 kilometres (60 or 80 miles) out to sea, where it can be distinguished as brown and silt-laden by contrast with the blue of the sea.

In the nineteenth century, explorers noted that the Congo River water was three degrees cooler than the sea water as well as lighter, and that it stayed separate from the sea water, feathering out over the surface of the sea like a fan. The fresh water was also turned in a regular curve towards the north by the northward flow of the Benguela Current, and could be detected as much as 485 kilometres (300 miles) away. This was similar in scale to the effect of the river water at the mouth of the Amazon, which freshens the sea water as much as 320 kilometres (200 miles) along the Guyana coast. The volume of water pouring out of the Congo was, and is, enormous – almost as great as the discharge of the largest river in the world, the Amazon.

By the nineteenth century, when explorers were arriving to make a determined effort to discover the Congo's source, there were slave ports at the mouth of the river – Moanda and Vista. The initial impression, that the Congo mouth was a single huge channel, turned out to be false. There are minor distributary channels as well, making a delta.

AN ANCIENT ROMAN BEAUTY

(1485)

In April 1485, workmen digging along the Appian Way in Italy uncovered a stone sarcophagus. It was displayed in Rome and attracted
huge crowds. As many as 20,000 people went to see it in one day –
because of the amazing state of preservation of the body it contained.
Rumours circulated that when the body had been found a lamp was still
burning beside it. The event was so sensational and created such hysteria
that the Pope ordered the body to be secretly reburied at once. But
before that happened a drawing was made and attached to a detailed
description of the body; the two were sent in a letter by Bartolommeo
Fonte to Francesco Sassetti, and luckily they have survived.

*You have asked me for tidings concerning the woman's body recently
found on the Via Appia. I can but hope that my pen is equal to describing
the beauty and charm of this body . . . Labourers looking for marble
suddenly broke through a brick vault twelve feet deep. Here they found a
marble sarcophagus. When they opened it, they discovered a body lying
on its face, coated with a greasy but fragrant substance to the thickness
of two fingers. When they cleared away the perfumed coating they looked
upon a pale face with features so clear that it seemed as if the girl might
have been buried that very day. Her long black hair was fastened in a
knot and parted in a manner suitable to a maiden; it was also covered
with a snood of silk and gold.*

*Tiny ears, a delicate forehead, black eyebrows – and finally eyes of a
curious shape, with the whites showing below the lids. Even the nostrils
were unimpaired and so soft that they yielded to the slightest pressure of*

a finger. The lips were red and slightly parted, the teeth small and white, the tongue scarlet. Cheeks, chin, throat and neck seemed warm as life. The arms hung from the shoulders in such a perfect state that they could be moved in any direction. On the lovely long fingers the fingernails were firmly rooted. Breast, abdomen and loins, however, had been pressed to one side, and disintegrated after removal of the aromatic coating. The back, hips and buttocks, on the other hand, had retained their shape and their wonderful curves; likewise thighs and legs, which during life must have displayed even greater beauties than the face.

In short, here was a sublimely beautiful girl from the days when Rome stood at the pinnacle of her glory. The sarcophagus bears no markings – we know neither this maiden's name, her origin nor her age.

This happened at a time when people were beginning to develop a serious interest in antiquity, and classical antiquity in particular. The discovery of the girl from ancient Rome became the wonder of the year in the Rome of 1485. Fifteenth-century people were able to look at the girl's body and feel that it was someone they knew, someone they cared about. They wanted to know her name, which family she belonged to, how old she was. Statues and monuments and ruins had survived from ancient Rome, but this was very different. She was the most poignant link with – almost a survivor of – the age of Augustus, and certainly an ambassadress for the ancient world. The discovery of the ancient Roman girl was one of the events that drove the Renaissance forwards. The classical past suddenly had an immediacy and a humanity that made it important to find out more about it.

THE CAPE OF GOOD HOPE
(1488)

The Portuguese were very persistent in their attempt to find a way round Africa. Their determination was remarkable in that there need not have been a sea route round Africa at all. The Atlantic could have been an enclosed, landlocked basin. Ancient accounts of the voyages of Necho and Hanno were available and it is just possible that the Portuguese endeavour was based on a reading of these accounts. But we today know the geography of Africa well enough to see which corroborative details make the ancient accounts credible, and it is hard to see how the Portuguese, who knew far less, could have been persuaded by them. Even with the knowledge of the early circumnavigations, sailing on south was very much an act of faith.

Then, in 1488, Bartholomew Dias reached the southernmost tip of Africa. It was a momentous discovery. In December 1488, Dias returned to tell the King of Portugal, John II, about the exciting discovery. He had not only discovered the southernmost tip of Africa – he had sailed round it. In his epic two-year voyage, Dias had sailed so far south (to 35 degrees South) that he had lost sight of the North Star, which had sunk below the northern horizon. He had been blown south by a strong wind, losing sight of land for thirteen days. When at last he had been able to turn back he found that the coastline of Africa was trending eastwards. He had at last found the southern coast of Africa.

Dias spotted native herdsmen on the South African coast and landed in order to meet them. Unfortunately they were unable to understand one another, and the herders were so alarmed by the sight of the Portuguese caravels that they drove their livestock inland as fast as they

68

could to get away from them. In view of the terrible later history of the white colonisation of southern Africa and the dispossession of the black inhabitants, one cannot help thinking that this instinctive initial reaction was the right one. The arrival of the whites in southern Africa was bad news for the indigenous blacks.

Dias told the King of Portugal he had named the great southern cape with its table-like mountain the Cape of Storms, but the King wanted him to change that to the Cape of Good Hope, because of what it promised for the future. What it promised, of course, was the long-hoped-for sea route to India. It later transpired that it was a false good hope, in that another cape lay in the way. There was another headland to round; Cape Agulhas, a short distance to the south-east, was the true southernmost tip of Africa. But the Cape of Good Hope was seen as the turning point, and it still seems to be that, partly because of its thin, tapering shape, and the curious way in which it sharply separates the warm tropical water on the eastern side from the cold Antarctic water on the western side. When you sail south from the Cape of Good Hope, you have a powerful sense of being at the meeting place of three oceans: the Atlantic Ocean to the west, the Indian Ocean to the east and the Southern Ocean to the south.

THE NEW WORLD: COLUMBUS'S REDISCOVERY

(1492)

The epic first voyage of Christopher Columbus across the Atlantic Ocean to discover the New World is one of the best-remembered facts of European history. Given the momentously historic nature of his achievement, Christopher Columbus himself remains a surprisingly shadowy figure. The events of his early life are uncertain. His son later recorded that he went to the University of Pavia, where he studied astronomy, geometry and cosmography, a reminiscence that clearly establishes Columbus as an educated man. Yet the story that Columbus himself told was significantly different. He claimed that he had gone to sea at the age of fourteen, which is at odds with the university education. Psychiatrists have a technical term for the tendency that some people have to make up stories about themselves – confabulation. Sometimes a psychological instability lies behind it. There seems to have been a rational purpose to Columbus's confabulation. The overall picture that emerges is that he knew rather more about the geography of the world, especially of what we now call the Western Hemisphere, than he made out at the time.

In 1474, after consulting the Florentine cosmographer Paolo Toscanelli, Columbus hit on the revolutionary idea of reaching India by sailing west instead of east. The success of such a voyage depended on the now widely accepted idea that the Earth is a sphere, and quite a small sphere at that. Thanks partly to an error of Ptolemy and partly to a bit of exaggeration of his own, Columbus underestimated the size of the Earth and overestimated the size of Asia. These two miscalculations together brought China to the position that North America occupies, and the East Indies to the position occupied by the West Indies. In fact Columbus got the latitudes of China and Japan wrong and he was looking for Japan in the West Indies (too far south) and China in Mexico (also too far south). But there was at least land that corresponded.

Was all of this happening by coincidence, by chance, as we have been led to believe? Or was it arrived at by a process of reasoning back from reports of secret landfalls already reported from across the Atlantic? Certainly Columbus knew about reports of driftwood picked up 400 leagues (2,220 kilometres/1,380 miles) west of Cape St Vincent, which implied that there was land not far off in that direction.

Columbus needed a patron for his planned westward voyage to the Orient. He patiently negotiated for seven years with Ferdinand and Isabella of Castile before they finally agreed to sponsor him.

It is still not known to what extent Columbus prepared the discovery of the New World, for example by studying reports of now-forgotten unofficial earlier voyages across the Atlantic, or had it prepared for him by others. Toscanelli may have given him more information than we know about. The possibility that Columbus lied about his education suggests that there was concealment. If Columbus did indeed have a university education, then he may well have thoroughly researched the physical geography of the North Atlantic basin and known in outline what he would find – long before setting sail. Recent research strongly suggests that the existence of a landmass across the Atlantic was already known, and that the Columbus voyage was a 'show discovery', a kind of formal ribbon-cutting ceremony.

However it came about, on 3 August 1492 Columbus set sail on his historic voyage across the Atlantic, in command of a small ship, the *Santa Maria*, accompanied by two even smaller ships, the *Pinta* and the *Nina*. He had eighty-seven men with him. After reaching the Canaries, morale fell. The *Pinta* had already lost her rudder and they had put in at Tenerife to refit. There was talk of Portuguese caravels patrolling in the area with orders to intercept the Spanish-sponsored voyage of discovery. Columbus's superstitious sailors saw a meteor fall into the sea and the vast depressing plains of seaweed known as the Sargasso Sea. They were thoroughly frightened.

Then, on 11 October, two months after setting sail, some significant objects were found floating in the sea: some pieces of driftwood and a branch covered with berries. When they saw this they knew land could not be very far away. In fact land was sighted the next day. Columbus called it San Salvador, now thought to be Watling Island in the Bahamas. In the custom of the time, Columbus put on his Sunday-best clothes for the formal landing, and went ashore as if in a historical pageant, which in a way it was, bearing the royal banner of Spain. The Pinzon brothers carried banners of the Green Cross (Columbus's device). It was a fine tableau made for the painters of historical scenes, and designed to be just that. It was an entirely self-conscious piece of history-making, just like the first Moon landing, with Neil Armstrong's carefully rehearsed first words spoken on the Moon.

Columbus went on to visit Cuba and Haiti, founding a small colony there before setting sail for home.

A second voyage with a larger squadron set sail in September 1493, reaching Dominica in the West Indies in November. This time Columbus was directed specifically to deal kindly with the inhabitants of any new lands and to try to convert them to Christianity. The third voyage in 1498, this time with six ships, led to the discovery, now often forgotten, of the mainland of South America. Columbus had for a long time believed that a landmass existed there, and once again it must be suspected that earlier travellers, perhaps blown a long way off their intended courses, had reported the existence of such a continent.

Columbus's voyages of discovery have an air of having been planned. It is almost as if he was following an itinerary. A comparison between maps of Columbus's voyages and maps of Captain Cook's is revealing. The map of Cook's zig-zagging exploration of the South Pacific really does look like a groping in the darkness of unknowing, while the map of Columbus's voyages implies foreknowledge.

A final, fourth, transatlantic voyage in 1502–4 explored the southern coastline of the Gulf of Mexico. Columbus was stranded for a whole year in Jamaica, where his crew behaved badly and he himself suffered badly from illness. The lawless behaviour of his men alienated the natives, who had initially been friendly and hospitable, and food was often in short supply as a result. Columbus finally set sail for Spain again in September 1504, arriving at Sanlúcar in November. He was too ill then to go to court to report on his adventures, so his son Diego went instead. After many years of hardship and ill treatment, Columbus died at Valladolid in Spain on 20 May 1506.

Opinion is still divided about Christopher Columbus and the 1492 voyage. Some scholars still believe that Columbus was the first European navigator to cross the Atlantic, that he really was the first European to visit the New World. Others think he knew the width of the Atlantic before he set sail because Portuguese ships had already crossed it unofficially, accidentally blown across by the trade winds. If that is so, the Columbus voyages were in effect a publicity stunt, a formal grand opening of the New World to Spanish and Portuguese colonisation. Columbus's ill-concealed formal education in astronomy, cosmography and geometry certainly point to a level of navigational and geographical expertise that might be required to replicate voyages that had already been undertaken, perhaps by Portuguese sailors. And why did he try to conceal that? Either way, Columbus's voyages expanded the horizons of Europeans in an instant and opened the way to European colonisation of North and South America.

In a very short time, the native Americans would come to regret the voyages of 'discovery' by the Europeans, which led to their humiliation, subjugation and disinheritance, the destruction of the Aztec and Inca civilisations, and the wholesale destruction of the ancient ways of life of the first peoples of the New World. The ultimate consequence of the 1492 Columbus voyages was the European takeover of the continents of North and South America.

THE CAPE ROUTE
TO INDIA
(1497)

Henry the Navigator died in 1469, the year when Vasco da Gama was born. Da Gama's voyages of exploration would see the ultimate fulfilment of Prince Henry's programme of exploration, the main aim of which was to find a sea route round Africa. Da Gama was the first to find it and sail it – at least since Hanno in the fifth century BC.

Da Gama was chosen by King Emanuel I of Portugal to find a sea route to India by way of the Cape of Good Hope, which was at that time reckoned to be the southernmost tip of Africa. He set sail from Lisbon on 9 July 1497 with three ships, taking four months to reach St Helena Bay just north of the Cape Peninsula in southern Africa. The segment of the voyage round the Cape of Good Hope itself was a difficult one because of storms and mutinies. In spite of these difficulties, da Gama was able to reach Malindi on the East African coast early in 1498.

From Malindi onwards, da Gama was in known waters, the long-familiar trade routes of the north Indian Ocean, and therefore much easier. He was able to pick up a skilled pilot from Indian merchants at Malindi to help him navigate across the Indian Ocean to Calicut on the Malabar coast.

Vasco da Gama returned to Lisbon in triumph. The king was delighted with this totally successful enterprise and ennobled da Gama. The little chapel at Belem on the Tagus estuary where da Gama and his crew had prayed before setting off was demolished to make way for a magnificent new church to commemorate the historic voyage. Its extravagant architecture was full of references to the sea and seafaring, and it became in itself a new national monument. Everyone was aware that a corner had been turned, that this was a great moment in European, indeed world, history.

The great voyage of Vasco da Gama is justly famous as the first European sea voyage to India, opening up a brand new trade route round Africa, a more reliable route to the Far East. It also opened, immediately, a new phase of European colonisation. Da Gama himself founded Mozambique, the second European colony in southern Africa. The voyage marked the beginning of the highly controversial domination of the subcontinent of India by Europeans, just as the Columbus voyage marked the beginning of the domination of the Americas by Europeans.

NEWFOUNDLAND: JOHN CABOT'S REDISCOVERY

(1497)

John Cabot's name is well known, but the man behind the name remains elusive. He was born in about 1455 at Gaeta near Naples, with the name Giovanni Caboto, and he was the son of a merchant. He seems to have spent some time in Genoa, but by 1461 he was living in Venice. In 1482, he married a Venetian woman, Mattea, and they had three sons, Ludovico, Sebastiano and Sancio.

Cabot traded in spices with eastern Mediterranean ports and became a skilled mariner. In about 1490, Cabot moved with his family to Valencia in Spain. The reason was probably that as an ambitious man he wanted to be in the Iberian peninsula where the frontiers of exploration and commerce were being pushed back. The ruling elites of both Portugal and Spain were keen to find new routes to the East in order to tap its wealth without the hindrance of the Mediterranean and the powers who controlled it. The Italians had a virtual stranglehold on the spice trade.

Cabot was unable to find an interested sponsor in Portugal or Spain. The Portuguese were looking for their route to the East round the south of Africa; the Spanish thought they had reached the East in the New World. Cabot turned to England, and in particular to the merchants in the port of Bristol, where he settled. He approached the English king, Henry VII, with a scheme to reach Asia by sailing west from England across the North Atlantic. He argued that this would be a shorter route than Columbus's more southerly route. This time Cabot was lucky. He got the backing he needed from the Bristol merchants, who had been sponsoring exploratory voyages into the North Atlantic from about 1480. Some scholars think that sailors from Bristol may have reached Newfoundland and Labrador even before Cabot sailed. But Cabot had an official backer. He had letters patent from Henry VII authorising him to sail to 'all parts of the eastern, western and northern sea' to discover 'whatsoever islands, countries, regions, provinces of heathens and infidels, in whatsoever part of the world placed, which before this time were unknown to all Christians.' And of course whatever Cabot achieved would be in the name of the English Crown.

There was a first, abortive voyage in 1496. Very little is known about it other than some stray remarks made by John Day, an English merchant, in a letter to Columbus. Day wrote succinctly, 'He went with one ship, he had a disagreement with the crew, he was short of food and ran into bad weather, and he decided to turn back.' Much misery in few words.

The 1497 voyage was more successful. If Cabot kept a log of his journey, it has disappeared. If he made a map, it too has disappeared. The main evidence is a few maps made at the beginning of the sixteenth century that contain information possibly acquired by Cabot and letters written by contemporaries commenting on the voyage. The result is that historians disagree about what actually happened.

John Cabot's ship was called the *Matthew*, probably in honour of his wife, Mattea. She was a small ship, with a capacity for 50 tons of cargo. She had a deck, a high sterncastle and three masts, the two forward masts carrying square sails and the after mast carrying a triangular lateen sail. About twenty people sailed on the *Matthew* when she left Bristol in May 1497. Cabot probably took her across to Cork, along the south coast of Ireland, and some distance north along the west coast of Ireland before turning west into the Atlantic. He probably set his westerly course at a latitude of about 54 degrees North, west of County Mayo.

How far south he may have drifted from this latitude is open to endless speculation and debate. Some historians believe that he held to this latitude, others believe he drifted far to the south as a result of magnetic variations affecting his compass and the effect of the Labrador

Current. But on 24 June, after thirty-five days at sea, John Cabot sighted land. The big question is: where was this land? Cabot was back in Bristol on 6 August after taking just fifteen days to return across the Atlantic. This means that he spent a whole month exploring the region.

If he held to his original latitude of 54 degrees North, he would have made landfall at Indian Harbour about halfway along the north-east coast of Labrador, so there is a strong chance that John Cabot discovered Labrador. He might well have sailed south while exploring the coastline during July, or have been driven south during the Atlantic crossing. Either way, Cabot is likely to have encountered Newfoundland, which he is always credited with discovering. Initially the island was named Terra Nova, and it is likely that Cabot himself christened it with this name. Some people think Newfoundland is the 'Vinland' known to the early Norse explorers of the area, but Vinland could as easily have been Labrador. Either way, both Newfoundland and Labrador had been visited by Europeans before – by Bjarni Herjólfsson in 986 and by Leif Ericsson in 995.

Newfoundland was a significant rediscovery. It is the sixteenth largest island in the world. It also stands at the mouth of the St Lawrence, creating the Gulf of St Lawrence, the world's biggest estuary. When Cabot visited Newfoundland, there was a native population, the Beothuk (meaning 'people') who seem to have originated in Labrador. Their culture is now extinct, and the last Beothuk died in 1829. The Beothuks were the people the Norse explorers described as *skraelings*. The very first conflicts between Europeans and North Americans occurred in 1006 at L'Anse aux Meadows, when groups of Norsemen tried to set up permanent settlements along the coast of Labrador and Newfoundland. The *skraelings* responded so violently that the Norsemen withdrew and gave up all idea of settling there. The Beothuks were too rough for the Vikings.

When contact was renewed after the 1497 Cabot voyage, it was estimated that anything up to 5,000 Beothuks were living in Newfoundland.

At L'Anse aux Meadows, archaeologists have discovered remains of the one and only authenticated Norse settlement in North America.

This is thought to be Leif Ericsson's settlement, which was inhabited only from 999 until 1001, and it emphatically proves that John Cabot did not discover Newfoundland, but rediscovered it 400 years after Leif Ericsson. Perhaps others came across the Atlantic in between. The Irish Saint Brendan is alleged to have made the voyage across and Welsh folklore has a Prince Madoc landing in North America in 1170. The Scots claim that the Earl of Orkney, Henry Sinclair, sailed to the New World in the late fourteenth century. The Portuguese claim that a Portuguese expedition in 1431 reached the far side of the Atlantic.

Tradition has it that John Cabot landed on Newfoundland at Cape Bauld, at the northernmost tip of Newfoundland. This is supported by a document in the Spanish National Archives written by a Bristol merchant. It says that Cabot landed 2,900 kilometres (1,800 miles) west of Dursey Head in Ireland. Dursey Head is 51 degrees 34 minutes North, and a landfall in that latitude would put Cabot's crew within sight of Cape Bauld. The same letter mentions an island that Cabot sailed past to go ashore; this fits the Cape Bauld theory, as Belle Isle is nearby.

The Cabot rediscovery was an important step in establishing the presence of a North American continent. It also led, during the next 200 years, to the development of a transatlantic fishing industry. In 1498–1500, Portuguese explorers, among them Miguel and Gaspar Corte-Real, visited Greenland, Labrador and Newfoundland.

Starting in 1501, an English syndicate consisting of three Azorean and two English traders made further voyages to Newfoundland. From 1504 onwards Breton, Basque, Portuguese and English fishermen started crossing the ocean to fish on the Grand Banks of Newfoundland. The Irish fishermen who went across to Newfoundland called it Talamh an Eisc, the Land of the Fish.

In 1583, when Sir Humphrey Gilbert formally claimed Newfoundland as an English colony, he found lots of English, French and Portuguese fishing vessels in the harbour at St John's, though there was still no permanent settlement there. It proved difficult to get a permanent colony established, but from 1610 onwards there was a small settlement at Cuper's Cove. The establishment of a permanent colony was essential for the English claim to stick, and by 1620, English fishermen from the West Country had successfully ousted all the non-English settlers from the east coast. French fishermen continued to dominate the south coast. The French formally ceded the whole island by the Treaty of Utrecht in 1713, which can be taken as marking the formal completion of the enterprise that John Cabot initiated.

But when John Cabot arrived back in Bristol in August 1497, he thought he had visited China, that he had found a new and shorter route to Asia. He had not returned with anything of value – no furs, silks or spices – but Columbus too had returned home virtually empty-handed. Cabot had found what everyone thought was the shortest route to wealth. He was regarded as a great hero. He was Henry VII's Columbus. Lorenzo Pasqualigo, a Venetian living in London at the time, commented that 'he is called the Great Admiral and vast honour is paid to him, and he goes about dressed in silk, and these English run after him like mad.' John Cabot was a great celebrity. Henry VII was very pleased, granting him a gift of £10 'to hym that founde the new isle'; he later granted him a pension of £20 a year.

In February of the following year, the English king granted Cabot his second letters patent. This time he was commissioned to take six ships and sail them to 'the land and iles of late founde by the said John.' The voyage began in May 1498. The flotilla set sail. It is known that there was a storm and one ship returned home damaged, but absolutely nothing else is recorded. Cabot disappeared utterly from history. The 1498 voyage is a complete mystery. Given the terms of the letters patent, it is likely that some of the ships recrossed the Atlantic, revisited Newfoundland and explored the island in greater detail. But whether any of the ships returned to England with additional information is impossible to tell.

There is a tradition that Cabot's ship was wrecked not far from Grates Cove and that he got ashore with his son Sancio and some of the crew. Once ashore, they died either of starvation or at the hands of the aggressive Beothuk people. This voyage confirmed that Cabot had not after all discovered a quick and easy route to Asia. He had not found the great cities of an exotic eastern civilisation, but a lonely and pitiful death on a rocky inhospitable shore. The light dawned in England and Spain that Cabot and Columbus had not discovered the short route to the East but a New World, a bleak and daunting continent in between. It must have come as a great disappointment to Cabot's financial backers in Bristol.

BRAZIL
(1500)

Amerigo Vespucci (1454–1512) was a Florentine merchant, explorer and cartographer. He worked for Lorenzo and Giovanni de' Medici and in the year of the Columbus voyage, 1492, they sent him to work in their Seville agency. He was to play a leading role in two major voyages along the eastern coast of South America.

Vespucci undertook four major voyages. On the first, in 1497, Vespucci sailed with the Spanish captain Juan de la Cosa on an expedition organised by King Ferdinand. The intention was evidently to discover if the main landmass of Asia lay close to the island of Hispaniola that had been discovered by Columbus, or far away from it. The leader of this expedition was Vicente Pinzon, who had captained the *Nina* on Columbus's first voyage. Vespucci was accompanied by the pilot and cartographer Juan de la Cosa, who had also sailed with Columbus in 1492.

According to the first published letter attributed to Vespucci, they made landfall at 16 degrees North. This was probably the Guajira Peninsula in Colombia, the northernmost point of South America, or it could have been the east coast of Nicaragua. From there they followed the western coastline of the Caribbean and the Gulf of Mexico, clockwise, right round until they emerged into the Atlantic between Florida and Cuba.

This first voyage was important in confirming that there was a landmass with a continuous coastline to the west of the islands of the Indies. It also confirmed the shape of the Caribbean sea and the Gulf of Mexico. The spectacular array of islands in the Greater and Lesser Antilles, stretching from Cuba in the west to Grenada in the east, was in effect enclosed in a colossal bay.

When the expedition returned to Spain, a famous map was produced, showing Cuba as an island for the first time.

The second voyage, which took place in about 1499–1500, was commissioned by the Spanish, with Alonso de Ojeda as the fleet's commander. The intention of this expedition was to sail right through the Atlantic Ocean, round the southern tip of Africa and into the Indian Ocean. It was what the Portuguese had been striving to do for decades, but had just achieved in the Vasco da Gama voyage. Whether the aim was to show the Portuguese that Spain could achieve just as much, or to verify what the Portuguese had reported about the voyage, is not clear. The approach was very different. The Portuguese had picked their way carefully along the western coast of Africa, bay-hopping, whereas the Spanish fleet sailed wide of the landmass. In doing so, they hit and discovered the coast of South America, striking it somewhere along the coastline of Guyana. At that point, the fleet split up. Vespucci continued to sail southwards along the coast of South America.

Vespucci sailed across the mouth of the Amazon on the equator. He went on and reached latitude 6 degrees South before turning back to explore the south America coastline from Guyana north-westwards. He saw the delta of the River Orinoco and the island of Trinidad before returning to Spain by way of Hispaniola.

The third voyage (1501–2) was sponsored by the Portuguese and led by Gonçalo Coelho. Vespucci and Coelho and their companions set sail from Lisbon and headed for Cape Verde, where they met two of Pedro Cabral's ships returning from India. In his letter to Lorenzo de' Medici written from Cape Verde, Vespucci declared his wish to visit the lands that Cabral had explored. This implies that he was about to set a westward course to sail to Asia, as on the 1499–1500 voyage.

When they reached the coast of Brazil, they sailed south-westwards along it until they reached the bay, where Rio de Janeiro was later to stand. According to the account we have, truthful or not, the expedition reached the latitude of Patagonia before turning back. One reason for doubting it is that in order to reach Patagonia, Vespucci must have crossed the exceptionally wide estuary of the River Plate. If he did, he could not fail to have noticed it, yet the account does not mention this major feature. The maps the Portuguese made immediately following the voyage do not show any land south of 25 degrees South, which seems a likelier point of turning back.

During the expedition, Vespucci mapped the stars of Alpha Centauri and Beta Centauri and the constellation Crux. These were stars known to the ancient Greeks, but because of a slight shift in the Earth's axis they were in Vespucci's time permanently below the horizon and forgotten as far as observers in Europe were concerned. When he got back to Lisbon, Amerigo Vespucci wrote to Lorenzo de' Medici that the landmasses he had seen were much larger than expected. They were also different from descriptions of Asia. What he had been exploring must therefore be a New World, a previously unsuspected fourth continent. Until that moment everyone in Europe had thought in terms of three continents – Europe, Africa and Asia – even after Columbus. Now there were four. It was a very important moment in European consciousness.

Until this time, the discoveries in the New World by Columbus and Cabot had been interpreted as Asian. Vespucci saw that this was not so, that an entirely New World lay on the far side of the Atlantic. It was a revolutionary concept. In a real sense, Vespucci was the discoverer of the New World.

So little is known of his fourth voyage, which may have happened in 1503–4, that some think it never took place.

Two accounts of the voyages of exploration attributed to him were published in 1502–4. Vespucci's achievements became more widely known. Then in 1507 the map-maker Martin Waldseemüller produced a world map on which he labelled the new continent 'America', apparently in honour of Amerigo Vespucci. In a book he produced to accompany the map, *Four Voyages of Amerigo Vespucci*, Waldseemüller published one of Vespucci's acccounts. This led to criticism that Amerigo Vespucci was trying to steal Columbus's thunder. But probably Vespucci was an innocent victim. Letters of Vespucci's that came to light in the eighteenth century show a different side to Vespucci and imply that that the 1502–4 accounts that came out under his name were not actually written by him at all. The letters were informal communications to Lorenzo de' Medici about his voyages. The middle one of the three was actually written during the early part of the third voyage; it was sent to Lorenzo from Cape Verde before Vespucci crossed the Atlantic.

It is said that Vespucci was unaware that people were referring to the new continent by a variant of his own name; there is no way of knowing now. Columbus was no longer around – he died in 1506 – to contest the claims that Vespucci was the discoverer of the New World.

In 1508, after these few but very important voyages, Vespucci in effect retired from active service. The post of Pilot Major of Spain was created for him by King Ferdinand; in this new and lavishly salaried role he was responsible for setting up at his house a school for pilots of future voyages of exploration. He was being turned into a new Henry the Navigator. In 1512, he died of malaria, but not before teaching the science of navigation to students such as Ferdinand Magellan. Vespucci even developed a fairly accurate method for finding longitude – without chronometers – though that claim has been seen by some as incredible, and providing further grounds for disbelieving what the writer had to say, whether that writer was Vespucci or someone else. In the story of the Vespucci voyages, we are plagued incessantly by the unreliability of the documentary sources. Ultimately, we cannot be sure who wrote what, still less whether what we are reading is true.

One further puzzle remains. It has for a long time been accepted that Amerigo Vespucci gave his name to the Americas – or rather that Waldseemüller paid him that honour. The publication of the falsely attributed letters led Martin Waldseemuller to use Vespucci's name on his 1507 globe and map. Like many authors of his day, Vespucci used a Latinised form of his name to sign his published writings, *Americus Vespucius*. Waldseemüller, we are told, decided on a feminine form of Americus, America, as the name for the new continent.

But it is possible that the name America came from a completely different source. Alfred Hudd, a Bristol antiquary, proposed in 1908 that America was named after Richard Amerike, the Bristol merchant who financed John Cabot's voyage of discovery to Newfoundland in 1497. This much was proved by some documents at Westminster Abbey. Waldseemüller is alleged to have included in his map and on his globe information deriving from English voyages across the Atlantic, and he may have had access to an earlier, English, map which incorporated this material. Perhaps the new territory on the far side of the Atlantic appeared on the English map with the name 'America' in honour of Cabot's sponsor, and perhaps Waldseemüller simply incorporated the name from the now-lost English map. The Richard Amerike theory has recently been revived and is now a popular alternative to the Amerigo Vespucci theory.

THE PACIFIC OCEAN
(1513)

The Spanish discoverer of the Pacific, Vasco Nùñez de Balboa, was seventeen when Columbus made his epoch-making voyage in 1492. Like many other adventurous young men of his time, Balboa decided to go to the Spanish colonies in the New World to make his fortune. In 1501, he sailed with Rodrigo de Bastidas to make a preliminary reconnaissance of the Caribbean coastlines of Colombia and Panama. Then he settled in Hispaniola (modern Haiti), where he tried his hand at raising pigs and failed.

At the same time, Alonso de Ojeda and Diego de Nicuesa obtained formal licences to colonise the region explored by Bastidas. Ojeda sailed to the north Colombian coast with 300 men in 1509, and Nicuesa sailed to Panama with 700 men. Things did not go well. There was hostility from the native Americans, and disease and food shortages took a great toll. Within months the thousand men had dwindled to under a hundred. Ojeda returned to Hispaniola, leaving the survivors of his colony in the charge of Francisco Pizarro while they waited for a relief expedition to arrive under Martin Fernandez de Encisco. Encisco arrived with a remarkable stowaway. Balboa had hidden in a barrel that was loaded on board in Hispaniola – to escape from his creditors. Balboa was physically strong, intelligent and wilful and, just as soon as he was out of the barrel, quickly established himself as the group's leader.

Because of his earlier reconnaissance voyage, he had the advantage of substantial knowledge of the region. He persuaded the men to abandon the unsuitable and unhealthy site Ojeda had selected for their camp at San Sebastian. Instead, they were to cross the Gulf of Uraba (now called the Gulf of Darien) to set up a new camp on the Isthmus of Panama. It was to be called Santa Maria la Antigua, or Darien. When they arrived there, he usurped Encisco's authority, which had really only been nominal once Balboa was out of the barrel, and sent him back to Spain. Balboa saw Nicuesa as another potential rival. He was collected along with other survivors and brought to Darien before being sent off in a leaky and poorly supplied vessel.

By now Balboa was in undisputed control of the embryonic Spanish colonies of Colombia and Panama. In 1510, that authority was formally recognised by King Ferdinand of Spain, who conferred on him the title Captain General and Interim Governor of Darien.

Balboa was now a fully fledged conquistador. He extended the Spanish conquest westwards along the Caribbean coast of Central America and inland, either conquering the native population by force or forming alliances by diplomacy. Balboa's men accumulated hoards of gold ornaments as they went. They also heard stories about a sea to the south which was bordered by kingdoms that were fabulously wealthy, loaded with gold.

But Balboa had made a serious and dangerous enemy out of Encisco, whom he had not only ousted but humiliated. Back in Madrid, Encisco was poisoning Balboa's reputation at the Spanish court. Eventually, Encisco was able to persuade King Ferdinand to replace Balboa with the elderly Pedrarias, who was sent with a company of 1,500 men.

Balboa got wind of this impending coup, and set about a coup of his own. He decided he would find this 'South Sea' that the native Americans had told him about. A major discovery would save his position. He set off with a small number of Spanish supporters and a much larger number of friendly natives, with the specific intention of 'discovering' the South Sea. The thousand natives took him to the narrowest part of the Isthmus of Panama. There they fought their way through the swamps and forests of the difficult hill country. It took them twenty-four days to climb up to the peak of Darien, which they reached on 25 September 1513.

From the summit he saw that what the natives had said was true. He saw the huge expanse of the Pacific Ocean stretching away to the south. Realising the significance of his discovery, Balboa marched all the way down to the Pacific coast and into the sea at the Gulf of San Miguel. In a magnificently theatrical gesture, he waded into the Pacific and claimed the South Sea and all the lands that bordered it for Spain. It was slightly absurd, but he knew he had to do something to defend his now-precarious position. As luck would have it there were pearl fisheries nearby, so there was something in the way of treasure to send back to Spain too.

The king did not go back on his appointment of Pedrarias as captain general of Darien, but he did make Balboa governor of the South Sea province and two adjacent provinces. The king was pleased with the pearls and gold Balboa sent him, and for five years a frustrated Pedrarias had to share authority with the piratical Balboa. Balboa was not above sending back reports, Encisco-style, complaining about his rival's maltreatment of friendly natives. Pedrarias tried to improve the situation by offering Balboa his daughter in marriage.

In the end, Balboa overreached himself. He had four ships built on the Pacific coast of Panama with a view to sailing off on another conquest expedition. Then he was summoned to a meeting with Pedrarias. On his way to it, Pizarro intercepted and arrested him. Balboa was accused of treason and condemned to death. He was beheaded in January 1519.

The discovery of the South Sea – it was left to Magellan to name it the Pacific Ocean later – added a new element to the European conception of the world. What had so far been discovered of the Americas had until recently been interpreted in Europe as part of eastern Asia. Presumably the South Sea, in that context, would be considered to be the Indian Ocean. The change in perception had been made by Amerigo Vespucci a few years earlier, though. America was a New World. Here was a new ocean, and it would be left to Magellan to find out how vast it was.

THE EARTH'S ROUNDNESS: MAGELLAN'S CIRCUMNAVIGATION
(1519–21)

Ferdinand Magellan's exploring career began in 1504, when he enlisted as a volunteer for the voyage to India of the first Portuguese viceroy, Francisco de Almeida. He served in India again in 1508 and was wounded at the Battle of Diu in 1509. Later that year, Magellan embarked from Cochin in southern India on a voyage that was intended to reach the Spice Islands, but the expedition was attacked and halted at Malacca. In 1510, he was rewarded for his service with the rank of captain. He distinguished himself again at the capture of Malacca under Albuquerque. After that he was assigned the task of sailing from Malacca to the Spice Islands; he came back with reports of abundant spices.

Magellan returned to Portugal in 1512 and the following year he accompanied an expedition to capture the town of Azamor in Morocco. During this action, Magellan was wounded and lamed for life. He was accused of trading with the Moors and as a result of this fell out of favour with King Manuel of Portugal, who gave him to understand that his country would have no further use for his services.

Magellan responded to this doubly crippling adversity with great spirit. He was always a man of action, and never a man of letters; he left no written record of his remarkable career. He coped with King Manuel's snub by renouncing his Portuguese citizenship and offering his services to the court of Spain. In particular he offered to Charles V an ambitious scheme which was in effect an extension of the Columbus project – to reach the Spice Islands by the westerly route. Columbus had sailed west apparently under the impression that there was just one ocean between Europe and the Spice Islands; after the discovery of the Americas, Magellan knew that there were two oceans. He would have to sail across the Atlantic and the Pacific. What Magellan set out to do was therefore far more ambitious and courageous than Columbus's Atlantic crossing of just twenty years earlier.

He hoped to find a sea passage to the south of South America, even though none had been discovered; it was still possible that the South Atlantic was a landlocked basin. He is said to have declared boldly that he would sail as far south as latitude 75 degrees South in search of the sea passage through to the Pacific.

In planning this ambitious and risky expedition, Magellan had help from Faleiro, an astronomer, and Christopher de Haro, a financial backer who bore a grudge against the King of Portugal. On 22 March 1518, Magellan and Faleiro, as joint captains general, signed an agreement with Charles V by which they would receive five per cent of the profits of the expedition. The government of any lands conquered along the way would rest in their hands and those of their heirs.

On 10 August 1519, Magellan set sail from Seville with five ships and 270 men. Faleiro decided not to travel with him after all; he had cast his horoscope and found that the expedition would be fatal to him. Statistically, he was probably right. Only one of the five ships, the *Vittoria*, would actually make it back to Spain at the end of the voyage.

While sailing south along the coast of Argentina, Magellan dealt with a formidable mutiny among his own men and also met the natives, to whom he gave the name 'Patagonians', meaning 'Big Feet'. In this way, Magellan inadvertently named the region of Patagonia. Then he found his way through the winding strait that still bears his name, the Magellan Straits separating the mainland of South America from Tierra del Fuego. At that time it was assumed that Tierra del Fuego, the Land of Fire, was the northernmost promontory of a huge southern continent, and was shown as such on maps, though eventually it proved to be an island.

In November 1519, Magellan's small fleet sailed into Balboa's Great South Sea, which Magellan flatteringly named the Pacific Ocean.

By this time, one of the ships had been wrecked and another had turned back to head for home. Later a third ship had to be burnt and scuttled in the Pacific because so many men had died that only two ships could be properly manned. Then the two remaining ships became separated, and one of them was captured by the Portuguese.

The enormous size of the Pacific Ocean came as a great shock and crossing it came close to killing everyone on the expedition. The Magellan voyage is regarded as the first successful circumnavigation of the world, but it came very close indeed to being a total disaster. It took Magellan ninety-eight days to cross the Pacific, a huge empty expanse of sea, a blue wilderness. In all that journey, he discovered only two islands, both of them small, uninhabited and sterile. His crews had to manage without fresh provisions, including fresh water. They suffered terribly from scurvy. They ended up eating sawdust, oxhides and rats.

At last they made landfall in some islands that were inhabited. Magellan unflatteringly named the islands the Ladrones because the inhabitants were thieves. This was Guam.

Magellan himself was killed in a fight with natives in the Philippines. His ship nevertheless returned home to Spain, complete with a massive cargo of cloves, commanded by the last surviving Spanish captain, Juan del Cano. Del Cano reached Spain on 6 September 1522, becoming the first man to sail right round the world in a single expedition. Of the 270 men who had set off at the start of the voyage, only eighteen made it back to Spain after this epic tour of the Earth. Magellan did not make it back to Spain, but, falling at Mactan, he died at a point further to the west than the longitude of his earlier furthest east in the Moluccas. In that sense, Magellan *did* go right round the world.

The significance of the Magellan circumnavigation was enormous. It showed conclusively, for the first time, that the Earth was a sphere. It also demonstrated the size of that sphere. The shape and size of the Earth were established. On a smaller scale, it revealed the enormous size and emptiness of the Pacific Ocean. It also supplied Patagonia, the Straits of Magellan and the Pacific Ocean with their names.

EXPLORING PERU
(1530–38)

The earliest attempt to explore the western part of South America was in 1522. Pascual de Andagoya was told by native South Americans of a gold-rich land called Viru, on a river called Piru (or Peru). Andagoya explored part of what is now the Colombia-Ecuador border before falling ill. When he returned to Panama, he spread stories about the gold of Peru, which caught the attention of Francisco Pizarro. Pizarro formed a partnership with de Luque, a priest, and Almagro, a soldier, to explore and conquer the south, dividing its wealth equally among them.

The first expedition to conquer left Panama in September (1524), but failed to reach Peru because of bad weather, hostile natives and food shortage, and returned to Panama. Two years later a second expedition was mounted. Though small – only 160 men – Pizarro divided his forces. Pizarro explored the swamps of the Colombian coast while Almagro returned to Panama for reinforcements. Bartolomeo Ruiz, Pizarro's pilot, meanwhile sailed on south with a third group, crossed the equator and captured a native balsa raft, which was found to be carrying gold, silver and emeralds. Ruiz then sailed north to find Pizarro, to find him and his men exhausted and in difficulties. Then Almagro arrived from Panama with welcome reinforcements and supplies.

The new governor of Panama declined to sponsor a third expedition in 1527; instead he sent a couple of ships off to fetch Pizarro and the others back. But Pizarro refused. He drew a line in the sand for his men and pointed: 'There lies Peru with its riches; here Panama and its poverty. Choose!' Just thirteen men decided to stay with him. Even Ruiz left, though with the intention of getting reinforcements and eventually returning to Pizarro. By 1528 Almagro and Luque were back with Pizarro and exploring north-west Peru. There they were welcomed by the Tumpis people, whose chief was festooned with silver and gold. Pizarro's exploration was still motivated by the desire to find great riches in gold and he went on, exploring as far as 9 degrees South.

As the third expedition was being prepared, the new governor of Panama, Pedro de los Rios, stopped it. The conquistadors decided that Pizarro must appeal in person to Charles V at Toledo. Pizarro impressed the king with his account of the wealth of Peru. Before leaving for Italy, Charles promised to support him, and it was Queen Isabella who signed his licence to conquer Peru; Pizarro was named 'Governor of New Castile' and, well in advance, given complete authority in Spain's new empire.

Before returning to the New World, Pizarro persuaded his brother Hernando and other friends to join him, among them Francisco de Orellana, who would later discover and explore the River Amazon. Pizarro was unable to raise the full number of crew to meet the terms of his licence, so he had to sail clandestinely from Spain to the Canaries in January 1530. There he waited for two more vessels. Pizarro's third and last expedition embarked from Panama for Peru in December 1530.

Landing on the coast of Ecuador, Pizarro met with opposition from the native Punians, and fighting followed. Hernando de Soto was despatched to explore, and he eventually returned with an envoy from the Inca king and an invitation to a meeting. The Inca king Atahualpa had recently defeated his brother Huascar, and Pizarro understood that to conquer Peru he had to destroy Atahualpa. Pizarro and a small force of fewer than 170 soldiers marched for two months to Cajamarca, where Atahualpa was waiting for him. Atahualpa could easily have destroyed the Spanish interlopers, but he did not feel threatened by them. There were no more than 200 Spaniards in his empire, while he had an army of 80,000; he had no reason to fear the intruders. Pizarro attacked the Inca army immediately, won, and captured and executed Atahualpa the following year. Then Pizarro invaded Cuzco and completed the conquest of Peru. The conquest was unscrupulous, violent and bloody. Pizarro naturally glossed over the atrocities he had committed when writing back to the Spanish king, smoothly describing the new acquisitions: 'This city [Cuzco] is the greatest and the finest ever seen in this country or anywhere in the Indies. We can assure your Majesty that it is so beautiful and has such fine buildings that it would be remarkable even in Spain.' Pizarro went on to found a new capital city, Lima, on the central coast.

After an inevitable quarrel among the conquistadors, a group of Almagro's supporters stormed Pizarro's palace in Lima and killed him.

In Peru, Pizarro has increasingly come to be regarded as a kind of criminal, and this is perfectly understandable. In the age of European imperialism, he was held up as an iconic, heroic figure, but he is now seen as an aggressor, an invader, a killer. He was to an extent an explorer, but only incidentally.

THE ST LAWRENCE RIVER

(1534–41)

Jacques Cartier was a Breton with expertise in navigation and cartography. In 1534, 1535–36 and 1541 he made two voyages to explore the St Lawrence River, the major river that connects the Great Lakes and empties into the Gulf of St Lawrence on the Atlantic coast.

The background purpose of the exploration was to find the fabled north-west passage. This was the sea route round the north of North America that would enable Europeans to trade with China. In April 1534, Cartier left the port of St Malo, his home town, with two ships. After twenty days he sighted Newfoundland. After following the coast of Newfoundland, Cartier systematically explored the whole coastline of the Gulf of St Lawrence. Following orders from the French king, Francis I, in the following year Cartier sailed up the great river that emptied into the head of the Gulf of St Lawrence. He entered the river on 10 August, which was the feast day of St Lawrence, and he named the river accordingly.

Cartier sailed on up the broad estuary as far as Stadacona. This native American village was to become the site of the city of Quebec. Then he sailed on to another village called Hochelaga and saw the Ottawa River and some rapids. Believing that China lay beyond the rapids, Cartier named them Lachine Rapids. He also named a conspicuous hill Mont Réal, which later became the site of the city of Montreal. He had sailed a long way inland from the open Atlantic, but Cartier had still ascended only halfway to Lake Ontario, the first of the Great Lakes. He sailed back down to Stadacona to overwinter. On his voyage home he held a course down the centre of the Gulf of St Lawrence, passing to the south of Newfoundland and sailing for the first time through the Cabot Strait, the Gulf's main exit into the Atlantic.

Cartier set off on his third voyage of discovery in 1541. He retraced his earlier course up the St Lawrence as far as Lachine Rapids. His hope was to set up a French colony in Canada, but the weather conditions were too severe and his crew were afflicted with scurvy, so the expedition had to be cut short. In 1542, he had to return to France, where he lived in retirement in St Malo.

Cartier's carefully planned and mapped voyages clarified the geography of the Gulf and estuary of St Lawrence, a large and complex feature of eastern Canada. They also formed the basis of France's claim to Quebec as a colony.

THE MISSISSIPPI RIVER

(1541)

The Mississippi was discovered by Hernando de Soto, one of the Spanish conquistadors who had joined Pizarro in the 1530s. He had become phenomenally rich as a result of his share of the Inca treasure.

In 1539, de Soto organised the biggest of the early Spanish exploratory expeditions. It ranged across the south-eastern quadrant of the United States with the dual aim of finding gold and a sea passage to China. We now know that North America is a huge continuous landmass, but on the knowledge available in 1530 it might have been an island group, with sea channels passing through.

The exact route de Soto followed is still being debated and discussed among historians. The first part of it, as far as Mabila in Alabama, is generally agreed. After that, there are historians (and local pressure groups) who favour a southerly route through Mississippi, Arkansas and Texas; there are others who argue for a northerly route through Tennessee, Kentucky and Indiana. Historical heritage has a cash value in terms of the tourist industry, and the dispute has become as much commercial as historical. Most of the encampment sites have been built over, and the only one that has produced solid archaeological evidence of de Soto's presence is the Apalachee village of Anhaica, about a mile east of the Florida Capitol building at Tallahassee in Florida; this, de Soto's first winter encampment, was discovered in 1987.

Sailing from Cuba, de Soto landed 620 men from nine ships at Charlottte Harbor in Florida. De Soto's men soon sighted Juan Ortiz, a young Spaniard who had gone to Florida in search of a lost earlier expedition and been held captive by the Uzica tribe. The Uzica chief's daughter had pleaded for Ortiz' life when her father ordered him to be roasted alive. Ortiz was rescued and joined the de Soto expedition as its lead guide; he knew the country and the language. He also organised a system for recruiting local guides along the route to deal with tribal dialects. Many of the Spaniards on de Soto's expedition were suspicious of Ortiz, because he continued to dress like a native North American. As with Lawrence of Arabia, Ortiz' exotic dress attracted deep suspicion.

After overwintering in the western panhandle of Florida, the Spanish turned towards the north-east through Georgia and South Carolina, following rumours of gold. No gold appeared, and de Soto headed north into the Appalachians. After that he turned south to the Gulf of Mexico to rendezvous with his ships bringing fresh supplies from Havana. On the way, de Soto was lured into an ambush at Mabila. The Choctaw chief Tascalusa tried to trap him there; de Soto managed to fight his way out, but forty Spaniards were killed in the battle.

De Soto took his men north into Tennessee to spend the winter. On 8 May 1541, de Soto's expedition reached the Mississippi River. It is not known for certain whether de Soto was the first European to set eyes on the Mississippi, but he was certainly the first to report it in documents. De Soto's discovery was profoundly important to him. The wide river represented a major obstacle to his journey of exploration. It took him about a month to have floats built, to transfer all his men and supplies across the Mississippi, and all this under the noses of hostile natives.

After wintering on the Arkansas River, de Soto moved on more erratically. Juan Ortiz had died, making the task of communicating with the native Americans much harder; getting food and finding directions became more difficult. The expedition penetrated as far into the interior as the Caddo River. There the Spanish clashed with an extremely aggressive tribe called the Tula. The expedition fell back to the Mississippi Valley, where de Soto himself died of a fever in May 1542. In an attempt to intimidate the native Americans, de Soto had promoted the idea of himself as an undying sun god. His followers therefore had to conceal his death. They tried to sink his body in the middle of the Mississippi at night, but the natives saw what they were doing and guessed the truth.

De Soto's long journey of exploration was a complete failure in his own terms. The Spanish found no gold, and they found no sea route to

China either. Over half of the members of the expedition died. No colonies were founded. It was a disaster. After de Soto's death, the decision was made to abort the expedition. But a great deal had been achieved that was of geographical value. The broad outlines of the physical geography of the south-east quarter of the United States were now known, along with its western boundary, the Mississippi River. The horses that escaped from the expedition established the first populations of mustangs in North America. The pigs de Soto brought in introduced pork to the South. The friction between de Soto and various native tribes forged a hostile relationship between natives and Europeans that would be reinforced thereafter. The Spanish also introduced diseases that wiped out the native populations of several of the areas visited. The de Soto expedition's descriptions of native culture were to be the only European accounts of the Mississippian culture at its peak. It was a huge and very mixed legacy.

THE COURSE OF THE
RIVER AMAZON
(1541)

Discovering the Amazon was one of the great discoveries of what is often called the great age of discoveries, simply because of the river's sheer size. It is one of the major features of world geography – the largest river in the world by discharge (volume of water), almost the longest river in the world (the Nile is slightly longer), and with the largest catchment area in the world.

Vicente Pinzón was the first European to sail into the river from the Atlantic in 1500. He named it Rio Santa Maria de la Mar Dulce, which was too long to catch on and became shortened to Mar Dulce ('Sweet Sea'). The river mouth Pinzón sailed into was a huge gulf over 320 kilometres (200 miles) across.

The exploration of the great rivers of Africa was still going on in the nineteenth century, with various adventurers finding this reach or that and struggling to find the sources. With the Amazon, it was spectacularly different. The entire course of the river was discovered all in one go – and by accident. Francisco de Orellana was governor of Guayaquil on the Pacific coast. He led a group of Spaniards inland from Guayaquil, passing through Quito to reach Gonzalo Pizarro's camp near El Barco. The idea was to explore the area east of Quito, which was believed to be rich in metals and cinnamon. The expedition ran out of food and Orellana volunteered to take a party down the River Napo in search of food supplies. The Napo was one of the northern headstreams of the Amazon though the Spaniards did not know that that was what it was. The intention was to use it for local transport, starting on 26 December 1541, but the river's current was so strong that Orellana's party could not go back upstream. They were swept away from Pizarro's camp and carried on further and further into the interior of South America. There was no going back.

This epic journey took place in 1541–42. The account of the journey was written by Friar Gaspar de Carvajal, Orellana's chaplain, who kept a journal. He described many difficult encounters with groups of native South Americans as they passed their villages on the river bank – and many close escapes.

On 5 June 1542, after nearly six months' sailing down the upper Amazon, Orellana arrived at a substantial village. A public square in the village contained a large wooden relief carving of a walled city with enclosure, gates, towers with windows. The carving rested on the paws of two 'fierce lions', which were possibly jaguars. Between the lion figures was a hole through which libations to the Sun god were poured. One of the natives said that carvings like this symbolised their mistress, the ruler of the Amazons who expected offerings from the villagers of macaw and parrot feathers, which were used to line the ceilings of their temples. Close by in the public square was a ceremonial house in which were stored feather costumes used in ritual dances.

Orellana found a similar wooden carving made out of a tree trunk in the next village. Then the Spaniards became nervous as the gatherings of natives were getting bigger and therefore more threatening. They continued downriver under constant threat of attack until 7 June, when they captured a small village and stole food supplies from it.

In early June, the party passed Carreiro Island at the confluence with the Amazon's main tributary, the Rio Negro. They were struck by the fact that the two huge rivers continued to flow side by side in the joint channel, the white, mud-laden water of the Amazon on the right and the black, clear water of the Negro on the left, flowing along together but not mixing for many miles below the confluence. Then Orellana passed the confluence with the Rio Madeira, which he called Rio Grande because of its impressive size. There the north bank was lined with very large settlements built on the sloping valley side. Along the river banks trophy human heads were displayed on gibbets. The

Spaniards called this reach of the Amazon the Province of the Gibbets.

Further downstream, on 22 June they passed another town on the north bank with glistening white houses. Orellana and his men were unable to visit this town because the winds and the river current were too strong. The next day they were able to land at another town, the Town of the Street, which had a central street with houses along each side. Then the natives attacked the Spanish boats, firing so many arrows that the brigantines looked like porcupines. Carvajal lost an eye in this onslaught. The Spaniards were struck by the participation of women warriors in this attack; these 'Amazons' fought every bit as fiercely and bravely as the men. After seven or eight of the Indians were killed they lost heart and fell back. The outnumbered Spaniards made for the centre of the river, and fled downstream with the Indians chasing them. After that, Orellana avoided land. Whenever he saw a village, he saw groups of warriors assembled ready to attack them. He even avoided the uninhabited islands along the lower Amazon, because their adjacent river banks bristled with armed natives.

The party eventually reached the Atlantic on 26 August 1542, eight months after embarking. Carvajal's *Relación* (*Account*) was not published until as late as 1855, and not published in full until 1896.

THE SUN AS THE
CENTRE OF THE SOLAR
SYSTEM
(1543)

Places can be discovered, then forgotten and later rediscovered. As we saw, Newfoundland and the mainland of North America were discovered in the tenth century, and then again in the fifteenth century. It is the same with ideas. The place of the Sun in the universe, or at least in the solar system, has been known (or assumed) and then forgotten (or rejected) before being rediscovered again. The idea that the Sun is at the centre of the solar system is known as heliocentrism. Its converse, the idea that the Earth is at the centre, is known as geocentrism.

What we see when we look up at the sky is the Sun moving; the Earth feels stationary. It is rather surprising that many early systems of cosmology were counter-intuitive: they were heliocentric. In the ancient world this idea was arrived at through philosophy rather than astronomy. Vedic Sanskrit texts from ancient India include this idea. In about 800 BC, Yajnavalkya viewed the Earth as a sphere and the Sun as 'the centre of the spheres'. He knew that the Sun was much larger than the Earth and measured the distances of the Sun and the Moon from Earth as 108 times the diameters of each of the spheres; in fact, it is 108 for the Sun and 110 for the Moon. Another commentary, the Vishnu Purana of about 50 BC, made clear that the Sun was stationary; 'Of the sun, which is always in one and the same place, there is neither setting nor rising.'

Aristotle was a geocentrist. The first of the ancient Greeks to argue for heliocentrism was Aristarchus of Samos, in about 270 BC. He calculated the size of the Earth, and the distances of the Moon and the Sun, and concluded that the Sun was six times bigger than the Earth, which was a major underestimate. His arguments for a Sun-centred universe have been lost, but they were referred to by others, including Archimedes. It may be that his awareness that the Sun was much larger than the Earth led him to assume that it was more likely that the Earth moved round the Sun than the other way round. Plutarch mentions 'the followers of Aristarchus', which tells us that other astronomers in antiquity also thought the Earth moved round the Sun.

In Babylonia, the astronomer Seleucus adopted the Sun-centred system of Aristarchus in around 150 BC and according to Plutarch he may even have proved it. The Middle eastern scholar Qutb al-Din, in the thirteenth century AD, considered the possibility that the universe was Sun-centred. Generally medieval Muslims, like medieval Christians, accepted Ptolemy's Earth-centred universe. There were, even so, scholars who were critical of Ptolemy and ready to question geocentrism.

In medieval Christian Europe, the prevailing model was geocentric. In fact it was one of the fundamental principles of European Christianity that the human race was the central organic creation of the universe and the Earth, its home, was the fixed centre of the universe. Everything else revolved round it.

In the Renaissance, it was Nicolaus Copernicus (1473–1543) who was the first to dare to propose that instead the *Sun* was the centre of the universe, and that the Earth revolved round it. Today, we would see cosmology, the study of the universe, as a purely scientific pursuit. In the sixteenth century, it was regarded as the preserve of theologians.

The Bible, on which Christianity was founded, includes a few references to the nature of the Earth. That automatically made cosmology the interest area of theologians. The Church's view of the universe was not really derived from the Bible at all but from Ptolemy. Ptolemy's book *Almagest* was compiled in about AD 150. The Ptolemaic system was an amalgam of previous theories that put the Earth as a stationary object at the centre of a universe that revolved round it. Revolving close to the Earth were small concentric spheres, each with a planet or the Sun or Moon embedded in it. Outside was a larger, fixed, sphere which had the stars embedded in it.

Because the medieval Church had decided on the Ptolemaic model, in other words that the Earth was at the centre of the universe, Copernicus's statement that it was not automatically counted as a heresy. Some centuries before, the scholars of other cultures had put the Sun at the centre, for example in India and ancient Greece, but Copernicus was the first European to oppose the Church's view of the universe with such an idea.

Copernicus was studying law at Bologna when he met the famous astronomer Domenico Maria Novara da Ferrara. Copernicus was inspired by Novara's lectures and became his assistant, helping Novara with astronomical observations. It is thought that while he was in Padua Copernicus read some pages in Cicero and Plato reporting the opinions of the ancient world on the movement of the Earth. In the third century BC, Aristarchus of Samos described some of the theories of Heraclides Ponticus (the daily rotation of the Earth on its axis, the revolution of Mercury and Venus round the Sun) to propose the very first scientific model of a Sun-centred solar system. The Earth and all the other planets revolved round the Sun, the Earth rotated on its axis once a day, the Moon revolved round the earth once a month. The detail had not survived, so it was and still is only possible to speculate about the evidence that led Aristarchus to his conclusion. Interestingly, even in antiquity, this idea was seen as heretical. Plutarch, who was a contemporary of Aristarchus, accused Aristarchus of impiety because he was 'putting the Earth in motion'. So the heliocentric (Sun-centred) idea was controversial even in antiquity.

In 1504, Copernicus started to gather observations and ideas that were relevant to the hypothesis of a Sun-centred universe, though always as a sideline, a hobby. He never earned his living as an astronomer; instead he was employed as a civil servant.

In 1514, Copernicus wrote a *Little Commentary*, a handwritten summary of his developing ideas on a heliocentric universe, and circulated it among his friends. In 1533, Johann Widmannstetter delivered a series of lectures in Rome, outlining Copernicus's theory. Among those listening with great interest were Pope Clement VII and a number of cardinals. At this stage there seems to have been no overt criticism, only excitement at a wonderful new idea.

Rumours were spreading all over Europe about Copernicus's new idea, which scholars were hearing about second hand. He was urged to publish his theory in a book, but he was nervous – and justifiably so – of the consequences. He was probably worried about the possible denunciation of his work by scientists. On the other hand, other people had openly discussed the scientific evidence for the precise movements of the Earth, such as Nicole Oresme and Nicolaus Cusanus, and they had not fallen foul of the Church. He had no particular reason, at that stage, to fear the response of the Church.

The ramifications of his theory were enormous, and Copernicus was intelligent enough, and had a background that was broad enough, to realise that a great deal was at stake. It was a new idea, or a very old idea resuscitated, that had extraordinary importance. It has often been said that few other people have exerted such a far-reaching influence on human civilisation in general and on science in particular. Copernicus knew that many things were going to be changed by his idea. There is a conspicuous parallel here with Darwin and his big new idea, the evolution of species, in the nineteenth century. Both men were acutely aware of the importance of their ideas and of the upset they would cause; both shrank from the bitter controversy that would follow; both delayed definitive publication for a long time, postponing it until late in life.

Copernicus was a modest and moderate man. This is very clear from his writings.

I am not so enamoured of my own opinions that I disregard what others may think of them. I am aware that a philosopher's ideas are not subject to the judgment of ordinary persons, because it is his endeavour to seek the truth in all things, to the extent permitted to human reason by God. Yet I hold that completely erroneous views should be shunned. Those who know that the consensus of many centuries has sanctioned the conception that the Earth remains at rest in the middle of the heaven as its centre would, I reflected, regard it as an insane pronouncement if I made the opposite assertion that the earth moves.

When a ship is floating calmly along, the sailors see its motion mirrored in everything outside, while on the other hand they suppose that they are stationary, together with everything on board. In the same way, the motion of the Earth can unquestionably produce the impression that the entire universe is rotating.

So I feel no shame in asserting that this whole region engirdled by the Moon, and the centre of the Earth, traverse this grand circle amid the rest of the planets in an annual revolution around the Sun. Near the Sun is the centre of the universe. Moreover, since the Sun remains stationary, whatever appears as a motion of the Sun is really due rather to the motion of the Earth.

In 1539, the mathematician Georg Rheticus arrived in Frombork, where Copernicus was working on his definitive book. Rheticus became Copernicus's pupil and stayed with him for two years. During that time he wrote his own book, called *First Account*, which gave an outline of Copernicus's theory. Although Copernicus was writing a book himself, he was not at all sure he wanted to publish it. The favourable reception of *First Account*, together with Rheticus's enthusiasm, finally brought Copernicus round. He agreed to publish. He would give the book to his close friend the Bishop of Kulm, who would deliver it for printing in Nuremberg.

Copernicus died in May 1543, and it is said that the first printed copy of the book was put into his hands just before he died. In an early manuscript copy of the book, Copernicus specifically quoted Aristarchus and Philolaus as sources of his idea. He wrote, 'Philolaus believed in the mobility of the Earth, and some say that Aristarchus of Samos was of that opinion.' For reasons that Copernicus never explained, he cut that passage from the final version for publication. Probably he was unwilling to lean on pre-Christian scholarly sources for fear that opponents could quickly develop that into 'Copernicus subscribes to pagan ideas.'

Copernicus' great book, *On the Revolutions of the Celestial Spheres*, presented a rounded discussion of the heliocentric model of the universe, much as Ptolemy had offered for the geocentric model in his *Almagest* in the second century. Copernicus discussed the philosophical implications of his system, used astronomical observations to support the mathematical parameters of his model, and even presented astronomical tables predicting future positions of starts and planets. What he was doing was moving the heliocentric model from the realm of philosophical speculation to the world of scientific proof.

The next phase in the adoption of the heliocentric model came with the arrival of Galileo Galilei, who was to become the great champion of the Copernican heliocentric theory. After being appointed to the chair of mathematics at the University of Pisa in 1589, Galileo moved to Padua, where he taught geometry, astronomy and mechanics until 1610. It was at that time that Galileo made many of his discoveries. In 1610, Galileo published his observations of the moons of Jupiter. He saw that the moons were arranged in a line but one by one disappeared periodically, then reappeared. The only possible explanation was that they were disappearing behind Jupiter, that their movements corresponded to regular orbits and that the line of moons was in effect the common plane of their orbits. Galileo used these observations to argue in favour of Copernicus's heliocentric universe, and against the old Ptolemaic geocentric universe. The geocentric view of the universe had all celestial bodies revolving round the Earth, but Galileo's observations of the moons of Jupiter clearly demonstrated that they were revolving round Jupiter, not the Earth. Later, his observations of the phases of Venus similarly showed that Venus must be revolving round the Sun.

The telescope was giving the lie to the ancient Ptolemaic model that had its roots in Aristotle. Using his telescopes, Galileo became the first person to see mountains and craters on the Moon. He even tried to estimate the heights of the mountains from the length of their shadows. He described the surface of the Moon as 'rough and uneven, just like the surface of the Earth itself'. This was another departure from the teaching of Aristotle. But all these departures from the accepted view of the universe were leading Galileo towards conflict with the Church.

He went to Rome to demonstrate his new telescope to the distinguished philosophers and mathematicians there. Not long after, in 1612, the first opposition was voiced to the Sun-centred universe. Then, in 1614, came the critical moment when a priest formally and publicly denounced it as heresy. It was Father Tommaso Caccini who denounced Galileo's opinions from the pulpit of Santa Maria Novella, one of the great churches of Rome; he declared Galileo's theory dangerous and heretical. Galileo was ready to defend himself against this accusation, but in 1616 he was handed a formal reprimand by Cardinal Bellarmino, warning him not to advocate or teach the Copernican theory. The Church's position was made clear; the Pythagorean doctrine of the Earth's movement and the immobility of the Sun 'is false and altogether opposed to the Holy Scripture.'

Cardinal Bellarmino insisted that the Copernican system could only be vindicated if there was proof, 'a true physical demonstration that the Sun does not circle the Earth but the Earth circles the Sun.' Galileo thought the tides provided this proof and circulated his account of the tides in 1616. But Galileo's arguments regarding tides fall over themselves in their determination to prove the 'Galilean' relationship between the Earth and the Sun, and dismiss the Moon as of no importance. Now, we know that both the Sun and the Moon exert their separate pulls on the oceans, which is why successive tides at the same place vary in height.

In 1630, Galileo was in Rome again, to apply for a licence to publish *Dialogue Concerning the Two Chief World Systems*, which appeared in Florence two years later with the full permission of the Inquisition and the Pope. But then he was ordered to present himself at the Holy Office in Rome. It was nothing less than an inquisition.

Galileo entered into a dispute with a Jesuit called Grassi regarding the nature of comets. The debate became polemical. Grassi wrote *The Astronomical and Philosophical Balance*. Galileo wrote *The Assayer* as a riposte. Galileo's book is regarded as a masterpiece of polemical literature and it was widely acclaimed at the time. It even pleased the new pope, Urban VIII, who was the dedicatee. But this was a short-term victory. Because Grassi was a Jesuit and Galileo had in effect publicly humiliated him, Galileo alienated the Jesuits in general. How influential the Jesuits were in orchestrating the major trouble Galileo found himself in later is hard to tell, but Galileo and his friends became convinced that the Jesuits were responsible for bringing about his condemnation.

Galileo had to face the Roman Inquisition. The Church had decided that Aristotle and Ptolemy were right, that the Earth was fixed, stationary, and the rest of the universe turned round it. It leant on certain Biblical references in Psalms, Chronicles and Ecclesiastes, which said things such as 'the world is firmly established, it cannot be moved,' and 'the Lord set the Earth on its foundations; it can never be moved.' Galileo stood his ground, arguing that heliocentrism does not contradict those passages. He took the view that many modern people have taken subsequently, which is that the scriptural verses in question should not be taken as teaching but as poetry. The men who wrote those passages wrote from the vantage point of the terrestrial world, and about how things appeared from that vantage point.

Pope Urban VIII had asked Galileo to include arguments for and against a Sun-centred universe; he also asked for his own views to be incorporated. Galileo included a character called Simplicius to present the Earth-centred universe view in his *Dialogue Concerning the Two Chief World Systems*. Galileo could not resist outwitting Simplicius in order to make the case for a Sun-centred universe appear stronger. It was unfortunate that this made Simplicius, who was actually voicing the Pope's views, look a fool. Pope Urban was intelligent enough to realise that Galileo was making fun of him, and did not like it. Nor did he like the very obvious bias of the book, which was not what he had agreed to when he gave Galileo consent to publish.

Galileo found himself standing trial for heresy in 1633. He was required to recant his Sun-centred universe ideas, which were formally denounced as 'absurd, philosophically false, and formally heretical'. He was found guilty of 'following the position of Copernicus, which is contrary to the true sense and authority of Holy Scripture.' His *Dialogue* was banned and he would not be allowed to publish any more works at all. He was also sentenced to imprisonment, though this was later commuted to house arrest.

Stung by this incredibly reactionary experience, Galileo stayed for a while in the home of the Archbishop of Siena, who was a friend. Then he was allowed to return to his own home at Arcetri not far outside Florence. There he lived out the rest of his life under house arrest. He died in January 1642. But the Catholic Church could not turn its face from the reality of the universe for ever. Science moved on, increasingly independently of the Church, and of religious belief, finding out many new things about the cosmos that were not in the Bible. Eventually the Church had to come to an accommodation with the scientific perception of the universe, and with the memory of the deeply wronged Galileo. In 1718, the Inquisition's ban on printing Galileo's books was lifted; in 1741, Pope Benedict XIV gave permission for the publication of an edition of Galileo's complete works.

The final trace of official Church opposition to a Sun-centred universe vanished in 1835, when the uncensored original versions of Galileo's *Dialogue Concerning the Two Chief World Systems* and Copernicus's *On the Revolutions of the Celestial Spheres* were removed from the Catholic Church's Index of banned books. In October 1992, Pope John Paul II said that he regretted the way the Galileo controversy had been handled.

Copernicus's book, *On the Revolutions of the Celestial Spheres*, is often seen as the starting point of modern astronomy. Seeing the Sun as the centre of the solar system, and the Earth and the other planets as revolving at different distances round it, was not only a true observation – it made other deductions and the building of new knowledge possible. The Copernican view of the universe opened a new view of man's relationship with it; religion was bound to enter the picture. The Earth, the Sun, the stars all *looked* exactly the same after Copernicus as they did before, but now they meant something quite different. It was human perception that changed their meaning utterly, therefore it was perception that meant everything. That loss of absolutes meant that the foundations of medieval science and metaphysics had been removed. This was a key moment in human history; after it, science would move on without religion – and unfettered by its precepts.

OBSERVATIONS AND REFLECTIONS ON A CHANGING UNIVERSE

(1572)

The Christian Church took the same line as the (non-Christian) Greek philosopher Aristotle, who was somehow kidnapped as a pseudo-Christian. Aristotle held as a central principle that the stars were unchanging. The Danish astronomer Tycho Brahe was severely shaken when, on 11 November 1572, he saw that a bright new star had appeared in the constellation Cassiopeia. Today that sudden appearance is understood as a supernova, a star in the act of being destroyed in an enormous and catastrophic explosion. Tycho Brahe knew that the 'new star' as he saw it was more distant than the Moon and was therefore in what was supposed to be the unchanging realm of the fixed stars. When he published his finding in 1573, the full significance of the discovery was clear to everyone: he had exploded an important ancient belief in the constancy of the universe.

The Italian philosopher Giordano Bruno believed, as Copernicus did, that the Earth orbited the Sun. His book *On Cause, Principle and Unity* foreshadows Einstein's relativity. 'There is no absolute up or down, as Aristotle taught; no absolute position in space; but the position of a body is relative to that of other bodies. Everywhere is incessant relative change in position throughout the universe. The observer is always at the centre of things.' Bruno also believed that the universe was very large and that it contained an infinity of worlds like our own. This was seen by the Church as heretical. The Bible presented the Earth as the centre, the focus of the universe; to propose that there was an infinity of similar worlds was unforgivable. He was condemned to death for heresy and burnt at the stake in 1600.

THE LAW OF FALLING BODIES

(1599)

Galileo's experiment on falling objects is probably the most famous scientific experiment in history. The experiment involved simultaneously dropping objects from the Leaning Tower of Pisa in order to demonstrate that all objects fall at the same rate regardless of their mass.

Some historians believe that Galileo did not carry out this experiment at all, that it is no more than a legend. It certainly seems to be the case that other scientists carried out very similar experiments before Galileo, so he may not have needed to carry it out himself. The experiment was part of a growing disillusionment among scientists with the ideas of Aristotle, whose word had been regarded as sacrosanct throughout the Middle Ages. Aristotle held that heavier bodies fall faster than light ones.

In 1544, an Italian historian called Benedetto Varchi mentioned experiments that had disproved Aristotle's law. Then in 1576, Giuseppe Moletti, who had been Professor of Mathematics at Padua before Galileo, reported on a similar experiment. He declared that objects made of the same material but of different weights, as well as objects of the same volume but different substances, arrived at the ground at the same time when dropped from the same height. This was a clear statement of the law of falling bodies and evidently based on experiment. Again in 1597, Jacopo Mazzoni at the University of Pisa reported seeing objects falling at the same speed regardless of their weight, and also fragments of an object falling at the same speed as the complete object.

In 1586, Simon Stevin reported on some experiments with two lead balls, one ten times the weight of the other, which he let fall from a church tower in Delft. The two balls fell 9 metres (30 feet) to the ground, and landed at the same moment. Some regard Stevin as the first scientist to carry out the definitive falling bodies experiment.

Galileo may or may not have repeated the experiment from the Leaning Tower of Pisa in 1599. In 1604, he nevertheless went on to prove experimentally that falling bodies obey the law of uniformly accelerated motion. All objects fall at the same rate, whatever their mass. Galileo's claim to have performed these experiments was challenged in the twentieth century by a French historian, Alexandre Koyré. He claimed that the experiments described to determine the law of acceleration of falling bodies needed more accurate measurements of time than were available to Galileo. Koyré proposed that Galileo arrived at the law deductively, rather than through experiment. But in the 1960s Galileo's experiments were replicated using Galileo's technology, and produced results with the same level of accuracy reported by Galileo. Galileo has been vindicated as a scientist.

By establishing the law of acceleration of falling bodies, Galileo went a long way towards establishing mechanics as a science, and prepared the way for Newton's work later in the seventeenth century.

III
THE AGE OF
ENLIGHTENMENT

POMPEII
(1594)

In AD 79 the violent eruption of Mount Vesuvius overwhelmed two Roman cities, Herculaneum and Pompeii. It was a disaster that was remembered for a long time – but it was eventually forgotten. The disaster was really only recovered as an historic event when exploration of the Pompeii site began in 1748, in an area called 'Civita'.

There was an earlier rediscovery, in 1594, which was a kind of misfire. In that year a local landowner, Count Muzzio Tuttavilla, decided to build an aqueduct to his villa at the foot of Mount Vesuvius. The line of the aqueduct passed across the site of the lost city. Tuttavilla's workmen unearthed the remains of ruined buildings and even found an inscription, which read 'decurio Pompeis'. This referred to a town councillor, a decurion, at a town called Pompeii. Count Tuttavilla seems not to have made any connection with this place name and the city overwhelmed in the catastrophic eruption of AD 79. Not every discovery is valued.

The effective rediscovery of Pompeii came, again quite by accident, in 1748. The historic excavations started on 23 March in that year. The work of excavating Pompeii was relatively easy as the pumice that covered the city was light and unconsolidated. In the mid-eighteenth century, people were mainly interested in recovering objects, and works of art in particular. The objects thought suitable for the private collection of Charles III, the Bourbon king, were pulled out of the ash and taken to Naples, where they are still on display at the Museo Nazionale. Some of the wall paintings were cut from the walls and mounted in frames. Along the way, a great many artefacts were lost or destroyed. Once an excavated villa was stripped of its valuables – looted, in effect – it was backfilled as being of no further interest.

Many scholars of the time, notably the high-profile archaeologist Johann Winckelmann, protested vehemently about the mistreatment of the ancient site. As a result of this pressure, the rate of despoliation was reduced, but the removal of wall paintings continued. By the end of the eighteenth century, two large areas of Pompeii had been laid bare, mainly by Karl Weber and Francesco La Vega. These two men wrote accounts of their excavations and made detailed plans of the buildings they had uncovered. Charles III had been extremely jealous of his collection of antiquities from Pompeii, and banned uninvited visitors; the price for breaking his ban was high. Visiting Naples for the first time in 1756, Winckelmann was annoyed as well as frustrated by the king's ban, and managed to get round it. He saw the collection, and then published his account of them. The king was very angry.

When the French were in control in Naples, from 1806 to 1815, the approach to excavation at Pompeii changed. The French wanted to excavate the site more systematically, starting in the west and working eastwards, and using as many as 1,500 workmen at a time. They also designed tourist routes round Pompeii, so that visiting scholars and dignitaries could see the sight to best advantage. After the fall of Napoleon, Naples returned to the rule of the Bourbon monarchy, now in the person of Ferdinand I; the French style of excavation and management continued, but on reduced funding. In this way, by the year 1860, much of the western part of Pompeii had been excavated.

One major effect of the Pompeii excavations was to reinforce the classical revival in art and architecture. The artist Giovanni Battista Piranesi loved to sketch classical architecture, and he was the first to sketch the exhumed remains of Pompeii. He developed a taste for drawing ruins. One of his fully developed pieces was a grandiose engraving of the Villa Hadriana at Tivoli. It shows a magnificent classical world, broken down and overgrown with shrubs and ivy. This led to a major eighteenth century craze for picturesque ruins. Landowners built deliberately unfinished follies as set pieces in their landscaped parks and gardens.

Another effect of the excavations at Pompeii was to make the distant past more real, more reachable, than before. One house was a brothel.

It had a bar on the ground floor, where mulled wine was served to clients before they were ushered upstairs to be entertained by Aegle, Maria or Smyrna, the girls whose names were scratched on the wall. One of the excavators, Fiorelli, found hollows and cavities in the ash, which he suspected were the forms of human bodies preserved by the loosely cemented cinders. Fiorelli poured plaster into the cavities and when he chipped away the ash he revealed perfect casts of the inhabitants of Pompeii, just as they had died 1,700 years before. These casts, when exhibited, had a similar effect to the body of the Roman girl found in 1485, and gave a great impetus to the development of the science of archaeology.

The discoveries at Pompeii continue. One alarming recent discovery concerns the nature of the AD 79 eruption, which was of a particularly fast and lethal type; this has a profound significance for Naples, which is likely at some point in the future to experience the same kind of eruption. Another recent discovery is that beneath the remains of the Roman city are those of a Bronze Age settlement, which in its turn was destroyed by a volcanic eruption in about 1500 BC. Successive discoveries point to a pattern of successive volcanic catastrophes at the same place, with a clear message for the future.

SPITZBERGEN
(1596)

All through the fifteenth and sixteenth centuries, Europeans were pre-occupied with finding a sea route to the East. Some explorers tried to find a way round the north of North America – the North-West Passage – while others tried to find an ice-free route along the Arctic coast of Asia – the North-East Passage.

John Davis tried three times and failed to find the North-West Passage, and with that triple failure the English attempt to find it came to an end. Instead the merchants of Amsterdam took up the challenge, sponsoring a Dutch attempt. In 1594, they funded an expedition led by William Barents, who sailed on three voyages of discovery. Accounts of these voyages reported on 'the cruel Bears and other Monsters of the sea and the unsupportable and extreme cold that is found in these places.' They also spoke of trouble, hunger and danger.

Barents set off from Amsterdam with four ships and instructions to sail into the 'North Seas' (meaning the Arctic Ocean) and 'discover the kingdoms of Cathay and China'. In July 1594, Barents was off the south coast of Novaya Zemlya. From there he sailed before the wind, always sailing as far to the north as he could and hugging the coast. His crew tried to capture a live polar bear, which they had evidently not seen before, but the bear gave them such a bad time that they had to kill it and be content with taking its white pelt back to Amsterdam.

Sailing on further north, Barents encountered a field of sea ice and banks of fog. Then he sighted islands, which he named Orange Islands after William of Orange; there he saw 200 walruses or sea lions basking in the sun on the shore. He called them sea horses. 'The sea horse is a wonderful strong monster of the sea, much bigger than an ox, having skin like a seal, with very short hair, mouthed like a lion; it hath four feet but no ears.' After that, Barents was forced to make for lower latitudes, returning safely home after a voyage lasting three and a half months.

Barents' description of Novaya Zemlya was well received by the Dutch merchants, who encouraged him to carry on searching for Cathay and China. A second expedition was fitted out. It set off the following year, but too late to achieve much. It was Barents' third voyage that was the most significant. He set sail from Amsterdam with two ships in May 1596. By early June, he had sailed far enough north to reach the region where there was no night.

Sighting the North Cape of Norway, Barents this time steered north-west. On 9 June, he discovered a little island, which he named Bear Island. Barents sent a party ashore to climb a steep snow-covered mountain and get a better view of the area, but found it was too slippery to descend. 'We sat up on the snow and slid down, which was very dangerous'; there were many rocks at the foot of the slope, where they could easily have broken arms or legs. Barents watched all this anxiously from the ship. The weather was once again misty, but they sailed on northwards until on 19 June they saw land again. This time 'the land was very great'. Barents and his men thought it must be a continuation to the north-east of Greenland, but it was a new land altogether. Barents had discovered Spitzbergen.

Barents was surprised by what he found there. Although the island group was situated at latitude 80 degrees North, very close to the North Pole, the climate was mild enough for grass and leafy trees to grow there; they also saw deer. Barents cruised along the coast without landing, then sailed back to Bear Island. From there he sailed eastwards again, across the open water now called Barents Sea, to make landfall again in the north of Novaya Zemlya. He found a good harbour there, but his ship was trapped there as sea ice closed in. He tried to get out during August, but it was impossible, and he had no choice but to spend the winter in that forbidding place. The ice heaped up higher and higher, threatening to destroy the ship. They fetched wood, built a snow house, and caught a few foxes to eat. They were in a fairly wretched state by Christmas, but cheered themselves with the thought that the sun would from then on rise higher in the sky. Even so, January, February and March found them and their ship still trapped.

It was only in mid-June that they were able to think of cutting a passage through the thinning sea ice to enable them to sail the ship or its boats out to open sea again. William Barents left a message in the house, explaining how they had come to be trapped there for ten months. He clearly did not expect to survive the journey home. They were unable to extricate the ship, and were going to try to escape in the two small boats. He was by this stage too ill to walk and had to be carried to the boats.

On 14 June 1597 the party set off, sailing round to Ice Point. Barents was too weak now even to sit up. 'Are we about Ice Point?' he said. 'If we are, then please lift me up; I must see it once more.' The wind suddenly got up and the ice closed in on them. They drew the boats out onto the ice. A few days later Barents died. Surprisingly, some of Barents' crew survived. On 1 November 1597, twelve gaunt men arrived in open boats in Amsterdam, still wearing bearskin coats and fox-fur hats, astonishing the merchants who had thought they must all be dead.

In 1871, Barents' winter quarters on Novaya Zemlya were rediscovered, complete with the expedition's pots and pans, tools and books. There were even the flute and pair of small shoes that had belonged to the cabin boy, who died there during that terrible winter of 1596.

HUDSON BAY
(1610)

In 1609, Henry Hudson received a commission from the King of England, James I, to find the North-West Passage. In June the following year, Hudson set sail in his ship, the *Discovery*. He followed the route explored by Martin Frobisher a quarter of a century earlier, reaching Frobisher Bay, a huge sea inlet at the south-eastern tip of Baffin Island. Frobisher Bay might have looked like an open sea channel – and therefore possibly the much sought-after North-West Passage – but it was not. It was a long fjord with a blind inner end. Cumberland Sound, an even wider sea inlet to the north, was also a blind inlet.

Hudson's instinct, to ignore those two possibilities and sail to the south along the south-western coast of Baffin Island, turned out to be right. There were, even at this early stage, signs of restlessness and rebellion among the crew. Skirting Resolution Island, Hudson found his way to the west blocked by ice, so in early July he turned south into Ungava Bay. He saw an island to his north-west, which he gave the very seventeenth century name Desire Provoketh; now it is known by its Inuit name, Akpatok (Place where auks are caught) Island. Ungava Bay was sheltered, but it was shallow and subject to huge tides (with a vertical range of 16 metres/53 feet), so the *Discovery* was pulled about by strong tidal currents. The crew were close to mutiny.

Hudson seems to have been bad at raising morale; he was at this point writing in his journal that he was 'in despair', a poor state of mind for any expedition leader. Nevertheless, he was able to produce a map from an earlier expedition, to show the crew that they had sailed 480 kilometres (300 miles) further than anyone had sailed before and therefore should be ready to go on. This cheered them enough to get them to work clearing the ship of ice, but he had made a bad mistake in seeming to allow his crew to participate in making the decision to go on. It was not until 16 July that Hudson realised that he was in fact trapped in a bay. He made for the north-west to get out of it.

After sailing north-westwards along the broad channel separating Baffin Island from the mainland of Canada for 645 kilometres (400 miles), Hudson was vindicated when it turned out to be open at its western end. Hudson was convinced that this was the entrance to the Pacific Ocean. Just before entering it, the expedition discovered Digges' Island. This was an imposing island with tall basalt cliffs 610 metres (2,000 feet) high. The crew went ashore. They were surprised to find it grassy, like England, with deer, flocks of fowl and a great waterfall. They also found stone houses built by the Inuit, with dead birds hung up inside to cure. Hudson summoned his crew back to the ship by firing guns. Some of the crew wanted to be allowed to go back on to the island, but Hudson set sail before they could plunder the Inuit larders.

But by this time summer was over and winter sea ice was beginning to form. The weather grew colder, the days shorter, and the environment was desolate and threatening. Hudson's crew split into factions. One of them wanted to turn round and head for England; the other was loyal to Hudson. Hudson steered the *Discovery* south into the huge bay later named in his honour, Hudson Bay, promising the crew that they would be sailing into a warmer climate soon. There was also the possibility that the bay would connect back to the Atlantic. The anti-Hudson crew members wanted him to turn back into the Hudson Strait so that they could get back to England before winter set in, but Hudson refused.

Although the bay was large enough to take them several degrees of latitude further south – the southern part of James Bay lies at the same latitude as London – it was still extremely cold. In James Bay they were close to the heart of a huge landmass, and the winters were very cold there. Hudson had been wrong about it being warmer to the south; he knew about latitude, but apparently not about continentality. He was also wrong about there being a connection back to the Atlantic; James Bay was a *cul de sac*, as he discovered by tracing its coast in October. By this stage it was too late to do what the malcontents on the crew wanted, which was to turn back. The *Discovery* was trapped in Hudson Bay by sea ice.

There had been some talk about mutiny among the crew during the voyage south through Hudson Bay. Now, during the long winter, it became commonplace. In spite of his experience, Hudson came across to his crew as incompetent. This was because he sometimes failed to be decisive, and he lacked authority.

One of the dissident crew members, Jouet, jeered at Hudson for hoping to see Java by Candlemas. Hudson ordered Jouet to be tried for mutiny, reminding the crew that Jouet had behaved treacherously before, as early in the voyage as Iceland; his behaviour had been insubordinate in Ungava Bay too. He demoted Jouet, cut his pay, and replaced him with Bylot. Wilson (who was unpopular with the men) was made bosun. The evidence against the mutineers was damning, but Hudson offered them pardon if they behaved well from then on. But Prickett and other crew members went on throwing doubt on Hudson's judgement, seamanship and leadership, and the old resentment quickly boiled over.

The apparently pointless wanderings of the *Discovery* in James Bay at the southern end of Hudson Bay only served to annoy and demoralise the crew. But Hudson was in difficulties. The water was incredibly shallow: in many places it was less than 3 metres (10 feet) deep as much as 24 kilometres (15 miles) offshore. To make things worse, the seabed was littered with large boulders (glacial erratics); the ship got stuck on some of them. The *Discovery* was hauled aground in the south-east corner of the bay so that the crew could spend the winter ashore. It was a miserable winter. Williams the gunner died. Hudson said Greene could have Williams's heavy grey cloak; this sounds like an act of kindness, but by tradition Hudson should have allowed the cloak to be auctioned, with the proceeds going to the dead man's next of kin. Then Hudson capriciously changed his mind and gave the cloak to Bylot instead. Hudson then quarrelled with and struck Staffe, who was one of the crew members who had remained loyal to him. The temperature fell and morale sagged.

In June 1611, when the sea ice disintegrated and melted back and the ship was once more afloat, Hudson made his worst mistake of all. The *Discovery* was able to sail again. By this stage, most of the crew wanted to return to England. Hudson was rationing food in such an extreme way that the crew suspected he was reserving a stock of food for himself. They later found out that he was. But more to the point was that Hudson was single-minded about his commission, and he startled the crew by announcing that the *Discovery* would be resuming its voyage westwards. The crew mounted a mutiny. They put Hudson with his son John in a boat, together with all the sick crew members, and then set sail for England. The nine men abandoned in the small boat managed to row fast enough to keep up with the *Discovery* for several days, but eventually, as they tired, they fell further and further behind until the *Discovery* disappeared over the horizon.

The small boat and its abandoned crew were never seen again. Henry Hudson and his son John were never seen again either. No one knows what happened to them. They may have died of hunger and hypo-thermia in the open boat. They may have made their way to the shore of Hudson Bay and set up camp there, to wait for the rescue party that would eventually come from England. In 1631, Captain Thomas James found the remains of a wooden shelter on Danby Island. This may have been erected by the men in the open boat; the ship's carpenter was among the abandoned men. In an expedition of 1668–70, Captain Zachariah Gillian found similar remains that appeared to have been left by an English crew sixty years earlier.

When the mutineers returned to England, four of them were put on trial. Surprisingly, they were acquitted. The mutiny was blamed on Hudson, who had a reputation as an indecisive captain.

Hudson's achievement was the discovery of Hudson Strait, the major navigable sea channel that separates Baffin Island from the mainland of Canada, and Hudson Bay and James Bay, major features of the Canadian Shield. He also confirmed – in effect at the cost of his own life – that Labrador was not an island.

THE LAWS OF PLANETARY MOTION

(1609–19)

The astronomer Tycho Brahe was a master of quantitative observation. His assistant, Johannes Kepler, proved to be the master of theory that would make sense of Brahe's observations. Perhaps inevitably, given their very different strengths, the two men did not get along well personally. Brahe seems to have distrusted the younger Kepler, who he thought, justifiably, might well eclipse him. As a result he kept some of his data back.

The task Brahe set Kepler was to explain the orbit of the planet Mars, which was giving him particular problems. Some historians think Brahe deliberately gave Kepler this very difficult problem to solve in order to keep him busy while Brahe himself worked on his own theory of the solar system undisturbed. Ironically, it was the data Brahe gave him relating to the orbit of Mars that enabled Kepler to formulate the laws of planetary motion. And it was this achievement that gave Kepler a far more prominent place in the history of astronomy than Brahe.

Kepler was a firm believer in the Copernican theory of the solar system. The problem with the Martian orbit was that Copernicus had correctly put the Sun at the centre of the solar system, but incorrectly given all the planets orbits that were circular. Within the Copernican system, the detail of planetary motion could only be explained by introducing epicycles. An epicycle is a movement along a small circle while also moving along the arc of a much larger circle, rather like the movement of the Moon round the Earth while the two bodies pass together along the much larger curve of the Earth's orbit round the Sun.

Kepler was eventually forced to admit to himself that the planetary orbits were ellipses, and not the circles required. It seems incredible today that an ancient Greek philosopher could have held that kind of hold over the minds of scientists as late as the seventeenth century, but his grip over the medieval Church had been even greater and, in a way, even more extraordinary. Kepler concluded that Aristotle was wrong and that the orbits of the planets had to be elliptical – and he was right. Often in illustrations the orbits are drawn as exaggerated ellipses, but this is rather to create an illusion of looking at the plane of the orbits from an angle, to make the system appear more three-dimensional. In fact the elliptical orbits of the planets are very close to being circular.

Brahe had unintentionally helped Kepler to his conclusion by giving him the puzzle of the Martian orbit, because that was the most markedly elliptical of the orbits for which Brahe had data. Pluto and Mercury have quite markedly elliptical orbits too. Kepler managed to get hold of Brahe's data after Brahe's death. He may have obtained it by means that were not strictly legal, but it was fortunate for the development of astronomy that he acquired it. Having come to the conclusion that the planets' orbits were ellipses, he was able to assemble his Three Laws of Planetary Motion.

The First Law is that the orbits of the planets are ellipses, with the Sun at one focus of the ellipse (generally there is nothing at the other focus). The Second Law is that the line joining the planet to the Sun sweeps out equal areas in equal times as the planet moves round the ellipse. This is an elegant way of describing the fact that the planet travels fastest when it is closest to the Sun, at what is called its perihelion, and slowest when it is furthest from the Sun, at its aphelion.

Kepler's Third Law is more complex; it states that the ratio of the square of the revolutionary periods for two planets is equal to the ratio of the cubes of their semi-major axes. Put more simply, the time it takes for a planet to orbit the Sun increases rapidly with the radius of its orbit. Mercury, which is very close to the Sun, therefore takes only eighty-eight Earth days to orbit while Pluto, which is a very long way from the Sun, takes 248 Earth years to travel round its orbit.

Modern astronomy has improved the accuracy of the measurements that Kepler was using, and added greatly to the number of measurements. Even so, the mathematical relationships that Kepler stated as laws have proved to be true.

ASTRONOMICAL DISCOVERIES: GALILEO GALILEI AND NICOLAS DE PEIRESC

(1609–10)

Aristotle proposed that the Moon was a perfect sphere. Even with the naked eye, when there is a bright and clear full Moon, it is possible to see that the surface of the Moon is uneven. When Galileo Galilei used the newly invented telescope in 1609, he saw that the surface of the Moon was pockmarked with craters; he could also see mountains.

The significance of this discovery was that people began to think of the Moon as another world, a place where there are landforms such as craters and mountain ranges, rather than a celestial, idealised, 'heavenly' body. It was part of a major shift towards a scientific rather than a religious approach to the universe. The discovery that Aristotle was wrong, in this as in other matters, was a shock to the Church, which had pinned many of its assumptions and certainties on Aristotle's teachings.

Galileo went on improving his telescope, increasing the magnification. He built one that made objects look twenty times larger than they were in reality. In January 1610, he used this model to look at the planet Jupiter and saw the four largest moons of Jupiter. Galileo published this observation and other observations made using his telescope in a book he called *The Starry Messenger*.

In the same year, the French scholar Nicolas de Peiresc used a telescope to discover the Orion nebula. The stars of the Orion constellation were plain to see with the naked eye, but the faint cloud of glowing gas which is the Orion nebula only became clearly visible with the telescope.

CAPE HORN
(1616)

Some geographical discoveries are more clear-cut than others. The discovery of Cape Horn, the southernmost headland of South America, is one that has been contested. One problem is that there are at least three 'furthest-south' points. There is a southernmost point of the mainland of South America, which is on the Brunswick Peninsula south of the Chilean port of Punta Arenas. To the south of that, beyond Magellan's Strait, is the large triangular island of Tierra del Fuego. There is a southernmost point on Tierra del Fuego, which is on the Beagle Channel not far from the easternmost tip of the three-cornered island; this 'furthest-south' is sometimes called False Cape Horn. Then there is a scatter of small offshore islands to the south of the Beagle Channel, each of which has a southernmost point. Horn Island is generally agreed to be the southernmost of these. Logically, the best contender for Cape Horn is the southernmost point of Horn Island.

The earliest possible contender for the act of discovery is Francisco de Hoces. He was a member of the Loaisa expedition and in 1525 his ship, the *San Lesmes*, was blown by a gale past the South Atlantic end of the Strait of Magellan. De Hoces was blown as far as 56 degrees South, which is indeed the latitude of Cape Horn. There he claimed 'they thought to see Land's End'. But if he was blown 'southwards' along the eastern coast of Tierra del Fuego, de Hoces is more likely to have seen Cape San Diego, the south-eastern tip of Tierra del Fuego, and not Horn Island at all.

Another candidate for discoverer of Cape Horn is Sir Francis Drake, who passed through the area during his circumnavigation of the world in 1577. He sailed on board the *Pelican* from the Atlantic to the Pacific through the Magellan Strait. But he was also caught in a storm, which is thought to have blown him well to the south of Tierra del Fuego. The expanse of open water led Drake to guess that Tierra del Fuego was an island rather than the northern tip of a great southern continent. But this does not really amount to a discovery of Cape Horn.

Cape Horn was first seen and rounded on 29 January 1616 by the Dutch mariners Jacob Le Maire and Willem Schouten. They sailed from the South Atlantic through the strait separating Tierra del Fuego and Staten Island, naming the strait the Strait of Le Maire. From there they sailed south-west and round Cape Horn, which they named in honour of Willem Schouten's birthplace, Hoorn in the Netherlands. Hoorn was also where the ship had been fitted.

NEW ZEALAND
(1642)

New Zealand was discovered by Abel Tasman. He was born in the Netherlands in 1603 and at the age of thirty joined the Dutch East India Company. In 1638, he sailed from the Netherlands for Batavia (now Djakarta in Indonesia) in command of the *Engel* and in 1642 he was given the task of finding the legendary Southern Continent, which had long been assumed to exist in the Southern Ocean. This unknown southern continent, sometimes sketched in speculatively on world maps and labelled Terra Australis Incognita, was believed to occupy the area we now know as the South Pacific. Tasman was commissioned by his company to take possession of all the lands he was to discover and land on during his voyage – and claim them for the Netherlands. He was given two ships, a long narrow ship called the *Zeehan* and a small warship, the *Heemskerck*, which was to act as the flagship. Tasman took with him the great surveyor and hydrographer Frans Visscher.

On 13 December 1642, Tasman caught his first sight of New Zealand, which he described in his journal as 'a great land, lifted high'. What he saw was the stretch of coast between Hokitika and Okarito, the middle of the west coast of the South Island with the impressive range of the Southern Alps behind it.

Tasman was not sure what he had discovered. He wondered if it might be the western edge of the great southern continent. In 1616, his fellow countrymen Willem Schouten and Isaac Le Maire had discovered Le Maire Strait and the island to the east of it, Staten Island, to the south-east of Tierra del Fuego. Staten Island was perhaps the northern tip of the same southern continent. Tasman accordingly wrote in his journal, 'To this land [New Zealand] we have given the name of Staten Landt, in honour of Their Mightinesses the States-General, since it could be quite possible that this land is connected with Staten Landt, though this is not certain. This land looks like being a very beautiful land and we trust that this is the mainland coast of the unknown south land.'

In fact it was only a few months later that Hendrik Brouwer proved that the two Staten Landts were not connected.

On 18 December, Tasman anchored at Taitapu Bay (which is now called Golden Bay). The crew were sent ashore in two small boats to survey the area and find fresh water. The crew returned and then, that evening, lights were seen on land. Two canoes appeared with natives on board, blowing some sort of wind instrument. The canoe people called out to the Dutch, but they were unable to understand one another and the canoe people paddled off. There were further meetings, initially friendly, but then the natives seemed intent on boarding the ships. One of the Maori canoes was paddled fast at one of the small Dutch boats, deliberately ramming it and killing four Dutch sailors. The Dutch fired at the retreating natives. By this time there were as many as thirty Maori canoes in the bay. Tasman set sail for the north, naming the bay Murderers Bay as he left. He sailed along the rest of the west coast of South Island and then along the west coast of the North island. He gave the name of the north-western tip of the North Island Cape Marie van Diemen, after the Governor General of Batavia's wife. After that he headed away for Batavia, without himself ever having set foot on New Zealand soil at all.

What Tasman established was that there was a west coast to New Zealand, but what lay to the east remained completely unknown. In 1643, it was still possible that that coastline marked the western edge of a huge landmass stretching thousands of miles eastwards towards Tierra del Fuego. At least Abel Tasman had the honesty to admit that he did not know what he had found, except that it looked as if it might be very beautiful.

THE RINGS OF SATURN, THE ROTATION OF MARS AND THE MARTIAN POLAR CAPS

(1655–66)

The invention of the telescope in 1608 by the Dutch spectacle maker Hans Lippershey opened up the possibility of making all sorts of new discoveries about astronomy.

One of many discoveries made with the aid of the newly invented telescope was the discovery in 1655 of the rings of Saturn and Saturn's fourth satellite, by the Dutch physicist Christiaan Huygens.

Another discovery of Huygens was the rotation of Mars. In 1659, he sketched the surface features of Mars. He noticed that when he returned to make new observations the features he was drawing had moved across the Martian disc. He realised that this meant that Mars was rotating. Seven years later, in 1666, the Italian-born French astronomer Gian Cassini was able to measure the time it took for Mars to turn once on its axis. He found that a Martian day was forty minutes longer than an Earth day.

Like Huygens, Cassini observed the surface features of Mars closely. He was the first to observe that Mars has polar ice caps, much like the Earth.

BOYLE'S SCEPTICAL CHYMIST

(1661)

Robert Boyle was one of the first modern scientists. His great merit as a scientific researcher was that he conscientiously followed the principles laid out by Francis Bacon in his book *Novum Organum*. At the same time he was careful to affirm that he was no-one's disciple: he was his own man. He often said that, in order to keep his judgement free of bias from any of the current philosophical theories, he refrained from studying any of them. What he was interested in was scientific experiments and the evidence they could supply; only then could he judge the merits of the theories. He did not like hypotheses. He liked knowledge. Facts.

Boyle's great book was *The Sceptical Chymist, or Chymico-Physical Doubts & Paradoxes Touching the Spagyrist's Principles,* published in 1661. Though a modern scientist, he had one foot in the Middle Ages, believing in alchemy, like the great Isaac Newton. As an alchemist he believed in the possibility of transforming metals into other metals, and even carried out experiments in an attempt to achieve it; interestingly, this experimenting necessarily entailed the hypothesis that metals could be transmuted. Alchemy was still at that time technically illegal. There was a statute from the time of Henry IV that forbade the 'multiplying' of gold and silver, evidently because if someone did succeed in making gold out of base metal they would undermine the currency. So, technically, what Boyle and others like him were doing was striving to do something illegal. Boyle was instrumental in getting this law repealed in 1689. Presumably by this time it was becoming apparent that no one would ever create gold, so the act was redundant.

What Boyle expounded in *The Sceptical Chymist* was a modern approach to chemistry. Chemistry was the science of the composition of substances, not just a branch of alchemy or pharmacy. He developed the modern view of elements as the undecomposable constituents of material bodies. He understood the distinction between mixtures and compounds and set up some procedures, which he called analysis, for finding out what they consisted of. He also supposed that elements were made up of particles.

Boyle had discovered a whole new approach, a more scientific and more rational approach to chemistry. This was all the more surprising given his involvement in alchemy.

THE RELATIONSHIP BETWEEN PRESSURE AND VOLUME

(1662)

The relationship between pressure and volume was discovered by two friends and amateur scientists, Richard Towneley and Henry Power. They brought their theory to the attention of Robert Boyle who, characteristically, devised experiments to test the theory and then published the results in 1662. It is likely that Boyle's assistant Robert Hooke, who actually built the apparatus and developed the improved vacuum pumps needed for the experiment, helped Boyle to quantify the law. Of the two men Hooke is believed to have been the better mathematician.

The French physicist Edme Mariotte discovered the same law independently of Boyle, so sometimes the law is referred to as Mariotte's Law or the Mariotte-Boyle Law. But given that Mariotte's discovery came fourteen years after Boyle published it, there seems to be little justification for naming it after Mariotte. It would be fairer to call it the Towneley-Power-Boyle-Hooke Law – if rather unwieldy. So, Boyle's Law it has to be.

Boyle's Law states that the volume of a gas increases when the pressure decreases at a constant temperature. There are twenty-three gas laws, but Boyle's Law is the most fundamental of them. It also states that the relationship between pressure and volume is constant, but only within a system where the range of pressure and temperature is not extreme. When temperatures or pressures are very high there are deviations from the law. At the time when the law was framed, these deviations were not significant, because technology was limited. But as technology has advanced there are more situations, for example within machines, where temperatures or pressures are very high. Boyle's Law nevertheless works perfectly well as a description of the natural world.

Boyle's Law can be expressed by the equation $pV = k$, where p is the pressure of the system, V is the volume of the gas and k is a constant value representative of the pressure and volume of the system. From this simple equation it follows that increasing the volume of a fixed quantity of gas will decrease its pressure. Conversely, reducing the volume of a fixed quantity of gas (compressing it) will increase its pressure. The law can be used to predict the result of introducing a change in volume or pressure to a fixed quantity of gas.

MICRO-ORGANISMS

(1665)

The existence of micro-organisms or microscopic organisms was discovered over a period, from 1665 to 1683. The discovery was made by two Fellows of the English Royal Society, Robert Hooke and Antoni van Leeuwenhoek.

In 1665, Hooke published the first depiction of a micro-organism, a microfungus called *Mucor*, in his *Micrographia*. Following on from that, Leeuwenhoek observed and described microscopic protozoa and bacteria. These discoveries were of the utmost importance scientifically. They were made possible thanks to the skill of Leeuwenhoek and Hooke in making and using simple microscopes that were yet able to magnify up to 250 times.

The huge importance of micro-organisms in causing and spreading infectious diseases was not appreciated straight away. The link between infection and micro-organisms was not to be made for over 150 years. Later it was also to become clear that micro-organisms are important in recycling chemical elements in the biosphere – carbon, oxygen, sulphur and nitrogen. In fact they are indispensable components of ecosystems. Micro-organisms are essential for the production of bread, cheese, beer, antibiotics, vaccines, vitamins and enzymes. Modern biotechnology rests on microbiology as its foundation; microbiology in turn rests upon micro-organisms. The science of microbiology in effect began with the discovery of micro-organisms.

NEWTON'S LAWS OF GRAVITY

(1666)

Robert Boyle and Robert Hooke lived at a time when great strides were being made in science, especially in England, where there was a kind of scientific renaissance. The greatest scientist of the age was undoubtedly the English genius Isaac Newton.

Like many of his contemporaries, Isaac Newton left London for the relative safety of the provinces when plague broke out in London. In 1666, Newton withdrew to rural Lincolnshire and there made his first steps in understanding gravitation. The moment is one of the most famous moments in the history of science – an iconic *Eureka* moment. He was in his garden when he saw an apple fall from a tree. It made him realise that there was a force pulling the apple to the Earth and he extended the image to much larger bodies. He 'began to think of gravity extending to the orb of the Moon.' He wondered if the Moon was being held in its orbit round the Earth by this force of gravity, but he did not publish anything about it for eighteen years. This was a big idea, an idea of exceptional importance, and it needed mulling over.

He turned away from it for a time, to the study of light and the construction of telescopes. After a range of experiments on sunlight refracted through a prism, he came to the conclusion that rays of different colours are refracted or bent by different amounts. This, which was an important discovery in itself, suggested to Newton that the indistinct, fuzzy, coloured-edged images seen through Galilean telescopes might be due to the coloured rays of light having differing focal lengths. This led on to the abandonment of the refracting telescope of Galileo and the invention of a new type of reflecting telescope, one that would produce a much sharper image – and lead to further discoveries out in space.

The Royal Society was in those days, like many other academic institutions since, a bear garden of bitter rivalries. One of its Fellows, Robert Hooke, boasted to Edmond Halley and Christopher Wren that he had discovered all the laws of celestial motion. This was a vain boast, and Halley admitted that Hooke had done no such thing. Wren, in his own words 'to encourage enquiry', said he would give a prize of a book to the value of forty shillings (£2) to the person who found the answer to this problem. Like Halley, Wren was unconvinced by Hooke's boast, but hoped to flush him out with the prospect of a prize, even a small prize, and make him publish his laws of celestial motion so that others better equipped than himself (ie better equipped than Wren) could evaluate them.

Halley afterwards visited Cambridge and discussed the matter with Newton. Newton was a remarkable man in many ways, but it is remarkable in the extreme that in the context of this query, he was prepared to give Halley a mathematical formula that would explain the movements of heavenly bodies by deploying his theory of gravitation. It was one of the most incredible gifts one scientist could give to another, and Halley was a very grateful and appreciative recipient. He well understood the value of Newton's great new theory, which was probably why Newton trusted him with it.

After the Cambridge visit, Halley wrote in a letter to Newton that he (Newton) 'had brought the demonstration to perfection.' In great excitement, Halley reported back to his fellow members of the Royal Society that Newton had shown him the draft of an important paper with the title *De Motu Corporum (On the Motion of Bodies)*. It was in the publication of this paper in 1684 that Newton gave his first public account of his theory of gravitation. Shortly afterwards, in 1687, he expounded the theory more fully in his great work, *Philosophiae Naturalis Principia Mathematica*, a major publication that was generously financed by Edmond Halley.

In *De Motu Corporum*, Newton had simplified the functioning of the solar system by treating the Sun and all of the planets as simple points in his equations. He quickly realised that this was a gross distortion of the nature of the system and that to treat the Sun, which is very large, as if it carried the same weight in the equation as the much smaller bodies of the planets was a misrepresentation. Logically, the much larger Sun must have a stronger pull. Then, in 1685, he came up with the crucially important idea that the gravitational pull of a heavenly body must be proportional to its mass. This idea he immediately refined to allow for distance, because objects a long way away cannot have the same gravitational pull as those close at hand.

Then Newton came upon one of his most important discoveries, or inferences – that bodies attract one another with a force that is proportional to the product of the masses of the two and inversely proportionally to the square of the distance between them. In this way he neatly summarised two very important ideas, that large objects exert a larger pull than small ones, and that objects near at hand exert a larger pull than similar sized objects far away.

Like many of the greatest ideas, Newton's law of gravitation seems very obvious, even self-evident, once it is said. But until Newton it seems no one had had even thought it, let alone said it. This was one of the great moments in history that completely changed the world. After that first expression of Newton's law of gravitation, science and people's perception of the universe were different.

Isaac Newton's epic work, the *Principia Mathematica*, explained how the universe worked. Newton established a comprehensive scheme for the mechanics of the solar system that would be used for 200 years and more, though it was to be added to in the twentieth century by Einstein. Newton's model for the solar system, with the principle of gravitation at its heart, was to be of great benefit to all subsequent astronomers and physicists – and not least to astronauts.

PHOSPHORUS
(1669)

As we have already seen, discoveries can be made, forgotten and re-discovered. This is as true for scientific discoveries as for geographical discoveries. The earliest discovery of an element for which we know the name of the discoverer is that of phosphorus, though it is possible that it had been discovered before – along with other elements formally discovered later.

It was common practice for alchemists to heat vinegar or urine along with earths and metals to cause chemical changes. Henning Brand was a German merchant who was also an amateur alchemist. In 1669, he was heating urine in the absence of air and this produced a white deposit at the bottom of a retort. This burnt out immediately, producing a dark, choking smoke. An outstanding property of the burning was that it produced a bright light that was strong enough to read by. Brand was able to read his alchemy books by its light.

Brand's discovery was important in its own right, but it was also immortalised when it became the subject of an historical painting by Joseph Wright of Derby.

Brand realised he had found something significant, and wrote about it to the philosopher Gottfried Leibniz. He in turn credited Brand with discovering phosphorus when he came to write his *Story of the Invention of Phosphorus* in 1710. Leibniz mentioned that Brand was an impoverished merchant who had hoped to get rich by converting base metals into gold. As was the standard alchemical practice at the time, Brand kept his experimental method to himself at first, but then he sold the secret on to a German physician, Johannes Krafft, who demonstrated the properties of the newly discovered substance as a kind of entertainment round the courts of Europe.

The method for manufacturing phosphorus leaked out, and it was not long before other scientists were making phosphorus for themselves, including Robert Boyle in 1680. Boyle's assistant, Ambrose Godfrey Hanckwitz, adapted the process for industrial-scale production and began to export phosphorus to the European mainland. Hanckwitz founded a pharmaceutical firm in London, which was named Ambrose Godfrey. The use of urine to make phosphorus went on until 1775, when it was discovered that bones could be used instead. In 1769, bone had been shown by J. G. Gahn to contain calcium phosphate.

Phosphorus is a highly reactive element, and is therefore never found as a free element in nature. Phosphorus is a literally vital element. It is a component of DNA and RNA and is an essential element in all living cells. Commerically, phosphorus is very important as the basis of agricultural fertilisers. It is also used in the manufacture of explosives, matches, fireworks, pesticides, detergents and toothpaste.

MEASURING THE SPEED OF LIGHT

(1675)

In the seventeenth century, scientists began speculating about the speed of light. Kepler and Descartes thought light travelled instantly, that it was infinitely fast. Bacon and Galileo thought it travelled very fast but at a finite speed. Galileo is sometimes credited with being the first person to attempt to find the speed of light. He and his assistant stood a measured distance apart, each with a lamp that could be covered or uncovered. Galileo uncovered his lamp and the moment the assistant saw the light he uncovered his. By measuring the length of time that passed between uncovering his lamp and seeing the light from his assistant's lamp, Galileo was able to calculate the speed of light. In practice, the light travelled too fast for him to measure; 'if not instantaneous, it is extraordinarily rapid,' he said. He estimated that light travels at least ten times faster than sound.

In 1675, a Danish astronomer called Ole Roemer was observing the eclipses of the moons of Jupiter. He noticed that the times of the eclipses seemed to vary according to the relative positions of Jupiter and the Earth. When the Earth was close to Jupiter, the orbits of Jupiter's moons appeared to run faster. When the Earth was far away from Jupiter, the orbits appeared to slow down. Roemer reasoned that the actual orbital velocities could not be affected by the distance of the Earth, and that the apparent time difference must be due to the extra time the light was taking to travel to the Earth. The distance variation involved was the diameter of the Earth's orbit, and estimates of that were available to Roemer. From this he demonstrated to the French Royal Academy of Science that light travelled at a finite but very high speed that *could* be

147

expressed in measurements, though he avoided giving a speed in units that we can recognise today.

Many people since then have commented on Roemer's discovery, giving inferred figures that have ranged from 120,000 to 210,000 miles per second. Roemer's paper implies that the lower limit for the speed of light must be 84,000 miles per second, but he allowed that it might be much higher than that. It seems that Huygens was the first to take the next daring step, and offer a figure for the speed of light. Roemer sent his results to Huygens in a letter before he published them. In 1690, Huygens' book *Treaty on Light* was published. In it he said that Roemer's results had not been published, which was no longer true. The truth was that Huygens had Roemer's data as early as 1675 and used it to present his own version of the speed of light in a lecture in 1678. Like Roemer, Huygens was less interested in giving an absolute figure for the speed of light, but he gave the calculations with some rounding down, leading to a speed of 127,000 miles per second. But without the rounding down, he would have arrived at 140,000. Then, in 1694, Edmond Halley noticed that one of Roemer's figures, a figure for a transit time, was incorrect; it should have been seventeen minutes, not twenty-two. Making this change and recalculating, Halley arrived at a speed of approximately 180,000 miles per second. And this was based squarely on Roemer's work.

In 1728, the English physicist James Bradley calculated the speed of light in a vacuum to be 187,000 miles per second. Bradley used what is called stellar aberration to arrive at this figure. Stellar aberration is the apparent shift in the positions of stars in the sky resulting from the Earth's shifting position as it passes along its orbit round the Sun.

In 1849, The French physicist Hippolyte Fizeau arrived at a figure of 194,000 miles per second for the speed of light. He devised a simple experiment, shining a light between the teeth of a rapidly rotating toothed wheel. He positioned a mirror about 5 miles away, which sent the light beam back between the same teeth in the wheel. The wheel had more than 100 teeth round its edge and rotated hundreds of times per second. This enabled Fizeau to measure small fractions of a second.

Fizeau ran the wheel at various speeds, and it was possible then to find out at what speed the wheel was turning too fast to allow the light to pass through the gap, out to the mirror and back again through the same gap. Then he knew the distance the light travelled (ten miles) and the time it took to travel that distance. By dividing that distance by the time taken, he calculated the speed of light.

In 1926, Fizeau's experiment was repeated by Léon Foucault, though using a rotating mirror instead of a toothed wheel. He repeated and refined the experiment, re-running it over a period of fifty years, and got a speed of 186,293 miles per second. This is very close indeed to the present-day measurement, which is 186,282.4 miles per second. Edmond Halley, using Roemer's data, also had it about right.

The speed of light has many implications for us. The fact that it is very fast indeed makes it easy for us to function in our everyday lives. We see things happening around us to all intents and purposes instantaneously. If it were not so, we could not anticipate any danger, we could not drive safely; we could not co-ordinate our actions with those of other people. But because light travels at a finite, not an infinite, speed, it is possible for us to see, far out in the universe, things that happened long ago. I recently wrote a book, *Britain 3000 BC*, in which I reconstructed what life in Britain was like at the time when the circles at Avebury and Stonehenge were first laid out. In it, I reflected on what neolithic people would have seen in the night sky. My first thought was that the sky would have looked slightly different; for one thing, the Pole Star would have been a different star. Then I realised that, out in the next spiral arm of our own galaxy, there are stars whose light was starting on its way towards us in 3000 BC, so we are actually seeing *now* what those stars were like five thousand years ago: stars such as the Ring Nebula in Lyra or the Rosette Nebula, or the Poop of the old constellation of Argo with its cluster of 500 stars near Sirius. We can literally look back into the past and see the universe as it was. And the further away we look, the further back in time we look. We can see the history of the universe.

If we look through a telescope at a quasar that is a billion light-years away, we are seeing the light that left that object a billion years ago.

There are many implications here. If the claims of the creationists were right and the universe is only 6,000 years old, we would not be able to see any objects more than 6,000 light-years away from us. The very fact that we are seeing objects several billion light-years away proves that the universe itself must be several billion years old – at least. Some creationists have attempted to explain this with a theory that the speed of light has slowed down exponentially since the creation. It has even been argued that the speed of light has slowed down since Roemer measured it in 1675, but the figures simply do not bear this out. The universe is several billion years old.

THE WAVE THEORY
OF LIGHT
(1678)

Christiaan Huygens was the first person to put forward a comprehensive theory of light. Huygens proposed that light moves in waves
and demonstrated how waves might interfere to create a wave front,
propagating in a straight line. This wave theory of light soon had a
powerful competitor in the corpuscular theory of light put forward by
Isaac Newton. Newton did not believe that light was a continuous
entity, but composed of small particles. By using this theory, Newton
was able to explain the phenomenon of reflection quite easily. He was
also able, though with more difficulty, to use it to explain refraction
though a lens. Newton's particle theory of light therefore went
unchallenged for more than a hundred years.

Then, in the early nineteenth century, Young and Fresnel carried out
double-slit experiments. These showed that when light passes through
a grid an interference pattern is created that is very similar to the
interference pattern produced by waves in water. The experiments gave
some support for Huygens' wave theory. They did not displace the
Newtonian particle theory of light altogether, but by about 1850 it was
Huygens' wave theory that dominated scientific thinking. Then
Maxwell came up with an explanation of light as propagated by electromagnetic waves. Maxwell's idea was verified by experiments, and after
that Huygens' wave theory was widely accepted.

Today, physicists and chemists regard all matter as exhibiting both
wave-like and particle-like properties. There is a reconciliation of
Huygens' and Newton's theories in what is called wave-particle duality.
Duality is a major concept in quantum mechanics, which implicitly

regards old concepts such as 'wave' and 'particle' as fundamentally inadequate to describe or explain natural phenomena.

The idea of duality is rooted in that seventeenth-century debate over the competing theories of Huygens and Newton. Following Einstein, many scientists have taken the view that all particles also have a wave nature, and that this holds for elementary particles and also for compound particles such as atoms and molecules. It can even be argued that wave-particle duality applies to macroscopic objects, though their wave properties cannot be detected because the wavelengths are very short.

NIAGARA FALLS
(1678)

It was in 1678 that the missionary and explorer Louis Hennepin discovered Niagara Falls. The thirty-eight-year-old French Franciscan, who had been in Canada for only three years at the time, was so staggered and moved by his discovery that he fell to his knees at the awe-inspiring sight. He was the first non-native North American to see it. He said, 'The universe does not afford its parallel.'

There are two main waterfalls, the Horseshoe Falls (53 metres/173 feet high) on the Canadian side and the American Falls (21 metres/70 feet high) on the US side, the two being separated by Goat Island. The falls were created as the last cold stage ended, about 12,500 years ago, at a time when the area became ice-free and meltwater filling the newly formed Great Lakes spilled over the Niagara Escarpment on its way to the Atlantic Ocean. The original waterfall was at Queenston-Lewiston and it has since then cut back about 24 kilometres (15 miles).

Niagara Falls are not very high, but unusually wide. An enormous quantity of water pours over the falls – the outflow from all four of the upper Great Lakes, amounting to about one-fifth of the world's fresh water. It has peak flows of 5,700 cubic metres (201,300 cubic feet) per second, making it not only the most impressive but the most powerful waterfall in North America. It is an important source of hydro-electric power and also a major tourist attraction. There was even a plan in the 1960s to remove the boulders from the foot of the American Falls to double their height and make them more impressive, but it was dropped because it would have been too expensive.

HALLEY'S COMET
(1682)

At one time it was believed that comets appeared just once. What the astronomer Edmond Halley showed was that they follow regular orbits round the Sun, like the orbits of the planets but much longer. They only become visible when they are relatively near to us. Halley studied the path of a comet that appeared in the sky in 1682 and was able to show that this and the two comets that appeared in 1531 and 1607 (and described by Apianus and Kepler) were in fact one and the same comet returning every seventy-five or seventy-six years. He was able to predict that it would return and reappear in 1758, 1835 and 1910. It did, and so it was named after him.

But although he takes the credit, Halley was not the first to see Halley's Comet as a recurring visitor. When it appeared in the sky in 1066, it was seen by the English as a portent of disaster. Something terrible was going to happen. The monk Eilmer of Malmesbury wrote ominously, 'You have come then, have you, you source of tears to many mothers? It is a long time since I last saw you; but as I see you now you are far more terrible than before. I see you as brandishing the downfall of my country.' As a boy Eilmer had indeed seen this grim visitor with its message of doom once before, seventy-five years earlier, in 989. He was right about the downfall of his country too. The Normans were about to invade.

The most recent appearance of Halley's Comet was in 1986. It will not be seen again until the summer of 2061.

DETERMINING
LONGITUDE
(1735)

With longitude, we come to one of those discoveries that could not have been made without an invention. In the early eighteenth century, it became a matter of urgency to discover longitude, in the sense that every sea captain needed to be able to find out where exactly he was, even he was out on the open sea, well out of sight of land. The need was widely recognised: somebody had to discover a way of finding longitude.

The British government offered a prize to whoever could find a simple and practical method for determining, exactly, the longitude of a ship at sea. The prize was offered by way of an Act of Parliament in 1714, and the award of the prize was to be administered by a newly created Board of Longitude.

In the early days of navigation at sea, people usually kept within sight of land. It was easy, with a little practice, to recognise the coastline of your own home territory and the coastlines of your neighbours' territories. By learning lists of landmarks, it was possible to memorise long itineraries and find your way, coastwise, round long distances of the shores of Britain. This is what happened in the prehistoric period, and what went on happening to a great extent in the Middle Ages too.

The problems started when sailors lost sight of land. One significant clue to the ship's position was the altitude of the Sun in the sky. On 21 March and 21 September, the equinoxes, the Sun is overhead at midday on the equator. The angle the Sun makes with the horizon is known as the Sun's altitude. If the observer was on the equator, latitude 0 degrees, the sun's altitude was 90 degrees. If the observer was at the North or South Pole, latitude 90 degrees, the Sun's altitude was 0 degrees. It was therefore possible for people to calculate their latitude very easily from the sun's altitude (latitude = 90 – altitude).

Latitude told navigators how far north or south they were, but not how far east or west. To pinpoint their position exactly, which is what they needed to be able to do, they needed this second co-ordinate. They needed to be able to fix their longitude. This could not be read from the Sun's position or the position of any other heavenly body either.

This uncertainty about longitude was one reason why early maps were very inaccurate. It was also a reason why ships went aground on reefs.

When Christopher Columbus sailed west across the Atlantic Ocean, he discovered land on the far side of the ocean, partly because of a misconception about the size of the Earth, and partly because Portuguese sailors had already made the crossing unofficially. But he was at least partly convinced that when he reached the Caribbean he had reached what we now call Indonesia, and that is how the islands of the Caribbean came to be known as the West Indies, to distinguish them from the East Indies, which were the real Indies.

The map of the world could only be drawn accurately if there was an accurate way of determining longitude. Navigation could only be made safe if sea captains had a way of determining their location with two co-ordinates instead of one. During and after the great voyages of discovery of the fifteenth and sixteenth centuries, the absence of a way of measuring longitude became an acute problem. People were sailing long distances out of sight of land, and frequently getting into difficulties. Even with dead reckoning, which was calculating a position by sailing in a known compass direction at a measured speed for a measured length of time, captains could still not be certain where they were in relation to features shown on inaccurately drawn maps.

The situation was brought to a head by a particular incident. In 1707, Sir Cloudesley Shovel was returning home to England in command of a squadron of ships after an unsuccessful attack on the French port of Toulon. Sir Cloudesley was on board his flagship, the *Association*, sailing north under full sail when he ran into rocks near the Isles of Scilly on 22 October 1707. The *Association* was badly holed and those on board the

St George, one of the other ships in the squadron, watched helplessly as the flagship sank in less than four minutes. The ship sank so quickly that everyone on board, Sir Cloudesley included, perished.

The *Association* and four other ships in the squadron were wrecked on the Gilstone Reef. In all, more than 1,600 and perhaps as many as 2,000 men were drowned in the disaster. It was one of the biggest peacetime disasters in British history and rightly regarded as a national catastrophe. Up to 2,000 men, five ships and the commander-in-chief were lost. The *Association* was also carrying a vast amount of treasure. There were chests of gold and silver coin and plate that were put on at Gibraltar by British merchants. There were chests containing British government funds for the war in France. There were chests containing Sir Cloudesley's own cash and still others containing regimental funds and silverware. The financial loss alone was colossal.

The squadron had sailed northwards onto a known reef and therefore Sir Cloudesley must have mis-navigated. The visibility was very poor that day and he and his officers had been unable to navigate by eye. He was either further to the east or west than he had believed, or the maps were inaccurate and had misled him. In other words he had not been aware of his longitude, or the longitude of the reef.

The outcome of the wreck of the *Association* was the offer of a huge cash prize for the invention of an instrument that could accurately measure longitude. A British Parliamentary committee consulted scientists, Sir Isaac Newton among them, and they advised that a seaworthy clock that could be trusted to keep accurate time would supply the information needed – a chronometer. The level of accuracy the committee required was the calculation of the longitude of the port of arrival in the West Indies at the end of a voyage from England; this meant that the chronometer had to keep accurate time for at least six weeks.

For twenty-three years there were no contestants for the substantial cash prize, apart from the Revd William Whiston and Revd Humphry Ditton. They entered a scheme based on ships kept moored at fixed intervals along the major shipping routes. Each night at midnight, each ship would fire an exploding rocket a mile into the air. This would be heard and seen 135 kilometres (85 miles) away, and it would inform navigators whether they had to correct their shipboard clocks. This ingenious scheme was no good, because the moored ships would each have needed clocks that were as accurate as the desired chronometer anyway. It was a circular solution to the problem.

After a very long struggle, this prize was eventually won by John Harrison, who invented the ship's chronometer. In fact Harrison manufactured several clocks that were so accurate that they lost no more than one second per month, which was more than accurate enough for the purpose. The main problems Harrison had to overcome were those of making the chronometer seaworthy. Because ships swayed and pitched so much, it was impossible to use a conventional pendulum clock. The chronometer had to carry on working regardless of big changes in temperature and humidity too.

In 1730, Harrison met Edmond Halley, who was the Astronomer Royal and also a member of the Board of Longitude. Halley looked at Harrison's plans and saw that, if the chronometer worked, it would solve the longitude problem. Harrison was encouraged to build his chronometer with a view to a trial, and he completed the first one, H1, in 1735. It was given a successful sea trial to Lisbon. The Board was favourably impressed and awarded Harrison £500 to enable him to build an improved model that would take up less deck space. H2, which was completed in 1739, was narrower and taller than H1. H2 did not have a sea trial, and Harrison went on refining and redesigning until he produced H4. This was Harrison's most famous invention. It was a great advance on the earlier chronometers because it was much smaller. It was just over 12.7 centimetres (5 inches) in diameter, like a large pocket watch. It was technologically very impressive, and a beautifully intricate piece of craftsmanship.

Harrison's H4 chronometer was given its transatlantic sea trial in 1761. On arrival in Jamaica it proved to have lost just five seconds, which amounted to an error of one minute of longitude. With this triumph, John Harrison qualified for the award, but the Board of Longitude failed to pay up. George III himself intervened when he saw Harrison's final version, H5, in 1772, and forced the Board to pay Harrison his prize money.

The rigorous testing of Harrison's chronometer had proved its worth, yet almost incredibly Captain Cook set off on his earlier voyages without it. In July 1771, though, James Cook set sail from Plymouth with the *Resolution* and the *Adventure* with a copy of Harrison's H4 chronometer on board. This enabled Cook to make far more accurate charts of his discoveries than were ever previously possible. It also accurately fixed John Harrison's place in history. John Harrison's invention enabled navigators and explorers to pinpoint locations with far greater accuracy than ever before. As a result, the regional and world maps produced in the later eighteenth and nineteenth centuries were far more accurate than the charts Sir Cloudesley Shovel had been using in 1707. It also became possible for ships' captains to navigate their courses more accurately – and safely. The chronometers were difficult to manufacture, and not susceptible to mass production, so their use spread slowly, but by 1850 every vessel in the British navy was carrying *three* Harrison chronometers. Harrison himself did well out of his invention, making a total of £23,065 in prize money.

THE BERING STRAIT
AND ALASKA
(1728–41)

Vitus Bering was born in 1681 and grew up in the town of Horsens in Denmark. He joined the Russian Navy as a sub-lieutenant in 1703, and served in the Baltic Fleet during the Great Northern War. In 1710, he went to serve in the Azov Sea fleet in the Russo-Turkish War. After 1715, he became involved in voyages of explorations, as part of a large-scale project devised by Peter the Great.

Bering was sent on a series of exploratory voyages along the north coast of Asia, leading up to a voyage to Kamchatka, near the Bering Strait. With the authority of the tsar behind him, Bering travelled overland to Okhotsk, crossed to Kamchatka and acquired and fitted out a ship, the *St Gabriel*. In 1728, on board the *St Gabriel*, Bering sailed northwards along the Asian coast until he could see no more land. It was in this way that Bering found that separating Asia from North America there was a channel of open sea; it would become known as the Bering Strait.

In 1729, he searched the Bering Strait to check that the Asian mainland did not extend across it. In doing so, he rediscovered one of the islands in the Diomede group, earlier discovered by Dezhnev. In 1730, Bering returned to St Petersburg. During this harrowing journey, Bering was very ill and five of his children died.

The tsar commissioned Bering to undertake another voyage of exploration, and he went back to Okhotsk in 1735. Here he had two new ships built, the *St Peter* and the *St Paul*, in which he sailed in 1741 – for North America. The expedition was to confirm the existence of the sea channel separating Asia from North America and chart the north-west coast of North America. Bering and his crew set off on a course south-east from the Commander Islands, about halfway across the Bering Strait. This was because others on the expedition insisted that there was land in that direction. Had they sailed due east, they would soon have made landfall in Alaska. As it was, they headed out into open water in the direction of Hawaii, thousands of miles away. By the time Bering changed course to the north-east, they had sailed hundreds of miles out into the North Pacific, missing all of the islands of the Aleutian chain.

So far, Bering's voyage of discovery had been little short of a fiasco. Then, on 26 July 1741, it was not Bering but Captain Aleksei Chirikov who sighted 'some very high mountains, their summits covered in snow, their lower slopes we thought covered in trees. This we thought must be America.' It was. Chirikov's ship had become separated from Bering's in a storm and so reached Alaska some days ahead of Bering. Chirikov landed and made contact with the native people well before Bering reached Kayak Island.

After reaching Alaska, Bering and his men were running low on fresh water and were forced to turn and head back towards Siberia. On the return voyage, Bering saw islands in the Aleutian chain. As they ran out of supplies, and Bering became too ill to command his ship, they attempted a landing on one of the islands, but strong winds blew the *St Peter* on to some rocks. The ship was wrecked. The entire crew were by now ill with scurvy; twenty-eight of them died of it. Bering himself died in December 1741. The survivors managed to stay alive on the island (a small island in the Commander group) by eating seals and fish. Eventually the ship's carpenter built a 12-metres (40-foot) boat from the wreckage of the ship and forty-six out of the original seventy-seven men on board made it by sea back to the Asian mainland. This second *St Peter* was seaworthy enough to remain in service along the Kamchatka coast for another twelve years. The carpenter, Starodubtsev, was awarded honours by the government and went on to build more ships.

The Bering voyages were unsatisfactory in many ways. Probably Bering was the wrong man to lead such expeditions. At the age of sixty, he was too old and vulnerable in 1741 for such an undertaking. His major discovery, the Bering Strait, was one of those discoveries that had been made before and forgotten. We now know that Semen Dezhnev made a voyage into the Bering Strait in 1648, and may even have crossed to Alaska; the documentary record of this voyage was 'lost' in Siberian archives and only came to light after Bering's voyage, serving to show that it had been unnecessary.

The verification of the existence of the Bering Strait in 1741 was redundant. In 1732, four years after Bering's first voyage, a Russian named Mikhail Gvozdev, used one of Bering's old ships to explore the strait and investigate the 'big land' on the opposite side. Bering's name has been attached to the discoveries of the Strait and Alaska largely, it would seem, because of the royal patronage and consequent official profile that his voyages had. Native Russians had been there before him. But the genuine and major achievement of Vitus Bering was the systematic acquisition of geographical knowledge about the easternmost region of Asia, co-ordinated by Peter the Great. Bering's own highly detailed map of Siberia and the Russian Far East shows how successful this systematic approach was.

NICKEL
(1751)

In 1751, the Swedish scientist Axel Fredrick Cronstedt was attempting to extract copper from a mineral called niccolite. To his surprise, instead of getting copper his experiment produced a silvery-white metal. He recognised that this was a new metal and he named it nickel after the niccolite from which it came. This was the moment when nickel was discovered in the western world, though it was already known elsewhere. An alloy that included nickel was in use in China as far back as 235 BC. This metal alloy, called *paktong*, was made of nickel, copper and zinc and it was used for making cooking utensils and other metal objects.

Later, it emerged that the new metal was actually an element: a shiny, silvery element with an atomic number of twenty-eight. It proved to be malleable; it could be hammered into thin sheets. Of the three ferro-magnetic elements, nickel, iron and cobalt, nickel is the least magnetic; but when all three ferro-magnetic metals are made into an alloy they make an unusually strong magnet.

The presence of nickel in iron-nickel meteorites (between five and twenty per cent nickel) distinguishes them from rocks or minerals produced in the Earth. The crystal structure of this meteorite nickel shows that it cooled and crystallised very slowly, probably deep inside asteroids.

Trace nickel is important to animal health, and is significant in the transmission of genetic codes.

CARBON DIOXIDE
(1754)

Carbon dioxide was one of the many important discoveries made by the great Scottish scientist Joseph Black. Based at the University of Edinburgh, he carried out experiments to discover the properties of carbon dioxide, which he named 'fixed air' in 1754, and he became the first person to isolate the gas in a perfectly pure state. One of his experiments involved putting a flame and some mice into a container of carbon dioxide. The mice died and the flame went out. Black concluded that the gas was not combustible and not breathable.

In 1756, Black showed the relationship between carbonates and carbon dioxide.

His isolation of carbon dioxide from air was an historic moment, as it showed that air was not an element, as many people had believed: instead it was composed of many different elements.

In 1761, four years after being made Regius Professor of the Practice of Medicine at Glasgow, Black discovered the principle of latent heat. He found that applying heat to boiling water does not result in immediate evaporation, nor does applying heat to ice produce instant melting. From these phenomena he inferred that the boiling water and the ice must be able to absorb heat in a latent form. This discovery of latent heat, which is regarded by some science historians as Black's most important discovery, opened the door to a new branch of study – thermal science. Black also demonstrated that different substances have different specific heats. All of this work was important in pure science terms, but also proved to have very significant implications for the development of the steam engine.

It was therefore no coincidence that Joseph Black was a friend of James Watt, the great pioneer of steam engines; nor was it a coincidence that Watt started his studies of steam power at Glasgow University in 1761, just when Black was discovering latent heat. Black was a member of the Poker Club, and counted among his friends David Hume, Adam Smith and other key members of the Scottish Enlightenment.

Discovering carbon dioxide had many repercussions. Commercially, carbon dioxide is used in the carbonation of drinks, as a refrigerant, and in fire extinguishers. In the USA alone, about seventy-seven million tons of carbon dioxide are manufactured commercially each year. Because the concentrations of carbon dioxide in the atmosphere are so low, it is not considered economic to extract it from the air but, given today's great crusade to reduce carbon dioxide emissions, there is a heavy irony in the huge scale of deliberate commercial carbon dioxide manufacture.

Identifying the distinctive role of carbon dioxide as an element in the Earth's atmosphere was perhaps Black's greatest contribution to human knowledge. Carbon dioxide exists in the Earth's atmosphere in very small quantities; the concentration is about 0.033 per cent. The role of this atmospheric carbon dioxide in maintaining or altering the temperature of the atmosphere is now assumed to be an established scientific fact, though there is no scientific evidence of a cause-and-effect relationship between temperature and carbon dioxide concentration. The relationship must be regarded as unproven, given that over the last 200 years temperatures have *fallen* as well as *risen* while carbon dioxide concentration has only risen. Carbon dioxide is released into the atmosphere when carbon-containing fossil fuels are burnt. Because of the marked increase in fossil fuel consumption from the Industrial Revolution onwards, and especially since 1850, the levels of carbon dioxide in the atmosphere have risen. Major climatic changes have been predicted as a result of this increase in carbon dioxide but, as mentioned already, there is no evidence of a connection – no evidence that would have satisfied Joseph Black.

MAGNESIUM
(1755)

Until 1755, magnesia was confused with lime; then Joseph Black demonstrated that the two were completely different substances. It was Joseph Black who first recognised magnesium as an element in 1755, though it was not isolated until 1808, by Sir Humphry Davy. It was first prepared in coherent form in 1831 by Bussy, and some historians believe that more credit should go to Bussy than to Davy, on the grounds that Davy only observed that magnesium oxide was the oxide of a newly recognised metal. Davy himself would not have minded this slight. He gave up his prestigious job at the Royal Institution on what seems to have been a pretence of being ill, delivered a farewell lecture, married a rich widow, took a knighthood and toured the continent for two years together with his new wife and his assistant, Michael Faraday. Davy himself said that the greatest discovery he ever made was – Michael Faraday.

Magnesium is the eighth most common element in the Earth's crust, but in nature it is never found on its own, uncombined. It is found in large deposits in minerals like dolomite and magnesite. Magnesium can be prepared commercially by the electrolysis of fused magnesium chloride obtained from brine and sea water.

Magnesium is used in flares, fireworks, incendiary bombs and photography. It is very light, one-third lighter than aluminium, so alloys of magnesium are used in the construction of planes and missiles. Magnesium hydroxide (milk of magnesia) and magnesium sulphate (Epsom salts) are used in medicine. Magnesium is an essential element in both animal and plant life. Chlorophyll, for instance, is magnesium-centred.

HYDROGEN
(1766)

Hydrogen was first identified as a substance distinct from other flammable gases in 1766. The man who made this discovery was Henry Cavendish, but the newly identified gas was not named for another twenty-two years. Antoine Lavoisier gave it its name in 1783.

Cavendish went to Cambridge in 1749 and left four years later, like many other young gentlemen of his age, without troubling to take a degree. He was a very solitary person who formed no close relationships; it was said that he had an additional staircase built onto his house so that he would not have to meet his housekeeper. His one social arena was the Royal Society Club, whose members dined together before the weekly meetings. It was at the Royal Society that Cavendish gained the respect of his contemporaries. He was even secretive about his scientific work, keeping many of his findings from his fellow scientists. Long after he died in 1810, his papers were searched, and they revealed that Cavendish himself had anticipated several discoveries now credited to other men: Ohm's Law, Richter's Law of Reciprocal Proportions, Dalton's Law of Partial Pressures and Charles's Law of Gases – it was an impressive list of unclaimed or wrongly attributed discoveries.

Cavendish made hydrogen by combining metals and concentrated acids. Others, such as Robert Boyle, had made hydrogen gas, but Cavendish is credited with its discovery because he was the first to recognise the true nature of hydrogen as an elemental gas. Cavendish did not use the name hydrogen, but called his discovery 'inflammable air'. He noticed that the gas reacted with oxygen, which was then known as 'dephlogisticated air', to form water. As Lavoisier and Watt made the same observation, there is disagreement about who should really take the credit for identifying hydrogen: is it Cavendish, Watt or Lavoisier?

Cavendish was also responsible for determining the composition of the Earth's atmosphere. He found that eighty per cent of it is phlogisticated air, which we would now identify as nitrogen, and twenty per cent dephlogisticated air or oxygen. Cavendish also discovered that 0.8 per cent of the atmosphere was a third gas, which was not identified for another hundred years, when William Ramsay and Lord Rayleigh discovered it was argon.

Hydrogen is ordinarily a colourless, odourless and tasteless gas. It is also the lightest (least dense) gas known. It is a vital element on the Earth, as its molecules react with oxygen molecules to form water. Hydrogen burns in air with a hot blue flame; it can be used for welding, but also has to be handled with care as it is highly flammable, forming easily ignited explosive mixtures with air or oxygen.

OXYGEN

(1774)

Oxygen had been produced in experiments by several chemists before 1774. What was distinctive about Joseph Priestley's experiment was that it led him to conclude that the gas was a distinct element. Another scientist, Carl Wilhelm Scheele, discovered oxygen at about the same time and in the same way, but Priestley is usually credited with the discovery. Both Scheele and Priestley made oxygen by heating mercuric oxide. Neither of them called the new element oxygen. Priestley called it dephlogisticated air and Scheele called it fire air. The name oxygen was given by Antoine Lavoisier.

Priestley reflected on his discovery later,

I cannot, at this distance of time, recollect what it was that I had in view in making this experiment; but I know I had no expectation of the real issue of it. Having acquired a considerable degree of readiness in making experiments of this kind, a very slight and evanescent motive would be sufficient to induce me to do it. If, however, I had not happened, for some other purpose, to have had a lighted candle before me, I should probably never have made the trial; and the whole train of my future experiments relating to this kind of air might have been prevented. Still, however, having no conception of the real cause of this phenomenon, I considered it as something very extraordinary; but as a property that was peculiar to air that was extracted from these substances, and adventitious; and I always spoke of the air to my acquaintance as being substantially the same with common air. I particularly remember my telling Dr Price, that I was myself perfectly satisfied of its being common air, as it appeared to be so by the test of nitrous air; though, for the satisfaction of others, I wanted a mouse to make the proof quite complete . . .

On the 8th of this month I procured a mouse, and put it into a glass vessel, containing two ounce measures of the air from mercurius calcinatus. Had it been common air, a full-grown mouse, as this was, would have lived in it about a quarter of an hour. In this air, however, my mouse lived a full hour; and though it was taken out seemingly dead, it appeared to have been only exceedingly chilled; for, upon being held to the fire, it presently revived, and appeared not to have received any harm from the experiment.

Priestley also wrote and spoke of another characteristic of his newly discovered gas.

This air is of exalted nature. A candle burned in this air with an amazing strength of flame; and a bit of red hot wood crackled and burned with prodigious rapidity.

In other words, he discovered that oxygen was an aid to combustion.

Oxygen was a very important discovery, not least because it is the third most abundant element in the universe. It is very important to us because it makes up twenty-one per cent of the Earth's atmosphere. It also accounts for nearly half the mass of the Earth's crust, two-thirds of the mass of the human body and ninety per cent of the mass of water. It is an element that is essential to most forms of life, and essential for combustion too.

Liquid oxygen combined with liquid hydrogen makes an excellent rocket fuel. Oxygen can be relatively easily extracted from the air by fractional distillation; large quantities of it are used in the conversion of pig iron to steel.

CAPTAIN COOK'S SOUTH PACIFIC VOYAGE
(1775)

The first voyage of exploration Captain James Cook made to the southern hemisphere was considered such a huge success that he was given command of a second voyage. This time he was to take two ships, the *Resolution* and the *Adventure*, to discover the unseen southern continent, Terra Incognita (the Unknown Land) or Terra Australis (the Southern Continent), that was for some reason thought to fill the area actually occupied by the South Pacific.

As far as its main goal was concerned it was a disappointing voyage. Between 1772 and 1775, Cook took his ships in a zig-zag course through the South Pacific, getting as far as 71 degrees South. It was a surprisingly high latitude to reach. Cook saw floating ice, but no landmass; he did not sail quite far enough south to sight Antarctica. The Antarctic coastline south of the central South Pacific lies at about 75 degrees South. The Antarctic coastline south of the Indian Ocean lies just on the Antarctic Circle, at just over 66 degrees South. Cook came very close to discovering Antarctica, but was just unlucky. Nevertheless, by sailing so far south, Cook put his ships seriously at risk from floating ice.

He headed for Easter Island, whose geographical position he was able to establish accurately for the first time. He discovered several previously unknown islands, including New Caledonia. On the way home, Cook crossed the South Atlantic at a high latitude, and discovered that there was no large landmass there either. It was an incredible voyage of discovery, truly epic in scale. In this one voyage,

Cook's ships travelled the equivalent of three times round the world and produced surveys of the Pacific that effectively redrew the world map. And it was a world map without a great southern continent.

Captain Cook's achievements were certainly under-acknowledged and under-rewarded during his lifetime. Cook's voyages produced an astonishing amount of information about the geography of the Pacific and South Atlantic Oceans. He returned to Britain with detailed descriptions and accurately surveyed charts. His exploits were the talk of Europe, and everyone was intensely excited about the exotic new world that was suddenly opening up. Cook's discoveries showed conclusively that there was no large landmass in the Pacific Ocean, that the Pacific was virtually empty of land, apart from the hundreds of small islands, which were scattered across it like stars in the night sky. Any large 'Unknown Land' that might exist – if it existed at all – must lie in very high latitudes, beyond 71 degrees South. Cook prepared the way for the discovery, later, of a smaller Antarctica.

URANUS
(1781)

Up until 1690, there were known to be just six planets in the solar system: Mercury, Venus, Earth, Mars, Jupiter and Saturn. The seventh planet, Uranus, was first discovered in 1690 by John Flamsteed, but unfortunately he did not realise what he had found. He thought it was a star, not a planet and labelled it 34 Tauri. After that, because of Flamsteed's misleading identification, the object was frequently noticed by astronomers, but disregarded. William Herschel, who was a German living in England, built himself a telescope. This in itself was a major project and it took him a long time to build a working telescope with a 16.5-centimetre (6½-inch) reflecting mirror that would give clear images.

The trouble Herschel took in building his telescope was rewarded on 13 March 1781, when he pointed it in the direction of the constellation of Gemini. Seeing the large blue object that Flamsteed had seen, he realised that it was a lot closer than the stars making up the distant constellation. He understood that he had found either a planet or a comet and began to record its movements. The behaviour of the body was not like that of a comet, so he realized he had discovered a new, seventh, planet.

George III was fascinated by Herschel's project and rewarded him; Herschel in turn wanted to name the new planet after his benefactor, 'Georgium Sidus' but the new name did not stick. Some wanted to call it 'Herschel'. Others wanted a classical name to match the names of the other planets – and even follow the genealogy of the classical pantheon. Mars is the son of Jupiter, Jupiter is the son of Saturn, and Saturn is the son of Uranus. So there was a proposal to call the new planet Uranus and in 1850 the name Uranus was officially adopted.

TUNGSTEN

(1783)

Sometimes it is hard to be sure who has made a discovery, either because two or three scientists are working on the same problem at the same time or because the discovery is a staged process, with several people contributing.

Tungsten was identified by the Swedish chemist Carl Wilhelm Scheele in 1781, but not isolated until two years later, 1783, by the two brothers Juan José and Fausto Elhuijar at Vergara in Spain. So there is some dispute about the true discoverer of tungsten. To make things more complicated still, two years before Scheele identified the new element, in 1779, Peter Woulfe examined the mineral wolframite and concluded that it must contain a new element. In recognition of Woulfe's contribution to the process of discovery, an alternative name for tungsten is wolfram. The name tungsten comes from a Swedish phrase, 'tung sten', meaning 'heavy stone'; tungsten has a density that is almost twice that of lead.

Tungsten is not a common element, ranking fifty-seventh in abundance in the Earth's crust. Tungsten as a metal is silvery-white and lustrous, but the element is usually obtained as a grey powder. The main ores containing tungsten are scheelite and wolframite. Tungsten is useful for making filaments for electric lamps, electron tubes and television tubes. Because it has a very high melting point (3,422 degrees Celsius/ 6,191.6 degrees Fahrenheit), it has many industrial uses in high-temperature environments where other metals would melt. Many high-speed tool steels are tungsten alloys, such as the alloys used for ultra-high-speed dental drills.

THE AGE OF THE EARTH

(1785)

Whether you search for evidence of the age of the Earth depends on your view of time.

In archaic societies, there are two views of time. One is linear, the other cyclical. If a society believes that time is cyclical then time has no beginning (or end) and nor does the Earth. Adhering to the idea that time is cyclical is very natural. Day follows night follows day, always. Full moon follows new moon follows full moon, always. Summer follows winter follows summer, always. There are generational cycles too, when old people die and are replaced by young. There are short daily cycles, there are medium-length annual cycles, there are long generational cycles, so why not much longer cycles too? On the other hand, the events of one day are not the same as those of the previous day. They could not be; if an elder in the community died yesterday he could not die today as well. There is an implication here that time could be both cyclical and linear at the same time.

Plato proposed a 72,000-year cycle, in which 36,000 years are a Golden Age of order and 36,000 years are a descent into disorder and chaos. If a society believes that time is linear, then it must believe that time had a beginning (and will have an end), and that the Earth itself was created at a particular moment. Many archaic societies that believe in linear time have creation myths, sometimes elaborate stories that seek to describe how the Earth came into being. The Book of Genesis is one example among many.

There is a tendency, though not an inevitable tendency by any means, for more sophisticated, 'advanced' societies to believe in linear time. This entails developing creation theories (which are also, we often forget, elaborate stories) that seek to describe how the Earth came into being. The Judaic belief system holds that the Earth was created, and assumes that time is linear. The Christian and Islamic belief systems were built upon these ultimately Judaic assumptions. From the point of view of declining numbers of committed believers, western civilisation should probably now be regarded as post-Christian, but many of the old notions have survived, and the linear concept of time is one of them.

The traditional Jewish calendar begins in 3760 BC, and this date is taken as the date of the Earth's creation. From this flows the dialogue, the discussion about the age of the Earth. Christians and Muslims, inheriting this Jewish calendar, continued to consider the events re-counted in Genesis, and began to question the date, which was not included in the holy texts but deduced by Jewish scholars. Because no date is mentioned in the scriptures, it could not be a matter of heresy to question the date.

One famous attempt to arrive at a date for the age of the Earth was that of James Ussher. Ussher was a very distinguished churchman and bible scholar, the Protestant Archbishop of Armagh. What he attempted to do was to construct a chronology of the whole of human history, right back to the Creation. He deployed historical sources relating to the Middle East and the Mediterranean. He also used the Bible, interpreting it in the most literal way. To reach a date for the Creation, he used the genealogies that are included in the Bible and in that way reached back to Adam, the first man, who was created in the first week of the world's existence. By following this route, Archbishop Ussher arrived at the moment of the creation of the Earth. It was the evening of Sunday 23 October 4004 BC. This date, which was the first Sunday after the autumn equinox in 4004 BC according to the old Julian calendar, was duly published in his *Annals of the World* in 1650.

One intriguing aspect of Archbishop Ussher's reasoning is that he arrived at a date that was not far off the traditional date from the old Jewish calendar. One reason for a convergence on this period as a beginning for human history is that it was within a few centuries of the

176

invention of writing, and so also within a few centuries of the very earliest historical records. But Ussher made one serious mistake, which was to follow the Bible in equating the creation and age of the human race with the creation and age of the Earth.

The English astronomer and mathematician Edmond Halley attempted to find a different route to a date for the physical creation of the Earth. Instead of relying on documents, he argued that purely physical evidence could be used. He reasoned that the oceans have become salty as a result of thousands of rivers all over the world dissolving small amounts of soluble minerals out of the rocks they flow across. When water is evaporated from the ocean surface those soluble salts are left behind. So, as a result of the continuous global water cycle, more and more salt has been building up in the oceans. Halley argued that it should be possible to calculate how long it would take for an initially freshwater ocean to reach its present level of saltiness. Without putting a figure on it, Halley argued that it must have taken a very long time for the oceans to become so salty, therefore the Earth cannot be young. But he also argued that the Earth cannot be infinitely old or the oceans would be totally saturated with salt, like the Dead Sea. What Halley was trying to prove was that the Earth was not infinitely old: that it did have a beginning.

Halley ducked the really difficult task of making the calculation. It was not until the 1890s that John Joly, an Irish geologist, attempted it. He came up with a figure of eighty to ninety million years for the age of the Earth. This was an improvement on Ussher's 5,654 years, but still a serious underestimate of the Earth's age. Halley's method failed because it was too simple. It took no account of the ways in which salts can be taken out of the ocean; large quantities, for instance, have become trapped in sedimentary rocks and lifted out of the oceans by earth movements.

Halley's method failed, ultimately, to achieve an age for the Earth but at the same time it did make intellectually respectable the idea that the Earth had an age that was much older than human history. It also made respectable the process of scientific reasoning from natural processes, independently of historical documents or religious texts.

George-Louis Leclerc, the Comte de Buffon, was an eighteenth-century geologist who became convinced from his studies that the Earth must be very ancient. He estimated the time it would take for a completely molten Earth to cool to its present state. He also carried out some small-scale laboratory experiments on cooling iron spheres to help his calculations. He arrived at an age for the Earth of 75,000 years, which was a major advance on Ussher's figure. In 1862, Lord Kelvin, the British physicist, re-examined Buffon's calculation and came up with a date of ninety-eight million years. He seems to have frightened himself with this big number, which he later retracted to twenty to forty million years. Both Buffon and Kelvin were thwarted in their attempts to arrive at a rate of cooling because they did not know about the heating effects of radio-activity. The Earth was keeping itself warm by the natural radioactivity in its rocks.

In 1785, the Scottish geologist James Hutton first published his landmark book *Theory of the Earth* (a revised and expanded edition came out ten years later). In it he incorporated his own detailed observations of geological exposures. The sedimentary rock layers themselves showed that there had been repeated cycles of erosion in the landscape, cycles separated by episodes when the land was lifted up by earth movements. This Earth history itself implied that very long periods of time must have elapsed.

Hutton concluded that the Earth was millions of years old, but he was unable to arrive at even a roughly estimated date. He concluded with undue pessimism that the repeated cycles of erosion and uplift had destroyed the history of the Earth. He was right to suspect that at any one location repeated erosion cycles might have removed completely long stretches of geological history, like a book with many of the chapters torn out. But he overlooked the possibility that the missing chapters might be seen in differently damaged copies of the same book elsewhere, and that they could be found by following the distinctive sedimentary rocks (the page numbers) across country. One of James Hutton's great contributions was his discovery that studying exposures (and later boreholes) of rock layers could tell the story of the Earth's history. Another was introducing the idea of 'repair'. With the Biblical background a very strong influence, previous views of the Earth's history had presumed an initial creation, when everything was made, followed by progressive decay or erosion. What Hutton introduced was the very significant idea that the Earth had repeatedly renewed itself, with the evidence of repeated erosion cycles and intermittent uplift recorded in the stratigraphy of the rocks. His work would form the basis of much of the progress in geology that was made in the nineteenth century.

Hutton may not have been able to offer a date, but he did establish an appropriate new stance in relation to the problem of the age of the Earth. His awestruck tone in the face of what seemed certain to be an immensely long time scale was entirely new, entirely appropriate. 'The result, therefore, of our present enquiry,' he wrote, 'is, that we find no vestige of a beginning – no prospect of an end.'

URANIUM
(1789)

The German chemist Martin Heinrich Klaproth discovered uranium in 1789. He was analysing a mineral called pitchblende and discovered in it a black powder. Klaproth concluded that this powder was a new element, which he named uranium, after the newly discovered planet Uranus. This was not quite right, as the powder was actually one of uranium's oxides rather than uranium itself.

It was only in 1841 that the pure metallic element was isolated, by the French scientist Eugène Péligot, and not until 1896 that Antoine Becquerel, also French, discovered the radioactive properties of uranium.

Up until the time, when nuclear fission was discovered in 1939 by Otto Hahn and Fritz Strassmann, the main use of uranium (and mainly its oxides) was in pigments. A distinctive yellow-green fluorescent glass was made, which was fashionable for glass vases in the late nineteenth century. But the subsequent discovery that uranium and its compounds are highly toxic has severely curtailed their use outside the controlled environments of nuclear power stations. Today, the main use of uranium is as a nuclear fuel for generating electricity.

THE MACKENZIE RIVER
(1789)

The discoverer of the Mackenzie River in north-west Canada was Alexander Mackenzie. He was born in 1764 at Stornaway on Lewis, but severe economic depression in the Hebrides forced Mackenzie's father Kenneth to emigrate to New York. Kenneth Mackenzie's wife had died, and he decided to emigrate with his two sisters and his son Alexander, leaving his two daughters behind. Just months after arriving in America, the Mackenzies found themselves embroiled in the American Revolution. Kenneth joined the King's Royal Regiment of New York under Sir John Johnson, was commissioned lieutenant in 1776, but then died suddenly in 1780. The young Alexander Mackenzie had been left in the care of aunts, who first took him to Johnstown in the Mohawk Valley, where Johnson had large estates. Then, when conditions there became difficult for loyalists (to England), the aunts sent him to Montreal to go to school. This was how Alexander Mackenzie came to be in Canada.

He was a sturdy and high-spirited boy and he was attracted to the idea of becoming a fur trader. In 1779, he joined the firm of Finlay and Gregory. In 1784, he was trusted sufficiently to undertake a deal with 'a small adventure of goods' in Detroit. This was so successful that he was offered a share in the business, on condition that he was prepared to be posted in the far west. He was happy to accept. The British fur traders were now trading further into western Canada following the ceding of Canada to Britain in 1763. Coincidentally, this thrust to the west happened at a time when the American Revolution was threatening to deprive Montreal of its share in the trade in the area to the south of the Great Lakes.

There was now not only expansion of fur trading into the north-west, but sharp competition to trade there too. It was an unpoliced wilderness, and furs were obtained by fair means if possible, and if not by foul.

There was more security in pooling partnerships, and there was a notable pooling of nine partnerships in 1779, leading to the formation of the North-West Company in 1784. In response to this, Mackenzie's firm enlarged to five members: Gregory, MacLeod, Pangman, Ross and Mackenzie. Mackenzie was assigned to the English River department. The North-West Company wanted to expand its trading right across the North American continent. In pursuance of this, they declared an intention to explore 'at their own expense, between the latitudes of fifty-five and sixty-five, all that tract of country extending west of the Hudson's Bay to the North Pacific Ocean.' The declaration went on to propose that in return for this work the NWC should have exclusive rights to the fur trade in the north-west. Nothing formal came of this, but the NWC made it its business to acquire as much geographical knowledge of the region as it could lay hands on. Peter Pond was a major source of their information. He had travelled and questioned Indians, and produced a map of the area north of Lake Athabasca.

Pond's map was accurate in outline, and showed a river flowing north to the Great Slave Lake. Another river flowed out of the lake to the Arctic Ocean. Afterwards, Pond saw accounts of Captain Cook's third Pacific voyage and found that Cook had mistakenly identified an inlet as an estuary, naming it Cook's River. Pond then jumped to the conclusion that 'Cook's River' was really the mouth of the large river that flowed out of the Great Slave Lake. In a map dating from 1787, there are still some streams draining towards the Arctic Ocean, but the main river is now shown flowing west to the Pacific, based on Pond's unjustified hunch.

Pond made another miscalculation, one that was to be important to Mackenzie, and that was an underestimate of the distance between the Athabasca and the Pacific. By this time, there had been no proper calculations of longitude in the area Pond was mapping, and he placed the lake 1,125 kilometres (700 miles) too far west.

Pond's career in the fur trade was to be cut short. He was a violent man, suspected of killing a rival trader, Jean-Etienne Waddens in 1782, and he was involved in a fight five years later with John Ross, sent out by Gregory MacLeod to compete with Pond; at the end of that brawl

Ross had been shot dead. The result of Ross's death was the amalgamation of Gregory, MacLeod and the North-West Company. Pond, remarkably, was not excluded from the new partnership, but it was understood that the 1787–88 season would be his last in the west.

Pond returned to his post on the Athabasca River in October 1787, supported by Mackenzie. They agreed quite well, though Mackenzie knew Pond was a murderer; Mackenzie wanted to learn what he could from Pond the trader and Pond the explorer. When Pond finally left in the spring of 1788, Mackenzie was in charge. He made plans at once to descend the large river that runs out of the Great Slave Lake, the river now known as the Mackenzie. He was expecting it to flow as indicated on Pond's map, a relatively short distance west, where it would empty into the Pacific. That Mackenzie had these expectations is confirmed by a letter written by Isaac Ogden after he had had conversations with Pond, who had clearly not change his mind about the course and length of the river. Ogden was given to understand that Mackenzie was 'to go down the River, and from thence to Unalaska, and so to Kamskatsha [Kamchatka], and then to England through Russia, &c.' A very ambitious journey of exploration was envisaged – even if Pond's map was correct.

It is also clear from Mackenzie's account that his journey was officially sanctioned. Its title says that the 'voyage' was undertaken by order of the North-West Company and that the purpose was to find a passage by water through to the Pacific. Mackenzie revelled in the huge challenge he had taken on. He set off on 3 June 1789 with four French Canadians, a young German, a Chipewyan Indian and an assortment of native 'wives'.

Progress by canoe down the upper Slave River was slow. The party encountered many rapids. Then there were delays because of ice on the Great Slave Lake. But once the canoes were on the Mackenzie River they made fast progress. Mackenzie and his party went down the river at incredible speed, following its whole length, 1,730 kilometres (1,075 miles), in just fourteen days. They were travelling at an average speed of more than 120 kilometres (75 miles) per day – a truly extraordinary speed on a journey of exploration in unknown territory.

At first, Mackenzie must have been reassured that the river followed a generally westward course. It was what Pond's map had led him to expect. Then, after about 480 kilometres (300 miles), at the Camsell Bend, the Mackenzie swung round towards the north. It went on flowing towards the north, and it dawned on Mackenzie that the river was not after all going to take them to the Pacific. He must have cursed the murderous Pond. He did not know what to do. On 10 July, when he and his party were only two days away from the Arctic Ocean, he wrote in his journal, 'I am much at a loss here how to act, being certain that my going further in this Direction will not answer the Purpose of which the Voyage was intended, as it is evident these Waters must empty themselves into the Northern Ocean.' Perhaps he realised that struggling back against the current would have been an appalling endeavour, and he decided to continue to the sea, 'as it would satisfy Peoples Curiosity tho' not their Intentions.'

The river opened out into a large expanse of open water. It was misty, so Mackenzie could not be absolutely sure whether he had reached the Arctic Ocean, or just another large lake. Mackenzie and his party spent four nights on Whale Island (now Garry Island) off the river mouth and observed the rise and fall of the tide. It was indeed the sea.

Then the return journey was begun, reaching Fort Chipewyan on 12 September. Mackenzie had achieved a long journey of exploration, more than 4,830 kilometres (3,000 miles), in just 102 days, and found the entire course of one of the world's greatest rivers. Later he came to be proud of what he had achieved, but at first Mackenzie was frustrated; he had been sent to find a short water route to the Pacific, one that would be commercially beneficial to his company, and he had failed to find it. His partners too were disappointed, but still increased his five per cent share in the company to ten per cent. He had after all discovered the 'Grand River'.

THE WEIGHT OF
THE EARTH
(1798)

Henry Cavendish carried out what has become know as the Cavendish experiment to measure in a laboratory the force of gravity between masses. The equipment Cavendish used for this was designed and built by John Michell, a geologist. Michell sent the apparatus to Cavendish in crates, but died before the experiment itself took place. The equipment consisted of a torsion balance to measure the gravitational attraction that existed between two lead spheres, each weighing 160 kilograms (350 pounds), and a pair of much smaller lead spheres, each weighing 725 grams (26 ounces).

By using this equipment, Cavendish was able to deduce the mean density of the Earth. He measured it as 5.448 times greater than that of water. Cavendish conducted his measurements twenty-nine times to arrive at this average value. The experiment was often misreported as an experiment to measure the Earth's mass, when it was specifically to measure its density, although it was then possible to calculate its mass. From his results he was also able to calculate the gravitational constant, G, which was not to be used until a hundred years later, in 1873.

Henry Cavendish carried out his famous experiment in an outbuilding in the garden of his estate at Clapham. For years afterwards, neighbours would point the building out to their children, telling them that that was the place where the world was weighed.

THE ROSETTA STONE
(1799)

Following the French occupation of Alexandria in July 1798, Napoleon's officials set up an Institute of Egypt with a view to improving scholarship in many different fields. The Institute produced its own scientific journal. Eventually much of the new research was published between 1809 and 1828 in a massive, multi-volume, *Description of Egypt.*

The scholars who travelled with Napoleon's army carried out surveys and compiled a comprehensive map of Egypt's antiquities; the science of Egyptology was launched. This intensive programme of research led to some major discoveries, and one of the most important of these was the Rosetta Stone. This is an imposing slab of black basalt, about 114 centimetres (45 inches) high with a polished flat surface inscribed with lines of writing. It was found during the Napoleonic survey of Egypt, at the village of Rashid a few miles from the coast of the western Nile Delta. Rashid was known as Rosetta by Europeans.

The exact circumstances of the discovery in July 1799 are unknown. It was said by some that it was found lying on the ground and by others that it was built into an old wall which the French soldiers ordered to be demolished when they were extending a fort. This second story is supported by the Institute's map, which shows Fort Julien on the Nile's west bank, in the neighbourhood of Rosetta. The man who discovered the stone was an engineer, Pierre Bouchard, who headed the demolition team.

The great importance of the Rosetta Stone lay in its inscriptions, which consisted of the same text in three different scripts. The first was in hieroglyphs, which were in use in 1000 BC, and the second was demotic, a cursive script that evolved from hieroglyphs and dated from about 643 BC. The third was Greek. Scholars realised immediately that the Rosetta Stone provided the key to deciphering the two older scripts.

Nineteenth-century French scholars could read ancient Greek, so they were able to use that to decipher the demotic and hieroglyphic texts.

To enable scholars to work on the task of decipherment, two lithographers coated the stone with printer's ink, laid sheets of paper on it, and then applied rollers on top of the paper in order to make prints of the writing. Copies of the prints were sent off to scholars all over Europe to work on. A French translation of the Greek text was made by Du Theil in Paris, and he showed that the stone was a monument to the gratitude of some priests of Alexandria to Ptolemy Epiphanes. The text was translated into Latin in 1801 and English in 1802.

In that year, the French scholar Silvestre de Sacy started deciphering the demotic text. He started with the proper names in the Greek text and found their translation in the demotic section. A Swedish diplomat recognised the words for 'temples' and 'Greeks'. In 1814, the Englishman Thomas Young made the important discovery that demotic words were not all alphabetically written, and that led him to compare the demotic script and the hieroglyphs. He looked for repeated Greek words, counted the number of times they were repeated, and looked for the same numbers of repeated Demotic signs. This enabled him to identify the signs for 'and', 'king', 'Ptolemy' and 'Egypt'. Then he identified the name 'Ptolemy' in the hieroglyphic section and spotted that some hieroglyphs were phonetic values.

The French scholar Jean-François Champollion was reaching similar conclusions. Both Young and Champollion used other script discoveries as well to help them, such as a bilingual text found at Philae in 1815. In 1822, Champollion published his decipherment of the hieroglyphic forms of many of the Roman emperors of Egypt. Young had come to an *impasse*, but Champollion went on to unravel the general system of hieroglyphs.

When Napoleon was defeated and exiled, French control in Egypt gave way to British control, and a dispute arose over ownership of the Rosetta Stone. General Jacques Menou, who thought he owned it, refused to give up the stone to General Hely Hutchinson; 'You want it, Monsieur le Général? You can have it, since you are the stronger of the two of us. You may pick it up whenever you please!' It weighed almost a ton. A Colonel Turner eventually arrived to collect the stone, which was stored in an Alexandrian warehouse with Menou's personal belongings, awaiting return to France. The Rosetta Stone was shipped to England on board HMS *l'Eyptienne* (which had also been captured from the French), arriving at Portsmouth in February 1802. It was taken to London, where plaster casts were made for four British universities, before being put on public display in the British Museum, where it can still be seen.

The Rosetta Stone was a turning point in the development of Egyptology. Not only did the stone capture people's imaginations, it actually provided, within itself, the key to deciphering the two scripts of ancient Egypt. And once hieroglyphs were decipherable, much more could be learnt about the ancient civilisation of the pharaohs.

IV
THE NINETEENTH-CENTURY WORLD

THE ATOMIC
STRUCTURE OF
MATTER
(1803)

The idea that matter is made up of atoms has been around for a long time. Leucippus of Miletus first had the idea in about 440 BC. Together with his pupil Democritus of Abdera, Leucippus refined and developed it. Most of their writings are lost, but their ideas were quoted by others. Aristotle quoted from them, mainly in order to argue against them. Many of their ideas come to us, rather oddly, from a poem by Lucretius, written in about 60 BC, and which was itself lost for more than a thousand years before being rediscovered in 1417. The poem is called *De Rerum Natura* (*On the Nature of Things*).

Democritus held that everything is composed of atoms, particles of matter that are too small to be seen. These atoms are irreducible; they cannot be further split up. The Greek word *atomos* means 'uncuttable'. Matter can be disintegrated into atoms, and also reintegrated from atoms. Leucippus held that there are voids, empty spaces between atoms, though there are no voids within atoms. We now know, thanks to Rutherford's discovery of the nucleus in 1911, that this is not true as atoms are mostly empty space. Leucippus and Democritus thought that atoms must be the same all the way through, though we now know, thanks to J. J. Thomson's discovery of the electron in 1897, that they possess an internal structure.

Aristotle was strongly opposed to the idea of the atom. Because of his immense authority, his inexplicable politico-intellectual power in the ancient and medieval worlds, the atom disappeared from view. Because

Aristotle did not believe in atoms, they did not exist. Because the Catholic Church accepted Aristotle's position on most issues, ideas of atoms were anti-Aristotelian and came to be regarded as in some way godless. There were a few 'heretics' who went on speculating about the atom idea, but it was not a mainstream idea by any means. To support the views, or the alleged views, of Democritus was to court danger. Democritus was believed to have said that the universe has no end, and that it was not created by any outside power.

It was in 1803 that John Dalton put the atom back onto a scientific basis. Dalton wrote his first table of atomic weights in his notebook dated September 1803. In 1830, in a lecture to the Manchester Literary and Philosophical Society, Dalton said, 'Under the date of September 3 1803, I find in my notebook *Observations on the ultimate particles of bodies and their combinations*, in which the atomic symbols I still use were introduced. On the 23rd of October the same year I read my Essay on the absorption of Gases, at the conclusion of which a series of atomic weights was given for twenty-one simple and compound elements.'

Although Dalton had found the atomic weights of a number of elements in 1803, he did not publish his results until 1805. He produced a book entitled *A New System of Chemical Philosophy*, and it is only in the closing pages that he discusses his reintroduction of atomic theory. The atomic theory Dalton proposed was straightforward. Chemical elements are made of atoms. The atoms of an element are identical in their masses. Atoms of different elements have different masses. Atoms only combine in small whole-number ratios such as 1:1 or 2:3.

The idea that elements are made of atoms was not by any means new in 1803. Democritus had said this over two thousand years earlier. But when Dalton re-expressed it, it was a genuine re-discovery. Dalton's atoms have invariably been taught to students as being similar to smooth, structureless billiard balls; models of molecular structures invariably show them in this way. But Dalton himself did not actually rule out the possibility that atoms might have some interior structure, that there might be subatomic particles. It was rather that his theory did not reach that far. Dalton knew that the technology of, for example, microscopy in the early nineteenth century did not allow the interior structure of an atom to be investigated. Unlike some modern physicists, Dalton was cautious: he was not prepared to speculate about areas where knowledge was impossible.

Dalton's idea that all atoms of a specific chemical element must have the same weight is now known to be untrue. Isotopes, that is, variants of elements, would not be discovered for a hundred years.

In France there were scientists who resisted Dalton's atomic theory. Right through to the late nineteenth century there were senior academic chemists in France who used their seniority to punish junior colleagues and students for publicly supporting atomic theory.

An idea that is implicit in Dalton's theory is that atoms cannot be created and cannot be destroyed. Dalton expressed this vividly: 'We might as well attempt to introduce a new planet into the solar system, or to annihilate one already in existence, as to create or destroy a particle of hydrogen. All the changes we can produce consist in separating particles that are in a state of cohesion or combination, and joining those that were previously at a distance.' This idea was not really a Daltonian discovery. Antoine Lavoisier had already framed the Law of Conservation of Mass in chemical reactions.

What we are seeing is not really a single moment of discovery, but a gradual and jerky progress towards a collective realisation of the nature of matter. The discovery was a process in which many different scientists participated in a kind of dialogue across the centuries. Dalton's atomic theory was built upon and extended almost at once, in 1811, when the Italian chemist Amedeo Avogadro discovered that the atoms in elements combine to form molecules.

Atoms were a fundamental discovery, the literal building blocks of the universe. It has been estimated that there are one trillion trillion trillion trillion trillion trillion atoms in the universe. A number like that is impossible to imagine. Nearer to home, there are more atoms in a tumberful of water than there are tumberfuls of water in all the oceans of the world.

ANTARCTICA SIGHTED
(1820)

The existence of Antarctica was assumed by ancient Greek philosophers long before any Europeans ventured that far south. In 450 BC, Parmenides divided the Earth into five climatic zones arguing that the zones in the far north and far south were uninhabitable. He had no direct knowledge of this, but inferred it, correctly, from the way temperatures fell away from southern to northern Europe. In about 322 BC, Aristotle gave a name to the extreme south. The extreme north lay under the constellation of the Bear (the Great Bear is commonly known as The Plough), and the name 'Arctic' (*Arktikos*) came from *Arktos*, 'Bear'. So the southern equivalent was named Antarctic (*Antarktikos*). The geographer Ptolemy later added the proposition that this southern region was occupied by a large landmass, so far undiscovered – *Terra Australis Incognita.*

At the time when the European navigators were reaching out to explore the unknown regions of the world, classical knowledge was being revived. With it came the idea of the great unknown southern continent. Even though successive voyages failed to find it, people still went on believing that it must exist. As late as the late eighteenth century, Captain James Cook had combed the South Pacific trying to find it, and he failed.

Maybe people had caught sight of it long before but the event had gone unrecorded. There is an interesting Polynesian legend, which has it that in about AD 650, at the time when Micronesia and eastern Polynesia were being colonised by western Polynesians, an adventurer did sail south. His name was Ui-te-rangiora, and he made a great sea journey south from Fiji, past New Zealand. He reached a place where 'things like rock' grew out of the sea. These were presumably icebergs.

The explorer named the sea Tai-uka-a pia, which means 'sea foaming like arrowroot.' The legend seems to describe an early voyage into the Southern Ocean, going far enough south to encounter sea ice and icebergs, just as Cook did in 1773–74.

Cook was impressed by the sheer desolation of the place. He wrote, 'I can be so bold as to say that no man will venture further south than I have done, and that the land to the South will never be explored.' It was a rash boast, and within half a century he was proved to be wrong. The impetus to Antarctic exploration came from the whaling and sealing industries. Interested businessmen sponsored several expeditions in the early nineteenth century, such as those of Nathaniel Palmer and the Enderby brothers. Nathaniel Palmer is often credited with being the first person to catch sight of the mainland of the continent in 1820. Another American sealer, Captain John Davis, was the first to make a landing, in February 1821. When the Russian captain, Bellinghausen, led the first circumnavigation of Antarctica he could hardly believe what he was seeing when in January 1821 he caught sight of nine vessels, all sealers, anchored off the coast of what is now called Palmer Land.

THE RED LADY OF
PAVILAND
(1823)

Paviland Cave is a sea cave on the coast of the Gower Peninsula of South Wales. When it was excavated in 1823, a human skeleton was discovered buried inside it. The excavator, Dean William Buckland, was Professor of Mineralogy and Geology at Oxford, which gave his interpretation of the find great authority. Buckland decided that what he had found was the skeleton of a woman who was buried in the cave just before the Roman Conquest. In other words, she was an ancient Briton from the late Iron Age.

The bones were stained with red ochre, so the skeleton became known as the Red Lady of Paviland. And so she remained for ninety years, until 1913, when W. J. Sollas argued that she was a man and also that the skeleton dated from a much earlier time. Suddenly the find became that of an early Upper Palaeolithic man – the oldest known inhabitant of Britain.

The sea caves along the Gower coast were a good hunting ground for archaeologists, as we now know that twenty-two of the Gower's ninety-five caves were used as shelters by prehistoric hunters. Buckland found the skeleton in a shallow grave along with as many as 5,000 objects and bones. The man, 'Paviland Man' was buried with grave goods that included ornaments of shell, ivory and mammoth bones. The elaborate ceremonial treatment of the body has given us invaluable evidence of the wildlife that lived in the area at the time, in South Wales and on the floor of the Bristol Channel, then exposed as dry land. There were not only mammoth, but reindeer, hyena and woolly rhinoceros.

The advent of radiocarbon dating in the 1950s brought closer the possibility of a more precise date. A radiocarbon date of 18,000 years before present was produced. That meant that the owner of the skeleton had been living in South Wales at almost the coldest point of the last cold stage, when most of Wales would have been covered by ice. Later attempts to date the skeleton more accurately produced an older date, 26,000 before present. There was still no real confidence in the date, because the bone was known to have been contaminated by preservatives applied after the skeleton was recovered.

Recently, Oxford's Radiocarbon Accelerator Unit has developed a system that produce purer samples of bone collagen. The filtering technique can block out the microscopic particles of nineteenth-century preservatives, which were suspected of producing a falsely recent date. The new ultrafiltration technique was tried out on fragments of rib and collar bone from the 'Red Lady', and it produced a date of 29,000 years before present.

This very early date for the skeleton is highly significant in showing a surprisingly advanced stage of cultural development in Britain. The burial of the Red Lady was evidently accompanied by a funeral ceremony, and elaborate burials of this kind were not previously known to have taken place this early in Western Europe. There is an implication here that elaborate ceremonial practices surrounding death and burial may have started here, in Britain, and spread eastwards. The tradition in archaeology has always been 'light from the east' – that innovation and civilisation started in the east (often the Middle East) and spread westwards across Europe. So perhaps here we are on the brink of another important discovery – that some innovations were made in the west.

SILICON
(1824)

Jöns Jacob Berzelius is usually recognized as having discovered silicon in Stockholm in 1824. But Louis-Jacques Thénard and Louis-Joseph Gay-Lussac probably prepared amorphous silicon, a brown powder, as early as 1811. Deville prepared the second form of silicon, crystalline silicon, which is grey with a metallic lustre, in 1854.

Silicon is a very important element, making up one-quarter of the Earth's crust by mass. It is the second most abundant element, oxygen being the most abundant. It does not occur on its own in nature, but exists in many different forms in compounds such as silicates or as an oxide. The oxide includes materials such as sand, quartz, rock crystal, agate, flint, amethyst and opal. The silicate form includes feldspar (one of the minerals in granite), asbestos, clay and mica.

In the form of sand and clay, silicon is an essential material for the building industry.

Commercially prepared pure silicon is used a great deal in solid-state devices. The silicon is usually laced with very small, precisely measured amounts of boron, gallium, phosphorus or arsenic, to make transistors and solar cells. In microchips, silicon is a vital component in computers and other microelectronic devices.

THE INTERIOR OF
AUSTRALIA
(1824)

The interior of Australia was explored gradually during the European colonisation by many explorers in many separate expeditions. Probably the best-known expedition is the Burke and Wills expedition, which was an heroic attempt to cross the interior, an attempt that failed. The British colonisation began at Sydney, but for a long time expansion westwards from Sydney was impeded by the presence of a substantial mountain range, the Great Dividing Range, which runs the full length of Australia from north to south. The range was like a wall. Governor Gidley King went so far as to say that it was impassable, but in 1813 an expedition led by Gregory Blaxland succeeded in crossing the range. Once the Great Divide was crossed, other expeditions followed.

In 1824, Governor Thomas Brisbane asked Hamilton Hume and William Hovell to travel from Hume's station, close to the site of Canberra, to Spencer Gulf, west of the site of Adelaide. Hume and Hovell were covering their own costs, and consequently made their own decisions about where they would go. They discovered the Murrumbidgee and Murray rivers, crossed them both, and eventually reached the site of modern Geelong.

In 1829–30, Charles Sturt explored the same area, following the Murrumbidgee until it joined the Murray. Then he found the confluence of the Murray and the River Darling, following the Murray on to its mouth. Sturt in effect pieced together the physical geography of the entire Murray-Darling Basin. The headwaters of all of its rivers flowed from east to west, and that had given the early explorers the idea that they might empty into an inland sea in the heart of Australia. This turned out to be wishful thinking. The rivers all turned south, joining one another before reaching the sea near Adelaide. There was disappointment about the vanishing inland sea, but at least the Murray-Darling Basin was opened up to settlement.

In 1858–60, Charles Sturt successfully crossed Australia from south to north for the first time, crossing from Spencer Gulf to Van Diemen Gulf, right across the Simpson Desert.

The most famous Australian explorers were Robert Burke and William Wills. They set off on a well-equipped expedition from Melbourne in 1860, heading north for the Gulf of Carpentaria. They were unlucky. Both of them died during the return trip. The Stuart expedition and the Burke and Wills expedition together showed that there was no inland sea, at least in the eastern half of Australia.

ALUMINIUM
(1827)

Alum, which contains aluminium, was used by the ancient Greeks and Romans in medicines and in the dyeing process. Many of the clays used for making pottery in the ancient world also contained aluminium. No one understood that an element called aluminium was contributing the properties they valued.

By the Middle Ages that had changed, and aluminium was one of the elements to which the alchemists attached a special symbol. But it was not until much later that aluminium was thought of as a metal in its own right. In 1807, Humphry Davy proposed the name alumium for the metal, later agreeing to change it to aluminum. A little after that there was general agreement that an 'i' should be added so that the ending would conform to the 'ium' ending of most of the other elements. Aluminium is now the internationally agreed spelling of the element. Confusingly, in 1925 the American Chemical Society decided to revert to the spelling aluminum, and this is still in use in the United States.

Aluminium was first prepared, in an impure form, in Copenhagen in 1825 by Hans Christian Oersted. It was first isolated as an element by Friedrich Wöhler in 1827.

Aluminium is a distinctive hard silver-white metal. It has an oxide form that protects it from reacting with air and water. It does not occur freely in nature, but it is even so the most abundant metal in the Earth's crust, occurring in mineral form in rocks such as bauxite. Aluminium is an extremely useful metal. It is low-density, light, non-toxic, corrosion-resistant, non-magnetic, non-sparking. It also had high thermal conductivity. It is very easy to use in manufacturing objects as it is easy to cast, and it is both malleable and ductile. Aluminium finds many uses in kitchen utensils, aircraft fittings and the superstructures of ships.

THE SOURCE OF THE MISSISSIPPI

(1832)

Henry R. Schoolcraft discovered the source of the Mississippi River, Lake Itasca, in 1832. This is how he described his discovery.

Ozawindib announced that we had reached the primary forks of the Mississippi. We were now in latitude 47 degrees 28 minutes 46 seconds.

Up to this point the river had carried its characteristics in a remarkable manner. Of the two primary streams before us, the one flowing from the west, the Itascan fork, contributes by far the largest volume of water, possessing the greatest velocity and breadth of current. The two streams enter each other at an acute angle, which varies but little from the south.

Ozawindib hesitated not a moment which branch to ascend, but shooting his canoe out of the stronger current of the Itascan fork, entered the other. His wisdom in this movement was soon apparent. He had not only entered the shallower and stiller branch, but one that led more directly to the base of the ultimate summit of Itasca. This stream soon narrowed to twenty feet. It was manifest from the forest vegetation that we were advancing into regions of a more Alpine flora. The branches of the larches, spruce, and gray pines were clothed with lichens and floating moss to their very tops, denoting an atmosphere of more than the ordinary humidity. Clumps of gray willows skirted the margin of the stream.

It was found that the river had made its utmost northing in Queen Anne's Lake. From the exit from that point the course was nearly due south, and from this moment to our arrival at the ultimate forks, which can not exceed a mile and a half or two miles, it was evident why the actual source of this celebrated river had so long eluded scrutiny. We were ascending at every curve so far south as to carry the observer out of every old line of travel or commerce in the fur trade (the sole interest here) and into a remote elevated region, which is never visited indeed, except by Indian hunters, and is never crossed, even by them, to visit the waters of the Red River – the region in immediate juxtaposition north. This semi-Alpine plateau, or height of land for which we were now pushing directly, is called in the parlance of the fur trade Hauteurs de Terre. It was evident that we were ascending to this continental plateau by steps, denoted by a series of rapids, presenting step by step, in regular succession, widespread areas of flat surface spotted with almost innumerable lakes, small and large, and rice ponds and lagoons.

It was now seven o'clock p.m. and we had been in our canoe sixteen hours, and traveled fifty-five miles. It was not easy to find ground dry enough to encamp on, and while we were searching for it, rain commenced. We had pushed through the ample borders of the Scirpus lacustris *and other aquatic plants, to a point of willows, alders, and spruce and tamarack, with* Pinus banksiana *in the distance. The ground was low and wet, the foot sinking into a carpet of green moss at every tread. The lower branches of the trees were dry and dead, exhibiting masses of flowing gray moss.*

The night here, in a gloomy and damp thicket, just above the line of the river flags, and quite in the range of the frogs and lizards, proved to be one of the most dreary and forlorn. It was felt that we were no longer on the open Mississippi, but were winding up a tributary, nowhere over thirty feet wide, which unfolded itself in bog bordered closely with lagoons. Indian sagacity, it was clear, had led Ozawindib up this tributary as the best, shortest, and easiest possible way of reaching and surmounting the Itasca plateau, but it required a perpetual use of hand, foot, paddle, and pole.

At five o'clock the next morning we were on our feet, and resumed the ascent. The day was rainy and disagreeable. There was little strength of current, but quite a sufficient depth of water; the stream was excessively tortuous. Owing to the sudden bends, we often frightened up the same flocks of brant, ducks, and teals again and again, who did not appear to have been in times past much subjected to these intrusions.

We toiled all day without intermission from daybreak till dark. The banks of the river are fringed with a species of coarse marshland grass. Clumps of willows fringe the stream. Rush and reed occupy spots favorable to their growth. The forest exhibits the larch, pine, and tamarack. Moss attaches to everything. Water fowls seem alone to exult in their seclusion. After we had proceeded for an hour above Lake Plantagenet, an Indian in the advance canoe fired at and killed a deer. Although fairly shot, the animal ran several hundred yards. It then fell dead. The man who had killed it brought the carcass to the banks of the river. The dexterity with which he skinned and cut it up excited admiration.

At length, at half-past five o'clock in the evening, we came to the base of the highlands of the Itasca or Hauteurs de Terre summit. The flanks of this elevation revealed themselves in a high, naked precipice of the drift and boulder stratum, on the immediate margin of the stream which washed against it. Our pilot, Ozawindib, was at the moment in the rear; halting a few moments for him to come up, he said that we were within a few hundred yards of the Naiwa rapids, and that the portage around them commenced at this escarpment. We had seen no rocks of any species, in place, thus far.

The next morning a dense fog prevailed. We found the atmosphere charged with water and vapors, which frequently condensed into showers. It was five o'clock before we could discern objects with sufficient distinctness to venture to embark. We found the channel of the river strikingly diminished on getting above the Naiwa. Its width is that of a mere brook, running in a valley half a mile wide. The water is still and pond-like, the margin being encroached on by aquatic plants.

I had now traced this branch of the Mississippi to its source, and was at the south base of the intercontinental highlands, which give origin to the longest and principal branch of the Mississippi. To reach its Source it was necessary to ascend and cross these. Of their height, and the difficulty of their ascent, we knew nothing. This only was sure, from the representation of the natives, that it could be readily done, carrying the small bark canoes we had thus far employed. The chief said it was thirteen opugidjiwenun, or putting-down-places, which are otherwise called onwaybees, or rests. From the roughness of the path, not more than half a mile can be estimated to each onwaybee. Assawa Lake is shown, by barometric measurement, to be 1,532 feet above the Gulf. Having followed out this branch to its source, its very existence in our geography becomes a new fact.

The elevated parts of the route were open, with often steep ascents. We had been four hours upon it, now clambering up steeps, and now brushing through thickets, when our guide told us we were ascending the last elevation, and I kept close to his heels, soon outwent him on the trail, and got the first glimpse of the glittering nymph we had been pursuing. On reaching the summit this wish was gratified. At a depression of perhaps a hundred feet below, cradled among the hills, the lake spread out its elongated volume, presenting a scene of no common picturesqueness and rural beauty. In a short time I stood on its border, the whole cortège of canoes and pedestrians following; and as each one came he deposited his burden on a little open plat, which constituted the terminus of the Indian trail. In a few moments a little fire threw up its blaze, and the pan of pigieu, or pine pitch, was heated to mend the seams of the bark canoes. When this was done, they were instantly put into the lake, with their appropriate baggage; and the little flotilla of five canoes was soon in motion, passing down one of the most tranquil and pure sheets of water of which it is possible to conceive. There was not a breath of wind. We often rested to behold the scene. It is not a lake overhung by rocks. Not a precipice is in sight, or a stone, save the pebbles and boulders of the drift era, which are scattered on the beach. The waterfowl, whom we disturbed in their seclusion, seemed rather loath to fly up.

I inquired of Ozawindib the Indian name of this lake; he replied Omushkös, which is the Chippewa name of the elk. Having previously got an inkling of some of their mythological and necromantic notions of the origin and mutations of the country, which permitted the use of a female name for it, I denominated it Itasca.

Lake Itasca is indeed the source of the Mississippi, but a stream flows into the lake, and that stream comes a short distance from Elk Lake. Elk Lake was determined as the ultimate source of the Mississippi by a New

York journalist, Julius Chambers, though there are other lakes which also feed Lake Itasca.

Henry Schoolcraft's claim was formally contested in 1891 by Captain Willard Glazier, who claimed to have discovered the source himself. He produced a paper in Berne in which he made his claim. A Committee was set up to judge on his charges, and it concluded in August 1891 that Glazier's claim to be the discoverer of the Mississippi source was a pretence. The Mississippi sources really were discovered by Schoolcraft.

A couple of years later, the city of Minneapolis had its beginnings in St Anthony's Falls, which was discovered and given its name by Father Louis Hennepin, who had travelled with La Salle through the Great Lakes to try to reach the source of the Mississippi River, another natural wonder of North America. The Mississippi itself had first been stumbled upon back in 1541 by Hernando de Soto, and the following year his men had navigated the Lower Mississippi from its confluence with the Arkansas River.

The Mississippi became part of the white American consciousness fairly early on. Gradually, as the European colonists extended their territorial interests into the interior, they realised what extraordinary and unexpected natural wonders North America had to offer, and the sheer scale of the continent. At first they were looking for somewhere to live, for land that would support them, but the landscape gradually imprinted and impressed itself upon them. A bond between people and landscape developed, one that forged a national identity and would eventually support a struggle for independence and a fierce patriotism.

THE CORIOLIS EFFECT
(1835)

The Coriolis effect, which is sometimes called the Coriolis force, was discovered by a French engineer and mathematician – called Coriolis. His full name was Gaspard-Gustave de Coriolis. He was born in Paris in 1792 into an aristocratic family. His father took the family out of Paris for safety during the French Revolution and settled in Nancy where he became an industrialist. Gaspard-Gustave de Coriolis trained as a civil engineer, but his poor health led him to turn to teaching mathematics and mechanics at the Ecole Polytechnique in 1816.

Coriolis published an important work, *On the calculation of mechanical action*, in 1829. In this, he used the terms 'work' and 'kinetic energy' in their modern scientific senses for the first time. In 1835, he published his most influential work, *On the equations of relative motion of a system of bodies*. This paper described in outline what is now known as the Coriolis effect. It is a theory of relative motion in a frame of reference that is rotating. This has many applications in relation to the Earth's rotation, where an object might be moving along through the Earth's atmosphere, in any direction. As it does so, according to Coriolis, it is subject to an additional inertial force acting at right angles to its direction of movement.

One result of the Coriolis effect is that winds moving from a belt of high atmospheric pressure to a belt of low atmospheric pressure do not move directly from one to the other, but are deflected so that they move diagonally. The effect is useful in explaining the diagonal directions of airflow in many of the prevailing winds, such as the North-East Trade Winds. The Coriolis effect can be seen at work at all times in patterns of atmospheric air flow, and also in the circulation of ocean currents.

Later, in 1856, the American meteorologist William Ferrel constructed a very useful statement, which is in effect an observation about the way the Coriolis effect can be seen to work in nature. It is called Ferrel's Law; any body moving on or near the Earth's surface tends to suffer deflection to the right hand in the northern hemisphere and to the left in the southern. This elucidates some very large-scale phenomena, such as the circulatory movements of ocean water. For example, in the North Atlantic Ocean, the Gulf Stream moves north-eastwards towards the British Isles, curving towards the right as it does so and then turning into the Canaries Current, which flows southwards along the west coast of the bulge of Africa. Then the water curves to the right again to become the North Equatorial Current, which in turn swings to the right to join the Gulf Stream. The moving water in these currents is continuously obeying Ferrel's Law and displaying the Coriolis effect. Ferrel's Law is a restatement, in a physical geography context, of the Coriolis effect.

There is continuing debate about possible manifestations of the Coriolis effect on the medium or small scale. Are large rivers like the Mississippi affected by it? Are railway trains affected by it? You and I are probably not affected by it because our mass is too small and our speed is too low.

These *alfresco* applications of the Coriolis effect were not what interested Coriolis himself. His scientific paper grew out of his research into industrial machines with major rotating components, such as water wheels. Engines like these were a major feature of nineteenth century industrial engineering, and their properties and side effects were of great practical significance. But what Coriolis said about the additional inertial force was as true for the Earth as it was for the water wheel. He discovered a general principle that was extremely useful in helping to explain the dynamics of some of the major geographical systems – and they evidently apply on other planets too.

Coriolis also wrote *Mathematical theory of the game of billiards*, which was far less useful.

OZONE
(1839)

The Dutch experimenter Martinus van Marum (1750–1837) was the first person to notice ozone. He was interested in the properties of electricity and hired the English instrument maker John Cuthbertson to build him a large frictional electrostatic generator at Haarlem in the Netherlands. In a description of his experiments, van Marum mentioned that 'persons within 3 metres (10 feet) experienced a sort of creeping sensation over them as if surrounded by a spider's web.' He could also smell a distinctive odour coming from his generator. This was the smell of ozone gas, though van Marum did not identify it as such. He described it as 'the odour of electrical matter' but did not identify the gas as an allotrope of oxygen, which is what it was.

The true discovery of ozone came in 1839. The German scientist Christian Schönbein noticed the same characteristic smell when conducting experiments, and gave the gas that was producing the smell ozone, a word deriving from the Greek *ozein*, meaning 'scent'. Schönbein therefore gave ozone its name. He was also the first person to research the reactions between ozone and organic matter.

Following Schönbein's announcement of his results in 1840 there were many studies on the disinfection mechanism of ozone. Werner Von Siemens in Berlin became the first person to use an ozone generator to manufacture the gas. The French chemist Marius Paul Otto launched a company to manufacture ozone installations for water purification. In 1906, Nice became the first town to be equipped with an ozone installation for the treatment of drinking water, and the practice quickly spread to other countries. During World War I, the use of chlorine as a chemical weapon led on to its deployment as an alternative disinfectant to ozone, and ozone production then fell away, though ozone is still used in France.

THE ICE AGE
(1840)

LOUIS AGASSIZ AND COMPANY

The discovery that the Earth had experienced a great Ice Age was one of the most momentous discoveries of the nineteenth century. We often think of evolution as being the most epoch-making discovery of that century, but in its way the discovery of the Ice Age was more important. It had even more ramifications, in the end, as we shall see, even leading to the current prevailing anxiety about global warming.

There is a heavy irony in the fact the man we have to regard as the principal discoverer of the Ice Age, Louis Agassiz, spent most of his time trying to promote a view of biology that trenchantly criticised and went against the grain of Charles Darwin's theory of evolution. It seems that Agassiz did not himself realise the worth of his own greatest idea. In 1869, almost thirty years after he published his book about the Ice Age, Agassiz wrote about himself, 'I have devoted my whole life to the study of Nature, and yet a single sentence may express all that I have done. *I have shown that there is a correspondence between the succession of Fishes in geological times and the different stages of their growth in the egg – that is all.* It chanced to be a result that was found to apply to other groups and has led to other conclusions of a like nature.'

Louis Agassiz, who remains one of the great enigmas of history, was born in 1807 in the French-speaking part of Switzerland. He studied biology and medicine, taking a doctor of philosophy degree at Erlangen and a doctor of medicine degree at Munich. Although it looked as if he was heading towards a career in medicine, his main interest at that time was zoology. After that he went to Paris to study comparative anatomy under Georges Cuvier, who was at that time the most famous naturalist in Europe. Agassiz's work on the *Fishes of Brazil*, published when he was only twenty-two, so impressed Cuvier that Cuvier handed Agassiz his own notes and drawings for a planned publication on fossil fish. When Cuvier died early in 1832 the two men had known each other for barely six months, yet Cuvier had learnt to respect the younger man and Agassiz in turn always regarded himself as Cuvier's intellectual heir. For the rest of his life, Agassiz defended and promoted Cuvier's ideas on animal classification and geological catastrophism.

After Cuvier's death, Agassiz became Professor of Natural History at the Lyceum of Neuchatel in Switzerland. For many years there he taught conscientiously and worked with great enthusiasm on various research projects including palaeontology and, starting in 1836, glaciology. It would be in the field of glaciology that Agassiz was to make his mark on history – and not notice it.

Living in Switzerland and observing the landscape objectively and scientifically, Agassiz was struck by the way in which the distinctive U-shaped troughs carved by the glaciers continued for many miles below the glaciers' snouts. It was as if the glaciers had once flowed much further down their valleys than they do today. It was a simple observation, but one with major reverberations when all its implications were realised. Several other writers had expressed the view that the glaciers had once been larger, but Agassiz pursued the idea and the evidence much further and built an integrated theory of the Ice Age.

Agassiz's major precursor was Jean de Charpentier (1786–1855), a German-Swiss geologist who studied Alpine glaciers. He began his adult life as a mining engineer, working in copper mines in the Pyrenees and salt mines in the Alps. In 1818, an incident happened which changed the direction of his life. An ice dam ponding back an Alpine lake broke, releasing a surge of water that killed many people. After that, Charpentier's attention was focused on the behaviour of glaciers. He saw erratics (boulders made of rock from somewhere else) as evidence that the Alpine glaciers had once covered a larger area. He saw the mounds of moraine (ice-deposited dumps of gravel and other debris) as more evidence that glaciers had once been longer. Charpentier took the idea no further than this; he had no idea how the glaciers had formed, expanded or retreated. He, in other words, presented Agassiz with one half of an idea.

Another precursor was Ignaz Venetz (1788–1859), another Swiss engineer and glaciologist. He studied glaciers in the Valais canton in the Alps. In 1821, he drafted a book, *Memoir on Temperature Variations in the Swiss Alps*, in which he proposed the revolutionary idea that much of Europe had once been covered by ice. The book was finally published in 1833, and was therefore available to Agassiz; it appeared seven years before Agassiz's *Study on Glaciers*. A third contributor to Agassiz's theory was Karl Schimper (1803–67), a German naturalist and poet who taught at Mannheim University. Schimper was a pioneer in the study of plant morphology, but he is best remembered as the man who proposed the idea of prehistoric warm and cold periods. We can see Schimper's idea as the forerunner of modern theories of ice ages and cycles of climate change. Schimper was reluctant to commit himself in writing, though, and never published his ideas. He discussed his theory of climate change with Agassiz and later came to regret it when Agassiz published and, understandably, got the credit for the ideas. But Schimper had only himself to blame.

When Agassiz became interested in glaciers and their behaviour in the 1830s, Charpentier, Venetz and Schimper discussed their views with him and persuaded him that the glaciers had retreated. He developed the hypothesis and published it.

Agassiz was much more than a borrower of other men's ideas. He observed glaciers in action. He went to the trouble of building a hut on the Aar Glacier, where he and his co-workers could study the structure and movement of the ice. He noticed that glaciers smoothed and polished the solid bedrock they passed over, abrading it with the sand and rock flour embedded in the ice. He noticed the distinctive parallel scratch marks (striations) in the same bedrock, produced by stones frozen into the ice. He then found exposed outcrops of bare rock on the valley floors and valley sides, miles down valley from the glaciers' snouts, where the same parallel scratch marks could be seen. He found the same features on the valley sides, high above the modern ice surface. The glaciers had once travelled much further down their valleys, and they must also have filled their valleys to a greater depth. That in turn meant that the climate must once have been much colder than it is today.

On the valley floors he found ridges and mounds of debris that had been bulldozed into position by the glaciers when they were much longer, and lots of parallel ridges marking stages in the retreat of the glacier's snout as it melted back. Strewn across the Swiss Mittelland, the lowland area that separates the Alps from the Jura Mountains, Agassiz saw angular blocks of rock that had originated in the Alps and could only have arrived in the lowlands rafted there by ice.

Agassiz put these pieces of evidence together and very quickly saw what they meant. There were signs of glacial action all over Switzerland, even where there was no longer ice, so once there had been ice over the whole country. Switzerland had at some point in the past been completely engulfed in ice. 'Great sheets of ice, resembling those now existing in Greenland once covered all the countries in which unstratified gravel (boulder drift) is found.' He had discovered the great Ice Age.

It was a moment of insight – simple and clear – and the world would never be the same again. Agassiz put his idea and his supporting evidence together in a book, *Etude sur les Glaciers* (*Study on Glaciers*), in 1840. Agassiz realised that the implications spread far beyond Switzerland. If the climate of Switzerland had once been much colder, then the climate of the rest of Europe must once have been much colder too, and the effects of that change in climate must be visible there too. He set to work on a second book, *Système glaciaire,* which was published in 1847. This included evidence of glaciation assembled from all over Europe.

Before that second book appeared, Agassiz had already left Switzerland for North America. In 1846, he went on a lecture tour there, and two years later he was appointed Professor of Natural History at Harvard. In North America, he saw more evidence for the Ice Age. As with all great new ideas, it changed the way he saw the world. It was now obvious that a global cooling had occurred at some time in the past, and that this cooling had had a spectacular effect on the middle to high latitude regions of the landmasses in the northern hemisphere. Unfortunately, Agassiz began to think that glaciers had overwhelmed the entire world and looked unsuccessfully for evidence of glaciation in Brazil. By this stage, Charpentier and Venetz were no longer supporting Agassiz; they knew he had gone too far in supposing that nearly all the land areas in the world had been covered by ice.

Agassiz seems to have regarded the Ice Age idea as a sideline, perhaps because he knew he had really borrowed, extended and publicized Charpentier's idea. He worked away at his ideas on comparative zoology and in 1860 he succeeded in opening the Museum of Comparative Zoology. He also worked towards the founding of a National Academy of Sciences in North America, which was created in 1863. He was an inexhaustible fundraiser for science projects, yet never found enough time to complete his own projects. His own pet project focused on comparative anatomy in animals. He pointed out the parallel development of animals. Darwin actually referred to Agassiz's work as supporting the principle of evolution, 'This doctrine of Agassiz accords well with the theory of natural selection.' Yet Agassiz was to go on opposing Darwin. He was not an evolutionist. He was probably the last scientist of any repute to go on rejecting evolution after Darwin published *On the Origin of Species*.

It was a strange career. Louis Agassiz was an academic of great distinction, so it is odd to see him so far ahead of his time in matters of climatology and geomorphology, where he was an amateur, yet so far behind in matters of zoology, when that was his specialist field. Agassiz made the mistake of bringing God into his academic work. He saw the Divine Plan of God everywhere in nature, and the principle of evolution was in conflict with that, so he could not accept it.

THE FOURFOLD GLACIATION MODEL

Agassiz's ideas on the Ice Age were developed by others after his death in 1873. In a way, his Ice Age was a development from, and a substitute for, the catastrophism of the eighteenth century. The catastrophists liked to see glacial drift and erratics as evidence of the Biblical flood, for which very little scientific evidence could be produced. The Ice Age in a way gave the catastrophists a new and more secure platform.

The Ice Age remained a single major event and it was in the remote past. But further work on the outwash deposits, the sands and gravels spread along river valleys by meltwater rivers, showed that there had been ice cover over Switzerland more than once. By the end of the nineteenth century, it was established by Albrecht Penck and Eduard Brückner that there had been four major phases of glaciation in the great Ice Age, which overall lasted two million years. Publication is key to progress in the development of ideas. The fourfold glaciation model developed in the 1890s was definitively published as *The Alps in the Ice Age* by Penck and Brückner in 1909. The four glacial episodes were named after rivers flowing northwards out of the Alps into Bavaria to join the Danube: Gunz, Mindel, Riss and Wurm. In these valleys, Penck and Brückner found that meltwaters had been released on four separate occasions, and these corresponded with four separate glaciations. The cold stages were separated by warm stages or interglacials, a term invented by Archibald Geikie in 1895.

By the 1920s, the picture of the Ice Age was still of four or five major episodes of glaciation separated by long stable periods of warmth. The Ice Age was seen as past, over, and it was even possible for a geographer to write a book in which the cold stages of the Ice Age were treated as 'climatic accidents'. Modern day, post-glacial, climate was still regarded as stable and unvarying. The Ice Age was an upheaval, a catastrophe that had happened to the Earth in the remote past, rather like the Biblical flood in which the eighteenth-century catastrophists had believed. It was still an anomaly.

The Penck and Brückner model of four major cold stages dominated the geographical literature of the twentieth century, but piecemeal research by successive generations of geomorphologists and scores of minor discoveries revealed that the glacial sequence was far more complex. By 1928, pollen analysis of the 'cold stage' sediments showed that the cold stages were not uniformly cold. The pollen of warmth-loving plants showed that there were short interludes within the glacials that were warm enough to melt the ice and allow vegetation to grow; these became known as the interstadials and the cold sub-stages they separate as stadials. In 1930, some glacial deposits that dated from before the Gunz glaciation were discovered in the northern Alps. This led to the discovery of a fifth glaciation, named the Donau. The fourfold glacial model had become fivefold.

By the 1970s, the fivefold glacial model had become twenty-fold, thanks to the discoveries made by continental geomorphologists working on the Central European tundra corridor between the British-Scandinavian ice sheets on the one side and the Alpine ice sheet on the other. One of the problems faced by geomorphologists in Britain is that repeated and comprehensive cover by ice in the later Pleistocene has wiped out much of the evidence for what happened in the early and middle Pleistocene. In the tundra corridor running across central Europe, the changes were less traumatic and in some places full sequences of deposits from each of the cold stages have been discovered. Cambridge researchers, especially Professor R. G. West, worked hard to assemble the fragmentary British record. They discovered that it has a one-million-year long gap in the middle, a chunk of recent prehistory about which we know virtually nothing.

THE BIRTH OF GEOMORPHOLOGY

Meanwhile geographers and geomorphologists were mapping the deposits laid down by ice sheets in successive glaciations, not just in the Alpine region where Agassiz had worked but in northern Europe where it was discovered that there had been ice caps covering Scandinavia and the British Isles. Another, even larger, ice sheet had once covered the whole of Canada and Alaska; that too had left suites of deposits that could be traced to several successive phases of glaciation.

One major development from these studies was the emergence of geomorphology, the science of landforms. Many of the lowland areas of Britain, for instance, could be interpreted as areas of glacial deposition, forming in the ablation zone of the glaciers and ice sheets. The highland areas could be interpreted as areas of glacial erosion, forming in the accumulation zone of the glaciers and ice sheets. The new perception of the processes of the Ice Age provided important conceptual structures for landscape studies. Geomorphology was not just the means for studying the products of the Ice Age, the Ice Age was supplying a disciplinary structure to the new science of geomorphology.

As the decades of the twentieth century passed, geomorphological studies of particular areas and particular landforms threw more and more light on the events of the Ice Age. In the lowland areas, where the ice sheets deposited their moraine, it is possible to see in sections exposed for a short time in working gravel pits how complicated the sequences of deposits are. Ice sheets deposit a chaotic jumble of rock particles (moraine or till). The meltwater streams that flow away from their margins deposit level spreads of sorted outwash sand or gravel. The two deposits are distinct and easy to identify. So, when we look into a gravel pit in the English Midlands, we do not see just a single thick layer of chaotic, unsorted moraine, which would tell us that an ice sheet had spread into and covered the area. What we see is perhaps ten or twenty thinner layers of moraine separated by layers of outwash sand. This interleaved sequence tells us that the ice sheet advanced into the area and melted back, and that the ice margin went forwards and backwards across the site of the gravel pit many times. This added an important new idea – that the climate varied enormously even during the cold periods of the Ice Age. The last cold stage of the Ice Age in Britain had at least six major stadials within it.

It was a short step from there to the realisation that the climate must have fluctuated during the warm periods that separated the cold periods as well, and that climatic change is going on all the time.

CASTING A COLD EYE ON THE FUTURE

With the advent of radiocarbon dating in the 1950s, a new shock discovery was that the last cold stage ended quite recently, only 10,000 years ago. Absolute dates for other events in the Ice Age brought disturbing new discoveries, that the last major cold period was a very long episode beginning about 73,000 years ago. Dating also showed that the last interglacial was short: only 20,000 years long at most and possibly as short as 10,000 years long. Then a realisation dawned that

216

the Ice Age was after all not a catastrophic event of the remote past, safely behind us. The period that had been safely labelled the Holocene to distinguish it from the Pleistocene Ice Age, or the Post-glacial to distinguish it from the Glacial, was actually an *inter*glacial. We were not at the end of the Ice Age at all, but in it, perhaps in the middle of it. Worse still, we might be living not just in an interglacial but at the end of an interglacial.

Based on these discoveries, George Kukla predicted that another cold stage of the Ice Age was about to begin; some climatologists and geomorphologists even named the imminent cold stage the Kukla cold stage. More recent research suggests that this interglacial is more likely to last 28,000 years, so the panic was unnecessary.

Then in the 1970s the warming trend of the first half of the twentieth went into reverse. Many climatologists warned that the interglacial was ending. The next cold stage was about to begin. The fact that they were wrong, that within twenty years they would be panicking about runaway global warming, is a side issue. The significant fact is that the climatic variations of the past, the temperature fluctuations of the Ice Age, were suddenly being seen as part of the present – and part of the future. Instead of the climatic upheaval being part of the past, we were in the middle of it. Now we live with catastrophe.

Geologists studying the remoter past, long before the two million years of the Pleistocene Ice Age, have discovered that there have been similar ice ages before. The earliest one detected, called the Huronian Ice Age, took place about two-and-a-half billion years ago. The next, which is well-documented in the rocks, took place from 850 to 630 million years ago. This, the Cryogenian, was not only a long ice age, it was very severe and it may be that during it the entire planet was engulfed in ice, to form what has been called a Snowball Earth. It is thought that this ended very suddenly, releasing large volumes of water and water vapour. Some geologists think (controversially) that this catastrophic deglaciation could have stimulated the great surge in the evolution of life which began in the following Cambrian Period.

Another Ice Age (Ordovician-Silurian Periods) occurred from 460 to

430 million years ago and another from 350 to 260 million years ago Carboniferous-Permian Periods).

Improving records of temperature change come mainly from sediments on the ocean floor. They show that in the rundown towards the Pleistocene Ice Age the world gradually cooled down starting about forty million years ago with the development and growth of the Antarctic ice sheet. Specifically, this event happened because continental drift took the continent of Antarctica over the South Pole. The global cooling intensified slightly between six million and three million years ago, then there was even more rapid cooling but with much bigger fluctuations. The Ice Age that we are living through is not just a time when there are plunges into glacial conditions but a time when the climate varies very widely.

THE QUEST FOR CAUSES

Studies of these alarming climatic changes have led to a great many new discoveries as scientists in several disciplines have tried to find explanations for them. A key question raised by Agassiz's discovery is 'Why does the Earth experience Ice Ages?' Some scientists favour volcanic activity as an explanation. Periods when a series of large-scale volcanic eruptions throw vast quantities of ash into the atmosphere are likely to be phases of cooling and there is plenty of evidence both from recent records and from antiquity that very large-scale ash eruptions do result in global cooling. Probably the biggest volcanic eruption of the last 100,000 years was the eruption of Toba in northern Sumatra in 73,000 BC. The eruption deposits that can still be seen imply that one billion cubic kilometres (240 million cubic miles) of solid rock were ejected in an eruption that may have gone on for ten days. The ash veil from the Toba eruption cut out a significant amount of the Sun's light and heat. Global temperatures plummeted and rapid ice sheet growth followed. This event shows up in the temperature graphs derived from sea-bed sediments as a steep fall in temperature, a drop of 7 degrees Celsius (12.6 degrees Fahrenheit). This was more than enough to trigger the start of the final cold stage of the Ice Age.

218

But within the temperature record for the last million years patterns have been discovered, and this means that volcanic activity cannot be the main cause of the cooling across the Ice Age as a whole. Volcanic eruptions follow a regular pattern. But within the temperature changes it is possible to see the influence of three major astronomical cycles, at three different time scales. These are variations in the tilt of the Earth's axis, the rotation of the Earth's axis, and slight variations in the shape of the Earth's orbit round the Sun. The rhythmic pulse of the cold stages, with peaks of intense cold every 100,000 years, is strong evidence of overall control by these Milankovitch cycles, which were discovered by Milutin Milankovitch.

Milankovitch (1879–1958) borrowed Croll's 1864 idea that variations in the Earth's orbit might be the cause of the climatic changes that produced the Ice Age. Milankovitch published a number of separate elements of his idea before finally publishing his integrated theory in 1941 under the impenetrable title *Canon of Insolation of the Ice Age Problem*. At first there was widespread scepticism as it was thought the astronomical variations were far too slight to have such a large-scale effect on the climate system. But when the temperature record from deep-sea sediments was assembled in the 1970s, there was widespread agreement that the Milankovitch cycles were responsible for most of the temperature variations.

The rest could be explained by feedback processes. One feedback effect is the Earth's albedo. As the Earth begins to cool, snow and ice cover becomes more extensive, so more of the Sun's heat is reflected back into space. That leads to further cooling, which means that the area under snow and ice gets larger, and so on.

Another major discovery, published in 1988, is the way in which the Tibetan Plateau acts as a carbon dioxide 'scrubber'. William Ruddiman, Flip Froelich and Maureen Raymo have proposed that this huge mountain area was lifted up progressively over the last forty million years as India drove northwards into Asia, creating a geographical environment that can draw down vast quantities of carbon dioxide into its rainfall and rivers. The formation of the plateau intensified the Asian monsoon, greatly increased rainfall, and created high rates of mechanical and chemical weathering. That chemical weathering by the rivers has taken large volumes of carbon dioxide down into the oceans. This drawing down of atmospheric carbon dioxide over a long time scale has been responsible for reducing the CO_2 level in the atmosphere over a forty-million-year period. It has also been responsible for gradually lowering temperatures.

Raymo and her co-workers believe that about half of the uplift of the Tibetan Plateau has occurred in the last ten million years, and the cooling effect has recently been more marked as a result. Once the average temperature was down to a certain threshold in middle latitudes, the temperature variations due to the Milakovitch cycles began to cause a yo-yo effect with climatic systems oscillating between glacial and non-glacial conditions.

Perceptions of the sort of world we live in have changed enormously over one-and-a-half centuries, and mainly because of a chain of discoveries that began with the discovery of the Ice Age. Agassiz's mad idea that the whole world was once covered in ice is, perhaps surprisingly, now regarded as a real possibility, though not in the Pleistocene Ice Age. We can no longer think of the Ice Age as a catastrophic event that is safely behind us. The picture emerging from modern geology is that periodic Ice Ages have occurred and they are long-lasting, going on for at least thirty million years. Our Pleistocene Ice Age has only been under way for two million years. It has only just begun.

THE ROSS SEA, MOUNT EREBUS AND THE ROSS ICE SHELF
(1841)

Several separate voyages to Antarctica took place in the mid-nineteenth century to explore and define its coastline. From 1838 to 1842, an American, Charles Wilkes, led a six-vessel squadron on a voyage that lasted four years. In 1840, Jules Vermont d'Urville discovered Adelie Land and claimed it for France. At the same time, James Clark Ross began his important voyage of discovery, setting sail from Hobart in the *Erebus* and *Terror* in November 1840.

After a week's sailing, Ross's ships made landfall in the Auckland Islands, where they found two notice boards. One announced that Charles Wilkes had visited the island on 10 March 1840. The other announced that d'Urville had landed there the very next day. Ross sailed on, encountering the first whales and icebergs on 27 December and the Antarctic Circle on 1 January 1841. After that, the floating pack ice became a bigger problem to navigation, until on 9 January Ross broke through into open water again.

Ross had discovered the Ross Sea. His aim was to reach the South Magnetic Pole, but before he could reach it he encountered land and not only land but mountains. The earlier sightings of the Antarctic coast had been sightings of the edge of the ice sheet, but here there was exposed bedrock. After his initial disappointment that he was not going to be able to sail to the magnetic pole, Ross became excited by the idea of discovering 'the southernmost land'. Ross and his party saw some mountains that they named the Admiralty Range.

On 27 January, he formally claimed Franklin Island for Britain, and the next day they were staggered to see a huge erupting volcano. Dr Hooker wrote in his notebook, 'All the coast one mass of dazzling beautiful peaks which, when the sun approached the horizon, reflected the most brilliant tints of golden yellow and scarlet, and then to see the dark cloud of smoke, tinged with flame, rising from the volcano in a perfectly unbroken column, one side jet black, the other giving back the colours of the Sun – this was a sight so surpassing everything that can be imagined. It really caused a feeling of awe to steal over us at the consideration of our own comparative insignificance and helplessness, and at the same time an indescribable feeling of the greatness of the Creator in the works of His hand.'

The volcanic peak soared 3,780 metres (12,400 feet) above sea level. Ross named it Mount Erebus, and the smaller extinct volcano to the east Mount Terror.

Then, almost incredibly, as the ships sailed on south came another great discovery, a long low white line in the distance extending from one horizon to the other. As they sailed closer to it they saw that it was a vertical cliff of ice, perhaps 60 metres (200 feet) high and perfectly flat and level at the top. This, the edge of the Ross Ice Shelf, was obviously the furthest south that they were going to be able to sail. As Ross said, 'We might with equal chance of success try to sail through the cliffs of Dover.' He named it the Victoria Barrier, but it was later renamed after Ross himself, the Ross Ice Shelf.

Ross followed the barrier for 320 kilometres (200 miles) before the Antarctic winter began to set in, bringing this major voyage of discovery to a close. Ross was delighted with it, not least because so much had been achieved without any casualty, injury or loss of life; everyone went home safe and well. That really was something to be proud of.

NEPTUNE

(1846)

The planet Neptune was formally discovered in 1846. Galileo's drawings show that he observed it on 28 December 1612, and again a month
later, though without realising what he was looking at. When he saw it
very close to Jupiter, Galileo thought Neptune was a fixed star. Because
he did not identify it as a planet, Galileo is not regarded as its discoverer.
Galileo's mistake is understandable. Neptune is so far from the Earth that
it appears virtually stationary, even viewed through a modern telescope.

Following the eighteenth-century discovery of the planet Uranus,
Alexis Bouvard published astronomical tables of its orbit in 1821. Later
observations of Uranus showed that it was deviating from the positions
indicated by the tables. These irregularities, or perturbations as they are
called, led Bouvard to wonder whether there was another massive body
far out in the solar system, large enough to have a gravitational pull on
Uranus and distort its orbit.

Following the same line of thought, in 1843 John Couch Adams
calculated the likely orbit of a hypothetical additional planet to account
for the perturbations of the orbit of Uranus. Adams sent his calculations
to Sir George Airy, the Astronomer Royal, who wanted some clarifica-
tion, but Adams did not pursue the matter, apparently feeling
discouraged by Airy's reply. In 1845–46, another astronomer, Urbain le
Verrier, made his own separate calculations and met with the same tepid
reception in France. But then Airy saw le Verrier's published estimate of
the planet's location and was struck by the convergence of le Verrier's
work with that of Adams. Airy realised that action was needed to verify
the two independent predictions and persuaded James Challis, the
director of the Cambridge Observatory, to look for the missing planet.

While Challis searched for it in vain, le Verrier wrote to Johann
Gottfried Galle at the Berlin Observatory, to ask him to search for it as

well. On the day le Verrier's letter was received in Berlin, 23 September 1846, Neptune was discovered within hours by Johann Galle. Its location was within one degree of the place predicted by le Verrier, and rather further (twelve degrees) from the location predicted by Adams. When he heard about the discovery, Challis at Cambridge checked his results and realised that he had in fact seen the new planet twice, but had overlooked his own sightings through carelessness.

Naturally, because it was such an important discovery, there was heated argument about who had made it. Was it Adams? Le Verrier? Challis? Galle? Bouvard? Or Heinrich d'Arrest, the student at Galle's side who had supplied him with the means of identifying the new planet? An international consensus shortly afterwards emerged that le Verrier and Adams deserved joint recognition for the discovery. Recent (1990s) research on the contemporary documents has suggested that le Verrier deserves more credit than Adams.

As with Uranus, it was not immediately clear what the new planet should be called. At first it was referred to as 'le Verrier's planet' or 'the planet exterior to Uranus'. Galle proposed calling it Janus. Challis proposed Oceanus. The French wanted to call it Leverrier, simultaneously (and fair-mindedly) renaming Uranus after Herschel. Adams proposed renaming Georgian Uranus. Le Verrier proposed calling his own planet Neptune. Soon, Neptune was adopted internationally; the adoption of a name from classical mythology was in line with the names used through the rest of the solar system.

Neptune is the furthest known planet from the Sun, and the fourth largest in terms of its diameter, the third biggest in terms of its mass. It is slightly more massive than Uranus. Uranus and Neptune are very similar to each other in size and character, except that Uranus is relatively colourless and Neptune is an intense blue. Neptune is also an exceptionally windy planet, with wind speeds of a thousand miles per hour. The 1989 *Voyager 2* fly-by revealed that Neptune has (or at any rate had at that time) a Great Dark Spot in its southern hemisphere, comparable with Jupiter's Great Red Spot.

THE CURE FOR CHILDBED FEVER

(1847)

In the early nineteenth century, many women died giving birth to their children as a result of puerperal fever, or childbed fever. Childbed fever was common in obstetric hospitals and often fatal, with as many as one-third of the cases ending in death. The man who discovered how to cut the incidence of childbed fever was a Hungarian doctor, Ignaz Semmelweiss, who was born in 1818. His father decided that Ignaz was to become an advocate in the service of the Austrian government bureaucracy, so he was sent to Vienna in 1837 to study law. Once in Vienna, the young man became more attracted to the idea of a career in medicine. It seems his father did not object, and he enrolled in the medical school.

After a year in Vienna, Semmelweiss returned home to Pest, to continue his medical studies there. But he was dissatisfied by the backwardness of Pest University compared with Vienna, and he went back to Vienna in 1841. The medical school was considered progressive, combining laboratory medicine with bedside practice; it was generally regarded as one of the leading centres for medicine for the next hundred years. This made the reaction to Semmelweiss's discovery at the Vienna General Hospital all the more disappointing. After graduating, Semmelweiss took a course in midwifery, was trained in surgery and diagnostic and statistical techniques. After this thorough training, Semmelweiss became an assistant in the First Obstetrical Clinic at the Vienna General Hospital.

Semmelweiss was working in the Vienna General Hospital when he noticed that it was general practice for doctors to pass from patient to patient without washing their hands. They even went straight from performing an autopsy on a diseased corpse to a living patient without washing their hands. Semmelweiss hypothesised that on the doctors' dirty hands there were particles that were being introduced into the women's bodies, and that it was these particles that were responsible for causing the childbed fever.

As so often in this kind of breakthrough, Semmelweiss's moment of insight came as a result of a particular incident. In 1847, his friend and co-worker Jakob Kolletschka died as a result of an infection that he picked up when his finger was accidentally cut with a knife during a post-mortem examination. The post-mortem examination of Kolletschka himself showed that his body had reacted in exactly the same was as the women who were dying of childbed fever. Kolletschka had died of puerperal fever. Semmelweiss inferred from this that Kolletschka had died as a result of contamination from the corpse by way of the knife.

Semmelweiss carried out a statistical study of the death rate statistics from his own clinic, the First Clinic, with those from the Second Clinic. Here his training in statistics paid off. He found that the death rate in the Second Clinic was significantly higher than in the First Clinic, and that this was due to doctors and students carrying infected 'particles' from the room where the autopsies were carried out to the patients in the wards of the First Clinic.

He discovered from trials that childbed fever could be virtually eliminated by introducing the practice of systematic handwashing in clinics. It was dirty hands that caused the fever. He found that if staff washed their hands in chlorinated lime solutions the death rate from childbed fever fell from twenty per cent to one or two per cent – a major improvement. Semmelweiss soon afterwards extended his hygiene regime to include washing instruments between patients as well.

Rather surprisingly, Semmelweiss did not rush to tell his superiors what he had discovered. He did not want to commit his findings on paper. Perhaps he sensed that the reaction would be hostile – which it was. After a time Ferdinand von Hebra wrote two articles outlining what Semmelweiss had discovered, and these drew some support from foreign physicians and one or two senior physicians in Vienna.

But Semmelweiss then encountered a problem. The prevailing mind-set was to attribute a decline in health and even disease to different causes in different people. Each patient was regarded as unique, with unique reasons for being ill. The approach that Semmelweiss was following looked forward to the Western approach to medicine in the twentieth and twenty-first centuries. This is a much more mechanistic approach. Patients displaying the same suite of symptoms are suffering from the same ailment or infection, with the same cause and requiring the same treatment. Semmelweiss advocated a general solution to the problem, which was regarded as absurd and therefore largely rejected or ignored. The doctors at the hospital were naturally reluctant to admit to having been responsible for so many deaths, and this defensiveness made them doubly resistant to Semmelweiss's findings.

This resistance to a new idea is quite common. Even highly qualified scientists, trained to evaluate objectively, sometimes have difficulty in facing up to a new discovery. The way Semmelweiss's discovery was greeted, or rather not greeted, is a classic example of this type of unreasoned blanket rejection. In fact it is such a classic that it has even given its name to this kind of behaviour – the Semmelweiss Reflex. It entails the dismissal or rejection out of hand of any information or idea without thought or inspection.

Even so, Semmelweiss at this stage had some influential supporters. Unfortunately he then got into political difficulties. This was the Europe of the 1848 revolutions, and Semmelweiss was an active liberal. When, in reaction to the revolutionary movement, a conservative government gained power in Vienna in 1848, Semmelweiss lost his job. A well-meaning colleague, Skoda, gave a lecture on the discovery to the Imperial and Royal Academy of Sciences in 1849, but unfortunately there were mistakes in the text, which Semmelweiss had neglected to correct, so the lecture was unconvincing. Semmelweiss was given a further opportunity to present his findings in person in 1850, which was more successful, but then he abruptly left Vienna without warning any of his supporters and returned to Pest. After this string of unfortunate incidents, he stood no chance of convincing the academic community in Vienna.

In Pest, Semmelweiss took charge of the maternity ward at St Rochus Hospital from 1851 until 1857. There he introduced his new hygiene regime and successfully reduced the death rate from childbed fever to less than one per cent. He became a conspicuous success in his profession, gaining a chair in midwifery at the University of Pest in 1855, and turning down a similar chair in Zurich. Meanwhile, back in Vienna, in the ward where he had virtually eradicated childbed fever the death rate had gone back up to thirty-five per cent.

In 1861, he wrote a book about his cure for childbed fever, and this influenced Joseph Lister, who was later to develop the idea of antiseptic practice further. A number of hostile reviews prompted Semmelweiss to lash out. He was angry at the medical profession's indifference to his discovery. He started writing outspoken open letters to high-profile obstetricians throughout Europe. He accused them of irresponsibility and murder. Semmelweiss believed strongly in his discovery and he was so convinced that it could save thousands of lives that his letters became almost libellous. He began ranting; he had a nervous breakdown. Even his wife thought he might be losing his mind. In 1865, he became violent and was confined to a mental asylum where he was beaten up by the guards. He died there only fourteen days after being admitted.

Ignaz Semmelweiss's discovery – that hygiene was the answer – was ahead of its time. It was only some years later that the medical profession realised that he was right. It was only after Louis Pasteur developed his theory that diseases were caused by germs that hygiene was seen as the standard route to stopping diseases from developing. Pasteur's discovery in other words provided the rationale for Semmelweiss's earlier discovery. Semmelweiss has been called the father of antiseptic medicine. He has also been called the saviour of mothers.

VICTORIA FALLS

(1855)

Looking back over the history of geographical exploration in the nineteenth century, it is easy to get a quite false sense that it was all about the acquisition of geographical knowledge for its own sake. That was very far from the truth. We saw with the early nineteenth-century exploration of the coastline of Antarctica that there was a very specific impulse behind it, which was the commercial interests of the whalers and sealers, who needed to know where the coastline was, and where there might be usable harbours. Once that coastline was established, there was a noticeable lull in exploration before a new series of expeditions, with entirely different motives, was launched to find out about the interior of Antarctica. With the exploration of Africa, the impetus came not from whaling or sealing, but from elsewhere. With Africa, the impetus came from a great moral crusade in the wake of the abolition of the slave trade.

The outline of Africa was already discovered and known in some detail by the early nineteenth century, but not the interior. There was a perception that in order to eradicate them completely, slavery and the slave trade would have to be dealt with at source. It was not so much the source of the Nile that the explorers were looking for as the source of the slaves. Finding navigable rivers and passable road routes into the interior was essential to the drive to clean up Africa.

The Scottish missionary and explorer David Livingstone had been hoping the Zambezi would prove to be a great navigable waterway to the interior of Africa, so in 1855 he was disappointed to find the way blocked by the world's most impressive waterfall. The native Africans obviously knew all about the Zambezi, and about the waterfall too, but no European knew about them. It was in early November 1855 that

Livingstone travelled to see the place the Africans described to him as 'the smoke that thunders'. He and his party approached in canoes, and they could see clouds of spray and hear the roar of the water miles away from the falls.

After twenty minutes' sail from Kalai we came in sight, for the first time, of the columns of vapour appropriately called 'smoke', rising at a distance of five or six miles, exactly as when large tracts of grass are burned in Africa. Five columns now arose, and, bending in the direction of the wind, they seemed placed against a low ridge covered with trees; the tops of the columns at this distance appeared to mingle with the clouds. They were white below, and higher up became dark, so as to simulate smoke very closely. The whole scene was extremely beautiful; the banks and islands dotted over the river are adorned with sylvan vegetation of great variety of colour and form. No one can imagine the beauty of the view from anything witnessed in England. It had never been seen before by European eyes; but scenes so lovely must have been gazed upon by angels in their flight. The only want felt is that of mountains in the background. The falls are bounded on three sides by ridges 300 or 400 feet in height, which are covered with forest, with the red soil appearing among the trees.

When about half a mile from the falls, I left the canoe by which we had come down thus far, and embarked in a lighter one, with men well acquainted with the rapids, who, by passing down the centre of the stream in the eddies and still places caused by many jutting rocks, brought me to an island situated in the middle of the river, and on the edge of the lip over which the water rolls. In coming hither there was danger of being swept down by the streams which rushed along on each side of the island; but the river was now low, and we sailed where it is totally impossible to go when the water is high. But, though we had reached the island, and were within a few yards of the spot, a view from which would solve the whole problem, I believe that no one could perceive where the vast body of water went; it seemed to lose itself in the Earth, the opposite lip of the fissure into which it disappeared being only 80 feet distant. At least I did not comprehend it until, creeping with awe to the verge, I peered down into a large rent which had been made from bank to bank of the broad Zambesi, and saw that a stream of a thousand yards broad leaped down a hundred feet, and then became suddenly compressed into a space of fifteen or twenty yards.

The entire falls are simply a crack made in a hard basaltic rock from the right to the left bank of the Zambesi, and then prolonged from the left bank away through thirty or forty miles of hills.

In looking down into the fissure on the right of the island, one sees nothing but a dense white cloud, which, at the time we visited the spot, had two bright rainbows on it. From this cloud rushed up a great jet of vapour exactly like steam, and it mounted 200 or 300 feet high; there condensing, it changed its hue to that of dark smoke, and came back in a constant shower, which soon wetted us to the skin.

On the left of the island we see the water at the bottom, a white rolling mass moving away to the prolongation of the fissure, which branches off near the left bank of the river. The walls of this gigantic crack are perpendicular, and composed of one homogeneous mass of rock. The edge of that side over which the water falls is worn off two or three feet, and pieces have fallen away, so as to give it somewhat of a serrated appearance. Upon the whole, it is nearly in the state in which it was left at the period of its formation. On the left side of the island we have a good view of the mass of water which causes one of the columns of vapour to ascend, as it leaps quite clear of the rock, and forms a thick unbroken fleece all the way to the bottom. Its whiteness gave the idea of snow, a sight I had not seen for many a day.

NEANDERTHAL MAN
(1856)

The defining discovery of what has become known as Neanderthal Man was made in the Neander Valley (Neanderthal) near Düsseldorf in Germany. It was in August 1856 that the partial skeleton of this pre-historic human being was found: a skull cap, two thigh bones, three bones of the right arm, two bones of the left arm, part of the pelvis, pieces of a shoulder blade and some ribs. The quarrymen who found the bones – the bones, they thought, of a *bear* – gave them to an amateur naturalist, Johann Fuhlrott, who in turn handed them on to the anatomist Hermann Schaaffhausen. The discovery was announced in 1857.

The name Neanderthal Man was coined by the Anglo-Irish geologist William King in 1863. But, in spite of the high profile given to this moment of discovery, skulls belonging to the same species or sub-species had been found before. One was discovered in Forbes' Quarry in Gibraltar in 1848 and another – really the first discovery – was found at Engis in Belgium in 1829. One reason why the Neander Valley find stuck in people's minds is that news of the find was coincidentally released just two years before the publication of Darwin's book *On the Origin of Species*, and that made the Neander Valley bones a particular focus of interest. An association of ideas emerged.

Knowledge of this early precursor of the modern human race was significantly extended when an almost complete skeleton of a Neanderthal man was found in 1908 at La Chapelle-aux-Saints in France. The palaeontologist Marcellin Boule studied this skeleton and published one of the earliest illustrations of Neanderthals, together with his scientific findings and his unflattering description of a shuffling, bent-kneed, hairy creature with no more than 'rudimentary intellectual abilities'. Boule was intent on ruling Neanderthal Man out as an ancestor of modern man – he was simply too savage. This has remained, for most of us, the abiding image of the Neanderthal people.

Subsequent palaeontologists have seen another side, a more human side, to Neanderthal Man and they have tried to rehabilitate the poor but memorable image that Boule created.

The remains of Neanderthal Man have now been discovered at more than eighty sites across Europe, the Middle East and western Asia. The bone assemblage gathered represents fewer than 500 individual people, half of whom were children. Along with the remains of these relatively few people, several hundred thousands of stone tools have been found.

The individual Boule found and studied is now known to have been an old man suffering from arthritis, and the bent and stooping posture was simply a result of his arthritic condition. There is no reason to suppose that the young and healthy Neanderthal people were stooped. The idea that they were brutish and savage may also be incorrect. There is archaeological evidence that Neanderthal people cared for their sick and elderly. In 1957, the remains of an old Neanderthal were found in a cave in Iraq. The fact that he had been battered but his injuries had healed shows that he was cared for until his death.

A problem we have is that the reconstruction drawings and paintings, once seen, are very hard to put from our minds. Many of these are extremely unreliable. Many details, such as hair length and style, eye colour, grooming, clothing, deportment and manners simply cannot be retrieved from the meagre archaeological remains; they are supplied by the artist's imagination, which in turn is often influenced by memories of Boule's savage brutes.

Modern dating techniques have allowed archaeologists to make new discoveries about old finds. It appears that the Neanderthals had evolved by 130,000 years ago and became extinct in Europe about 30,000 years ago. No Neanderthals are known to have survived after this. Even so, it looks as if there were Neanderthals living in Europe at the same time as modern human beings, *Homo sapiens*, and that the two species co-existed for about 10,000 years. Whether that co-existence was peaceful and friendly or competitive and hostile is not known, and it is hard to see how evidence to answer that question could be discovered. The Neanderthal people made their toolkits in what is known as Mousterian style, using soft hammers made out of bone, antler and wood to make their stone tools. Towards the end of their time, they started using what is called the Chatelperronian tool style, which is more advanced, and it is thought that they may have learnt the new technique from incoming modern people. This suggests that there may have been a certain amount of mixing, communicating and interplay. Whether they ever interbred is being hotly debated.

Because of the time when they were living in Europe, the Neanderthals had to cope with major climatic and environmental changes. They were living in a landscape that was repeatedly plunged into Arctic conditions. It has been suggested that this is why they were short and robust in build with big noses (to warm the cold air as they inhaled). On average, adult male Neanderthals were about 1.65 metres (5 feet 5 inches) tall.

Perhaps the outstanding significance of the Neander Valley find is that it was the starting point of the science of palaeoanthropology. Coming as it did at almost the same moment as the publication of Darwin's revolutionary ideas on evolution, the discovery of Neanderthal Man became a marker for the study of human evolution.

LAKE TANGANYIKA
(1858)

The search for the source of the Nile was the great obsession of a group of mid-nineteenth century explorers and adventurers, perhaps the best-known of whom were the missionary David Livingstone and the fiery adventurer and linguist Sir Richard Burton. Burton translated the *Arabian Nights* into English and wrote about his extensive travels in South America, Western Asia and Africa. After a haphazard education, Burton joined the army of the English East India Company in 1842, serving in Sind (southern Pakistan). Burton used this posting as a springboard for various escapades which often involved travelling disguised as a native; he was a good enough linguist to be able to do this. He even penetrated the Muslim holy city of Mecca, disguised as an Arab. His account of these travels, published in 1855, made him famous throughout Europe.

His first journey of exploration with John Hanning Speke was into Somalia, where both men were wounded – Burton in the face by a spear that pierced both cheeks. Burton again wrote about his exploits in a book, *First Footsteps in East Africa*, in 1856.

In 1857, Burton returned to Africa, this time commissioned by the British Royal Geographical Society to find the source of the Nile. Again he was accompanied by Speke. They set out from the island of Zanzibar, which was the centre of the East African slave trade and had become the starting point for most expeditions into the African interior. They spent six months in Zanzibar, which Burton enjoyed; he spent his time learning Swahili and measuring African men's penises. The conventional, prudish Speke was unsettled by Burton's behaviour. By the time the two men set off on foot into the interior, the friction between these two very different men was beginning to surface. Speke was irritated by Burton's refusal to indulge his own interest in game: 'Captain Burton, being no sportsman, would not stop for shooting.'

Five months later, Burton and Speke and their bearers arrived at Tabora, a base for slave trafficking 965 kilometres (600 miles) from the Indian Ocean. Talking to the local people, Burton heard that there was somewhere to the west an enormous lake, 'slug-like' in shape. He jumped to the conclusion that this might be the legendary Tears of Isis, which the ancient Egyptians believed was the source of the Nile. Burton and Speke set off again, crossing the hills of Unyamwezi, and sighted the enormous lake they were anticipating – Lake Tanganyika.

The discovery of this huge natural feature, a major feature of Africa's physical geography, was an important achievement. Burton went on believing that it was the source of the Nile, though eventually it would prove not to be that but the source of another great river, the Congo.

By this stage, both of the Englishmen were too ill to walk. Speke had eye problems and Burton had an ulcerated jaw. They made camp at Ujiji, a village that would later make its name as the place where Stanley met (and supposedly found) David Livingstone. Burton again talked to the natives, who told him a river called the Rusizi flowed out of the northern end of Lake Tanganyika. This was good news as far as Burton was concerned, as it made it more likely that Lake Tanganyika was the source of the Nile; the Rusizi was probably the headwater of the Nile. Still very ill, Burton hired two canoes and after an extremely difficult and arduous journey reached the Rusizi. But he then found that the Rusizi flowed *into* the lake, not out of it.

Burton and Speke went back to Tabora. There the two men had a blazing row. Burton's informants told him that two week's march away to the north was a lake that was even bigger than Lake Tanganyika. Speke wanted to go and see it, Burton refused, and Speke set off alone. Burton's explanation of his behaviour later was that he was still lame and that there was no need for both of them to go. When Speke returned he confirmed that there was indeed a gigantic lake to the north, which he had named Victoria after the queen, and expressed the view that it was the source of the Nile. He would later write, 'Captain

Burton greeted me on arrival . . . I expressed my regret that he did not accompany me as I felt quite certain in my mind that I had discovered the source of the Nile. This he naturally objected to, even after hearing all my reasons for saying so, and therefore the subject was dropped.'

It turned out that Speke was right and Burton was wrong, but Speke had only visited the southern shore of Lake Victoria and spent three days there; he had no evidence at all of which way it drained. It could have had a river overflowing from it to the west which formed a second headstream for the Congo. It is only subsequent events and hindsight that have vindicated Speke. He *happened* to be right.

Burton went on giving all of his attention to Lake Tanganyika. The falling out between the two men may seem childish, but they were two very different Englishmen alone in a very difficult and hostile environment, thrown on each other's company; any issues were likely to be blown out of proportion. It was unfortunate that the focus of the quarrel was the issue about the lakes, which was central to the entire expedition. Speke wrote to the Secretary of the Royal Geographical Society later, 'B. is one of those people who can never be wrong, and will never acknowledge an error.' Even so, by the time they got back to Zanzibar, and they both had to be carried there, they were still outwardly on friendly terms.

They parted in April 1859, Burton convalescing in Aden while Speke set off for England. Speke undertook to delay revealing the results of the expedition until Burton arrived in London. Then Speke embarked for England, with some dramatic irony, on board HMS *Furious*: it was Burton who would shortly be furious. When Burton arrived in London a month later he found that not only had Speke blurted out his find, but his claim to have discovered the source of the Nile had been accepted by the Royal Geographical Society. The Society had even commissioned him, Speke, to head another expedition to acquire definite proof that Lake Victoria really was the Nile source.

Lake Victoria was a very big lake, and finding its outfall was no simple matter. The Speke expedition did not produce proof of his claim. It now seemed as if Burton's and Speke's cases were about equal. The British

Association for the Advancement of Science called a meeting in Bath, at which Burton and Speke were to present their respective cases for Lake Tanganyika and Lake Victoria. The day before the main meeting was due to take place there was a preliminary meeting at which Burton and Speke ignored each other. A few hours later Speke shot himself. One version of events is that he shot himself by accident while climbing a stile. But it may be that the prospect of being the victim of a frenzied tongue-lashing by a furious Burton – the Burton who could never be wrong – was too much for Speke to face, even if he was sure in his own mind that he *had* found the source of the Nile.

Sir Richard Burton was devastated by the news of Speke's death. According to his wife, he 'wept long and bitterly' and was in a grief-stricken state for 'many a day'. More bitterness was to follow, when Henry Morton Stanley proved that the White Nile did indeed flow out of Lake Victoria. Speke had been right all along.

THE FIRST (NEARLY) COMPLETE DINOSAUR SKELETON

(1858)

The dinosaur family, *Dinosauria*, was officially defined in a two-hour speech by Sir Richard Owen in 1842. The specific known dinosaurs at that time were Megalosaurus, Iguanodon and Hylaeosaurus. They were all known from fragments found in Europe. No complete specimen of a dinosaur skeleton had so far been discovered. In the middle of the nineteenth century all that changed. Some complete skeletons were discovered in North America, and they enabled scientists to create a more accurate picture of what the dinosaurs looked like and the way they behaved.

It was Ferdinand Vandiveer Hayden who discovered the first dinosaur remains in North America in 1854 while he was exploring the upper Missouri Valley. Hayden and his team found a collection of isolated teeth close to the confluence of the Missouri and Judith rivers. The find was described the palaeontologist Joseph Leidy two years later. Shortly after that, Leidy was describing the first near-complete dinosaur skeleton in the world, *Hadrosaurus foulkii*, named after its discoverer, William Parker Foulke.

In the summer of 1858, William Parker Foulke, who was an amateur fossil hunter, was on holiday at Haddonfield, New Jersey. He heard that twenty years earlier, in 1838, the workmen in a local marl pit had found some gigantic bones there. William Hopkins took the huge bones to his house and displayed them there. Foulke decided to try to find some more. He spent some weeks in the late summer and autumn of 1858 directing a team of hired labourers, whom he had digging ankle deep in thin grey mud. Eventually, they dug up the bones of an animal that was bigger than an elephant but with the structural features of both a bird and a lizard. Foulke had discovered the first almost-complete skeleton of a dinosaur. Only the skull was missing.

The site of the find is today marked by a tombstone-like monument at the point where a suburban road, Maple Street, gives way to woodland; just beyond the stone is the ravine where the dinosaur was found – *Hadrosaurus foulkii*. One outstanding feature of this Hadrosaurus was that it had small front limbs and large back limbs. This was a clear indication that the creature had walked on its back legs and not on all fours. Some dinosaurs could have been bipedal, like people, and highly unusual for a reptile. It stood 2.4 metres (8 feet) high at the pelvis, probably with its upper body thrust forward, and was 7.6 metres (25 feet) long overall, with a long heavy tail.

Foulke's two-legged dinosaur was mounted for public display, and visitor numbers at the Academy where it was on show trebled. Right from the start, the general public was fascinated by dinosaurs, and that fascination has continued ever since. For a long time, Foulke's Hadrosaurus was the only dinosaur on display, the only one available. Copies of it were made to put on display elsewhere in North America – and Europe too. Hadrosaurus became a kind of mascot in Haddonfield; in 2003, the people of Haddonfield even unveiled a bronze statue of their dinosaur.

The first time that skeletons of complete dinosaurs were found in quantities was at Como Bluff in Wyoming, and in the Garden Park area of Colorado. These were discovered in the late 1870 and they were the spur to the First Great Dinosaur Rush. This was driven mainly by two palaeontologists, Edward Cope from Philadelphia and Othniel Marsh from Yale. At first they were friends, but as the hunt for dinosaurs developed they became bitter rivals. It is said that they even went so far as intercepting one another's shipments of fossil bones in transit. But at least they raised public awareness of the spectacular fauna of the Jurassic period. A Second Great Dinosaur Rush took place in the badlands of the Red Deer River in Alberta, Canada, starting in 1910. Here again, there was intense rivalry to commandeer the finds, between Barnum Brown of the American Museum of Natural History in New York and C. H. Sternberg of the Canadian Geological Survey, though this time the rivalry was friendlier. Their finds illuminated the reptile world of the Cretaceous period.

EVOLUTION BY
NATURAL SELECTION
(1858–59)

The English naturalist Charles Darwin developed his ideas on evolution as a result of observations he made during the exploratory voyage of the *Beagle*. Embarking on the *Beagle* voyage was to be the most momentous decision of Darwin's life. It turned out to be an epoch-making voyage, not just because of the huge volume of data which Darwin collected, but because of the freshness and originality with which the young and inexperienced young man interpreted what he saw. Darwin's mind and the nineteenth century's collective mind were opened wide by that five-year voyage (1831–36) round the world of HMS *Beagle*. The intellectual journey of those years left Darwin with a huge bank of data that would occupy him for the rest of his life, feeding him with ideas that he would find hard to digest. By the end of the *Beagle* voyage, when Darwin was still only twenty-seven, he already knew where the principal academic minefield was – the origin of species – and where the evidence for it lay.

He saw that the finches living on various Pacific islands were different, and concluded that they had become different while separated on their different islands. He was also strongly influenced by a chance reading of the essay *On Population* by Thomas Malthus, which argued that animals compete to survive; Darwin realised the profound truth of this statement and that this competition to survive could be what was driving evolution forwards. The struggle for existence would lead to the extermination of individuals and families with unfavourable variations. Malthus had provided him with a mechanism, a dynamic, a *reason*, for evolution.

Darwin went on mulling over his extensive evidence for five years. Then, in 1844, he wrote a 321-page paper summarising his arguments and clarifying them for his own reference. This was in effect a rough draft of the book that was to cause such a stir in 1859. Darwin was a cautious and sensitive man, and he probably understood the anger and pain that his book would cause when eventually published.

He was nudged towards publication when, in June 1858, Alfred Russel Wallace sent him a copy of a paper he had written on the Malay archipelago which, to Darwin's surprise, contained a summary of the same idea as his own on natural selection. Wallace asked for Darwin's opinion on his paper and also wanted Darwin to forward his opinion to Sir Charles Lyell. Darwin wrote to Lyell, who had been warning Darwin that he should publish his ideas, 'Your words have come true with a vengeance – that I should be forestalled.' Darwin discussed the situation with his friends, a situation now fraught with all sorts of ethical snags, and was persuaded that the best solution was for him and Wallace to submit a joint paper based on Wallace's paper and his own 1844 sketch. This was read at the Linnaean Society on 1 July 1858 at the same meeting as Wallace's Malay paper.

Now that news of his (and Wallace's) ideas on evolution were out, Darwin set to work to argue the case for natural selection fully, again under pressure from his friends. This turned into the great and profoundly influential book *On the Origin of Species by Means of Natural Selection, or the Preservation of Favoured Races in the Struggle for Life*, which was published on 24 November 1859. In it, Darwin presented evidence that the plants and animals we see today were not created in their present form, but evolved from earlier forms, and are continuing to evolve into new forms. Darwin's theory was based on what he called natural selection. The various members of a species are all slightly different from one another. The individuals with differences that make them more able to compete are more likely to survive, and pass on these advantageous differences to their descendants.

The idea of evolution by natural selection was extremely controversial, as it appeared to contradict the version of creation laid out in the Bible. In addition to being offensive to those who believed in the fundamental and literal truth of the Bible, it implied that living creatures were controlled entirely by physical laws. It offended people in a third way by appearing to argue that people were descended from apes.

The book had an explosive impact on the Western world, an impact that is now hard to imagine. Given the enormous hostility that evolution generated, it was not surprising that Darwin, who was essentially a shy and unassuming man, had delayed for a long time before publishing. Luckily, he had supporters like the naturalist Thomas Huxley, who were happy to speak out assertively on behalf of his ideas in public debates.

The storm of controversy reached a climax in 1861, when at the British Association meeting in Oxford there was a noisy verbal duel between Thomas Huxley and Bishop Samuel Wilberforce of Oxford ('Soapy Sam'), who was against Darwin. Darwin was not the sole originator of the theory of evolution by natural selection. As we have seen, Wallace was thinking of it at the same time. But Darwin was the first to argue the natural selection theory through in a way that was comprehensive and backed up with sufficient evidence for a significant number of fellow scientists to find it acceptable. Darwin took the crude evolutionism of Erasmus Darwin and Jean-Baptiste Lamarck and grafted onto it his own idea of natural selection; this raised evolution from a hypothesis to a theory that could be verified.

Cultures and civilisations are by their nature conservative and resistant to large-scale change. This is how they defend themselves and maintain their identity. Darwin's great achievement lay in changing Western science, steering it well away from religious fundamentalism and towards a new and frightening idea that the emergence of the human race might be a result of mere chance. He did not say that – he was far too cautious and circumspect a man – but it was an implication: that was where his ideas would lead. Darwin's discovery changed the thought worlds of the nineteenth and twentieth centuries, not always to the good. Darwinian theory was partly responsible for the extremes of the Nazi belief in a Germanic-Nordic master race; it justified or seemed to justify the cruelty of that (largely imaginary) master race towards the Jews. It rationalized the death camps and the eugenics programme.

Darwin's theory of evolution is widely accepted, though many modern geneticists and geologists believe that evolutionary changes often occur in sudden jumps, rather than slowly and gradually.

HELIUM
(1868)

It is surprising that the element helium was ever discovered. It is a colourless, tasteless, non-toxic gas and an inert element. It is the least reactive of all elements. It is surprising that we can detect it. It is nevertheless an extremely important element as it is the second most abundant element in the universe.

It was a French astronomer, Pierre Janssen, who stumbled upon the first evidence of the existence of helium in Guntur in India in August 1868. While observing a total solar eclipse, he saw an unknown spectral line signature – a bright yellow line - in the Sun's chromosphere. It was this association with the Sun that led to the element being named after the Sun. Janssen did not at that time recognise that he was seeing evidence of a distinct and hitherto unidentified element, but thought the signature indicated sodium. It was in October of the same year that the English astronomer J. Norman Lockyer also observed the yellow line in the solar spectrum. He named it the D3 line, because it was close to the (known) D1 and D2 lines of sodium. Lockyer rightly deduced that this new spectral line was being produced by an element that exists on the Sun but was then unknown on the Earth. It was Lockyer and the English chemist Edward Frankland who named the new element helium after the Greek name for the Sun, Helios.

Helium is the second lightest element in the universe and is thought to have been created in the Big Bang. Subsequent generation of helium is the result of nuclear fusion of hydrogen inside stars. On the Earth, helium is a rare element, most resulting from the radioactive decay of heavier elements. Reserves of helium are fund in natural gas fields.

Helium has a range of uses, in deep-sea breathing systems, inflating balloons, providing lift for airships and as a protective gas with many industrial applications, such as arc welding. Through much of the universe, helium exists in a plasma state. In this state, the helium electrons and protons are not bound together, and this gives it high electrical conductivity. The charged particles are strongly influenced by electrical and magnetic fields. It is in this way that, in the solar wind, together with ionised hydrogen, they interact with the Earth's magnetic field to produce the Northern Lights.

THE PERIODIC TABLE OF ELEMENTS

(1869)

The ancient Greek philosopher Aristotle declared that there were four fundamental elements: air, earth, fire and water. These reacted with one another to create other elements; fire and earth reacted together to create lava. Once the true multiplicity of chemical elements began to be discovered in modern times, the Aristotelian theory was abandoned. Instead a new way of organising and classifying information about the elements was needed. The simplest shorthand way of summarising information of this kind is a table, and the table of elements came to be know as the periodic table.

When the table was first drawn up, subatomic particles had not been discovered, so some key characteristics of elements are not included. Elements can be put into a rank order according to their atomic mass. Then, if other properties are plotted against atomic mass, it is possible to see a periodicity or undulation to those properties as a function of atomic mass. The first chemist to notice these irregularities was the German Johann Döbereiner. In 1829, he observed that there were groups of three elements with shared properties: chlorine, bromine and iodine; calcium, strontium and barium. Then other chemists saw other chemical relationships that went beyond the triads. Fluorine was added to the chlorine, bromine, iodine group. Sulphur, selenium, oxygen and tellurium were seen as another group. Phosphorus, nitrogen, arsenic, antimony and bismuth were seen as another.

A major breakthrough in the classification of elements came in 1865, when the English chemist John Newlands saw that when elements are put in rank order of increasing atomic weight, elements with similar physical and chemical properties recurred at intervals of eight. Newlands likened this pattern to the recurrence of notes in music, where notes repeat in octaves. His law of octaves was ridiculed by some contemporaries. In the end, Newlands' law of octaves fell apart because it did not work for elements with relatively high masses, and when additional elements were discovered, such as helium and argon, they did not fit into his table either.

In 1869, a table classification of the elements was devised, almost simultaneously by a Russian chemist and a German chemist. The Russian chemistry professor Dmitri Mendeleyev arranged the elements in order of mass, but plotted a few elements out of mass sequence in order to allow them to match their neighbours in the table better. His table had a few empty cells in it, which allowed Mendeleyev to predict not only the existence but even the likely properties of elements that had yet to be discovered. Many of these were later discovered and the table turned out to predict their properties well. Three of these were discovered during Mendeleyev's lifetime: gallium, scandium and germanium.

Mendeleyev's key contributions to devising the table were the creation of a layout that drew attention to the recurring chemical properties of elements (the periodicity) and the provision of gaps predicting the future discovery of new elements. Mendeleyev started new rows in the table so that elements with similar properties would fall into the same columns ('groups'). His original table had periods of the same length. Today, the table has had to be modified, with progressively longer periods further down the table. Another modification came in the 1940s, when Glenn Seaborg identified the transuranic (beyond uranium) lanthanides and actinides; these are placed within the table or below it.

The periodic table expresses the nature of the elements so well and so naturally that it must be regarded as being as much a discovery as an invention. It is in use everywhere within the science of chemistry, supplying the most useful framework for thinking about and comparing different forms of chemical behaviour. The current standard table contains 118 confirmed elements, of which ninety-two are naturally occurring; the rest are produced artificially. The main table starts with H (hydrogen) in the top left hand corner, in Group 1, Period 1, and ends with Uuo in the bottom right hand corner, in Group 18, Period 7. The element Uuo was discovered in 1999, has not been officially named and has so far been produced in only one laboratory, so its status is still in doubt.

TROY
(1865–94)

The conventional version of events is that the site and remains of the Bronze Age city of Troy were discovered by Heinrich Schliemann in 1875. What actually happened is much more complicated.

The location of the ancient city of Troy, immortalized in Homer's *Iliad*, preoccupied a number of people in the eighteenth and nineteenth centuries. The only information about Troy and the Trojan War, until the late nineteenth century, was a cycle of poems known in antiquity as the Epic Cycle. This consisted of eight long poems, of which unfortunately only two, the *Iliad* and the *Odyssey*, have survived to the present day. They were written down between 750 and 500 BC, and were based on oral traditions that probably reach back to the time of the Trojan War in the thirteenth century BC. There was uncertainty in ancient times as whether this story was history, legend or poetry, and both the uncertainty and the debate about it persist to the present day. By the early nineteenth century, most scholars had come to the conclusion that it was poetry, pure fiction with no basis in fact at all. And if that was so, there was no point in looking for Troy because Troy had never existed.

It was an adventurer called Robert Wood who seems to have sparked off the modern quest – and the controversy that raged around it. Wood braved the local bandits to walk the landscape of north-west Turkey, which in his book he claimed matched Homer's description. Sceptics continued to regard Homer as simply a poet and story-teller, and the *Iliad* as a kind of novel. Troy, they argued, never existed at all. But others wondered whether there was at least some truth in Homer's story, and for there to be even some truth in it there had to be an Anatolian town called Troy.

In 1810, Lord Byron sailed into Beşika Bay, the small bay on the open Aegean coastline, and rode there at anchor for days, daydreaming about the Trojan War. Then he disembarked, apparently by chance on the very beach where it is now thought Agamemnon dragged the Greek ships ashore in 1250 BC, and set off to walk across the Plain of Troy, the battlefield where the Trojan War was fought. Byron's verdict was that the area was 'a fine field for conjecture.' But where was Troy itself?

Bronze Age villages and towns in the Middle East were often built of mudbrick. This meant that as the centuries passed and successive houses were built on the same site the crumbled remains created a low mound. These tells were a good indication to archaeologists of the previous existence of a settlement. There were several along the edge of the Plain of Troy. There was Hisarlik. There was also Bunarbashi a few kilometres to the south, and that had emerged as the favoured candidate for Troy by the middle of the nineteenth century.

Frank Calvert was the youngest of seven children in James and Louisa Calvert's English ex-pat family, living in the Hisarlik area. Frank was the quiet, unassuming, thoughtful sibling. He had an enduring passion for Homer and a firm conviction that what Homer wrote was historically true. As early as 1822, Charles Maclaren had identified the Hisarlik mound as a possible site of Troy. In 1847, Frank's brother Frederick bought about 10 square kilometres (4 square miles) of farmland which included part of the Hisarlik mound, and this turned out to be an historic decision. Frederick and James carried out their consular duties, and Frank acted as their secretary, writing and where necessary translating their letters. In 1874, Frank succeeded his brother James as American vice-consul at Cannakale, the nearby town, and from time to time was acting British consul too. During the 1850s and 1860s, Frank Calvert carefully excavated parts of the family-owned land, which included the Hisarlik mound.

Frank Calvert was sure Hisarlik was the right mound. When some German archaeologists excavated Bunarbashi and found nothing, Calvert was more than certain than ever about Hisarlik. He dug a few trenches and found walls and pottery, confirming that there had been a settlement at Hisarlik. He found the remains of the Temple of Athena and the Hellenistic walls raised by Lysimachus in about 300 BC, the later city of Ilion's magnificent defences, which Schliemann's excavations would shortly destroy.

But to mount a full-scale excavation he needed money, and the Calvert family did not have enough to fund it. After the Crimean War ended, Calvert confided his views to Heinrich Schliemann, a wealthy businessman who wanted to make his mark in archaeology and had the financial resources to fund a large-scale dig. Calvert owned the eastern part of the Hisarlik mound, while the Turkish government owned the western part. Schliemann was at that time still thinking of Bunarbashi as Troy; it was Calvert who persuaded him to switch his attention to Hisarlik, and later regretted it. In fact, from today's perspective, it would have been far better if Calvert had *not* drawn Schliemann's attention to Hisarlik; then more of the site would have been left for scientific excavation in the twentieth and twenty-first centuries. Less would have been destroyed. But Frank Calvert could not have known this at the time.

Schliemann started his radical and destructive excavation of the Hisarlik mound in 1870–73. He used as many as 160 workmen at a time to drive great trenches through the mound, against the advice of Calvert, who wanted a network of more modest trenches. Schliemann's brutal digging destroyed many of the remains of the beautiful city of Lysimachus, the later city in which he, Schliemann, was not interested, but it also unknowingly destroyed much of the Homeric citadel too. By 1872, Calvert had withdrawn his permission for Schliemann to excavate his own part of the mound, and it is not difficult to understand why. Schliemann was irritated by Calvert's refusal to co-operate. Then Calvert published an article in the *Levant Herald* in which he wrote damningly of Schliemann's evidence from the Troy excavations, 'a most important link is missing between 1800 and 700 BC, a gap of over a thousand years, including the date of the Trojan War.'

Schliemann was furious with Calvert. Schliemann was sure Troy II (the layer of remains second up from the bottom) was right for Homer's Troy, when he found what he called Priam's Treasure in its debris. Both the treasure and Troy II are now known to date from 2200 BC, too early by 1,000 years to have been the Troy of King Priam. But Schliemann knew inwardly that he had not really solved the problem. By 1879, he was writing, 'I thought I had settled the Trojan question for ever . . . but my doubts increased as time wore on.' Calvert had been right, but Schliemann never recanted and never expressed any gratitude for Calvert's extreme generosity in virtually giving him the discovery.

Schliemann's final campaign at Troy unexpectedly uncovered evidence that Troy VI, a much higher layer in the mound, was contemporary with Mycenaean Greece, the Greece of Agamemnon. The Troy that had contact with Agamemnon's Greece had to be Troy VI, not Troy II.

Schliemann died shortly after this devastating revelation, at Christmas in 1890, universally recognised as the discoverer of Troy. Calvert died in 1908, his contribution to the discovery entirely unacknowledged. After Schliemann's death, his assistant Wilhelm Dörpfeld continued the archaeological excavation at Troy. The real landmark excavation at Troy came in 1893–94, when the walls of the Troy VI citadel were discovered. Dörpfeld was impressed when he saw the great North-East Bastion and recognised from its ambitious and accomplished masonry that *this* must be the Troy of the Trojan War. Hosts of Homer scholars rushed to agree. One was Walter Leaf, who wrote, 'We shall therefore not hesitate, starting from the fact that the Trojan War was a real war fought out in the place, and at least generally in the manner, described in Homer, to draw the further conclusion that some at least of the heroes named by Homer's names, who did actually fight in that war.' This was going a bit too far, but the excitement was understandable.

The breakthrough that Dörpfeld made was that he had uncovered 'a past in which we had ceased to believe'.

So, who discovered Bronze Age Troy? Robert Wood, Frank Calvert, Heinrich Schliemann, Wilhelm Dörpfeld? It has become clear that Schliemann actually destroyed quite a large part of the interior of the citadel of King Priam's Troy; he in fact discovered virtually nothing of the period of Troy that interested him most. Frank Calvert's and Wilhelm Dörpfeld's contributions to the unearthing of Homeric Troy were much greater than Schliemann's.

One of the great remaining problems was that the walls of Troy as unearthed by Dörpfeld enclosed rather a small area. It is only 180 metres (600 feet) across. This is far too small a settlement to justify the colossal force that, according to Homer, the Greeks ranged against it. Once again there seemed to be good grounds for being sceptical. Many scholars who were prepared to believe that a town called Troy had existed in the Bronze Age and that it had been attacked by Greeks argued that the attack must have been much smaller in scale. Homer exaggerated the whole enterprise. Schliemann himself wrote at the end of his life, when plagued by doubts about what he had found, 'I wish I could prove Homer to have been an eyewitness of the Trojan War, but I cannot. Had Troy been merely this small fortified place, a few hundred men would have sufficed to take it, and Homer's story would be exposed as a total fiction.'

Many have gone on wondering whether the so-called city of Troy was in reality only the citadel and that there was a town outside its walls, standing on the gentle slopes to the east and south. The classical town of Ilion spread across these slopes, across two spurs and the intervening saddle, and it seemed likely that a Bronze Age town occupied the same area.

In 1988 another German archaeologist, Manfred Korfmann, launched a new attempt to find the Bronze Age town, and since then he has indeed proved its existence on the western spur, stretching southwards down the slope for about 460 metres (1,500 feet), at which point there was a major line of defence, a deep ditch. Thanks to Korfmann's work, late Bronze Age Troy is now seen to have been thirteen times larger than previously thought, with a population of up to 10,000 people. That made it one of the biggest cities of its day in Anatolia or the Aegean region, and most certainly a worthy target for a large-scale Mycenaean invasion. And that is in itself a significant discovery.

THE TUBERCULOSIS
BACILLUS
(1882)

From antiquity onwards, tuberculosis was one of the great scourges of humanity. Bone fragments from Egyptian mummies dating from as far back as 2400 BC show the symptoms of tubercular decay. Tuberculosis has been known by a variety of names over the centuries, phthisis and consumption being common alternatives, as well as the shortened form, TB. The naming of the disease phthisis appeared in ancient Greek literature. In 460 BC, Hippocrates declared that phthisis was the most widespread disease of his day; he noted that it was usually fatal. He also gave doctors the appalling advice that they should not visit patients in the later stages of the disease as the patients' inevitable deaths would damage the doctors' reputations.

By the seventeenth century, medical books were giving exact descriptions of the disease and its symptoms. In 1679, Sylvius discovered that patients suffering from tuberculosis developed cavities in their lungs. With the advent of X-rays much later, this symptom was one that could easily be identified. The infectious nature of the disease seems to have been picked up relatively late. It was commented on in the late seventeenth century, but it seems not to have had any effect on the way patients were looked after, and it went on being very common – even in England in the early twentieth century – for tuberculosis to wipe out entire families. The poet John Keats was a very typical case of someone who caught the disease after nursing a family member. Keats nursed his brother George until George died, then died from tuberculosis himself in 1821.

In 1720, an English physician, Benjamin Marten, became the first to wonder whether tuberculosis was caused by 'wonderfully minute living

*A man on board a sailing ship taking an observation of the Sun with a sextant
(above right) to try and find the magnetic pole.*
Original painting by Stradamus.

The discovery of the River Amazon was an amazing revelation because of the river's sheer size. It is one of the major features of world geography and the fact that its entire course was discovered all in one go and by accident makes it even more amazing.

The 'House of the Poet' in the ruins of Pompeii, Italy. The city of Pompeii was buried in AD 79 when the supposedly extinct volcano, Vesuvius, erupted. The ancient site was discovered when excavations began in 1748, and the discovery has shown us in amazing detail what town life was like under Roman rule.

Niagara Falls on the Niagara River in Ontario, Canada. The discovery of these magnificent falls in 1678 by Father Louis Hennepin was described by him as: '. . . a vast and prodigious cadence of water which falls down after a surprising and astonishing manner, insomuch that the universe does not afford its parallel.'

Here the Coriolos effect can be seen at work in nature at Wapusk National Park, Manitoba, Canada – a pair of whirlpools spinning in opposite directions. Freely moving objects on the surface of the Earth experience the Coriolis force and appear to turn to the right in the northern hemisphere and to the left in the southern – water movements are notable examples of this behaviour.

The ancient ruins of the Palace of Minos in Knossos, Crete, Greece, were discovered by Sir Arthur Evans in the early part of the twentieth century. Columns were a predominant feature of the Minoan architecture and many of the walls were highly decorated with frescoes. Thanks to this discovery we are able to learn much about the ancient Minoan culture.

The Dead Sea Scrolls were discovered by accident in 1947 when goatherds weres searching the cliffs along the Dead Sea and came across a cave containing jars filled with manuscripts. Their find, which included copies of biblical books and writings, not only caused a sensation when it was released to the world, but it still continues to fascinate to this day.

The discovery of the terracotta army in 1974 at Xian in China is now regarded as the Eighth Wonder of the Ancient World. Local farmers accidentally found a pit while digging a well, and uncovered thousands of life-size terracotta figures who guarded the tomb of the First Emperor of China, Qin Shi Huangdi, who lived over 2,200 years ago.

creatures.' He also believed that it was likely that people who habitually shared a bed with an infected person, or often had meals with him, or held conversations with him, would be very likely to become infected by inhaling the same air that had been emitted from the infected lungs. Marten quite rightly surmised that 'slightly conversing with a consumptive person is seldom or never sufficient to catch the disease.'

But a cure was a very long way off. In the eighteenth and early nineteenth centuries, sending patients from the cold, wet climate of Britain to the warm, dry climate of the Mediterranean countries was often prescribed as a remedy; it may have prolonged the lives of some patients, but it is not likely to have cured anyone. The introduction of the sanatorium cure was the first really significant step in defeating TB. Hermann Brehmer was a Silesian botany student suffering from TB. He was advised by his doctor to move to a healthier climate. He went off an expedition to the Himalayas, with the idea of curing himself and pursuing his botanical studies at the same time. He returned cured, and then in 1854 presented his PhD dissertation, which had the promising and eye-catching title, *Tuberculosis is a curable disease*. That year, Brehmer built a sanatorium among fir trees at Gorbersdorf, where he put his patients out on balconies to inhale continuous fresh air. The technique helped many patients, and sanatoria sprang up all over the Alps. They remained in use on a large scale right on to the mid-twentieth century.

In 1865, a French military doctor, Jean-Antoine Villemin, discovered that TB was transmissible from species to species. He demonstrated that the disease could pass from people to cattle and from cattle to rabbits. This was a revolutionary discovery in itself, but it led Villemin to the conclusion that the disease must be caused and spread by a micro-organism. This was an important scientific step forward, as up to that point there was a widespread belief that TB arose spontaneously in each affected organism. Many people thought of TB as a fact of life, and accepted it in a way that they did not accept the Black Death or other plagues. In the eighteenth and nineteenth centuries, the condition was associated with melancholia and otherworldliness, and some people believed it was actually brought on by those states of mind. Even the twentieth century psychologist Carl

Gustav Jung believed that at least half of the TB cases were psychosomatic; he thought that people with complexes breathed less deeply. That was anachronistic and mischievous nonsense. TB is and always was a physical illness; the melancholia is a *symptom*.

The major breakthrough came in 1882 when Robert Koch discovered a staining technique for preparing slides. The stain enabled him to see what was causing TB. It was indeed a micro-organism - *Mycobacterium tuberculosis*. Everyone was very excited by Koch's discovery, as they understood and anticipated that defeating TB was now possible. There would, however, be a long wait before the drug that could combat the bacillus was discovered or concocted. Meanwhile, the sanatoria did much to prolong the lives of TB sufferers, and also gave their family members and co-workers a better chance of remaining free of infection.

A technique was devised by the Italian Carlo Forlanini, which involved collapsing the lung by squirting compressed air through hypodermic needles into the pleural cavity. This rested the lung and improved its chance of recovery. How effective this unpleasant treatment was is unclear, but it had a good psychological effect on patients. Now they felt at last that doctors were actively doing something to help them to get better, instead of telling them, quite literally, to go away.

The discovery of X-rays by Wilhelm von Röntgen in 1895 and the invention of the X-ray photograph were also landmarks in the development of the treatment of TB. Now it became possible to see the pattern of damage, and the pattern of healing, in a patient's lungs. The progress of the disease, and also the impacts of various treatments, could now be monitored.

The French bacteriologist Albert Calmette used specific culture media to reduce the virulence of bovine (cattle) TB bacterium. This formed the basis of the BCG vaccine that is still in use today. Then, during World War II, came the ultimate breakthrough – chemotherapy. The treatment of infectious diseases by using chemicals, especially sulphonamide and penicillin, had been going on for some years, but these had proved ineffective against *Mycobacterium tuberculosis*.

From 1914 onwards, Selman Waksman was systematically screening soil bacteria and fungi. In 1939, while at the University of California, he discovered that certain fungi, especially *actinomycete*, inhibited the growth of bacteria. Then, in 1940, Waksman and his team isolated actinomycin, an antibiotic that was effective against the TB bacterium. This discovery proved to be a false dawn, as actinomycin was too toxic to use on people or animals. Then came success. In 1943, Waksman purified streptomycin from *Streptomyces griseus*. This inhibited the growth of the TB bacillus but was also relatively non-toxic. On 20 November 1944 the new antibiotic was given for the first time to a TB patient, a man who was critically ill. The advance of his disease was arrested and he made a rapid recovery. Streptomycin was to save tens of thousands of lives.

A succession of anti-TB drugs appeared during the 1940s and 1950s. This was necessary as, when using a single drug, resistant mutants started to appear within a few months. It was soon discovered that this effect could be overcome by using a combination of two or three drugs. At last, the global Great White Plague of tuberculosis was in retreat. When Waksman was awarded the Nobel Prize in Medicine in 1952, the Swedish academic hosting the banquet addressed him in these terms: 'You have discovered a new and powerful weapon in the deadly battle against one of the oldest foes of mankind . . . the gratitude due to you is of the kind that cannot be expressed.'

FLUORINE
(1886)

Fluorine in the form of fluorspar was described by Georgius Agricola in 1530, when it was used as a flux, a substance to aid the fusion of metals. In 1670, it was found that fluorspar treated with acid could etch glass. Fluorine as an element was first identified by Karl Scheele in 1771, but it was not isolated until 1886 by Henri Moissan. This was the culmination of over seventy years of continuous effort by several chemists. Deriving the element fluorine from hydrofluoric acid is a very dangerous procedure and several chemists were blinded or killed during experiments; they were known as 'fluorine martyrs'. Moissan was awarded the 1906 Nobel Prize in chemistry for his work, though he was to die at only fifty-four.

Fluorine is a halogen gas, yellowish, poisonous and highly corrosive. It is highly reactive, combining readily with most other elements, and as a result it does not occur in isolation in nature; it is found in compounds such as cryolite, apatite and fluorite.

Fluorine is a dangerous element, one that can cause severe burns when it comes in contact with skin. In spite of its negative properties, fluorine has a range of uses. Soluble fluorides such as sodium fluoride and stannous fluoride may be used as an additive to water supplies or to toothpaste to reduce the level of tooth decay. Their addition to public water supplies has generated controversy, partly on ethical grounds – is it justifiable to administer drugs to improve people's dental health without their consent? There are also concerns that long-term exposure to small doses of fluoride could be detrimental to health.

Fluorite is used in the process of refining iron, cryolite in the process of aluminium manufacture, sodium fluoride as an insecticide, fluorine for refrigeration and air-conditioning systems.

THE DEPTH OF THE ATACAMA TRENCH
(1890)

The Atacama Trench is a major feature of the Earth's surface, a deep furrow in the ocean floor running 5,900 kilometres (3,670 miles) from north to south about 160 kilometres (100 miles) off the Pacific coast of South America. It is about 65 kilometres (40 miles) wide and reaches a maximum depth of over 8,000 metres (26,000 feet) below sea level.

A landmark in its exploration came in May 1890, when the British cable-laying ship Relay discovered an exceptionally deep point in the trench. It was 7,635 metres (25,043 feet) below sea level. Subsequent surveys, as with the other ocean trenches, found points that were deeper still; the deepest point currently known is 26,460 feet (8,065 m) below sea level.

This major submarine landform is sometimes called the Peru-Chile Trench, sometimes the Atacama Trench and sometimes the Atacama Graben. The discovery and measurement of this and other trenches led on, eventually, to an understanding of the way in which the Earth's crust has moved around to create fold mountains and mid-ocean ridges, as well as trenches. The Atacama Trench in particular has resulted from the South American plate moving westwards to collide with the Nazca Plate. The eastern edge of the Nazca Plate is subducted beneath the South American Plate.

X-RAYS

(1895)

X-rays, also known as roentgen rays, were discovered by the German physicist Wilhelm Röntgen. He had been Professor of Physics at the Physical Institute at Wurzburg since 1888. On 8 November 1895, he noticed a phenomenon while he was working with the cathode-ray ultra-vacuum tube that had recently been invented by the English physicist William Crookes. When Röntgen passed a current through the cathode-ray tube, a piece of paper nearby that was painted with barium platinocyamide appeared to fluoresce brightly. What Röntgen had discovered was en effect caused by an invisible ray.

Röntgen found that he was able to use the invisible rays to 'see through' objects. Perhaps his most significant discovery was that he could use X-rays to take photographs of the interiors of people's bodies. As a demonstration he took a photograph of the hand of one of his colleagues. The bone structure showed exceptionally clearly. The rays could pass through skin and flesh very easily, denser tissue less easily and bone not at all, so it was possible to look inside someone's body. This was an historic image, which has been reproduced often to illustrate this landmark in diagnostic medicine. It was one of the great breakthroughs in medicine. By providing doctors with a brand-new and wholly unexpected diagnostic tool, it changed the quality of medical care throughout the twentieth century.

Röntgen was awarded the first Nobel Prize for Physics in 1901. In 1903, The German surgeon Georg Perthes made the first observations that X-rays could inhibit cancerous growth. So even at this very early stage, another major use emerged for Röntgen's magic rays. They could not only diagnose – they could *cure*.

THE GREENHOUSE EFFECT
(1896)

THE INITIAL DISCOVERY

Like many great discoveries, the greenhouse effect was made in several steps and not all at the same time. A pioneer of the idea was John Tyndall, a Victorian alpinist who had firsthand knowledge of glaciers. He had become convinced by the evidence that Louis Agassiz offered of a great Ice Age in 1840, and believed that thick layers of ice had covered much of northern Europe within the past 100,000 years. What was puzzling was how such radical and wrenching climate changes could happen. Tyndall thought it could be to do with a change in the composition of the Earth's atmosphere. As early as the 1820s, and the work of Joseph Fourier, the idea had been available that gases in the atmosphere could trap heat from the Sun, though no evidence for this was produced.

John Tyndall tried to discover experimentally whether any gases were capable of doing this. He found that water vapour was the most important; carbon dioxide could trap heat too, although the concentrations of this gas were extremely low.

After Tyndall came the Swedish scientist Svante Arrhenius, who was similarly attracted to the problem of explaining the mysterious drop in temperature associated with the Ice Age. In 1896, Arrhenius calculated that halving the current concentration of carbon dioxide in the atmosphere might have lowered the atmospheric temperature in Europe by up to 5 degrees Celsius (9 degrees Fahrenheit), which would be enough to initiate an Ice Age. Then Arrhenius turned to the question whether such a reduction of carbon dioxide levels would have been possible. He discussed it with Arvid Högbom, who had speculated about the carbon dioxide cycle – the way that carbon dioxide moves by way of a variety of geochemical processes from volcanoes into the atmosphere, is then taken up by ocean water, and so on.

Högbom came up with calculations of the amount of carbon dioxide given off by factories, and came to the conclusion that human activity was adding as much carbon dioxide to the atmosphere as was being emitted or absorbed by natural processes. The added gas was a tiny amount. In 1896, the amount added by human activity was barely one-thousandth of the total atmospheric carbon dioxide. This was probably not enough to make a difference to the temperature of the atmosphere but, if the additions continued, they might. Arrhenius then made a calculation of the temperature of the atmosphere based on a hypothetical doubling of the carbon dioxide level, and estimated an increase of up to 6 degrees Celsius (10.8 degrees Fahrenheit) – major global warming.

Although the result of this calculation might have alarmed Arrhenius, he was relatively unconcerned because he was not expecting the burning of fossil fuel to accelerate. He assumed fossil-fuel consumption would continue at 1896 rates, and that would mean it would take perhaps as much as 3,000 years for the temperature to rise by six degrees. Högbom doubted whether the warming would be that great anyway, as the oceans would absorb five-sixths of the additional gas. Probably both scientists were fairly heartened by the idea that the cold country where they lived, Sweden, might become slightly warmer as a result. Another scientist, Walter Nernst, even wondered about the possibility of burning surplus coal in order to bring on the global warming a little faster! This is reminiscent of recent remarks by Vladimir Putin that global warming is not necessarily a bad thing for Russia.

Arrhenius wrote up his ideas on possible future warming in a widely read book in 1908. By then, coal was being burnt at a significantly higher rate than in 1896, and Arrhenius suggested that the warming effect might be felt within centuries rather than millennia. But these speculations were still subordinate to his main interest, which was the *cooling* effect that caused the Ice Age. Arrhenius was not really promoting the idea of the greenhouse effect or of global warming, merely pointing them out as the corollary of what he was arguing.

Then T. C. Chamberlin, an American geologist, started exploring the possible routes by which carbon dioxide might be recycled in the Earth's natural systems. The gas seemed to pass through the atmosphere, into the oceans, and become combined to form minerals like calcium carbonate, as well as passing through living things like trees. There were many variables here, which could explain variations in the amount of carbon dioxide present in the atmosphere at any one time. But Chamberlin and his contemporaries were still following up the problem of explaining the cooling necessary to produce an Ice Age. Their other interest was in explaining much longer-term changes in global climate, the gradual but large-scale shifts in temperature across millions of years.

Arrhenius's idea of carbon dioxide-related cooling and warming was in any case flawed. For one thing, he oversimplified the climate system. To take one example, he gave no consideration to the possible effect of variations in cloud cover on temperature. Another problem was that some laboratory experiments seemed to disprove the greenhouse hypothesis. Another Swedish scientist, Knut Angstrom, organised an experiment in which infrared radiation was passed through air with a carbon dioxide concentration rather lower than the average found in the atmosphere as a whole. When the concentration of carbon dioxide was reduced by one-third there was no measurable change in the amount of radiation passing through. The experiment showed that tiny traces of carbon dioxide were absorbing radiation to saturation level, but that when the concentration was raised it made little further difference. The crude spectrographs available at the time also showed that carbon dioxide only affected radiation in the bands of the spectrum that water vapour was blocking – and water vapour was a far more abundant greenhouse gas than carbon dioxide. The Angstrom experiments suggested that carbon dioxide was having only the smallest effect on atmospheric temperature.

REJECTION

The result, following publication in 1900, was that the scientific community (if it can ever be credibly described as such) closed ranks against the idea of a carbon dioxide-based greenhouse effect. In fact, Angstrom's laboratory experiment was flawed in several ways, not least in scaling down the thickness of the atmosphere to a glass tube in a laboratory. It made no allowance for the variations between the different layers of the atmosphere, which we know behave very differently. In the thin upper layers of the atmosphere, radiation may easily escape into space, and in those layers some additional carbon dioxide or any other greenhouse gas may make a significant difference. The scaling down also removed any possibility of simulating interactions between the layers of the atmosphere. In fact, it is this problem of scale and complexity that dogs every climate model, up to and including the most advanced computer models available today; the global climate system cannot be simulated. But, as far as the scientific community was concerned, Arrhenius was wrong and the carbon dioxide greenhouse effect was considered to be non-existent. It was a display of scientific dogmatism that we would do well to remember in the context of what is being said today about carbon dioxide.

There were a few lone voices who went on believing that Arrhenius was right. In 1931, an American physicist, E. O. Hulburt, pointed out that insufficient effort had been made to measure absorption coefficients accurately. Hulburt recalculated and came to the conclusion that halving the carbon dioxide concentration in the atmosphere would produce a fall in temperature of 4 degrees Celsius (7.2 degrees Fahrenheit), and that doubling the concentration would produce a rise of four degrees. Hulburt came to the conclusion that carbon dioxide variations therefore could after all have been responsible for the Ice Age. As is often the way, his paper published in the *Physical Review* was ignored because it was out of line with the current scientific consensus: it was the Semmelweis Reflex.

It is hard to believe now, but as recently as 1951 the American Meteorological Society's *Compendium* stated that the idea that raising the level of carbon dioxide in the atmosphere would raise the temperature 'was never widely accepted and was abandoned when it was found that all the long-wave radiation that might be absorbed by carbon dioxide is absorbed by water vapour.' One reason for dismissing variations in atmospheric carbon dioxide was that scientists knew that there was fifty times as much carbon dioxide dissolved in sea water. Whatever variations there might be in the atmosphere, the oceans would act as a buffer, stabilising the climate system. Some scientists looked to 'homeostatic regulation'. If there was more carbon dioxide in the atmosphere, this would act as a fertiliser, make vegetation grow more luxuriantly and in this way absorb the surplus gas. The Earth was a natural system that could regulate itself.

REDISCOVERY

A new champion of carbon dioxide arrived in 1938, in the shape of Guy Callendar, an English engineer who was also an amateur meteorologist. The greenhouse effect is one of those ideas that has been discovered more than once. This rediscovery was in effect a revival of the ideas of Arrhenius and Chamberlin. A number of climatologists had observed that early twentieth century weather records showed a warming trend. Callendar confirmed this when he compiled temperature figures from the late nineteenth century on to the 1930s. Then he compiled measurements of concentrations of carbon dioxide in the atmosphere, and these showed an increase of about ten per cent. Callendar then made the historic, and seemingly irreversible, assertion that the increase in carbon dioxide was responsible for and explained the warming trend.

The observation was in fact poorly based, as the correlation between the two variables is statistically poor. There were, even within the period Callendar was studying, decades when temperatures fell while carbon dioxide concentrations were rising; since Callendar's time we have had the additional major 'anomaly' of the 1970s, when temperatures fell while carbon dioxide levels were rising sharply. Unscientific though Callendar's work was, it was to prove a turning point as far as the scientific community was concerned.

Callendar's ideas were mainly developed with one eye on cooling in the Ice Age, just as the ideas of Tyndall and Arrhenius had been, rather than on future warming. The climatology textbooks of the 1940s and

1950s routinely included a reference to Callendar's idea, but even so most professional climatologists were doubtful. For one thing, the early measurements of carbon dioxide could not be regarded as accurate, and any trend would need to be monitored across a much longer period anyway. And all the same old arguments that had been levelled at Arrhenius were brought out again, including the masking of any carbon dioxide effects by those of water vapour.

REJECTION

Callendar's ideas did not deserve to be taken seriously. The alleged correlation between carbon dioxide and temperature did not work. He also could have seen, if he had looked up sunspot numbers, for instance, that the Sun had become progressively more active during the twentieth century, which would have given him an alternative explanation for the warming. But he also neglected several other real-world variables. He admitted that actual changes in the climate must depend on many interactions and many variations, such as cloud cover, which could not be reliably calculated. Sensibly, many scientists of Callendar's time believed that it was an area of pointless speculation, because the greenhouse effect theory was (still) not really anything more than that – a theory – and not susceptible of appropriate data gathering.

In fact, the major temperature changes that produced the cooling episodes in the Ice Age, the cold stages, and warming episodes separating them, the interglacials, are far more convincingly explained by astronomical variations. The so-called Milankovitch cycles, very small cyclical variations in the angle of tilt of the Earth's axis, the direction in which the axis points, and the shape of the orbit, are sufficient to produce the major temperature changes. There was no need to call into play carbon dioxide as an agent of change at all. Within the past two or three hundred years, variations in Total Solar Irradiance, the amount of solar radiation reaching the Earth's surface, have been shown to be sufficient to explain all the temperature changes, up to and including the past few decades. In other words, the original discovery of the greenhouse effect was after all not a discovery. Nor was its rediscovery by Callendar in the 1930s. It was a hypothesis. But the idea, the hypothesis, was now dangerously available. Modern proponents of carbon dioxide greenhouse effect like to see Guy Callendar as a pioneer, a trail blazer, when he was simply wrong – whatever is happening to the climate today.

THE COLD WAR SHIFT

The Cold War led to unprecedented funding for research into the atmosphere and the oceans, mainly as habitats for missiles, spy planes and nuclear submarines. But a great deal of scientific knowledge about the Earth was acquired, thanks to the extra funding. Improvements in the accuracy of laboratory measurements in the 1940s led to the discovery that the spectral bands where water vapour and carbon dioxide absorbed radiation did not exactly coincide after all. It was also discovered that in the upper atmosphere, where there was very little water vapour, carbon dioxide might be playing a more important role than hitherto realised. The early approach, of regarding the atmosphere as if it was a homogeneous whole, had been quite misleading. Looking at what was happening in the different layers of the atmosphere would be crucially important, and it would prove to be very difficult to measure.

This is a moment where discovery meets invention. The introduction of computers transformed many branches of science and made much more advanced calculation possible. By 1956, computers were sophisticated enough to handle huge sets of data, so they opened the possibility of assimilating and interpreting the processes of the atmosphere. A problem was then, and still is now, that we put excessive faith in what the computer screen shows us; the fundamental IT adage, 'rubbish in, rubbish out', is too often forgotten. The most advanced computer models of the global weather system generate very impressive and persuasive screen images, often animated to 'demonstrate' how global warming will progress, given this or that amount of additional carbon dioxide to the atmosphere. It looks real enough, and then comes the realisation that each pixel, each unit of information in the image, is perhaps the size of Wales or Massachusetts. In the climate system, which is known to be extremely volatile and unstable, the variations and interactions that occur within a region of that size are highly significant – yet they are being ignored. The model as whole, however complex, turns out to be a hopeless oversimplification of reality.

Nevertheless, two generations of physicists and climatologists have invested enormous faith in their models. After making his calculations, the physicist Gilbert Plass announced that human activity would raise the average global temperature at a rate of 1.1 degree Celsius (2 degrees Fahrenheit) per century. The calculations were, as usual, based on a simplified view of the climate system. They took no notice of variations in water vapour or cloud cover, and because of the general nature of the method they did not convince many scientists. One reviewer sternly noted that Plass's figures would be 'subject to many strong revisions'. But because the mathematics and the computer technology were way beyond the understanding of most people, nugget statistics like these were to form the incontrovertible bedrock of global warming doctrine; they gave those who wanted to believe in carbon dioxide-driven global warming the ammunition they needed. Interestingly, Plass was still trying, primarily, to explain the mystery of the Ice Age; if global temperature went on rising until the end of the twentieth century, Plass said, it would prove that carbon dioxide was behind it – a very odd piece of scientific reasoning indeed.

Another argument raged over the role of the oceans in absorbing carbon dioxide. Plass believed that carbon dioxide added to the atmosphere stayed there for thousands of years, while others thought the surface of the ocean could absorb it in a few days. The discovery of the radioactive isotope carbon-14, which made the invention of radiocarbon-dating possible in the 1950s, also made it possible to track the movement of carbon through its cycle. In 1955, Harry Suess discovered ancient carbon-14 in the atmosphere. The quantities of it that he measured were very small, and from this he deduced that the oceans must be taking up most of the carbon that was created by burning fossil fuels. Then in the 1960s Suess discovered that the percentage of fossil carbon in the atmosphere was far higher, suggesting that the oceans were after all not absorbing the additional carbon output. But the research results are ambiguous. They may not show a real change in the atmosphere – rather a change in research technique, or a variation in scientific accuracy.

Suess collaborated with Roger Revelle at the Scripps Institution of Oceanography. The results of experiments in measuring carbon-14 in the air and the ocean were reassuring; they showed that typically a molecule of atmospheric carbon dioxide was absorbed by the ocean within ten years. This was again reassuring in confirming that the ocean can readily absorb carbon dioxide. Revelle predicted that concentrations of atmospheric carbon dioxide would probably increase by not more than forty per cent and stabilise at that level after a few hundred years. Buried within this superficially reassuring statistic was an implication that was quite alarming. If carbon dioxide was a greenhouse gas and the ocean was unable to keep the concentrations of it in the atmosphere to their present level, the result would be hundreds of years of warming. This implication was missed by most scientists when Revelle's paper was published. In fact, the work of both Suess and Revelle was far less influential than the rather similar observations published by two Swedish meteorologists, Bert Bolin and Erik Eriksson. In 1959, they published their view that carbon dioxide concentrations in the atmosphere would rise, in spite of the ocean's capacity to absorb some of the gas.

It was at about this time that scientists began to warn the general public of the dangers of global warming. Those dangers were clearly worse because of increasing industrialisation and rising outputs of carbon dioxide. The problem with all of this, though, was that the big ideas were based on unreliable measurements of tiny parts of a huge and infinitely complex natural system. It was a speculation with some numbers added.

A major step forward was taken in the mid-1950s when, during the International Geophysical Year, a great many ambitious initiatives were launched. Many scientists were dissatisfied with the low quality of the carbon dioxide measurements, which were bound to vary locally, according to the proximity or otherwise of factories, and with time, according to wind direction. Revelle and Suess acquired enough funding

271

to hire Charles David Keeling to take precise carbon dioxide measurements all round the world. Keeling's intention was to establish an accurate picture of the carbon dioxide levels, with a view to repeating the exercise perhaps a decade or two later. In fact by only 1960, after taking readings in the relatively clean air of Mauna Loa and Antarctica, he showed that the gas levels had already risen. Cost forced the closure of the Antarctic station, but readings at Mauna Loa continued, and they still continue. The graph Keeling produced (Keeling's curve) has been reproduced again and again as the definitive evidence of a steady and inexorable rise in carbon dioxide levels. It is the icon of the greenhouse effect in the eyes of those who believe in it.

REDISCOVERY AGAIN!
In the 1960s scientists used another new invention, the systems diagram, to illustrate how the carbon cycle worked. This involved drawing a simple flow diagram with a box for each stage in the cycle. As measurements and estimates were added in, the scientists gained a clearer picture of the way carbon dioxide was being exchanged, but the key figure, the amount that was being drawn down into the oceans and forests, remained elusive. The systems diagram remained no more than an unfinished sudoku. This however did not stop the greenhouse effect enthusiasts from making rash predictions about future temperatures.

Many scientists at this stage, by the 1970s, still felt confident about stating publicly that they were unconvinced that carbon dioxide was driving a change in climate. By the 1990s that would change. But in 1970 the leading climatologist Helmut Landsberg dared to say that little was known about the way the human race might affect climate. He thought any effect carbon dioxide might have would be small, perhaps raising global temperature by two degrees over the next 400 years. Another leading climate expert, Hubert Lamb, was also doubtful about the effect of carbon dioxide. He pointed out that carbon dioxide could not be made to explain the many temperature variations of the last thousand years. Lamb also argued that the sharp cooling episode of the 1940s made nonsense of the greenhouse theory. And the years immediately following, the 1970s, were to be another episode of marked cooling that would support Lamb's position.

Keeling's curve, the spectacular graph of carbon dioxide measurements from Mauna Loa, actually gives the lie to the greenhouse effect. It displays a very regular annual zig-zag reflecting seasonal changes. This is superimposed on a very regular and continuous upward trend, almost a straight line, from 315 parts per million in 1959 up to 383 ppm in 2007. The twenty per cent increase in carbon dioxide over a period of just forty-eight years is worrying as a demonstration of atmospheric pollution. But it cannot be used to explain global warming. Temperature graphs for the same period do not show this consistent increase, but warming and cooling episodes. Right in the middle of it was the marked cooling of the 1970s, where Keeling's curve shows carbon dioxide continuing to rise. The two are clearly unconnected.

The greenhouse effect scientists ignored this but were puzzled by something else. Figures were available for the amount of carbon dioxide emitted by burning fossil fuels. Estimates were made of the take-up of carbon dioxide by the oceans and by vegetation. The numbers did not match. A significant amount of carbon had gone missing. The scientists did not fully understand the global system.

The greenhouse effect idea was then rescued by two events. One was the resumption, from 1980 onwards, of the warming required by the theory. The other was the analysis of ice cores newly obtained from Greenland and Antarctica. These contained millions of tiny air bubbles and the chemistry of this fossil air provided detailed evidence of temperature over a 100,000 year period, and also evidence of carbon dioxide. A Greenland ice core showed that at the coldest point of the last cold stage, around 20,000 years ago, there was only half as much carbon dioxide in the atmosphere as today. In 1987, an ice core from Vostok in Antarctica yielded a record of 400,000 years of temperature changes, reaching right back across four cycles of cold and warm stages. It showed, spectacularly, that warm stages were, and are, times of high carbon dioxide and cold stages times of low carbon dioxide. The assumption was made that the greenhouse effect had been proved, but two problems remain. One is that processes operating on a scale of thousands or tens of thousands of years do not necessarily show up on a time scale of centuries or decades – a point that Hubert Lamb made. The other is that the low carbon dioxide levels associated with the cold stages may have been the *result* and not the *cause* of the low temperatures, perhaps by way of the huge changes in the biosphere. In fact, in the 1990s precise measurements of the ice core data showed that the temperature changes came first and the changes in carbon dioxide levels came later, following after several hundred years.

We are left in a very uncertain world now, one where it is evident that the processes of the Earth's atmosphere, oceans and biosphere are inextricably linked together, but it is by no means clear exactly how they are linked. Perhaps the strangest aspect of the situation is that politicians, environmental pressure groups, a great many scientists in many disciplines, and even media celebrities like Sir David Attenborough are preaching the dogma of carbon dioxide-driven global warming with great vehemence as if it was an established fact – when as we have seen it is a very long way from proved. Scientists who dare to oppose the dogma are marginalised, sometimes even vilified. The pressure on academics to conform is as great as in the days of the Inquisition; to disbelieve in carbon dioxide-driven global warming is now a virtual heresy.

The graph of atmospheric carbon dioxide has risen steadily and persistently for the last 110 years, yet the graph of atmospheric temperature has gone up and down. The correlation between the two is weak. Conversely, the correlation between temperature and Total Solar Irradiance (TSI, controlled by solar radiation and terrestrial volcanic activity) is strong. Several scientists from the 1970s onwards have argued the case for the dominance of solar and volcanic control but they are marginalised. One commentator has remarked, 'Scarcely any reputable expert now doubts that CO_2 was responsible for warming since the 1980s.' So those who disagree are disreputable, then? Currently, debate is stifled.

Given the history of the ideas, TSI looks likely to be the next rediscovery in this complicated and alarming saga, though we must hope that that happens before any more nuclear power stations are built.

ELECTRON
(1897)

In 1874, G. Johnstone Stoney suggested that there was a fundamental unit of electrical charge in electrochemistry; he went on to estimate its amount and name it the 'electron' in 1894. During the next few years, several physicists proposed that electricity could be considered as being made up of discrete units. These very small units were given various provisional names, but for the moment they remained theoretical: their reality had not been demonstrated.

It was in 1897 that J. J. Thomson discovered that the electron existed as a subatomic particle while he was researching cathode ray tubes at the Cavendish Laboratory in Cambridge. A cathode ray tube is a glass cylinder containing two electrodes separated by a vacuum. When a voltage is applied across the electrodes, cathode rays are generated and these cause the tube to glow. Thomson discovered that the rays could be deflected by a magnetic field and came to the conclusion that they were made of tiny negatively charged particles. He called them corpuscles. When he measured their mass-to-charge ratio he found it was less than one-thousandth of a hydrogen ion. This meant that they were either very highly charged or very small in mass. Other scientists worked on the problem and proved that the corpuscles were indeed very small in mass. The mass-to-charge ratio did not vary with the choice of cathode material or the gas in the tube, and this led Thomson to the conclusion that his newly discovered corpuscles were universal; they were to be found in all materials.

The charge of an electron was measured more precisely by R. A. Millikan in an experiment in 1909. Now that sub-atomic particles (electrons and protons) had been proved to exist it was possible to look to them for explanations for the anomalies in the periodic table; other scientists started to look there for answers. In 1913, Henry Moseley devised the concept of the atomic number, and explained the periodic law (which governs the layout of the periodic table) in terms of the number of protons each element has.

The discovery of the internal structure of atoms was to open up many exciting new areas of physics in the twentieth century.

MALARIA CAUSED BY MOSQUITOES
(1897)

The human race has suffered from malaria for at least 50,000 years. The first documentary record of malaria comes from China in 2,700 BC. The word malaria itself comes from an Italian phrase meaning 'bad air'. The disease was also known as ague or marsh fever, because of its known association with swamps.

Malaria is caused by a protozoan parasite called *Plasmodium*, which is transmitted by the bites of infected female *Anopheles* mosquitoes. Malaria is widespread in the tropics and subtropics and it is estimated that it infects about 515 million people each year and causes between one and three million deaths. It is still a major problem. Most of the victims are young children in sub-Saharan Africa. Malaria is often associated with poverty, and indeed it is a major cause of poverty in Third World countries.

In the human body, the *Plasmodium* parasites multiply in the liver, and then infect the red blood cells. Symptoms of malaria include fever, headache, nausea and vomiting, usually appear between ten and fifteen days after the mosquito bite. Many of the superficial symptoms are similar to those of flu. Other symptoms include anaemia, light-headedness and tachycardia. In severe cases, when the blood supply to vital organs is disrupted, victims may pass into a coma and die.

The earliest effective treatment for malaria was the bark of the cinchona tree, which grows in the Peruvian Andes. The bark, which contains quinine, was used by the native inhabitants of Peru to inhibit the effects of malaria. When the Spanish arrived in Peru in the sixteenth century they picked up this treatment, found it effective and in the 1640s took it back with them to Europe.

The first major advance in scientific research on malaria came in 1880. A French army doctor working in an Algerian military hospital, Charles Laveran, spotted parasites for the first time. He saw them when he looked through a microscope at the red blood cells of people suffering from malaria. Laveran proposed that malaria was caused by a protozoan and then identified it; this was the first time anyone identified a protozoan as the cause of a disease. For this major breakthrough, Laveran was awarded the 1907 Nobel Prize in Medicine. The protozoan that Laveran saw was given the name *Plasmodium* by two Italian scientists, Ettore Marchiafava and Angelo Celli.

In 1881, a Cuban doctor called Carlos Finlay, who was treating patients suffering from yellow fever in Havana, suggested that it was mosquitoes that were responsible for transmitting disease, both to and from human beings. The clinching discovery was made by the British medic Ronald Ross. He was working in India when he finally produced proof that mosquitoes were indeed transmitting malaria in the way Finlay proposed. Ross proved that certain species of mosquito transmit malaria to birds, and he showed this by isolating malaria parasites from the salivary glands of mosquitoes that had fed on infected birds. Ross was awarded the 1902 Nobel Prize in Medicine for his discovery.

The work of Finlay and Ross was verified by a medical board in 1900. The discovery had enormous implications. New health measures were introduced during the building of the Panama Canal to reduce the incidence of malaria among the work force. Thousands of lives were saved during this and many subsequent health campaigns.

Malaria is best prevented by preventing mosquitoes from biting. At the personal level, mosquito nets and insect repellents are helpful. At the environmental level, draining areas of standing water where mosquitoes lay their eggs is a good way of reducing the mosquito population. At the present time there is no malaria vaccine; there are only preventative drugs, which have to be taken continuously to reduce the risk of infection. These are very effective for visitors from more economically developed countries, but too expensive for most of the people who actually live in the affected regions.

RADIUM
(1898)

In 1897, Pierre and Marie Curie were scientific researchers, he on crystal growth, she on the magnetisation of tempered steels. Their attention was caught by a phenomenon discovered in the previous year by Henri Becquerel. Marie Curie described what happened.

The discovery of the X-ray by Röntgen had excited the imagination, and many physicians were trying to discover if similar rays were not emitted by fluorescent bodies under the action of light. With this question in mind Henri Becquerel was studying uranium salts, and as sometimes occurs came upon a phenomenon different from what he was looking for: the spontaneous emission by uranium salts of rays of a peculiar character. This was the discovery of radioactivity.

The particular phenomenon discovered by Becquerel was as follows: uranium compound placed upon a photographic plate covered with black paper produces on that plate an impression analogous to that which light would make. The impression is due to uranium rays that traverse the paper. These same rays can, like X-rays, discharge an electroscope by making the air which surrounds it a conductor.

Henri Becquerel assured himself that these properties persist when the uranium compound is kept in darkness during several months. The next step was to ask whence came this energy, of minute quantity, it is true, but constantly given off by uranium compounds under the form of radiations.

The study of this phenomenon seemed to us [Pierre and Marie] very attractive and all the more so because the question was entirely new and nothing yet had been written upon it. I decided to undertake an investigation of it. In order to go beyond the results reached by Becquerel, it was necessary to employ a precise quantitative method. The phenomenon that best lent itself to measurement was the conductibility produced in the air by uranium rays. This phenomenon, which is called ionisation, is produced also by X-rays and investigation of it in connection with them had made known its principal characteristics.

For measuring the very feeble currents that one can make pass through air ionised by uranium rays, I had at my disposal an excellent method we had developed. This consists in counterbalancing on a sensitive electrometer the quantity of electricity carried by the current with that which a piezo-electric quartz can furnish. The installation therefore required a Curie electrometer, a piezo-electric quartz and a chamber of ionisation, which last was formed by a plate condenser whose higher plate was joined to the electrometer, while the lower plate, charged with a known potential, was covered with a thin layer of the substance to be examined.

Needless to say, the place for such an electrometric installation was hardly the crowded and damp little room in which I had to set it up. My experiments proved that the radiation of uranium compounds can be measured with precision under determined conditions, and that this radiation is an atomic property of the element of uranium. Its intensity is proportional to the quantity of uranium contained in the compound.

I undertook next to discover if there were other elements possessing the same property, and with this aim I examined all the elements then known, either in their pure state or in compounds. I found that among these bodies, thorium compounds are the only ones which emit rays similar to those of uranium. The radiation of thorium has an intensity of the same order as that of uranium, and is, as in the case of uranium, an atomic property of the element.

It was necessary at this point to find a new term to define this new property of matter manifested by the elements of uranium and thorium. I proposed the word 'radioactivity' which has since become generally adopted. During the course of my research, I had had occasion to examine not only simple compounds, salts and oxides, but also a great number of minerals. Certain ones proved radioactive; these were those containing uranium and thorium; but their radioactivity seemed abnormal, for it was much greater than the amount I had found in uranium and thorium had led me to expect.

This abnormality greatly surprised us. It became necessary to find an explanation. I then made the hypothesis that the ores of uranium and thorium contain in small quantity a substance much more strongly radioactive than either uranium or thorium. This substance could not be one of the known elements, because these had already been examined; it must, therefore, be a new chemical element.

I had a passionate desire to verify this hypothesis as rapidly as possible. And Pierre Curie, keenly interested in the question, abandoned his work on crystals (provisionally, he thought) to join me in the search for this unknown substance.

We chose, for our work, the ore pitchblende, a uranium ore, which in its pure state is about four times more active than oxide of uranium. Since the composition of this ore was known through very careful chemical analysis, we could expect to find, at a maximum, one per cent of new substance. The result of our experiment proved that there were in reality new radioactive elements in pitchblende, but that their proportion did not reach even a millionth per cent!

The method we employed is a new method in chemical research based on radioactivity. It consists in inducing separation by the ordinary means of chemical analysis, and of measuring, under suitable conditions, the radioactivity of all the separate products. By this means one can note the chemical character of the radioactive element sought for, for it will become concentrated in those products which will become more and more radioactive as the separation progresses. We soon recognised that the radioactivity was concentrated principally in two different chemical fractions, and we became able to recognise in pitchblende the presence of at least two new radioactive elements: polonium and radium. We announced the existence of polonium in July 1898, and of radium in December of the same year.

In spite of this relatively rapid progress, our work was far from finished. In our opinion, there could be no doubt of the existence of these new elements, but to make chemists admit their existence, it was necessary to isolate them. Now, in our most strongly radioactive products (several hundred times more active than uranium), the polonium and radium were present only as traces. The polonium occurred associated with bismuth extracted from pitchblende, and radium accompanied the barium extracted from the same mineral. We already knew by what methods we might hope to separate polonium from bismuth and radium from barium; but to accomplish such a separation we had to have at our disposition much larger quantities of the primary ore than we had. It was during this period of our research that we were extremely handicapped by inadequate conditions, by the lack of a proper place to work in, by the lack of money and of personnel.

Pitchblende was an expensive mineral, and we could not afford to buy a sufficient quantity. At that time the principal source of this mineral was at St Joachimsthal (Bohemia), where there was a mine which the Austrian government worked for the extraction of uranium. We believed that we would find all the radium and a part of the polonium in the residues of this mine, residues which had so far not been used at all. Thanks to the influence of the Academy of Sciences of Vienna, we secured several tons of these residues at an advantageous price, and we used it as our primary material. In the beginning we had to draw on our private resources to pay the costs of our experiment; later we were given grants.

We had to start them our chemical treatments in an abandoned storeroom. This was a wooden shed with a glass roof which did not keep the rain out. The only objects it contained were some worn pine tables, a cast-iron stove, which worked badly, and the blackboard which Pierre Curie loved to use. There were no hoods to carry away the poisonous gases thrown off in our chemical treatments, so that it was necessary to carry them on outside in the courtyard, but when the weather was bad we went on with them inside, leaving the windows open.

In this makeshift laboratory, we worked practically for two years. Then it became necessary for us to divide our work. Pierre Curie continued the investigations on the properties of radium, while I went ahead with the chemical experiments which had as their objective the preparation of pure radium salts. I had to work with as much as twenty kilogrammes of material at a time, so that the hangar was filled with great vessels full of precipitates and of liquids. It was exhausting work to move the containers about, to transfer the liquids and to stir for hours at a time, with an iron bar, the boiling material in the cast-iron basin. I extracted from the mineral the radium-bearing barium and this, in the state of chloride, I submitted to a fractional crystallisation.

The radium accumulated in the least soluble parts. The very delicate operations of the last crystallisations were exceedingly difficult to carry out in that laboratory, where it was impossible to find protection from the iron and coal dust. At the end of a year, results indicated clearly that it would be easier to separate radium than polonium; that is why we concentrated our efforts in this direction. We examined the radium salts we obtained with the aim of discovering their powers and we loaned samples of the salts to several scientists, in particular to Henri Becquerel.

During the years 1899 and 1900, Pierre Curie published with me a memoir on our discoveries.

The main result of our investigations and of those of other scientists during these years, was to make known the nature of the rays emitted by radium, and to prove that they belonged to three different categories. Radium emits a stream of active corpuscles moving with great speed. Certain of them carry a positive charge and form the Alpha rays; others, much smaller, carry a negative charge and form Beta rays. The movements of these two groups are influenced by a magnet. A third group is constituted by the rays that are insensible to the action of a magnet, and that, we know today, are a radiation similar to light and to X-rays.

We had an especial joy in observing that our products containing concentrated radium were all spontaneously luminous.

The Congress of 1900 offered us an opportunity to make known, to foreign scientists, our new radioactive bodies. This was one of the points on which the interest of this Congress chiefly centred.

We were at this time entirely absorbed in the new field that opened before us, thanks to the discovery so little expected. And we were very happy in spite of the difficult conditions under which we worked. We passed our days at the laboratory, often eating a simple student's lunch there. A great tranquillity reigned in our poor, shabby hangar; occasionally, while observing an operation, we would walk up and down *talking of our work, present and future. When we were cold, a cup of hot tea, drunk beside the stove, cheered us. We lived in a preoccupation as complete as that of a dream.*

Sometimes we returned in the evening after dinner for another survey of our domain. Our precious products, for which we had no shelter, were arranged on tables and boards; from all sides we could see their slightly luminous silhouettes, and these gleamings, which seemed suspended in the darkness, stirred us with ever new emotion and enchantment.

Marie Curie had the rare distinction of being awarded two Nobel Prizes, one in 1903 for Physics, which she shared with her husband and Henri Becquerel, and the other in 1911 for Chemistry. Pierre Curie died in a Paris street accident in 1906; he was run over by a carriage in a snowstorm.

Unfortunately, what the Curies had discovered was an extremely dangerous element. Radium is more than a million times more radioactive than uranium. The luminosity of radium led to its one-time use in luminous paints for watches, clocks, aircraft switches and instrument dials. At least a hundred watch dial painters who used their lips to shape their paintbrushes into points died as a result of the radiation. Radium was still used in this way until as late as the 1950s, even though twenty years earlier it had been found that workers exposed to radium by handling luminescent paints suffered serious health hazards. Sores, anaemia and bone cancer were identified as results of radium exposure. Marie Curie's own life may have been shortened by handling radium; she died at the relatively early age of sixty-seven. Her notes are still strongly radioactive a hundred years after she last handled them. The use of radium ceased soon after it was realised how dangerous it was and products containing radium – it had even been added to toothpaste and food – fell rapidly out of use. Radium is now in use only in controlled medical environments as a cancer treatment.

THE UNCONSCIOUS MIND
(1900)

SIGMUND FREUD

An idea of a part of the human mind as unconscious has existed since antiquity. The ancient Hindu texts, the Vedas, written between 2500 and 600 BC, contain the idea. Philosophers in the West developed the idea later, though not entirely independently of the early writings in the East. Baruch Spinoza, Gottfried Leibniz, Arthur Schopenhauer and Friedrich Nietzsche all had something to contribute to the idea of an unconscious mind – before Freud arrived on the scene. Schopenhauer's view of the human mind was influenced by his reading of the Vedas and the Jewish mysticism in the Kabbalah.

The great discoverer of the unconscious was Sigmund Freud. He had his own antecedents and influences, for example Jewish thought traditions, which helped him to develop his view of the unconscious. But he also drew on the findings of earlier medics. In 1884, an Austrian neurologist called Joseph Breuer told Freud about an experience he had had, in which hysteria was cured by hypnosis, a technique which had helped the patient to recall painful past experiences. The experience of recall had been a kind of catharsis. Freud was deeply impressed by this and he developed Breuer's cathartic technique to a point where it became the foundation stone of modern psychoanalysis. After absorbing Breuer's technique, using hypnosis, Freud developed another. He invented free association, which he used instead of hypnosis to find out what was going on below the surface of the conscious mind.

In 1893, Freud persuaded Breuer that he ought to publish his breakthrough in the treatment of hysteria, and so in 1895 Freud and Breuer together published a book called *Studies in Hysteria*.

Freud's take on the unconscious was a utilitarian one, one that well suited the Western mindset of the twentieth century. It involved a person-to-person (patient-to-therapist) examination of the human mind, and a particular human mind at that, with a view to solving the patient's psychiatric problems. It was a very new kind of intervention, within the human mind, to sort out behavioural and emotional disturbances. This approach to the unconscious mind was a long way from the Eastern mystical approach; it was not religious, not at all religious, but medical in nature. This therapeutic dialogue with the interior of the human mind was called psychoanalysis. While Freud and his followers drew generalities and common themes out of his case studies, the focus of the therapy was on the individual character of the unconscious mind of a particular patient.

Freud made his discovery about the nature of the unconscious mind while trying to help patients overcome neuroses. He got his patients to tell him their dreams, and he realised that these gave him access to what was going on in the dreamers' unconscious minds. Dreams, he believed, are the truthful expression of the unconscious mind. The inferences Freud drew from these therapy sessions were published in *The Interpretation of Dreams* (*Die Traumdeutung*), his landmark book published in 1900.

Freud took the view that consciousness is a relatively shallow surface layer of the mind, dealing with perceptions. Below the conscious layer of the mind is the preconscious and below that is the unconscious. The unconscious is a cellarage of instinctual desires, drives, needs and psychic actions, acting well below the perceptions of the conscious mind. This is the realm where significant psychic events take place.

Put more simply, in our everyday thoughts we do not have access to what is going on in our unconscious minds. Past experiences, thoughts and memories that the conscious mind has 'forgotten' reside for ever in the unconscious mind and from there they direct the conscious thoughts and feelings of the individual. This is where the therapeutic nature of the dialogue becomes useful: in helping to explain why an individual acts, thinks, feels as he or she does. The individual is thought of as not forgetting anything in the everyday sense of accidental memory loss. Instead the individual suppresses or represses certain memories or incidents because they are too difficult to deal with. Part of the therapy is to revive that repressed material, to put the patient back in touch with painful memories in order to deal with them properly.

Freud saw the conscious mind as the ego, and the unconscious mind as containing two parts, the superego and the id. The superego is in effect the part of the mind where the conscience resides. The id is the animal instincts.

One major change that this discovery brought was the introduction of a whole new approach to helping people in psychic distress of one sort or another. This was to extend from patients suffering from serious personality disorders that prevented them from functionally normally at all – people who earlier in the nineteenth century would have been written off as lunatics – across the spectrum to people who were simply unhappy. It has led on to other tiers of dialogue-based assistance such as grief counselling and crime victim support. The therapist acts as a mediator who tries to allow the patient's conscious mind to make contact with and understand the hidden and repressed contents of their unconscious mind.

An essential part of the mediation, right from the earliest days of psychoanalysis, has been the interpretation of the encrypted contents of the unconscious mind. The material is often stored or expressed in symbolic form, and the symbols have to be interpreted by the therapist. This is where Freud's method aroused suspicion – and still arouses suspicion. In The *Interpretation of Dreams*, Freud narrates his patient's dream, then identifies the symbolic content (which is a subjective matter, selecting the content that he is interested in), then identifies the sexual elements in it. The argument of the book is that dreams are disguised manifestations of repressed sexual desires. Once Freud has reached the sexual content of the dream he is well satisfied. Then he has arrived at his goal – '*the* interpretation' is the phrase he himself uses. Anyone reading *The Interpretation of Dreams* can see straight away that this tells us more about Freud's mind than about the patient's; several other interpretations are always possible. Probably a better title might have been *An Interpretation of Dreams*. In fact, Freud sorely tried the patience of many friends and colleagues as he too dogmatically developed his ideas. Many of them thought he was too insistent on the role of sex in the mind and especially in the role of repressed sexual urges. It was altogether too doctrinaire. This obsession was all too plain in his major and most famous publication.

Freud attracted a great following. His ideas understandably excited enormous interest and controversy in the early twentieth century. They were not just exciting and new and revolutionary – they were sensational. In 1902, he was appointed Extraordinary Professor of Neuropathology at Vienna University. He also started holding weekly seminars at his home. These were meetings of men who were thinking along similar, though not necessarily the same, lines, but all of them were adventurous explorers of the human psyche. In 1908, the informal weekly meetings at his home became formalised into the Vienna Psychoanalytical Society, which changed its name in 1910 to the International Psychoanalytical Association. It was a revolution in medicine, and a revolution in thought. It was akin to the surge of discoveries about the physiological workings of the human body when doctors and their students were formally permitted to dissect corpses.

CARL GUSTAV JUNG

Conspicuous among the followers who attended Freud's seminars were Alfred Adler, Ernest Jones and Carl Gustav Jung. In many ways, Jung was Freud's most outstanding pupil or disciple. It was he who became the International Psychoanaytical Association's first president. He and Freud told one another their dreams and interpreted them for one another; they became very close friends. But there came a parting of the ways. Jung said it was because Freud revealed something to him in total confidence and said that he could not own up to it publicly because it would reduce his authority. Jung felt this was inconsistent with what they were trying to achieve, and Freud's authority was not the most important consideration. The rift was complete and extremely bitter, and the truth of what passed between them has never been revealed.

John Freeman tried to tease something out of the elderly Jung when interviewing him for the television programme *Face to Face*. It was obvious that Jung knew more than anyone else about the workings of Freud's mind, but even in his final year of life Jung stoutly refused to betray the doctor's traditional oath of confidentiality. He smiled and said, 'There's such a thing as a professional secret.'

Freud was so bitter about Jung's departure that he refused to let Jung help him to escape from the Nazis. In 1938, Jung organised a go-between to deliver a substantial sum of money to Freud, literally on his doorstep, to enable him to escape, but Freud refused to accept it; the money was tainted because it had come from Jung. A plan that did not involve Jung succeeded, and the Freud family was safely moved to London. Freud died in London, of cancer, within the year.

Jung had a very poor relationship with his father, a Protestant pastor who was cold, stern and tyrannical. A Freudian bystander might have judged that Freud was playing a very dangerous game with the younger man by adopting the role of the dogmatic and dictatorial father, in effect making Jung relive an unpleasant experience that he had left behind. The more Freud acted the father, the more Jung played the role of the ultra-rebellious son. One tyrant father was quite enough. Probably this is what their colleague Ernest Jones thought, as he watched the personal and professional tragedy unfold. Quite apart from the personal dynamics of the situation, Jung probably needed to detach himself from the father-figure Freud, to put distance between them, in order to spread his wings and develop his own ideas.

He was to develop the idea of the unconscious in an even more ambitious way than Freud. But first he had a serious mental breakdown, brought on by the trauma of separation from Freud. The fact that he broke down so severely is an indication that the separation really was based on the deep-seated personal dynamics of the relationship, not on any professional disagreement. It lasted – significantly – for the duration of World War I. Jung even made the bizarre suggestion that the external struggle was a projection of his own breakdown, but that was part of his temporary insanity. He went on seeing patients during this period; one wonders whether he can have helped them in any significant way. It is known that he diagnosed one patient who was unfortunate enough to knock on his door for help as being in the final stages of syphilis. Jung gave him only weeks to live. The surprisingly level-headed patient went off to seek a second opinion; he turned out to be (merely) manic-depressive and lived on for another fifty years.

Emerging from his breakdown, Jung entered a long and fruitful period when he developed his own style of psychoanalysis, and his own view of the unconscious mind. He went on using Freud's method of trawling the contents of his patients' dreams as a means of access to the patients' unconscious mind, but analysed the dreams in a much looser and less doctrinaire way than Freud. He demonstrated his method in a comprehensive analysis of the published dreams of an anonymous American woman (known as 'Miss Miller'), whom it seems he never met. She was suffering from schizophrenia at the turn of the twentieth century. The demonstration analysis is a brilliant showcase of Jung's method, a *tour de force*. It was written in 1911 and first published in 1912, just before his breakdown commenced, as *Wandlungen und Symbole der Libido*. It appeared in 1924 as *Symbols of Transformation*. Jung himself said, 'This book became a landmark, set up on the spot where the two ways divided.'

It was a prophetic comment. *Symbols of Transformation*, now, nearly a century later, looks like an even more monumental landmark in the development of our understanding of the human mind. It is a truly wonderful book, though not easy reading. Jung opened with a reflection on Freud's sensational revelations. He knew that most people reading Freud's *Interpretation of Dreams* would be 'outraged by the novelty and seemingly unjustified boldness of his procedure', and that they would be 'morally indignant over the stark nudity of his dream interpretations'. He nevertheless hoped that people would stay calm, look beyond all that and 'turn away from the vast confusion of the present to glimpse the higher continuity of history.' That was very much Jung's approach: the panoramic, Olympian view.

He divided the unconscious into two parts, the personal unconscious and the collective unconscious. The personal unconscious is, in Jung's as it was in Freud's conception, a reservoir of material that has occupied the conscious mind at some stage but has been forgotten or repressed. We have easy and frequent communication between our conscious minds and the personal unconscious. For instance, we can consciously make an appointment with a dentist, and store that information in our memory. A week later we may be having a conversation with a neighbour and in the middle of it suddenly remember that we have to be at the dentist in half an hour; the information is suddenly presented to us by our personal unconscious, functioning as a PA.

The collective unconscious, which was Jung's specific and very great discovery, is an even deeper level of the human psyche. It contains the accumulation of inherited experiences and it has never been conscious. It is inborn. The collective unconscious is less accessible, and filled with ancient and mythic material. This ancient material exists in the form of archetypes, which may be primal images or situations.

The collective unconscious is an area of the psyche that can be distinguished from the personal unconscious by the fact that it does not owe its existence to personal experience and consequently is not a personal acquisition. The personal unconscious consists mostly of complexes. The collective unconscious consists mainly of archetypes, which are elementary or primordial thoughts. In mythological research, these are usually called 'motifs'. In the psychology of archaic societies, they correspond to Levy-Bruhl's concept of 'collective representations'. In comparative religion, they have been called 'categories of the imagination'. Jung's idea of the archetype, literally a pre-existing form, did not spring out of nowhere; it already existed in other fields of knowledge under other names. His big idea was that the collective unconscious consisted of a universal and impersonal suite of archetypes which is identical in all individuals, regardless of time, race or culture. It is not developed but is inherited. The collective unconscious gives definite form to certain contents of the psyche. The archetypes only appear in the conscious mind in some secondary form, but may have a powerful effect on it.

Myths and fairy tales are familiar expressions of the archetypes. So too are religious texts. Archetypes include trinity, quaternity, anima (a compensating feminine principle in men), animus (a compensating masculine principle in women), wheel, circle, child, father, mother (earth mother), maiden, wise old man, shadow, trickster. There are also archetypal situations, such as a transformation in a cave, the child surviving danger, rebirth. It is easy to see how myths, religious epics, fairy tales, children's stories and even adult novels might be made to resonate with an assemblage of archetypes – and this is what gives them their psychic power. Wagner's operas (the last of them completed when Jung was seven years old) are full of them, and that is why they strike us as so elemental and powerful; whether we *like* them or not is immaterial, but they activate our psyches at that deeper level.

The old Catholic Church was an enormous reservoir of archetypes, which resonated deeply in the hearts of European Christians through the Middle Ages. Seeing and hearing archetypes exercised externally was a way of putting people in touch with their innermost selves. By the 1930s, Jung came to see the Protestant Reformation as psychically destructive. The literal iconoclasm in the churches – the smashing of stained glass windows, the demolition of stone statues of saints, the destruction of saints' shrines – was paralleled by an intellectual and psychic iconoclasm. It resulted in a psychic catastrophe. Protestant Europe cut itself off from its archetypes. Jung was not advocating Catholicism as such, simply pointing out that it was an effective public stage for many archetypes. Had Christianity not prevailed in Europe, but the older pagan religions, then they might well have done the same job. But the rich symbolism of the medieval Catholic Church was swept away and replaced with – nothing.

Jung saw the world of the last two or three centuries as a world of growing impoverishment of symbols, a world of vanishing mysteries. As he wrote, significantly bringing his unsatisfactory father into the story, 'We inherited this poverty from our fathers. I well remember the confirmation lessons I received at the hands of my own father. The catechism bored me unspeakably. One day I was turning over the pages of my little book, in the hope of finding something interesting, when my eye fell on the paragraphs about the Trinity. This interested me at once, and I waited impatiently for the lessons to get to that section. But when the longed-for lesson arrived, my father said: "We'll skip this bit; I can't make head or tail of it myself." With that my hope was laid in the grave. I admired my father's honesty, but this did not alter the fact that from then on all talk of religion bored me to death.' Religion only works if there is mystery, and Protestantism drained off the mystery.

This spiritual impoverishment is why increasing numbers of people are getting into psychological difficulties. There is a vacuum. Attempts have been made to fill it with milk-and-water oriental mysticism, astrology, ley lines and the like, but they are poor substitutes for the richness of the old religions with their rich mythic brews of archetypes.

Another manifestation of the unconscious mind is the so-called 'compensating unconscious'. The unconscious sometimes works in an opposite direction to the conscious mind in order to ensure psychic balance. This, Jung argued, explains why people with a certain type of personality, especially if it is a strongly delineated personality, will occasionally and suddenly behave out of character. This may help us to understand how ruthless businessmen suddenly engage in bouts of sentimental philanthropy.

OBJECTIONS AND RESERVATIONS

Jacques Lacan adopted another approach, contending that the unconscious is structured like a language. In his view, the unconscious is not more primitive or archetypal than the conscious mind; both are linguistically based. Lacan's ideas on the structure of language were largely drawn from the work of Roman Jakobson and Ferdinand de Saussure. Because Saussure's model of language is regarded as obsolete and superseded, it follows that Lacan's entire model for the functioning of the mind as language-dependent must also be rejected.

These are but three examples, albeit major examples, of the way psychology has regarded the unconscious mind. Practitioners of psychology continue to disagree about the true nature of the unconscious mind. Meanwhile, in the larger world outside clinical and theoretical psychology, there have been any number of applications of these new ideas. Without Freud's *Interpretation of Dreams* there could have been no novel called *Sons and Lovers* by D. H. Lawrence. Without Jung's *Symbols of Transformation* there would have been no opera called *The Midsummer Marriage* by Michael Tippett.

Among philosophers, one of Freud's most distinguished contemporary opponents was Karl Popper. Popper argued that Freud's theory of the unconscious was not falsifiable, and because of this it was not scientific. He was not objecting to the idea of things happening in our mind that we are unconscious of, only that they are not falsifiable. By falsifiable, Popper meant testable. For a statement to be scientific it must be possible to make an observation or devise a physical experiment – and so prove it or disprove it. A proposition might be true, yet not be capable of proof. An example is the statement 'all men are mortal'. No amount of observation of any number of human lives could prove that this statement is true, because there might still be the child, perhaps born today, who will never die. Popper's discomfort about Freud was that what Freud said about the unconscious mind was not only unprovable but untestable.

The science theorist Adolf Grünbaum argued differently from Popper, that psychoanalysis might be testable but that there are serious problems with the evidence. This turned out to be true. David Holmes looked through sixty years' worth of research into the Freudian concept of repression – the 'burial' of unpalatable memories in the unconscious mind. What Holmes found was that there was no evidence for repression at all. This is true for many other hypotheses put forward by Freud. Findings like these (for example, the conspicuous lack of evidence that the unconscious behaves as Freud said it should) have led some psychologists to propose an unconscious mind that functions in different ways. One researcher wrote of a cognitive unconscious, another wrote of an adaptive unconscious, and another wrote of a dumb unconscious.

The philosopher Ludwig Wittgenstein believed that at a fundamental level Freud had confused causes and reasons. His method of interpretation could supply reasons for new meanings, but that was useless if what was required was a causal relationship. Wittgenstein gave an example. A therapist could throw some objects on to a table. The patient could give free associations for each of the objects and the therapist could give interpretations for them. The outcome would be the attribution of a meaning to each object – but the psychic causes would still remain obscure.

Many others have criticised Freud's approach to the unconscious but, as Bertrand Russell pointed out in 1952, often they have done so from the point of view of its applicability (or otherwise) in fields other than those that Freud had in mind. Whatever approach to the unconscious mind we choose to follow, there is no doubt that the speculation, research and theorising about it that has gone on for over a hundred years has enriched the world. The far-reaching ideas of Freud and Jung especially have given the twentieth century much of its character. It is hard to see how the art forms of first the novel and then the biography could have developed in the way that that they have without Freud. The insights gained have been sharp, but also destructive; it is scarcely possible to pick up a modern biography (of a deceased subject, at least) without having to wade through a disproportionate amount of speculation about the subject's sex life, and especially the skeletons in the cupboard, real or imagined. By a neat piece of irony, a 1990s biography of Jung revealed that he (allegedly) had a homosexual relationship as a teenager and then (allegedly) went on to become a seducer of his women patients. Freud would have loved both the revelation and the irony of it. Freud had opened a Pandora's box. He had let a genie out of a bottle, when he unleashed the sex demon as an explanation – no, *the* explanation – for human behaviour.

Jung's approach to the unconscious mind, and to the workings of the mind in general is immeasurably richer and more exhilarating than Freud's, which often seems squalid, mundane and over simplified by comparison. Jung's method not only explained the dreams and fantasies of disturbed patients, but also the content of great literature like Goethe or Shakespeare, or the content of ancient myths and religions. His approach opened a door to understanding modern phenomena like Adolf Hitler and UFOs. Freud opened a door not only onto the unconscious mind but on to the twentieth century way of looking at things. It would be good to think that Jung opened a door on to the twenty-first century way of looking. Time will tell.

THE PALACE OF MINOS
AT KNOSSOS
(1900)

Knossos is like Troy, an ancient city known in antiquity, known to Homer, and then lost to sight for many hundreds of years. Just as Heinrich Schliemann is invariably credited with discovering Troy, Arthur Evans is credited with discovering Knossos. But once again the story is more complicated than that.

Between 2000 and 1100 BC there was a Bronze Age city at Knossos in central Crete, but when people talk of Knossos they usually mean the biggest building in that city, the palace of Minos discovered by Evans in 1900. The palace is complicated – a big site with many chambers and passageways, and several building phases. It is further complicated by the assumptions, tastes and preferences of its main excavator and his alterations to the site. The palace was in use until the end of the Minoan civilisation, after which it gradually fell into ruins. In the classical period, it lay on the south-eastern corner of the city, either shunned as a taboo place or respectfully avoided as a great antiquity. In the classical period, 200–100 BC, coins minted at Knossos showed the mythical Minotaur and a Labyrinth. The Knossians were proud of their local legend about Minos, Ariadne, Theseus and the Minotaur, and the ruins of the palace were probably still pointed out as the Labyrinth.

The history of the site's rediscovery in the late nineteenth century explains how some of the mistakes were made. Antiquaries visiting the area were distracted by the visible remains of the classical town to the north. Pliny said that no trace of the Knossos Labyrinth remained, so no one with a classical education expected to see it. Less scholarly visitors wanting to see the Labyrinth were taken to Roman stone quarries at

Gortyn far to the south. Even so, it is odd that the Minoan building remained unrecognised until so late; there were some well-crafted blocks of masonry visible at the surface, which showed where it was.

Once the site was identified, there were political barriers to exploration. Because Crete was under Turkish control, any significant finds would have to be sent to Constantinople and the Cretan Assembly did not want anything to leave Crete, so any excavations that looked as though they might unearth anything significant were halted. During the long delay, an expectation grew that this was a Mycenaean palace.

Arthur Evans's major excavation of Knossos started in 1900. Evans described himself as the discoverer of the Palace of Minos at Knossos, but there was a good deal of activity on the site before that. In 1878, a local businessman from Heraklion, Minos Kalokairinos, opened trenches on the top of the tell at Knossos, the Kephala Hill, and found an oblong building, which he thought was the palace of Minos. He even drew a sketch plan of the building with the proud title 'le Palais de Minos'. At the same time, in London, Evans was viewing with great excitement the exhibition of Schliemann's finds from Troy.

In 1879, sensing that Kalokairinos was finding a site of great significance, the Cretan Assembly stopped his dig. Two years followed during which there was no excavation; Kalokairinos must have found this very frustrating, as his initial finds were very promising. In 1881, an American journalist called Stillman wrote a report on the site in which he described it as the Labyrinth of Daedalus. Daedalus was the legendary engineer and architect who was commissioned by King Minos to build a labyrinth to house the Minotaur. Stillman's choice of phrase is interesting because the labyrinth in the Knossos of legend was distinct from the palace of Minos: it was a separate building with a separate function. The palace was the dwelling for the king, the Labyrinth was the dwelling for the Minotaur.

In 1883, Arthur Evans toured the mainland of Greece, including Mycenae, another ruined ancient city that teetered on the brink between myth and Bronze Age reality. He visited Schliemann to discuss Schliemann's Mycenaean finds. At this point, Evans had not thought of excavating Knossos, but Schliemann had. He, Schliemann, was going to visit Knossos in three years' time and he may well have discussed this future project with Knossos in the context of the mainland Bronze Age palaces at Mycenae and Tiryns.

In 1886, Schliemann went to Knossos and was given a guided tour by Kalokairinos. Schliemann noted that it was 'a vast edifice similar to the prehistoric palace of Tiryns.' He wanted to purchase the site and excavate it, but was unable to reach an agreement on price. Two years later, Flinders Petrie discovered the destroyed remains of the Egyptian Labyrinth at Hawara, which was known to have been a temple. Evans was impressed by this discovery. The Roman author Pliny had described Hawara as the first labyrinth, Knossos as one of the first four, and Knossos had been modelled on Hawara. Now that the lost Hawara Labyrinth had been discovered, Evans began to think that the Knossos Labyrinth might be found too.

In 1889, Schliemann made one last attempt to buy what he now called 'the palace of the kings of Knossos', and failed. The next year Schliemann died, which changed the dynamics of European archaeology overnight. It is hard now to imagine, but Schliemann's rapid excavations and spectacular discoveries at site after site – Troy, Mycenae and Tiryns – made him the central figure in world archaeology. He was a figure of enormous and daunting authority, even if many of his co-scholars thought him devious and deceitful. Evans may have begun to see himself as Schliemann's potential heir and successor. Evans pretended to disapprove of Schliemann. Evans was a snob, and Schliemann was an ostentatious spender of what English snobs liked to call 'new money'. Evans was forgetting, as such people often do, that his own father had made the Evans family fortune out of a paper mill. Even so, Evans admired and envied Schliemann and it was not long before Evans was tying his finds in Crete to Homer, just like Schliemann at Troy and Mycenae.

In 1894, Evans visited Heraklion, where he met Kalokairinos and visited Knossos for the first time – but already *knowing* that he would find there a Mycenaean palace. Evans initially ridiculed Kalokairinos's idea that it was the palace of Minos, but I suspect that was again out of snobbery: what did Kalokairinos, a mere businessman from Heraklion, know about archaeology? Evans was later to adopt Kalokairinos's phrase exactly, though in English rather French, for the title of his great work on the site, *The Palace of Minos*. Perhaps he sensed that it made good copy. I think Kalokairinos's name for the site was a joke. His own name was Minos, after all. Perhaps if he had been named Yannis the misleading name would never have appeared on Kalokairinos's plan – or on the spines of Evans's much later multi-volume book.

Evans bought the site and in 1900 he started excavating, determined from the first day that he was going to uncover a Bronze Age palace. Because he was wealthy, he was able to take an independent line, and there was no pressure on him to justify his assumptions. He just went on finding evidence that fitted his initial assumptions about the site. There is a flicker of reconsideration in his pencilled notes when he comments that the walls are 'very complex, but hardly as Stillman proposes the Labyrinth itself.' Evans added later: 'No, on further examination I think it must be so.' This was never followed through systematically. Had Evans thought of the significance of this distinction, he would have remembered that – in the legend – there were two distinct buildings, the palace where the king lived and the house of the Minotaur. The Palace of Minos and the Labyrinth are two buildings. Which of the two was Evans excavating?

Evans first opened up the whole of the oblong building that Kalokairinos had sampled, and therefore in effect already discovered. There were well-preserved walls standing up to 1.8 metres (6 feet) high, with rows of giant storage jars along the west side. Then he found the Throne Room, which seemed to supply the evidence he needed that this was a palace, but it was tiny, and none of the rest of the building looked like a palace.

There was a major conservation problem, because the floors and wall veneers were made of soluble gypsum. The site could not be left open to the winter rains. This led Evans into reconstructing walls up to ceiling height and adding roofs. But he added some misleading features, such as the large staircase at the southern end, where there had been no staircase in antiquity; we know this from the pencil plans drawn by his architect. Evans's intention was to suggest to visitors that the southern end of the building was a kind of foyer to the chambers up on the first floor. Because the first floor had been destroyed, Evans felt free to say what he liked about it, so he described the Piano Nobile, as he grandly named the upper storey, as containing a suite of royal apartments.

Evans was nevertheless relieved to find the building continuing into a North Range, and then that joining an East Wing. Instead of a small oblong building, the palace was a huge irregular building planned round the four sides a rectangular Central Court. In the East Wing, Evans was relieved to find chambers he could call royal apartments. The centre-piece of these was the Hall of the Double-Axes, but it is still quite small. It is also oddly placed at the foot of a staircase, surrounded by small chambers and buried more than 6 metres (20 feet) below the level of the Central Court. It would have had no direct light, even from the east, because the high boundary wall of the palace rose only a few feet away in that direction. It was a dark and dismal cellar. The so-called royal apartments were claustrophobic, dungeon-like.

Evans nevertheless managed to sell his idea of the building as a palace by his vivid word pictures in his book and in his lectures, and also in the reconstruction paintings he commissioned from Piet de Jong. De Jong made the chambers look more spacious and airy by flooding them with light and by drawing the human figures smaller, which deceives the eye into seeing the rooms as fifty per cent larger than they are. Evans learnt several lessons from Schliemann the trickster. Evans worked for thirty years to promote the idea that he had been the discoverer of Knossos. He treated Minos Kalokairinos in much the same way that Schliemann treated Frank Calvert – with disdain and ingratitude – yet he was prepared to take over Kalokairinos's excavation, and his interpretation of the site as the Palace of King Minos.

Evans wrote four volumes about *The Palace of Minos*, full of references to its religious function. He argued that the Throne Room proved the site's royal character, but when describing the room he used words like sacral, shrine, chapter house, ceremony of anointing, ritual, religious; it 'teemed with religious suggestion' and reminded him of initiation sanctuaries in Anatolia. Yet the name Palace of Minos continues in use.

In 1989, my book *The Knossos Labyrinth* was published. Each room in the labyrinth is interpreted afresh, based on the archaeological evidence found in it. What emerges is that there are several suites of rooms dedicated to a wide range of religious rituals, opening onto the Central Court. The outside of the building is in effect the 'backs' of all of these suites; the 'fronts' face onto the Central Court. The Labyrinth was an inside-out building, which is why it was a puzzle-building to people of later periods – hence the maze idea. The idea of the enclosed sunken areas as places for initiation rituals was confirmed by a spectacular find on the island of Santorini, where a more complete Bronze Age initiation suite has been found, complete with wall paintings. The frescoes, both on Santorini and at Knossos, tell us what went on in the adjacent spaces and their precise cult significance. A long entrance corridor at Knossos, for instance, had on its walls a life-size frieze of Minoan worshippers walking in solemn procession towards an elaborately dressed priestess or goddess (part of this, reconstructed, can be seen in Heraklion Museum). And nearly all the frescoes at Knossos show religious ceremonies of one kind or another.

Where does all of this lead? It leads to the discovery that the Knossos Labyrinth was a huge temple – and probably of the same general type as was being built in Egypt and Anatolia at the same time. Arthur Evans did not discover the Palace of Minos because that has yet to be discovered. What he and Kalokairinos were excavating was, as Stillman said, the Labyrinth of Daedalus. The Central Court was the place where the spectacular bull-leaping ritual took place, an extraordinary display in which boys and girls and bulls appeared to dance dangerously together; and these rituals may have been partially remembered in the later story of Theseus encountering the bull-man at the centre of the Labyrinth.

THE CAUSE OF YELLOW FEVER

(1900)

Yellow fever was a great scourge in the tropics in the eighteenth and nineteenth centuries, a terrible plague. No disease, it was said, was so appalling in its symptoms, development and result, with the exception perhaps of cholera. It was particularly virulent among populations that were non-immune. People from mid-latitude cities in North America, for example, arriving in the port towns of the Mexican Gulf were especially likely to fall victim to the disease. Occasionally there were outbreaks of yellow fever well to the north. In one notorious epidemic of yellow fever in Philadelphia in 1793, ten per cent of the population died. In 1878, yellow fever invaded 132 towns in the United States, killing 15,900 people, and 4,600 in New Orleans alone.

The place where it was finally confronted and its cause traced was in Cuba. Specifically it was tracked down at the hospital at the Columbia Barracks, a garrison of 1,400 soldiers about 13 kilometres (8 miles) from the city of Havana. The year was 1900 and at that time Havana was in the grip of a yellow fever epidemic.

One theory was that poor hygiene or poor sanitation might be behind the disease, but applying every kind of sanitary improvement had made no difference whatever to the spread of the disease. Yellow fever was treated as if it was a disease of the same infectious type as cholera. Shotgun quarantine was applied; victims were kept in strictest isolation; yet still the number of cases grew. The nature of the disease was simply not understood. Several false claims had been made by medics or pseudo-medics. One had claimed that he had discovered the 'germ' that caused yellow fever. A doctor called Sanarelli claimed in Montevideo that he had successfully developed a technique of inoculation. He was treated as a hero, but only briefly. The bacillus Sanarelli had found was a strain of cholera and therefore nothing to do with yellow fever. But the US medics had to follow up the claim and a couple of them believed they had found corroboration for Sanarelli's claim when they investigated yellow fever cases at the Columbia Barracks.

In May 1900, a detachment of four medical officers from the US Army was ordered to Cuba to set to work to try to find the cause of yellow fever at the Columbia Barracks. The medics arrived there in late June. They were in a strong position to observe the spread of the disease as two nearby towns were in the midst of a yellow fever epidemic. The medical officers wondered whether insects might be spreading the disease, because of the stringent quarantine that was being exercised. Obviously mosquitoes were impervious to quarantine rules. In fact, mosquitoes had been proposed as the carriers of yellow fever by Dr Carlos Finlay of Havana; he was an enthusiastic supporter of the theory, but his view had not been taken seriously. Now the army medics thought that he might be right and felt bound to test the mosquito hypothesis. Dr Finlay was very excited at the prospect.

In August, Reed was unexpectedly recalled to Washington. Two of the remaining officers exposed the third, an assistant surgeon by the name of James Carroll, to mosquitoes. He had fallen ill with yellow fever within four days. Then under microscopes they studied slides of his blood. They had very mixed feelings about what they saw. The man did indeed have yellow fever, which was no cause for celebration – they had deliberately infected a co-worker with a dangerous illness, but the medical officers were elated that they had succeeded in manipulating the disease to that extent. They hardly dared to hope that they had the answer: that the illness was the direct result of being infected by the mosquito they had applied to him four days before.

The medical officers then found another soldier prepared to volunteer to take a mosquito bite. He just happened to approach the hospital buildings at the opportune moment. They wrote down his name, 'William Dean, Troop B, Seventh Cavalry.' He had never been in the tropics before and was therefore non-immune: an ideal guinea pig. Five days later he duly went down with yellow fever. The diagnosis confirmed, the medical officers sent a cablegram at once to inform Reed, who was now back in Washington, that they now had experimental evidence that yellow fever was transmitted by mosquitoes. The idea had been floated before, by Dr Finlay, and doubted; now they had confirmed it. It only remained now for Dr Finlay to single out eggs belonging to the carrier mosquito, hatch them and then send the sample insects to Washington for identification. The yellow fever mosquito responsible for yellow fever was identified as *Stegomyia fasciata*.

The team of medical officers responsible for the yellow fever break-through consisted of Major Walter Reed and Acting Assistant Surgeons James Carroll, Aristides Agramonte and Jesse Lazear. They were surprised and very gratified that they had made their discovery so easily and so quickly. When they arrived, they expected the undertaking to occupy them for two years.

Finding out that it was mosquitoes that caused, or at any rate carried, yellow fever – and only mosquitoes – made possible the building of the Panama Canal. It also made it possible to control and eventually stamp out the disease which had until then been the scourge of Cuba, Vera Cruz, Rio de Janeiro and New Orleans.

V
THE MODERN WORLD

HORMONES
(1903)

Claude Bernard and Charles Edouard Brown-Séquard were the first to introduce the concept of internal secretions within the human body, as early as the 1850s, though neither of these two researchers thought of the secretions as specific chemical messengers. That breakthrough discovery was made in 1903 by William Maddock Bayliss and Ernest Henry Starling. They showed that acid instilled into the duodenum, the part of the small intestine leading out of the stomach, stimulated a secretion by the pancreas. This was the first time scientists proved that one part of the human body was able to influence the behaviour of another part of the body that was remote from it. Bayliss and Starling gave the chemical messengers they discovered the name hormones, from a Greek word meaning 'impetus'. The particular hormone they discovered and described was secretin. It was secretin that they found was being secreted from the duodenum to stimulate the pancreas into secreting its digestive juice.

The discovery of secretin in 1902–3 was announced by Ernest Starling in his Croonian lectures to the Royal College of Physicians in 1905. It led on to the discovery of more and more such messengers that carry signals from one cell or group of cells to another, either by way of a special duct (exocrine hormones) or via the bloodstream (endocrine hormones). It transpired that all multicellular organisms, including plants, produce hormones to regulate the function of their different parts. In mammals, hormonal activity is ultimately master-controlled from the hypothalamus, acting on inputs it receives from the central nervous system. Hormonal secretion is also a response to more local conditions, including temperature, light and mental activity. Hormones are created within certain specialized cells, such as those in the thyroid gland, testes and ovaries.

Over the decades, more and more hormones have been discovered, along with their crucial roles in determining aspects of personality and behaviour. Hormones can stimulate or inhibit growth, affect mood, activate or inhibit the immune system, regulate metabolism, control the reproductive cycle and prepare the individual for some new activity, such as sex or fighting. A recent discovery is a class of hunger hormones (such as ghrelin and orexin) and satiety hormones (such as leptin and obestatin).

Important hormones in the human body include melatonin, serotonin, thyroxine, adrenaline, dopamine, angiotensinogen, angiotensin, gastrin, ghrelin, glucagons, inhibin, insulin, leptin, oxytocin, prolactin, relaxin, secretin, somatostatin, cortisol, aldosteron, testosterone, estradiol. More hormones are being discovered all the time. Their discovery has opened the way to new medical procedures. It is now possible to adjust irregular behaviour in various organs by administering doses of hormones. It is also possible to alter the behaviour of whole individuals, which is a more controversial ethical issue; in the field of competitive sport the use of performance-enhancing drugs has become a particular problem.

EINSTEIN'S SPECIAL THEORY OF RELATIVITY

(1905)

Newton's classical laws of physics were established in 1687. According to the Newtonian laws, the motion of a particle had to be described in relation to an inertial frame in which the particle, when not subjected to external forces, moved at a constant velocity in a straight line. Two inertial frames are related in that they move in a fixed direction at a constant speed in relation to one another. Time within the frames differs by a constant. All times can be related to an absolute time.

It was only in the nineteenth century that this view of the universe was challenged. It was known that sound needed a medium, an ether, to travel through and it was natural to propose a comparable ether for the transmission of light. By the end of the nineteenth century, scientists were proposing different ethers with different properties for the transmission of light, heat, magnetism and electricity. In the 1870s, James Clark Maxwell proposed a single universal ether, and he described his failed attempt to measure the effect of the (imagined) stationary ether's drag on the motion of the Earth. Following up Maxwell's ideas, Albert Michelson conducted his own experiments and concluded in 1881 that the hypothesis of a stationary ether was incorrect. He was encouraged to try again, but in 1887 he reported that he could find no evidence of a stationary ether; the velocity of light seemed to be independent of the velocity of the observer.

Then, while researching the Doppler shift, Woldemar Voigt produced some equations, which became known as the Lorentz equations, and these became the underpinning for the geometry of special relativity. Another major contribution came in 1889 from an Irish physicist,

George FitzGerald. He wrote a very short non-technical paper on the ether. In it he argued that the results of Michelson's experiment could only be explained if 'the length of material bodies changes, according as they are moving through the ether or across it, by an amount depending on the square of the ratio of their velocities to that of light.'

Completely independently, and without seeing FitzGerald's paper, Lorentz proposed the same thing. When Lorentz discovered that FitzGerald had already published the idea, he wrote to FitzGerald. FitzGerald's answer mentioned that he had indeed sent a paper to the journal *Science*, but did not know if they had ever published it. He was pleased that Lorentz agreed with him, because as he said, 'I have been rather laughed at for my view over here.' Lorentz was very careful from then on to acknowledge that FitzGerald was the first to propose the idea of the 'FitzGerald contraction'. Lorentz published the equations named after him (Lorentz) in 1899.

Another publication relating to special relativity was a paper by Henri Poincaré, *The measure of time*, published in 1898. By 1900, the idea of the ether as a substance was being questioned; it was now seen as 'merely space with certain physical properties'. In 1904, Poincaré came close to a theory of special relativity in his address to the International Congress of Arts and Science in St Louis. Observers in different frames will have clocks that will 'mark what one may call the local time. As demanded by the relativity principle, the observer cannot know whether he is at rest or in absolute motion.' He also said, 'It seems that this impossibility of demonstrating absolute motion is a general law of nature.'

There was a gradual run-up to the idea of special relativity, which came fully into existence in June 1905, when Albert Einstein's first paper on the subject was received. It stood out from the preceding papers on the subject in that it made no attempt to comment on or explain results of experiments, but simply and elegantly stated a new vision of the nature of the universe. In the introduction to his paper, Einstein stated that 'the introduction of a light-ether will prove to be superfluous', so that was one redundant idea out of the way. His theory was based on two principles. One is that the laws of physics take the same form in all inertial frames. The other is that in any inertial frame, the velocity of light, C, is the same whether the light is emitted by a body at rest or by a body in uniform motion. Einstein went on to deduce from his assumptions both the Lorentz equations and the FitzGerald contraction. The cluster of ideas made a coherent whole.

Einstein described the clock paradox. Two clocks C1 and C2 showing the same time start at point A. Clock C2 leaves A, moving along a closed curve to return to A; it will be found to run slow compared with clock C1, which has not moved. There is no real paradox, as C2 experiences changes in speed and direction, while C1 does not.

The initial paper was followed in September 1905 by a second short paper in which he proved the formula $E = mc^2$, which has become the icon of twentieth-century physics, a turning point in our perception of the universe.

Another paper on special relativity, not by Einstein but by Max Planck, was published in 1908. Planck was a 'big name', and it was very largely due to Planck's crusade for special relativity on Einstein's behalf that Einstein's work became noticed. Now it is Einstein rather than Planck whom we recognise and remember, but that was not how it looked in 1905. While Planck was a voice people were ready to listen to, Einstein was a nobody, a mere technical expert third class working at the patent office in Berne. We often forget that a great many ideas are published and forgotten, and a great many discoveries are made and ignored. It was by no means inevitable that anyone would take any notice of Einstein. Planck's support helped the theory to take off. Another publication in 1908 came from Hermann Minkowski. In this important paper, Minkowski demonstrated that Newton's theory of gravitation was not consistent with the theory of special relativity. That was equivalent to announcing that Einstein was making a bid to supplant Newton, that he was replacing Newtonian physics with his new view of the universe. The stakes were being raised.

Given the poor attitudes they had towards one another's work, it is surprising that the relativity pioneers came up with a consistent theory at all. Einstein was always reluctant to acknowledge any debt to the

Michelson experiments, in effect denying that he was influenced by them. Poincaré reacted to Einstein's landmark 1905 paper in a rather strange way. He lectured in Göttingen in 1909, on the subject of relativity, and failed to mention Einstein at all. Poincaré must have understood Einstein's paper and its overwhelming significance, but he declined to refer to it; in fact whenever Poincaré wrote about relativity he carefully avoided all mention of Einstein. Perhaps he regarded him as an interloper, an amateur. Einstein's response was equally pointed. He too avoided referring to Poincaré's work. Both Einstein and Poincaré acknowledged the contribution of Lorentz fulsomely. Lorentz, for his part, was less than convinced about the theory of special relativity and its dogmas. He was unhappy about the dogma that the speed of light could never be exceeded. He described that as a 'daring assertion', a 'hypothetical restriction'.

But relativity was very swiftly accepted, which is especially surprising in view of its utterly revolutionary nature. Lorentz and Einstein were jointly proposed for the 1912 Nobel Prize, but the prize committee was cautious. By the time it had made up its mind, Einstein's amazing mind had moved on – to make even more spectacular new discoveries, so he was never awarded a Nobel Prize for his theory of relativity.

THE BRITISH ANTARCTIC EXPEDITION

(1907–09)

With his experience on Scott's expedition of 1901–04 behind him, Ernest Shackleton was able to organise the British Antarctic Expedition of 1907. The new expedition's aim was to reach the South Pole, the pole round which the Earth rotated. Arriving on board the *Nimrod*, the party set up a base camp at Cape Royds on Ross Island in the Ross Sea. The 10-metre (33 feet) long hut they erected was prefabricated, and came from Humphreys' in Knightsbridge. The Shackleton Hut is still there, restored in the 1950s, and in 1997–98 the original layout of equipment and stores was re-established.

Shackleton's team included Professor Edgeworth David, a geologist from Sydney, and another geologist nominated by David, Douglas Mawson. There was another Australian, Forbes Mackay, a Sydney doctor. The three Australians were to become the first to climb Mount Erebus, Antarctica's highest mountain, in 1908. Mount Erebus, an active volcano, had been discovered in 1841 by James Clark Ross. It rises spectacularly from sea level in McMurdo Sound up to 3,794 metres (12,444 feet) above sea level and was not climbed until 1908.

The expedition divided into two. One party, led by Shackleton, made an abortive attempt to reach the South Geographic Pole. The other, the three Australians led by David, headed for the South Magnetic Pole. Shackleton's party failed to reach the South Geographic Pole, but on 16 January 1909 Mackay, David and Mawson reached the Magnetic Pole. This was a real achievement, given that David fell ill during the journey; Mawson displayed a real flair for leadership.

REACHING THE NORTH POLE
(1909)

By the beginning of the twentieth century, there were few corners of the northern hemisphere that still remained undiscovered and unvisited. The one outstanding unvisited place was the North Geographic Pole. With the North Pole, as with the South Pole, an international race quickly developed to be the first to get there. Teams from Norway, the USA and Britain competed to be the first to reach the North Pole.

The American Robert Peary, a commander in the US navy, made the earliest known attempt to reach the North Pole in 1893. After failing, Peary made two further expeditions, in 1898–1902 and 1905–06, and these failed too. The expedition of 1908–09 was going to be Peary's final attempt to reach the pole. On 5 September 1909, Peary came back from the Arctic to announce that he had reached the pole on 6 April after a thirty-eight-day sledge journey from Ellesmere Island's Cape Columbia. There was a simultaneous announcement that another American, Frederick Cook, had not only reached the pole but reached it a year before, on 21 April 1908. This took the edge off Peary's moment of glory, though Cook's claim was quickly exposed as fraudulent. Cook was unable to produce evidence of his movements across the Arctic ice and there was no corroboration for his claim. When he fled the exploration scene and was convicted for mail fraud in 1922 it seemed to confirm the total unreliability of Cook's polar claim.

But Robert Peary's claim to have reached the North Pole with his black servant Matthew Henson and four Inuit supporters also ran into difficulties. He too was unable to provide independent corroboration for his achievement, and was even reluctant to make his logbooks and diaries available for scrutiny. In the end a 1911 Act of Congress gave

Peary's claim formal recognition, but this was a politically motivated action rather than an academic evaluation. The scientists remained divided as to whether Peary had really reached the North Pole or not and the uncertainty continued long after Peary's death in 1920. One objection was that Peary was such an egotist, so bent on glory, that he was driven to invent his achievement; he had fallen short of reaching the North Pole before and there was every reason to believe that he had fallen short on this final expedition as well.

Henson had no skill at using navigational instruments, and nor had the Inuit, so they only knew that they had reached the North Pole because Peary told them they had. The one member of the team who had experience of using navigational equipment and was able to calculate latitude was Robert Bartlett, the ship's captain. Critics of Peary's honesty were and remain suspicious that Peary ordered Bartlett to turn back 225 kilometres (140 miles) south of the pole. In other words, Peary carefully excluded the one witness who could have confirmed exactly which latitude he reached.

One reason for doubting Peary's claim was that it seemed unlikely he could have made the journey there and back so fast; his travel was at a claimed rate of 48 kilometres (30 miles) a day through the final five days. It was known that early in the journey he was delayed for six days by a stretch of open water.

On the other hand, Peary had a substantial back-up team, consisting of twenty-two men, nineteen sledges and 133 huskies, who created the trail to the pole for him. He organised groups of men, called 'divisions', to travel on ahead of him, dropping off dumps of supplies and building igloos for him to use along the route.

A recent re-run of the trip to the North Pole in 2000 by Arctic experts Paul Crowley and Paul Landry revealed some significant points in Peary's favour. Crowley and Landry found that the return trip could be made at high speed, because the teams of huskies were able to follow their own urine trail. It looks as if the urine-marked trail confirmed in the dogs' minds that they were on their way *home*, which made them run with greater enthusiasm. The armchair geographers who had disbelieved Peary's 'impossible' sledge speeds turned out to be wrong; fast speeds really were possible after all. In fact the two-man Crowley and Landry team actually exceeded Peary's speeds on several days. So, the balance of probability now is that Peary and Henson really did reach the North Pole in 1909.

COMPETITION TO REACH THE SOUTH POLE
(1910–13)

The South Geographic Pole was known to exist, in that the Earth was rotating on its axis, and the southern end of that axis must exist somewhere in the interior of Antarctica. Reaching it became a point of honour. It had no scientific or geographical significance. It was more a matter of national prestige to mount an expedition to visit it – and plant a flag there.

Robert Falcon Scott led the National Antarctic Expedition in 1901–04, and was keen to go back to reach the South Pole. The new expedition, the British Antarctic Expedition, had two aims, which was almost certainly its downfall. It was to carry out an ambitious scientific programme, as well as reach the South Pole. One objective would have been better.

A twenty-five man team sailed from England aboard the *Terra Nova* in June 1910. When they reached Melbourne in Australia, they heard the news that Roald Amundsen, the Norwegian explorer, was also on his way to reach the South Pole. Suddenly the situation had changed; there was a race to the Pole. In January 1911, the British expedition established a base, complete with prefabricated hut, at Cape Evans on the Ross Sea. On 1 November, Scott set off on a trek to the South Pole with four instead of the planned three men he had planned and provisioned for – and taking the extra man meant that they were bound to run short of supplies.

Scott's party reached the South Pole on 17 January 1912, but they were bitterly disappointed to discover that Amundsen had got there already. He had in fact reached it a full month before, on 14 December. Now totally disheartened by failure, the Scott party started the long journey back to the base camp – 1,290 kilometres (800 miles). In spite of being the middle of the Antarctic summer, the weather conditions were very severe, and the intense cold took its toll. Before Scott's party could reach their supplies they ran out of food and died of hypothermia. The frozen bodies were found, still huddled inside their tent when a search party arrived in November 1912.

The Northern Party reached Cape Adare in February 1911, setting up camp there and carrying out a programme of scientific data gathering. This aspect of the expedition was a great success, but that was completely overshadowed by the death of Scott and his party. Opinion has remained divided as to whether the Scott expedition was a display of heroism or folly; certainly there were failures of organisation and planning.

The Norwegian Antarctic Expedition of 1910–12 was a very different sort of expedition. It was privately funded, meticulously and efficiently planned and it had but a single purpose, to reach the South Pole. Amundsen set up his base camp and hut, called Framheim after their ship, the *Fram*, at the Bay of Whales. Like the British huts, the Norwegian hut was prefabricated. The hut is now in a ruinous state after collapsing in the 1960s.

CONTINENTAL DRIFT
(1912)

The idea that the continents drift slowly across the surface of the Earth like gigantic floating rafts was first put forward in a systematic way by Alfred Wegener in 1912.

As with many other discoveries, there had been forerunners. The starting point for the earliest suggestion that continents might move sideways in relation to one another was the shape of the Atlantic Ocean. So the conception of the idea of continental drift came with the discovery of North and South America. Once a reasonably accurate map of the Atlantic Ocean coastlines was available it struck a number of people that the two coastlines were strongly parallel. Abraham Ortelius drew attention to it his book *Geographical Thesaurus* in 1596, suggesting that the Americas had been 'torn away from Europe and Africa by earthquakes and floods . . . The vestiges of the rupture reveal themselves, if someone brings forward a map of the world and considers carefully the coasts of the three continents.' Francis Bacon drew attention to the parallel coasts of the Atlantic again in 1620. The two coastlines looked like the edges of two adjacent pieces of a jig-saw puzzle. Perhaps once they were joined. Perhaps they were joined and then were torn apart.

ALFRED WEGENER

For a long time this was just regarded as a curiosity. It was only assembled as a coherent theory of the Earth in 1912, and then not by a geologist but by a meteorologist, Alfred Wegener. His idea that the Atlantic had once been 'closed' but had opened up was not new. It had been proposed in 1858 by Antonio Snider-Pellegrini.

Another of Wegener's interests was Greenland and it is possible that it was while watching floating ice floes that he conceived the idea that the continents themselves were 'floating' in an underlying denser layer. He matched the coastlines of Europe and North America, Africa and South America, and on paper reassembled the continents into one large supercontinent, which he named Pangaea. This world continent existed in the Carboniferous Period, about 300 million years ago, when it was surrounded by a world ocean which he called Panthalassa. Since the Carboniferous Period, the supercontinent has gradually broken up and the fragments have drifted apart. He first lectured on the outline idea of continents drifting in 1912, then assembled his evidence in a book, *The Origin of Continents and Oceans*, in 1915.

Wegener relied heavily on the fit of the coastlines and the matching of major geological features. He wrote, 'It is just as if we were to refit the torn pieces of a newspaper by matching their edges and then check whether the lines of print run smoothly across.' These lines of print were the rock formations that run out to sea on widely separated continents. The ancient flora and fauna contained in the rocks also matched across oceans that the living species could not possibly have crossed; they must have died, been incorporated in the rocks and then separated when the rock layers were disrupted long afterwards. One example was the *Glossopteris* fern, a fossil plant that flourished 270 million years ago. Its fossil remains can be found on the widely separated continents of Australia, India, Africa and South America. Wegener also pointed to the widely separated traces of a Carboniferous ice sheet in the same regions. Obviously it would be a remarkable ice sheet that would extend across those widely separated regions today, not least because India is now well north of the equator. If we visualise India and the southern continents clustered together near the South Pole, a Carboniferous Period ice sheet looks much more viable.

Wegener's idea drew attention and interest, but not widespread support. A major problem was the lack of mechanism. He thought the continents were rafts that moved through the layer below in the same way that a ship moves through water, displacing it, pushing it out of the way as it drives forward. But he could not suggest a force strong enough to force a continent to behave in this way. This lack of a mechanism was a serious stumbling block. He also believed, rightly as it turned out, that the continents continue to move today. The Americas had been moving apart from Europe and Africa for the past tens of millions of years. They are still moving apart; in fifty million years from now the Atlantic Ocean will be twice as wide as it is today. He was impressed by the results of a surveying expedition to Greenland, which seemed to show that Greenland was several hundred metres further west of Denmark in 1906 than it had been in 1870. This looked like marvellous evidence that the Atlantic was still widening. Unfortunately it was just a surveying error. When the measurements were re-taken several times between 1927 and 1948, the 1906 movement was not corroborated.

This meant that a key piece of Wegener's evidence was invalid. It also occurred to many geographers and geologists that the shapes of the coastlines were to a great extent an accident of current sea level. If sea level had been lower in the past, the coastlines would have been further out. The true edge of a continent was really the outer edge of the continental shelf, the area of shallow water surrounding the continent. If the continents were to be fitted together, they should be fitted along the edges of their continental shelves. These two 'mistakes' on Wegener's part and his failure to provide a driving force for moving continents meant that by 1950 there was widespread scepticism about the theory.

By the 1950s geologists were divided into two camps with regard to the issue of continental drift. There were the fixists, who believed the continents have always been where they are today, and the mobilists, who believed in continental drift. One eminent geophysicist, Sir Harold Jeffreys, thought continental drift was a crazy idea; the very fact that the Earth responds to internal stresses with earthquakes implied that the Earth's interior was rigid.

SEA-FLOOR STUDIES

But in the 1950s and 1960s there was a major shift in perception. The Cold War and the deployment of long-range nuclear submarines meant that the US Navy suddenly needed highly detailed maps of the sea floors. A major programme of ocean floor surveys was launched at the Scripps Oceanographic Institute on the Pacific coast. Detailed surveys of the ocean floor revealed that some hitherto unsuspected and dynamic forces had been at work, shaping the face of the planet. Some features were already known about. The HMS *Challenger* survey of the 1870s had shown the existence of continental shelves, areas of shallow sea less than 180 metres (600 feet) deep, and mid-ocean ridges like the Mid-Atlantic Ridge. The *Challenger* survey did not show the shape of the sea floor in detail, though.

The post-war survey used a high-precision echo-sounder, which gave far more detail. What it showed was that mid-ocean ridges have a very rugged relief with deep rift valleys and hundreds of volcanoes. There was an assumption that the Pacific Ocean basin had existed for a very long time, possibly since its crust was blasted out to form the Moon billions ago (a theory popular at one time), and that its floor would be blanketed with deep layers of sediment. The echo-sounder showed that the floor of the Pacific was surprisingly hilly; it was not as old as had been thought. Another survey grabbed some rock fragments from the deep ocean. What came up included some coral, which can only grow in shallow sea, so here was evidence that parts of the ocean floor had once been shallow sea and were now much deeper.

By 1956 it was possible for American cartographers Bruce Heezen and Marie Tharp to produce a detailed map – the first detailed map – of the world's ocean floor by using the thousands of bits of data from the survey vessels. As they produced their map, Heezen and Tharp made another discovery, that the mid-ocean ridges actually connect up with each other to form a continuous undersea mountain range that winds all the way round the world. This is a major relief feature that, before the *Challenger* survey had been completely unknown. The ocean basins are generally about 5 kilometres (3 miles) deep and the crests of the mid-ocean ridges are about 1.6 kilometres (1 mile) below sea level. This means that the mid-ocean ridges are usually about 3 kilometres (2 miles) high. The rifts along the crests of the mid-ocean ridges looked as if they must be formed by tension, and the many parallel transform faults that offset the ridges also appeared to show evidence of movement. The texture of the ocean floor implied that the Atlantic, for instance, was being pulled apart along the central axis of the Mid-Atlantic Ridge.

The Heezen-Tharp map was an icon of the new approach to the geography of the planet. It was widely reproduced, in the *National Geographic* magazine, in school and university textbooks, and as a wall map. Over time its accuracy has been improved; a fine new edition of it was published in 1977. It has become an icon of the new age in physical geography. Magnetic studies of the sea floor revealed further support for the idea of continental drift. A proton magnetometer measured the variations in the magnetic field on the flanks of the mid-ocean ridges. There were areas of stronger magnetism, areas of weaker magnetism. They were arranged in stripes, parallel to the crest of the ridge and, more significantly, the pattern on one flank of the ridge was a mirror image of the pattern on the other. Gradually geologists realised that they were looking at strips of ocean floor that had been formed at the same time on the crest of the ridge, magnetised to the same strength, and had then been moved out sideways from the ridge crest. This would explain the apparent newness of the crust forming the floor of the ocean basins.

In 1960, Harry Hess of Princeton University produced a manuscript hypothesis for the origin of the ocean floor. His idea was that the mid-ocean ridges were zones of upwelling in the Earth's mantle. The hot material was lighter than the surrounding material, which was why it was buoyant. When the hot mantle material reached the crust, it moved sideways. As it did do, it dragged the overlying crust with it, together with any continental crust that might be embedded in it. As the mantle material cooled it sank back towards the core to be re-heated.

ARTHUR HOLMES

This idea was in effect a revival of a hypothesis put forward by the brilliant English geologist Arthur Holmes (1890–1965), who made two outstanding contributions to our understanding of Earth history. Holmes came from a poor background in Newcastle, but was fired by an inspirational physics teacher, James McIntosh. He graduated in Physics in 1909 and under the supervision of Professor Robert Strutt he researched the measurement of geological time. As a result of this he produced the geological timescale in 1913. This is a diagram displaying the chronology of significant events in the history of the Earth, including dominant life forms, mountain building episodes and mass extinctions. We are so used to seeing this diagram that, like the London underground map, we take it for granted.

Holmes was barely twenty-three when he proposed his timescale. He was not only the first to propose the form of presentation, he was the first to appreciate that the Earth was billions of years old (1.6 billion, he thought), rather than millions as most scientists had thought until then. He went on working on the question of the Earth's age. By 1947, he had revised it back to 3.35 billion years. In 1953, Clair Patterson showed that meteorites were representative of the primeval Earth, which is what Holmes himself had suggested way back in 1913. The age of both the meteorites and the Earth was finally agreed to be 4.55 billion years.

Holmes included the first version of his timescale in his book *The Age of the Earth*, which immediately marked him as the world's leading authority on the subject. There were still many geologists who resisted his ideas, some of them still clinging to the idea that the Earth was only twenty million years old. Holmes worked for an oil company in Burma for a time, and returned to England in 1922 to find that the scientific establishment has swung in his favour.

By then the debate about continental drift was raging. Once again Holmes dared to flout the establishment, teaching his pupils that continental drift was a perfectly valid view of Earth history. Eventually he came up with a mechanism to explain how continents could be shunted around. His hypothesis was that there are convection currents within the mantle, driven by the heat from the Earth's core. These are more than adequate to explain the doming effect observed along the crests of the mid-ocean ridges, the sideways movements of continents, and the ocean trenches, which mark the zones where the cooling mantle material sinks back towards the core.

Holmes proposed his theory as early as 1931, though it was not picked up and appreciated at its full value until thirty years later. The convection current hypothesis provided the motor power for continental drift that Wegener was unable to find. The main objection to Wegener's continental drift theory had in effect been overcome. The fact that the science establishment went on shutting its mind to continental drift after 1931 is an example of the Semmelweis Reflex. Minds were closed to new information; people refused to listen.

By 1960, people were more ready to listen, and they listened to Harry Hess. Holmes was by then seventy. His theory of convection currents acquired the status of proven fact. We often forget that it does in fact still remain only a working hypothesis – though the only one available. At the end of his life (he died in Battersea in 1965) Holmes pointed out with characteristic modesty that 'mantle currents are no longer regarded as inadmissible'. He led a rather sad and poverty-stricken life, yet was described in 1932 as 'one of the few English geologists with ideas on the grand scale'. He was in fact one of the greatest geoscientists of the century, and it is a pity that his fellow geographers, geologists and geophysicists did not value what he was saying more highly.

In the 1960s, the convergence of evidence on the reality of continental drift was like an academic landslide. The realisation that ocean floors moved along like conveyor belts, carrying whole continents like crates on a production line, was a major breakthrough. Suddenly there were explanations for all the large-scale relief features on the Earth: mountain ranges, volcanoes, continents, mid-ocean ridges, ocean trenches, chains of sea-mounts. There were explanations for all the major geological events too: earthquakes, volcanic eruptions, geysers. There was an eruption of interlocking research results that amounted to the emergence of a completely new science, the science of plate tectonics. It was a very exciting moment, like watching the new volcanic island of Surtsey rising out of the Atlantic in 1963. Surtsey exploding out of the middle of the ocean seemed at the time to be a powerful symbol of the violent transformation that was wrenching apart the Earth sciences and shaping them into a new intellectual landscape.

But – who discovered continental drift? It is customary to give Wegener the credit, but many other people contributed ideas to make the theory work. As we have just seen, Arthur Holmes supplied the mechanism without which the theory would have remained a hypothesis rather than a discovery. Bacon noticed the coastline fit in the seventeenth century and Ortelius noticed it in the sixteenth century, so there were well-established precursors. Wegener himself was aware by 1929 that other people had had the same idea before him; he mentioned Franklin Coxworthy, Roberto Mantovani, William Pickering and Frank Bursley Taylor, though he had arrived at the continental drift idea without their help. As with many other major discoveries, it is really composed of a number of separate discoveries that are individually less significant, but linked to make something of high importance – in this case a completely new view of the way our planet works.

ATOMIC NUMBER
(1913)

The atomic number of an element tells us the number of protons (positive charges) in the nucleus. This discovery was made in 1913 by Henry Gwyn-Jefferies Moseley by using X-ray analysis. What he found was that certain line in the X-ray spectrum moved, by the same amount, each time the atomic number was raised by one.

The following year, Ernest Rutherford described the nature of Moseley's discovery. 'Recently Moseley has supplied very valuable evidence that this rule [atomic number increasing by one from one element to another] also holds for a number of the lighter elements. By examination of the wavelength of the characteristic X-rays emitted by twelve elements varying in atomic weight between calcium (40) and zinc (65-4), he has shown that the variation of wavelength can be simply explained by supposing that the charge on the nucleus increases from element to element by exactly one unit. This holds true for cobalt and nickel, although it has long been known that they occupy an anomalous position in the periodic classification of the elements according to atomic weights.'

It took some time for scientists to work out where the positive protons and negative electrons were located inside the atom. The electron, the first subatomic particle to be discovered, was itself not discovered until 1897. In 1903, J. J. Thomson speculated that the electrons were negative particles with mass, while the positive charge was diffused through the space of the atom. Then in 1911 Rutherford proposed his atomic model, which consisted of electrons orbiting round a nucleus, which was conceived as a dense concentration of positive charge. In 1913, Niels Bohr researched the location of the negative electrons within the atom, while Moseley did the same for the positive charges.

Moseley was a junior member of Rutherford's Manchester research group at the time when he launched into his atomic number work. It was Moseley who wanted to experiment with X-rays. Rutherford was unenthusiastic about this as a research technique, but went along with it.

Within a few months of the publication of Rutherford's paper on the nucleus, the true physical reality of the atomic number was proposed by A. van den Broek. He wrote, in 1913, 'if all elements are arranged in order of increasing atomic weights, the number of each element in that series must be equal to its intra-atomic charge.' What Moseley found was that the stepping of the atomic number corresponded to the stepwise movement of the so-called 'K' line of the X-ray spectra of the elements.

The atomic number assigned to each element by Moseley, was found to be an expression of the number of protons in the atoms of each element. Atomic number became a way of defining an element, as atoms with the same atomic number make up a particular element. The elements are now arranged in the periodic table according to the order of their atomic numbers, whereas originally atomic weight was used as the criterion.

THE GENERAL THEORY OF RELATIVITY

(1915)

Albert Einstein introduced the special theory of relativity in 1905 and developed the general theory of relativity in 1915. The special theory showed that there were limitations to Newton's three laws of motion; the laws break down as velocities approach the speed of light. The general theory of relativity showed that Newton's law of gravitation was also only approximately correct, that it breaks down when gravitation is very strong.

The special theory is valid for systems that are not experiencing acceleration. Newton's second law has it that an acceleration implies a force, so special relativity is only valid when no forces act. This means that it cannot be used where a gravitational field is present.

Among the important implications of special relativity are the relationships between mass and energy and between space, time and velocity. At speeds close to that of light, space becomes contracted in the direction of motion and time slows down. These are bizarre ideas in relation to our everyday world, because that world normally does not include anything travelling anywhere near the speed of light. But, bizarre though it still sounds, many experiments indicate that Einstein's special theory is correct, and that our common sense expectations of phenomena (as well as Newtonian physics) are incorrect as the speed of light is approached.

The general theory of relativity was a result of Einstein's superhuman attempt to remove the restriction on special relativity that no accelerations and no forces could be present. He attempted to do this so that he could apply his theory to gravitational force. It was an enormously challenging problem, one that took him ten years to solve. The general theory of relativity is nothing less than an entirely new theory of gravitation, a model to replace Newtonian gravitation.

Einstein's general relativity and Newtonian theory make similar predictions wherever the gravitational field is weak, in other words once again in the normal everyday world we live in. But there are several specific situations where Einstein predicts something that diverges from Newtonian theory, and his predictions have been proved correct. Einstein's theory predicts that light should bend in a gravitational field, and astronomical observation shows that such gravitational lensing does occur; light really does bend as a result of gravity. The general theory of relativity predicts that light emanating from a strong gravitational field should have its wavelength shifted towards higher values – a red shift. Again detailed astronomical observation indicates that a red shift does occur.

An electromagnetic field can have waves in it that carry energy in the form of light. A gravitational field can have energy-carrying waves in the form of gravitational waves. These are ripples in the curvature of space-time, ripples travelling at the speed of light. A problem here is that gravitational waves are too weak to be detected and so they have not been directly observed. They have nevertheless been indirectly observed in the binary pulsar. The arrival time of pulses from the pulsar can be measured very exactly. From these measurements it is clear that the rotation of the binary system is gradually decreasing. The rate of 'decay' or slowing down is very low indeed, around seventy-five millionths of a second per year. This rate of slowing is what would be expected for energy being lost to gravitational radiation, just as predicted by Einstein's theory of general relativity.

The Einstein general theory of relativity represents the best available model of gravitation. Newton's model is still very workable under conditions of low velocities and small gravitational fields: in other words, under most circumstances. It is only where velocities approach the speed of light or where gravitational fields are much larger than the Earth's that Newton's and Einstein's views of the nature of the universe differ.

General relativity unifies special relativity, Newton's law of universal gravitation and the new idea that gravitational acceleration can be described by the curvature of space and time. This extraordinary compilation of exotic and ambitious ideas still seems revolutionary almost a hundred years after it was first composed. Whether we should regard it as a discovery or an invention is uncertain, but if Einstein did stumble on the true nature of the universe in 1915 it must rank as a major discovery.

One important way in which general relativity is different from other theories of gravitation is in its use of the so-called Einstein field equations to describe the curvature of space-time. The field equations are a system of differential equations; their solution describes the 'shape' of space-time.

General relativity is the most successful gravitational theory available. It is almost universally accepted, it is substantiated by observations, and since 1960 it has been the basis of much of the science of astrophysics. Its first success was in explaining the anomaly in the observed orbit of Mercury. In 1919, Sir Arthur Eddington announced that observations of stars close to the disc of the eclipsed Sun confirmed Einstein's prediction that massive objects like the Sun can bend light. Since then many of the predictions of general relativity have been confirmed by observation and experiment. These include gravitational time dilation, the red shift of light and the expansion of the universe. Astronomers believe that some of their observations confirm the existence of general relativity's most remarkable and sinister predictions – black holes.

General relativity is justified by the equivalence principle. This states that free-falling observers are in inertial motion. The most obvious effect of gravity is that things fall. But this can be eliminated by introducing a reference frame that is in itself in free fall. In such a reference frame, the laws of physics are much as in the special theory of relativity. In this way, inertial observers may accelerate in relation to each other. Someone who is in a lift whose cable has broken will fall with the lift, yet experience weightlessness; objects will 'float' weightlessly with them. The experience of the unfortunate person in the falling lift will be very similar to those of someone in a rocket out in deep interstellar space, a long way from any source of gravity. Einstein's key insight was that there was no real difference between the constant gravity pull we know from everyday experience and the forces felt by an accelerating observer (or in technical language an observer in a non-inertial reference frame). The so-called force of gravity someone feels under their feet is a result of continuous physical acceleration, and this could easily be imitated by that same person travelling in a rocket that accelerates at the same rate as gravity. This is completely different from the universe that Newton described.

The impact of general relativity on the science of the last ninety years has been enormous. The effect of gravity on time was first measured, and therefore proved, in a laboratory experiment in 1959. It was then confirmed by astronomers. Gravity has also been shown to deflect light. The positions of stars close to the Sun's disc have been shown to shift as a result of the Sun's gravitational field – an effect seen many times since Eddington first observed the phenomenon.

Relativity was also able to account for the anomalies in the shifting orbit of the planet Mercury. The anomalies had been discovered in 1859 by Urbain Le Verrier, but remained unexplained. The fact that Einstein's gravitational field equations were able to explain the behaviour of Mercury was satisfying on two counts: astronomers were able to understand Mercury better, and Einstein's theory was validated. His equations were then used to explain and predict the anomalies in the orbits of other planets.

Relativity predicts that binary systems (two bodies rotating round each other) will emit gravitational waves that entail a loss of energy. Within the solar system there is no system large enough to display this effect. But a binary pulsar, which consists of two neutron stars circling on another, is certainly large enough, and significant amounts of energy are given off in the form of gravitational radiation. This in turn causes a decrease in the orbital period, a phenomenon that was measured for the first time in 1974.

The deflection of light by gravity sometimes has the side effect of producing multiple images of the star being observed or, if the star is relatively close, a brightening of the star. Observation of binary pulsars tells us that there are probably gravitational waves radiating from them. But gravitational waves rippling across space from the far side of the universe have yet to reach us – or have yet to be detected reaching us. A good deal of current research is being dedicated to finding evidence that they are arriving. A joint US-EU mission is expected to launch a space-based detector in 2009. If and when these gravitational waves are identified, they promise to tell us a great deal about the objects that are sending them. Some may contain information about the nature of the earliest phases in the development of the universe.

General relativity predicts that when an object becomes compact enough it will turn into a black hole. This is an area of space from which nothing can escape – even light itself. Speculation about black holes has gone on developing without very much in the way of proof that they exist. In cosmological models based on general relativity, there is a presumption that super-massive black holes lie at the centres of galaxies. These will have up to a few billion solar masses, and it is believed that they have played an important role in the generation of galaxies. Another important role of black holes is in converting gravitational energy into radiation energy. As dust or gas settle onto super-massive black holes, spectacularly luminous astronomical effects are created. But we need to keep sight of the fact that the direct evidence for the existence of black holes has so far proved elusive. Astronomers are still keenly searching for the 'shadow' that could mark the location of our own Milky Way galaxy's central black hole.

Einstein's theory is a picture of the way a whole universe functions, so it has become a useful basis for cosmology, the study of the universe as a whole. It has been elaborated to create cosmological models to show (or rather explore) the evolution of the universe over the last fourteen billion years from the Big Bang onwards. The resulting models have been very successful in matching the results of all observations of the universe. But they have also led to the conclusion that all the matter in the universe that is detectable via current astronomical techniques amounts to only ten per cent of the universe's total mass. This has led on to the almost mystical idea of an unknown 'substance' called dark matter. This has mass and therefore gravity, but does not interact electromagnetically, so that it cannot be seen. Startlingly, it is thought that ninety per cent of the mass of the universe consists of this dark matter.

Another disturbing feature of general relativity is the appearance of singularities. There are space-times that fulfil all the requirements of Einstein's theory, but have singularities with ragged edges. In other words, they have boundaries where the paths of light come to a sudden end. There is speculation that there are different classes of singularity. One possible future singularity, where world-lines end, is the so-called Schwarzschild solution, which is thought of as being a singularity within an eternal static black hole. Other space-times are thought to have a past singularity in which world-lines begin – big bang singularities. But these are ideas, possibilities, speculations; they are not facts or observations. They are *not* discoveries. *Not yet*.

Ninety years on, Einstein's discovery about the nature of the universe is still having repercussions, spawning more and more incredible new ideas.

INSULIN

(1922)

Frederick Banting (1891–1941) was the Canadian medical researcher who was the principal co-discoverer of insulin. After being wounded in World War I, Banting returned to Canada, completed his training as an orthopaedic surgeon at the Hospital for Sick Children in Toronto. Banting was dissatisfied with his job and hankered after what he thought would be a more productive role in medical research into diabetes. In the autumn of 1920, he had an idea how this might be done and he was impatient to try it. He began his research in 1921 in a laboratory at the University of Toronto under the general supervision of Professor John Macleod, who provided him with the lab space. Banting was allocated an assistant, a young graduate student called Charles Best.

Fred Banting and Charles Best worked with great intensity right through the hot summer of 1921, performing experiments on diabetic dogs. The experiments entailed isolating the pancreas and the hormone it secreted. Banting found that he was able to keep diabetic dogs alive with the extracted hormone. When Macleod returned from his summer holiday, Banting enthusiastically reported his success to him. Many medics were unimpressed by what they considered unsound physiology and crude experimental technique.

But Banting, Best and Macleod continued undeterred. The experimental work went on through the autumn, with Macleod now actively involved as well as a chemist called James Collip. Collip's role was to find ways of purifying the extracted insulin so that it could be safely injected into people. By the following year, 1922, the team had developed a technique for extracting insulin. The breakthrough was hailed as a major medical breakthrough, which gave hope to many human sufferers of diabetes all round the world. Word spread like wildfire. The life-saving insulin was discovered and within a matter of months it was in mass production.

It went into use straight away and began to extend the lives of millions of people round the world suffering from the endocrine disease diabetes mellitus. At that time there was no other treatment for the disease, and sufferers had little prospect of survival; they became blind and quickly died. The first patient to be experimentally injected with insulin, early in 1922, was Leonard Thompson. This test was spectacularly successful and the technique became the regular and life-saving method for treating what was otherwise a fatal disease. The treatment was even used on patients who were already in what looked like a terminal coma, and they made a full recovery thanks to insulin.

Success had come to Banting very quickly, considering that he had only started the research in 1921. He had a brilliant idea, chased it relentlessly and purposefully, and succeeded in making it work after only a few months. By 1923, he and Macleod were accepting a Nobel Prize for Medicine in Stockholm. Fred Banting was generous enough to share his award money with his assistant Charles Best.

TUTANKHAMUN'S TOMB
(1922)

The discovery in 1922 of the tomb of Tutankhamun is universally acknowledged as one of the most important archaeological discoveries of the twentieth century. The lost Egyptian pharaoh was found by the archaeologist Howard Carter, who was sponsored by Lord Carnarvon, a wealthy English aristocrat. Carnarvon had been funding years of painstaking searching in the Valley of the Kings – years in which nothing significant had been found. Carnarvon was rich, but inflation had begun to take its toll as the pound lost its purchasing power and he warned Carter that the 1922 season would have to be the last.

Carter managed to retain Carnarvon's interest when in 1921 a discovery was made in a store room at the Metropolitan Museum of Art in New York. Some ancient Egyptian objects that had been deposited there twelve years earlier were found to carry both the seal of Tutankhamun and the seal of the royal necropolis. So here at last was the confirmation that Tutankhamun really had been buried in the Valley of the Kings. On 22 November 1922, Carter's conscientious persistence finally produced a result; he located and uncovered a hitherto untouched royal burial. Finding it was a triumph; finding that it had not been robbed, like most of the other tombs in the valley, was almost unbelievable.

Carter's discovery has sometimes been presented as simply lucky, but he had planned over a four-year period to find Tutankhamun's tomb. He could not have known that all its sumptuous grave-goods would still be stacked inside it, but it was that particular tomb that he set out to discover. He had been through the list of pharaohs, and also the list of identified pharaohs' mummies found in the 1870s and 1890s.

Tutankhamun was unaccounted for, and Carter was sure from the movement of the pharaoh's court from Akhenaton's city at Tell al-Amarna back to Thebes that the missing pharaoh must have been buried in the royal necropolis of Thebes – the Valley of the Kings.

Carter even developed a theory to explain why the missing tomb had not yet come to light. A rare rainstorm, he suggested, had produced an exceptional flow of water down the valley side and sealed up the tomb entrance at the bottom of the valley side with debris. He turned out to be right. The tomb, when it was eventually discovered, was at the bottom of the valley side, and covered with debris. It was also disguised by having three other pharaohs' tomb entrances immediately above it: Amenmesses, Ramesses III, Ramesses IV. The excavation of those tombs and scattering of debris outside their entrances had more or less ensured that the entrance to Tutankhamun's tomb would stay hidden.

Howard Carter understood his ancient Egyptians and started looking near the tombs of Tutankhamun's near-contemporaries. In 1917, near the entrance to the tomb of Ramesses IV, Carter found the remains of workmen's huts, but he stopped working on them because he had decided that the Tutankhamun tomb must lie within a triangle he had drawn on his map – and they lay just outside his triangle. That is an indication of how methodical and disciplined Carter was. There may have been another reason, which is that the huts were very close to the entrance to the Ramesses IV tomb, which was a great magnet to tourists, and Carter hated being anywhere near crowds, especially crowds of tourists.

Carter's final season began in 1922 with a return to the area of the workmen's huts. By 3 November, he had uncovered enough of them to see their pattern and layout, and that they sat on about 90 centimetres (3 feet) of ancient soil. When the first of the huts was removed, to find out what was below the ancient soil, the energetic waterboy, playing with a stick in the soil, found a step cut into the rock. He quickly covered it up, realising at once what it meant, and ran to Carter to tell him what he had found. It was not long before Carter had unearthed a whole stairway going steeply down into the rock, and he knew from the design that this was a tomb entrance of the right period. Carter was both excited and apprehensive; even at this stage what he had found could still turn out to be an unfinished tomb.

Then Carter found a blocked doorway with necropolis seals attached to it. What lay beyond had not been disturbed for three thousand years. At the door's lintel some plaster had fallen away, so Carter made a small hole right through it, just big enough to shine a torch through. This was the most exciting moment in Carter's career; there was a hollow beyond, an open passageway, presumably leading to the tomb chamber. The temptation to go on and open the doorway and see what lay beyond must have been almost overwhelming, but it was late in the day, and Carter had to stop. He also felt honour-bound to call his patron out to witness the actual opening of the tomb. Carnarvon cabled to say that he would arrive in Alexandria on 20 November.

Typically elated and anxious by turns, because that was his nature, Carter was now worried by the arrival of hordes of tourists. Once Carnarvon had arrived, Carter got his workmen to clear the doorway, and only then did they find the seals of Tutankhamun. But Carter was depressed when they found scarabs and pots inscribed with the names of other pharaohs; he feared that this was going to be no more than some kind of dump of miscellaneous objects, brought here by Tutankhamun and deposited for safety.

Down a debris-filled sloping passage, 9 metres (30 feet) from the first doorway, was a second blocked doorway. Carter made a small hole in the blocking, pushed a candle through and looked in. 'At first I could see nothing, but presently as my eyes became accustomed to the light, details of the room within emerged slowly from the mist, strange animals, statues and gold – everywhere the glint of gold. For the moment – an eternity it must have been to the others standing by – I was struck dumb with amazement, and when Lord Carnarvon, unable to stand the suspense any longer, inquired anxiously, "Can you see anything?" it was all I could do to get out the words, "Yes, wonderful things." Then, widening the hole a little further so that both could see, we inserted an electric torch.'

Carter insisted that they only looked in before re-closing the hole and leaving the valley. But the reality was that the whole group of people present broke in and spent practically the whole night inside the tomb, going through chamber after chamber to see what was there, moving objects about, and then trying to disguise the fact that they had been in there. Their curiosity was understandable. Even the highly disciplined Carter could not help himself – he just had to see what was inside the tomb. And I would guess that in those circumstances any of us would have done the same. The official opening of the burial chamber did not take place for months, and it may be that Carter and Carnarvon returned for more sneak previews, but they successfully concealed their activities from everyone.

When the spectacular finds, especially the gold objects, were made public, the world was overwhelmed by their richness, refinement and beauty: the golden shrine, the pectoral, the gold dagger, the gilded statuettes of the king, and above all the gold mask from the sarcophagus, showing what the face of the young king Tutankhamun looked like.

The level of interest in the tomb of Tutankhamun and its treasure immediately after the discovery was unparalleled in history. The newspapers and magazines were full of pictures and descriptions. The artefacts that were brought out even had a major effect on art and architecture in the 1920s. It was as if, as far as the world at large was concerned, ancient Egyptian civilisation itself had been discovered, rather than just the burial of an obscure and relatively unimportant pharaoh. Obscure though he may have been in the three thousand years after he died, Tutankhamun is now the best-known pharaoh of them all, the one king of ancient Egypt whose name everybody knows.

WAVE MECHANICS
(1926)

One major problem in advancing new theoretical models, about light, time or atomic structure, is they ultimately have to be expressed in words and in terms that are already familiar. We get into difficulties when we try to describe, hypothesise, or even visualise a phenomenon that is completely unfamiliar; the images and words are often not available. A classic example of this was the atomic model put forward by Niels Bohr in 1913. It had great appeal, because it presented the atom as a miniature solar system, with minute particles orbiting round a nucleus, just like planets orbiting the Sun. It was easy to visualise, because an analogy was readily available. But that did not necessarily mean that it was true.

Many scientists felt intuitively that Bohr's model was right, because the microcosm, the world within the atom, reflected the macrocosm, the solar system, the larger world outside. Max Born wrote in 1923, 'An alluring result of Bohr's atomic theory is the demonstration that the atom is a small planetary system. The thought [that the laws of the macrocosm are reflected in the microcosm] exercises a great magic on mankind's mind. Indeed its form is rooted in the superstition (which is as old as the history of thought) that the destiny of men could be read from the stars. The astrological mysticism has disappeared from science, but what remains is the endeavour towards the knowledge of the unity of the laws of the world.'

But this intuition did not have to be true. The spiral structure of the Milky Way galaxy, for example, does *not* imitate the concentric shape of the solar system, nor is there anything existing in between the Earth-Moon system and the atom that has the orbiting structure of the solar system. So there is no special reason to suppose that spatial scales nest within one another like Russian dolls, even if we would like the universe to be structured in this way.

Wave mechanics had been available as an idea for many decades. As early as 1850, Jean Bernard Léon Foucault showed that light travels more slowly through water than through air. That was in line with what the wave theory of light predicted and contradicted what the corpuscular (particle) model predicted. The deduction was that light must be a wave phenomenon. But that presupposed that the reality must match one of the two alternatives available; perhaps a third possibility, one not so far thought of, was the reality. In 1923, Louis de Broglie proposed his wave-particle duality theory. According to this, particles including electrons could behave like waves. De Broglie's research supervisor was unsure whether his student's proposition was brilliant or ridiculous, so he sent it to Albert Einstein for a second opinion. Einstein replied cryptically, 'I believe that it involves more than a mere analogy'. Einstein supported de Broglie, which helped it to gain acceptance. The new wave model for light encouraged Erwin Schrödinger to assemble a wave mechanics model for the atom.

In 1926, Schrödinger wrote, 'My theory was inspired by L. de Broglie and by short but incomplete remarks by A. Einstein . . . I knew of [Heisenberg's] theory but felt repelled by the algebra, which appeared very difficult, and by the lack of visualisability'. The Heisenberg theory he referred to was quantum mechanics, proposed in 1925. Even Werner Heisenberg himself was nervous about his model being impossible to visualise. He referred to 'the disadvantage that there can be no directly intuitive geometrical model because the motion of electrons cannot be described in terms of the familiar concepts of space and time'.

The stresses that developed among the conflicting theories were intense, as were the personal strains between their champions. Heisenberg was outspoken in his condemnation of Schrödinger's ideas. 'The more I reflect on Schrödinger's theory the more *disgusting* I find it. What Schrödinger writes on the visualisability of his theory, I consider *rubbish*'. On the question of visualisability, Heisenberg repeated his conviction that what they were discussing could not be visualised; 'the electron and the atom do not possess any degree of physical reality as objects of daily experience.' The two men met and quarrelled passionately about the issue.

Schrödinger said to Bohr, 'You surely must understand, Bohr, that the whole idea of quantum jumps necessarily leads to nonsense.' Schrödinger objected to quantum jumps on common sense grounds. Bohr's answer was revealing. 'In what you say you are completely right. But that doesn't prove that there are no quantum jumps. It only proves that we can't visualise them. The pictorial concepts we use to describe the events of everyday life do not suffice to represent the process of a quantum jump. The processes with which we are concerned here cannot be the subject of direct experience and our concepts do not apply to them.' Bohr was even able to provide some ways in which we can visualise atoms; he used the uncertainty principle devised by Heisenberg in 1927 to clarify the duality between waves and particles. The uncertainty principle is the statement, made in the context of quantum physics, that locating a particle in a small region of space makes the momentum of the particle uncertain. It also carries the implication that measuring the momentum of a particle precisely makes the position uncertain.

PENICILLIN
(1928)

In 1928, Professor Alexander Fleming of Queen Mary's Hospital in London accidentally discovered a mould that attack harmful bacteria.

Fleming left a plate of *Staphylococcus* bacteria out in his laboratory for a few days. When he looked at the plate he noticed that that it had become contaminated with mould. He also noticed that around the mould were rings that were cleared of bacteria. It looked as if the mould must be producing a chemical that was killing the bacteria.

Fleming identified the mould as *Penicillin notatum*, which is the common mould that grows on bread. It kills many types of bacteria, not just *Staphylococcus*, and does no harm to the white blood cells found in human blood; this was an early indication that it was going to be safe to use on people. Fleming had difficulty in isolating the chemical from the mould, and it was to be some time before penicillin extracted from mould would be available to treat infections.

It was on 9 January 1929 that Fleming made his first trial use of penicillin on a human being. One of his assistants had an infected sinus. Fleming washed the man's sinus out with a broth of diluted penicillin. This proved to be very successful in destroying most of the *Staphylococci*. Two years later, in 1931, penicillin was used on two children at the Royal Infirmary in Sheffield. The children had contracted gonorrhoea from their mothers at birth and were suffering from gonococcal ophthalmitis. Penicillin reduced the infection. The new discovery was also used at Sheffield on a colliery manager with an eye infection.

With these first tentative treatments, a new age, the age of antibiotics, had arrived. But in spite of this early promise, the use of the new drug was slow to take off in the 1930s. Then in 1940, the Australian-British pathologist Howard Florey published an article in *The Lancet*, entitled

Penicillin as a Chemotherapeutic Agent. Together with his refugee collaborator Ernest Chaim, Florey had developed Fleming's penicillin into an agent that would become a major weapon against infections and disease. The three of them, Fleming, Florey and Chaim, were to be awarded the Nobel Prize for Medicine. But for the time being penicillin was in very short supply. The entire world supply of penicillin as it stood in 1942 was barely enough to treat just a single case of meningitis. It was only in 1945 that an Anglo-American research team developed a way of mass-producing penicillin, enabling it to be distributed widely on a commercial basis. After that, antibiotics became increasingly available to cure a very wide range of infections. It was one of the great leaps forward in modern medicine.

THE EXPANDING UNIVERSE

(1929)

The man who discovered that the universe was expanding was Edwin Hubble. He graduated at the University of Chicago in 1910, in mathematics and astronomy, but also with a great reputation as a boxer; boxing promoters saw him as a serious contender for the heavyweight championship against Jack Johnson. Instead Hubble took a very different career route. He accepted a Rhodes Scholarship to Oxford, studied law and then astronomy, which he sensed was a vocation.

It is hard to believe now, but in 1919 when Hubble started his career in astronomy it was still uncertain whether the Milky Way galaxy, our own galaxy, was the totality of the universe; some astronomers thought the universe might be much bigger and that our galaxy was just one of many galaxies scattered through space. Questions like that could only be answered with very high-powered telescopes. Edwin Hubble was fortunate in starting his career at the Mount Wilson Observatory, home of the largest, newest and most technically advanced telescope in the world. Using the new telescope, Hubble peered at the blurred clouds of cosmic light known as nebulae. Inside one of these, the Andromeda Nebula, he identified cepheids, variable stars that regularly change in luminosity.

Meanwhile, Henrietta Leavitt had luckily pioneered a method of using variable stars like these to measure distance. Hubble was able to use her method of distance measurement on the cepheids in Andromeda and he concluded that they were much too far away to be part of the Milky Way galaxy. Then he realised that the Andromeda Nebula was in reality a galaxy crowded with billions of stars. It was a momentous discovery. The universe consisted not of one galaxy, but a great many galaxies. He settled the controversy. He also settled the position of the Earth in the universe. Within 500 years, the human race had moved from believing that the Earth was the centre of the universe to seeing that it was an insignificant speck in an insignificant position in just one out of countless millions of galaxies.

This would have been a major contribution to science in itself, but Hubble went on to study the red shift in the light arriving from light sources outside our galaxy. The light received from a star or galaxy that is receding from us in the line of sight displays a red shift in its spectrum (a Doppler effect). Conversely, light from a star or galaxy that is approaching will display a blue shift. In 1929, Hubble measured the red shifts of distant galaxies and also calculated the relative distances of these galaxies from the Earth by measuring the apparent brightness of cepheids he found in each galaxy. When he compared the red shift and the relative distance, he discovered that the red shift increased as distance increased. Expressed in a slightly different way, as what is known now as Hubble's Law, the greater the distance between galaxies, the faster they move away from each other.

Since the red shift in the colour spectrum of a galaxy means that the galaxy is moving away from us, Hubble's result showed that the universe is expanding; expansion was the only explanation. Whichever way we look in the sky outside our own galaxy, there is red shift. Although this means galaxies are moving away from us in all directions, it does not mean that our galaxy is in any sense at the centre of the universe, the central point of the primal explosion. Intelligent beings in other galaxies would all see exactly the same thing; the space between the galaxies is getting bigger.

We now take for granted the idea that most of the stars and galaxies are moving away from us, that the reaches of empty space separating the galaxies are getting larger and larger, and that the red spectral shift is proof of that phenomenon. But Hubble was by no means convinced that that was what he was measuring. He observed and measured red shift, but was unsure whether red shift represented actual recession. In Hubble's own words:

In principle, the problem can be solved; a rapidly receding light source appears fainter than a similar but stationary source at the same momentary source. For velocities of a few miles or a few hundred miles per second, the dimming factor is negligible. But for extremely distant nebulae, where the apparent recessions reach tens of thousands of miles per second, the effects are large enough to be readily observed and measured. Hence, if the distances of the nebulae were known quite accurately we could measure their apparent faintness and tell at once whether or not they are receding at the rates indicated by the red shifts.

But it was at such great distances that Hubble got into difficulty. Because those stars and galaxies are very faint, there are inevitable errors in calculating their distances, so there was a catch. He wondered whether there was a way past the problem. As the intrinsic luminosity (brightness) of each galaxy is known, its apparent faintness can be made to give two distances, depending on whether the galaxy is regarded as stationary or receding. Hubble believed that if he did this systematically for all the galaxies, he would end up with two scales, one of which would lead to contradictions or serious practical difficulties. He found that one scale did in fact lead to inconsistencies, and it was the scale that included dimming produced by recession.

For this reason, Hubble was uncertain what it was he had actually proved. It was other scientists who took up his idea of an expanding universe, and made it the norm, the received wisdom, in the second half of the twentieth century.

Regardless of Hubble's own reservations about it, his idea marked a historic moment in our perception of the universe. The evidence, though very incomplete, was that the universe was finite and getting bigger all the time. As with many other discoveries, this discovery had a corollary. If the universe was and still is expanding, then if we go back in time the universe must once have been infinitesimally small. An expanding universe implied an origin in an explosion, which would in due course become known as the Big Bang. This Big Bang marks the origin of the universe as we know it.

The ancient Greeks were torn between thinking that the universe was finite and that it was infinite. They could not accept that it was infinite. But at the same time they could not imagine what would lie beyond the boundaries of the universe once you reached them. The idea of an expanding universe and the Big Bang that marked its beginning carried with it a new problem: what came before the Big Bang? Was there nothing at all – no universe, no space, no time? Or was there another earlier universe that perhaps had just imploded? There are still no answers to these questions.

Both Newton's and Einstein's equations allowed that the universe might implode. Gravitation, however weak, might in theory eventually have caused everything to rush together. The expanding universe in effect prevented that from happening; all the components of the universe have been flying outwards from the moment of creation. But does that rule out an eventual implosion, once the energy from that initial explosion has run out? The equations of the expanding universe have three possible solutions, each of which results in a different destiny for the universe. The outcome depends on three things: the mass of the matter composing the universe, the speed of the expansion and the relationship between these two.

The three possible types of expanding universe are described as open, flat and closed. An open or hyperbolic universe has a density below the critical density. It will eventually reach a fixed rate of expansion and after that go on expanding at that rate for ever. A flat universe, which has a density which is exactly the critical density, will also go on expanding for ever, but the rate of expansion will slow to a standstill after an infinite amount of time. Both of these two types of universe are never-ending; they will just go on expanding. After a time, in an open universe, all the galaxies beyond our Local Group will have shot away at speeds above the speed of light and we will never be able to see them, so the visible universe will be a smaller and smaller fraction of the total. Eventually, all the stars in all the galaxies will die and nothing will replace them and what will be left will be no more than a vast frozen emptiness. The third type of universe, the closed universe, will go on expanding but at a progressively slower rate until the expansion stops; after that, gravitation would lead to a gradual, though accelerating, implosion. The force of that implosion might set off another Big Bang, making the universe a cyclic creation, which would be consistent with many other aspects of its physical nature. In all three possible universes, the slowing down is caused by gravity.

Astrophysicists are deeply interested in discovering which of these universes we are actually living in, and they have been making increasingly accurate estimates of the two key variables: the rate of expansion and the average density of the universe. When there are accurate measures of the two variables, it will be possible to say which of the three universes ours is. The Sloan Digital Sky Survey is a large-scale project to measure systematically the density of galaxies across the heavens; this should enable astronomers to measure the density variable. There are three major projects trying to establish the geometry of the universe. The initial results all point in the same direction, to a density of the universe that is precisely the critical density. This evidence points to a universe that will never end, but continue to expand for ever but at a decelerating rate.

What Hubble introduced was not just the expanding universe but a new and grander concept of its scale and dynamics. Now, instead of thinking in terms of a universe consisting of just one galaxy – our own – we think in terms of a universe consisting of 125 billion galaxies. If each galaxy has the same number of stars as our (average-sized) galaxy, 400 billion, that means there are 50,000 billion billion stars in the universe. There are as many stars in the universe as there are grains of sand on the Earth. This huge inflation of scale in our conception of the universe began with Hubble.

Edwin Hubble was never awarded a Nobel Prize, but his contribution to modern human knowledge is incalculable, beyond any prizes. Stephen Hawking described Hubble's great discovery of the expanding universe as 'one of the great intellectual revolutions of the twentieth century'.

PLUTO
(1930)

Several astronomers became aware that irregularities in the orbits of the outer planets Uranus and Neptune existed, and there was an agreement that they might well be caused by a so-far undiscovered planet even further out from the Sun. One of these was the wealthy Bostonian astronomer Percival Lowell, who (it was later said) successfully predicted the missing planet's orbit. Lowell instigated the search for the planet, which he called Planet X, and it was eventually found in 1930 by his successors at the Lowell Observatory in Arizona. The method behind the discovery was the same as the one used in the 1840s by Urbain le Verrier, when he analysed perturbations in the orbit of Uranus to predict the existence – and the position – of the previously un-discovered planet Neptune. Lowell hoped that by tracking down Planet X he would re-establish for himself some scientific credibility. His reputation had been badly dented by his interpretation of his obser-vations of Mars. Through the telescope he saw lines on Mars, and he believed these were canals built by an intelligent civilisation; his fellow astronomers ridiculed the idea and the lines turned out to be optical illusions. Lowell searched in vain for the missing planet from 1905 until his death in 1916; it was a deep disappointment to him that he was unable to find it.

Lowell's widow then entangled the observatory he had set up in a decade-long fight to get the observatory's million-dollar legacy for herself. This meant that the search for Planet X stopped in its tracks. The work of the observatory did not resume until 1929. Then the director, Vesto Slipher, handed the task of finding Planet X to Clyde Tombaugh, a twenty-two year old farm boy from Kansas. Amazingly, Tombaugh found Planet X relatively quickly, within a few months.

Clyde Tombaugh made the discovery of the missing planet by comparing a photograph of the night sky taken on 23 January 1930 with two others taken on 20 and 29 January. He was using a machine known as a blink comparator, which enabled him to flick rapidly backwards and forwards between two plates to show up the movement of any light sources on the plates, and therefore the movement of planets across the backcloth of stars. Tombaugh saw the small point of light moving slightly from plate to plate and walked into Slipher's office, saying, 'Doctor Slipher, I have found your Planet X.' Further photographs were examined to confirm Tombaugh's finding and then Harvard College Observatory was notified.

It was not surprising that the planet had taken so long to identify, as it was very small and a very long way away. The discovery by Tombaugh has been represented as a triumph of scientifically reasoned discovery, but it was actually based on a misconception. Pluto is now known not to be massive enough to have any effect on the orbits of Uranus and Neptune. The discrepancy turned out to be the result of an earlier overestimation of the mass of Neptune. So the discovery was made by chance.

The Lowell Observatory had the right to name the new planet, and Tombaugh urged Slipher to decide on a name quickly, before someone else hijacked it. People wrote suggestions from all over the world. Constance Lowell, Percival Lowell's widow, proposed 'Zeus'. Then she proposed 'Lowell'. Then, even more startlingly, she proposed 'Constance'! Slipher disregarded these suggestions. It was an eleven-year-old English girl, Venetia Burney from Oxford, who proposed 'Pluto'. She was interested in astronomy and also in classical mythology. She thought Pluto, the alternative name of Hades, the Greek god of the underworld, an appropriate name for a dark and inhospitable world. Her grandfather passed the name to an Oxford professor, who cabled it to the USA. Pluto was officially named on 24 March 1930.

Pluto is very small, with only about 0.7 per cent of the volume of the Earth. Its diameter is only about two-thirds that of our Moon. It has an eccentric orbit; sometimes it is as far as 7.4 million kilometres (4.6 million miles) from the Sun, sometimes as close as 4.4 million km, which brings it inside the orbit of Neptune. The orbits of Pluto and Neptune are such, though, that they can never collide. The plane of Pluto's orbit is also unusual, being tilted at seventeen degrees in relation to the orbits of other planets. Another peculiarity of Pluto is that it has large moon, Charon, and the two bodies really revolve around one another. Some astronomers therefore like to treat Pluto and Charon as a binary system, but officially Charon is classified as a moon of Pluto, along with Nix and Hydra, two additional small moons that were discovered in 2005.

From the date of its discovery in 1930, Pluto was regarded as the solar system's ninth planet, but its status has slid as estimates of its size have gradually dwindled. Its status has also shifted in the last couple of decades as more discoveries have been made about the solar system. Many objects similar to Pluto have been found to exist in the outer reaches of the solar system, such as Eris, a scattered disc object that is twenty-seven per cent more massive than Pluto. The discovery of Eris and other ambiguous bodies led the International Astronomical Union to redefine the term 'planet', and the definition that was arrived at in 2006 excluded Pluto.

There are, according to the IAU resolution, three main conditions for an object to be regarded as a planet. It must be in orbit round the Sun. It must be massive enough to be a sphere as a result of its own gravitational force; its own gravity should pull it into a shape of hydrostatic equilibrium. It must have cleared the neighbourhood along its orbit. Because Pluto has such a small mass, it is unable to clear a path, and this is why is fails to qualify as a planet.

Pluto has had its full planetary status taken away. It now ranks as the second-largest dwarf planet in the solar system. It is regarded as the largest member of a distinct region of asteroids called the Kuiper belt. Pluto is a dwarf planet or minor planet. So too are Eris and Ceres.

ECOSYSTEM
(1930)

The term ecosystem was invented in 1930 by Roy Clapham to describe the physical and biological elements in an environment considered in relation to one another as a unitary system. In 1935, the British ecologist refined the concept, describing an ecosystem as an interactive system established between a group of living creatures and their biotope, the environment in which they live.

A central idea in the ecosystem concept is that living organisms are dynamically linked through a web of relationships with every other element that makes up the environment which they inhabit. The concept was early on developed to include the human ecosystem. Studies of the human ecosystem are grounded in the traditional idea of a dichotomy between man and nature, but what invariably emerges is that all species in an ecosystem are ecologically integrated with one another as well as with the inorganic elements of their environment.

Changes in any one of the interrelated environmental factors will result in changes to the nature of others – and the nature of the system as a whole. Environmental factors that may change include the availability of nutrients, temperature, the intensity of grazing by herds of wild animals or domesticated livestock, and the population density of species. A fire sweeping through a temperate deciduous woodland will destroy all the large trees and most of the herbs, flowers and shrubs growing on the forest floor. After a short recovery time, the community that once consisted of large trees becomes a community of grasses and herbaceous species; bluebells or bracken may take over. But there will also be tree seedlings growing on the cleared land, and eventually these grow to full size, shading out many of the smaller plants and re-establishing the original woodland canopy. Whether the secondary woodland that develops is as rich as the primary woodland depends on the proportion of the nutrients stored in the soil and how much has been leached out during the period when the soil was exposed to the air.

Ecosystems can be studied on a wide variety of scales. An ecosystem can be as small as a puddle or as large as the Earth. A human ecosystem may be as small as a house or as large as a nation-state. Often ecosystems are discussed and studied as if they had well-defined and impermeable boundaries (closed systems), though they are invariably, in reality open to external influences (open systems). Ecosystems include, coral reefs, rainforests, beaches, deserts, tundras, savannas, cool coniferous forests.

The ecosystem concept carries with it an implication of natural balances that will maintain it in a state of equilibrium – while it is in a natural state. The ecosystem approach enable researchers to study impacted or damaged ecosystems to assess the extent of the damage and the repercussions through the system. There is an implicit notion of ecological health lying behind such studies. Often ecosystems are able to repair themselves or rebound after a disruption; if, for instance, a clearing is made in a forest, natural processes will ensure that species from the surrounding forest recolonise the cleared area. Viewed in this way, ecosystems can be regarded as healthy or robust if they can rebound quickly and easily; they can be regarded as fragile and vulnerable if they rebound only very slowly and with difficulty.

The ecosystem idea provided a new framework for studies of vegetation, wildlife and human impacts – one that was to prove very fruitful in various disciplines including biology and geography. From around 1950 onwards there has been a preoccupation with the different kinds of human interference with ecosystems, such as the Brazilian rain-forests and the tropical coral reefs, generally with a view to showing that human impacts are undesirable. But ecosystems are mainly governed by chance events, and it is important to remember that they do not possess central nervous systems. An ecosystem is really the end result of millions of individual responses of organisms to other living and non-living elements in their environment. But because very large numbers of responses are involved, the fluctuations in all the individual variables in the environment are damped down; this is what gives an ecosystem its long-term stability or inertia.

In 2005, a major assessment of the Earth's ecosystems was carried out and published in the Millennium Ecosystem Assessment. It concluded that the Earth's ecosystems have altered more in the past fifty years than at any other time in history.

DEUTERIUM
(1931)

The existence of the element deuterium was predicted in 1926 by Walter Russell, who used gaps in his spiral periodic table to identify apparently undetected elements. The predicted element was first found spectroscopically in 1931 by a chemist at Columbia University, Harold Urey. Urey and his collaborator, Ferdinand Brickwedde, used the low-temperature physics laboratory in Washington DC to distil five litres of cryogenically produced liquid hydrogen down to one millilitre. This concentrated the deuterium, a heavy isotope of hydrogen, to a point where it became clearly identifiable when analysed spectroscopically.

Urey gave the newly discovered element the name deuterium from the Greek and Latin words for the number two. Deuterium had hitherto gone unnoticed because it constituted such a tiny fraction of the hydrogen found in most natural contexts. There is only one deuterium atom for every 6,500 hydrogen atoms in the waters of the oceans. As a result, there is not enough deuterium around to make any measurable difference to the atomic mass of the hydrogen.

Urey was awarded the Nobel Prize in Chemistry in 1934 for his discovery. He also successfully concentrated water in order to show deuterium enrichment. Gilbert Lewis prepared the first sample of pure 'heavy water', D_2O, in 1933. Heavy water is ten per cent denser than ordinary water.

Deuterium exists naturally in a very diluted state, but in large quantities. It accounts for 0.03 per cent of the weight of the hydrogen in the world's oceans. There is a lot of deuterium on Jupiter, where it accounts for about 0.6 per cent of the atoms.

The nucleus of deuterium is called a deuteron, containing one proton and one neutron. Neutrons were discovered at the same time as deuterium. The nucleus of the far commoner 'ordinary' hydrogen (sometimes called protium) contains no neutron.

Identifying the existence of deuterium added important information about the cosmos. Stellar fusion destroys deuterium. The only natural process that could create deuterium is the Big Bang; the existence of deuterium is one of the arguments in favour of the Big Bang theory over the steady state theory of the universe.

Deuterium is useful in that it can be used in nuclear fusion reactions, especially with tritium, because it yields a large reaction rate; it has been used for making electricity on a commercial scale. Measuring the natural variations in abundance of deuterium, alongside the abundances of heavy oxygen isotopes, makes it possible to trace the origins of the water on the Earth. The level of enrichment in rainwater, for instance, varies according to the climatic temperature in the area where the rain falls, so enrichment varies with latitude. Water that has originated as precipitation can therefore be traced to a climate of origin.

Heavy water experiments were carried out in Nazi Germany with a view to developing a nuclear reactor. These experiments were a major source of anxiety to the Allies, as they could lead to the production of plutonium, which in turn could be used to make an atomic bomb. After World War II ended, it was discovered that the Germans had not got very far with their experiments and in 1945 they were still several years away from developing an atomic bomb.

NEUTRON

(1932)

Before 1932, each atom was known to contain a positively charge nucleus that was surrounded by enough negatively charged electrons to make the atom as a whole electrically neutral. Most of the atom consisted of empty space; its mass was concentrated in the tiny nucleus. Scientists believed that there must be protons (hydrogen ions) as well as electrons. Some radioactive nuclei emitted positively charged alpha particles and neutral gamma radiation as well as beta particles. In 1920, Ernest Rutherford had hypothesised the existence of a neutral particle with roughly the same mass as the proton. He thought it might result from the capture of an electron by a proton. Rutherford's hypothesis stimulated a search for the missing particles, but the search was hampered by their lack of an electrical charge; most experimental techniques used electrical charge as a means of detection and measurement.

In 1928, a German physicist and his student, Walter Bothe and Herbert Becker, bombarded beryllium with alpha particles emitted from polonium. They found that this released a penetrating radiation that was electrically neutral, and they believed this radiation to be high-energy gamma photons. Four years later Irène and Frédéric Joliot-Curie further investigated the radiation discovered by Bothe, but got little further in unravelling the problem.

James Chadwick discussed the Joliot-Curies' results with Lord Rutherford, who did not believe what was happening. Chadwick repeated the Joliot-Curies' experiment, bombarding hydrogen atoms in paraffin with beryllium emissions, but also bombarding helium, nitrogen and other elements as well. When Chadwick compared the energies of recoiling charged particles from different targets, he was able to show that the beryllium emissions contained a neutral component with a mass that was about the same as that of the proton. Chadwick named this neutral particle the neutron. He received the Nobel Prize in physics for this work.

CIGARETTE SMOKE CAUSES CANCER
(1933)

A British biochemist called Ernest Kennaway was the first to isolate a pure cancer-causing chemical. Kennaway was also able to show in his laboratory tests of 1933 that a hydrocarbon produced from incomplete combustion can cause cancer in animals. These hydrocarbons were to be found in the exhaust fumes of cars and lorries – and in cigarette smoke. Inhaling cigarette smoke increased the risk of developing cancer.

These research results appear to be the very first medical evidence that that much-maligned monarch, King James I of England (and VI of Scotland), was right after all about the harmful effects of smoking tobacco. Over the next thirty or forty years, more and more evidence was to emerge from medical research that smoking was harmful. By 1953, the popular magazine *Reader's Digest* published an article on the harmful effects of smoking, and its title said it all: 'Cancer by the Carton'. The following year the American Heart Association published its findings that smokers were between 50 and 150 per cent likelier to die from coronary heart disease than non-smokers. More research along the same lines and with the same results came out the next year.

In 1963, the American Heart Association launched its first campaign against tobacco smoking. In 1964, the American Surgeon-General, Luther Terry, brought out a report entitled *Smoking and Health*; this confirmed that smoking was dangerous and that both lung cancer and heart disease could result from it. Within two years, packets of cigarettes were carrying health warnings. People nevertheless carried on smoking as if this information and advice did not exist. In the mid-1960s, the average American smoked ten cigarettes a day. In 1971, the Royal College of Surgeons in Britain reported that smoking cigarettes was causing as many deaths as the typhoid and cholera epidemics of the nineteenth century.

In 1972, a new slant on tobacco smoking emerged. The US Surgeon-General reported that passive smoking was a severe health hazard. In other words, people who chose not to smoke but who happened to be in the same rooms as people who were smoking were being significantly harmed by inhaling second-hand smoke. This had not previously been thought of as dangerous, which in itself is strange, and it led to increasingly vociferous calls to ban smoking in public places such as restaurants, offices and planes. The very next year the state of Arizona imposed a ban on smoking in public places in order to protect the health of people who had decided not to smoke.

The evidence that cigarette smoking causes a range of health problems, both to the smokers themselves and those around them, has been gradually mounting over a seventy-five-year period, three-quarters of a century. Some of the illnesses that result from smoking are extremely serious, the worst of them being heart disease and lung cancer. Curiously, many seasoned smokers continue to maintain that they had no idea when they took it up that smoking could be harmful. But it is very clear that as early as 1933 the information that smoking could cause cancer was already available; any smoker who is now below the age of seventy-five and able to read a newspaper had access to it and could have made the decision never to start smoking – even before reaching adulthood.

SUTTON HOO SHIP BURIAL

(1939)

Sutton Hoo in Suffolk is the site of two Anglo-Saxon cemeteries dating from the period AD 500 to 700. One of these was found to contain a ship burial in which the body had unfortunately not survived – but the rich grave-goods had. These treasures proved to be of enormous value in telling us a host of new things about culture and society in seventh-century England. The discovery of the artefacts was of particular importance because they shed light on a period that was poorly documented. This was the age of Arthur, a period hovering between history, myth and legend.

The cemeteries date from around the time when King Redwald of East Anglia was the commander-in-chief (bretwalda) of the English and therefore represent a distinct period of royal power. This helps to explain the wealth, quality and refinement of the grave-goods found at Sutton Hoo. The ship burial found in 1939 is what most people know about Sutton Hoo, but there were many burials and there was even a second cemetery.

Sutton Hoo is the bluff marking the eastern bank of the Deben estuary opposite Woodbridge harbour. It stands about 11 kilometres (7 miles) inland, close to the lowest fording place on the River Deben. The main cemetery has always been known about, because of the distinctive grave mounds in it, about twenty of them, rising slightly above the skyline when viewed from the Woodbridge side, which was probably intended as the public viewpoint. The second cemetery is about 460 metres (500 yards) upstream. It was discovered and partially explored in 2000 during construction work on the site of the Exhibition Hall. This cemetery also had burials beneath mounds, but the mounds have been ploughed away.

The owners of the Sutton Hoo site were a couple called Pretty, who moved there in 1926. Mrs Pretty became aware of local stories of 'untold gold' in the burial mounds. Mrs Pretty's nephew was a dowser and he picked up indications of gold from within the ship mound. There was some solid archaeological evidence that a ship burial had been found on the site already. In 1860, 'two bushels of iron screw bolts' were found when a mound was opened; these were almost certainly the nails or rivets used to secure the planks of a timber-hulled ship. But Mrs Pretty seems to have been happier to use folklore, dowsing and spiritualism for guidance.

Mrs Pretty approached Ipswich Museum, who supplied Basil Brown to take charge of an excavation. Brown had been a smallholder in Suffolk until his business failed; then he had taken to full-time Roman archaeology. Mrs Pretty showed Basil Brown the site and proposed that he start digging one of the biggest mounds. But Brown noticed that it had been disturbed and he decided instead to start with three smaller mounds in 1938. The finds from these were interesting, but they were only fragmentary as the graves had been robbed.

Mrs Pretty was still keen to see the big mound excavated, so in May 1939, Brown started work, again aided by Mrs Pretty's gardener and gamekeeper. They drove a trench in from the east end and soon started finding rows of rusted nails, still in position where they had held the now disintegrated planks of a ship's hull. As work progressed it became clear that this was the imprint of a large sea-going ship, and several weeks of work were needed to clear the cast of its hull. Then they reached the burial chamber amidships. As it happened it was exactly beneath the spot where Mrs Pretty had asked Brown to start digging the year before.

In June 1939, Charles Phillips of Cambridge University heard a rumour about the ship discovery, visited Ipswich Museum and managed to get in on the dig. Phillips realised the huge importance of what was being uncovered at Sutton Hoo, alerted the British Museum and the

Science Museum, and intervened to excavate the burial chamber himself. This sort of hijacking is fairly common practice in archaeology. He brought in a team of experts including W. F. 'Peter' Grimes, O. G. S. Crawford and Stuart Piggott. Meanwhile Basil Brown, now distinctly sidelined, continued with the work of clearing the rest of the ship.

The need for secrecy led to friction among those involved, and Charles Phillips antagonised two officials of Ipswich Museum, Moir and Maynard, respectively its honorary president and curator. Moir had founded the Prehistoric Society of East Anglia in 1908, and Maynard was its secretary. In 1935, Charles Phillips and his friend Graham Clark had taken control of the Prehistoric Society. In what looks like a calculated snub to Moir and Maynard, Phillips now systematically excluded them from the unfolding discoveries at Sutton Hoo. The world of scholarship is often far from gentlemanly.

The rich finds were the subject of an inquest held in Sutton village hall. The verdict was that it was safe to assume that the treasure had been buried without any intention to recover it, so it was the property of the landowner, Mrs Pretty. She nevertheless decided to hand the treasure over to the nation.

The ship burial had been missed by treasure seekers. Like Tutankhamun's tomb in the Valley of the Kings, it had somehow been overlooked. In the Middle Ages, the area had been crossed by boundary ditches to make enclosed fields, and one of these skimmed across the western side of the ship mound. Sixteenth-century treasure hunters had dug a pit into the centre of the mound, narrowly missing the burial chamber. The looters did not foresee that the burial and its grave-goods would rest so low down in the monument; it was right down in the belly of the ship, which was buried well below the level of the land surface. The treasure was not *in* the ship mound, it was actually *beneath* it.

This was clearly a major royal burial, the grave of one of the kings of East Anglia. The location is easily understood as the centre of a series of tidal estuaries – Alde, Butley, Deben, Orwell and Stour. These estuaries were entrance corridors for incoming migrants from Europe in the fifth and sixth centuries. Sutton Hoo was not the only cemetery focus; there were several others from the Bronze Age and later at other locations. Further up the Deben Valley there were cemeteries of much the same date as Sutton Hoo at Ufford and Rendlesham. At Snape, above a ford across the River Alde, there was another ship burial, similar to the famous one at Sutton Hoo. Bede mentions that King Aethelwold of the East Angles had a palace at Rendlesham. The area was evidently the seat of royal power in East Anglia.

The treasures found in the burial chamber amidships were found to be of an unprecedented quality, and certainly belonged to the early seventh century. But as World War II broke out the exposed cast of the ship had to be covered up for the duration of the war. It was covered with bracken and turf. The site was then, with incredible inappropriateness, used as a training ground for soldiers driving jeeps.

After World War II, a research team based at the British Museum resumed work on Sutton Hoo, re-excavating the ship mound in the late 1960s to try to resolve some of the questions left unanswered by the initial excavation. A plaster cast was taken of the impression left by the ship's hull. This made it possible to create a fibreglass facsimile of the hull itself. Then the pit was filled in and the ship mound was restored to look the way it did before 1939.

New investigations at Sutton Hoo, completed in 2005, were directed by Martin Carver. These spread across a wider area that included six other mounds. The soil was stripped off to find out how the mounds related to earlier uses of the site, and it turned out that the siting of the mounds was indeed related to earlier patterns (both Romano-British and prehistoric) of land enclosure. The cemetery was exclusively a royal burial ground in the sixth and seventh centuries, but it also appeared that the cemetery had been the scene of executions in the period after the royal burials; a gallows stood on one of the burial mounds. Large areas of the cemetery have been left for future archaeologists to investigate, using techniques as yet undreamt of.

The sea-going ship at the heart of the ship mound was 27 metres (90 feet) long, with tall upward-sweeping stem and stern posts. It was clinker-built (with the oak planks overlapping each other), fastened with rivets and beautifully crafted. The hull was strengthened with twenty-six wooden frames. There were oar rests along the gunwales, marking places for forty oarsmen. The body of the king was laid out in a timber chamber, surrounded by various objects: several wooden buckets, an iron lamp, a bottle, a small bell (probably for a dog's collar), a large round ornamented shield, a whetstone (possibly acting as a sceptre), a bronze hanging bowl from the Eastern Mediterranean, an Anglo-Saxon lyre in a beaver-skin bag, bronze cauldrons, ten silver bowls, two silver spoons, a great gold buckle, a magnificent sword – and the king's parade helmet. The helmet has become not only emblematic of the Sutton Hoo discovery, but an icon of that whole period of English history, the age of Beowulf. Helmets from this period are extremely rare finds, so to discover this one in good condition, and such a masterpiece of craftsmanship, was remarkable. The art and craft work from the ship at Sutton Hoo has become one of the cornerstones of the study of the arts in Britain in the sixth-to-ninth centuries.

LASCAUX CAVE PAINTINGS
(1940)

A French schoolboy by the name of Jacques Marsal made a spectacular and entirely unexpected discovery in a cave at Lascaux near Perigueux in 1940. What the boy saw, along both sides of the corridor-like cave passage was a frieze of prehistoric mural paintings, a painted procession of animals. The discovery was a truly historic moment. There is a popular tendency to see the history of archaeology as a sequence of great discoveries: the tomb of Tutankhamun in Egypt, Homeric Troy, the painted caves of the Old Stone Age. The discovery of the Lascaux cave paintings was certainly one of those popular historic landmarks.

There seems to have been a surge of artistic creativity round about the time when the late-glacial ice sheets reached their greatest extent. The European cave paintings, such as Lascaux in southern France and Altamira in northern Spain, date from the period 20,000–15,000 BC. The coldest point, the time when the ice was at its greatest extent and the sea level was at its lowest, was 16,000 BC. It is tempting to see the burst of creativity as response to extremely adverse environmental conditions. This was a climatic crisis far worse than the global warming that is the big scare story of the twenty-first century, with huge areas of northern Europe completely entombed beneath hundreds of feet of ice. It may well be that people were responding to the climatic crisis with some religious appeal for help. But we must not argue too far in that direction, as the number of dated finds is really too small to justify that inference, and some pieces of artwork have been found from significantly earlier times, when the climate was milder.

What did the drawings and paintings of animals in the caves mean to the people who painted and drew them? This leading question is almost impossible to answer. One possibility that has been proposed is that the major centres of art production, like Altamira and Lascaux, served as major religious or ceremonial centres and were the scene of important ceremonies that took place during regular, perhaps annual, gatherings of the people of each area. Alternatively, it may be that the production of the art was in the hands of particular chiefs or religious leaders, and that they used the creation of the art and the ceremonies that went with it to legitimise their authority. But these explanations are entirely speculative. One thing that is clear is that the art is not to be found uniformly across Europe, but concentrated in the areas that are known to have been most densely populated around 16,000 BC.

One of the painted panels at Lascaux shows a sequence of vigorous overlapping images of wild cattle, horses, ibex and red deer, painted in red ochre and black manganese dioxide. The Chauvet cave, which was discovered in southern France half a century later, has similar overlapping animal images. It was for a time seriously believed that the spectacularly vivid Chauvet paintings were too good to be true, and that they must be a modern forgery – but they are not.

Another image at Lascaux shows a wounded bison apparently knocking over a naked man. Nearby another bison defecates and there is a bird on a stick. Odd. There are also some puzzling rectangles and dots. It is very hard to work out what the image is about, if indeed it is supposed to be read as a single image at all, but it appears to be connected in some way with hunting magic. Other cave art also has animals that might well have been targeted for hunting as the main focus of interest. The pictures are certainly not landscape art in any sense that we understand.

Most of the Stone Age art that has so far been discovered in caves and rock shelters has been found in southern France and northern Spain, but that may only be because we have not been looking hard enough elsewhere, and there are lots of caves all over Europe. In fact, only recently some prehistoric cave sketches or engravings have been discovered in caves in England, first in Derbyshire, then at Cheddar in Somerset – and there may well be more.

Some caves are accessible enough and young Jacques Marsal was able to walk straight into the Lascaux cave. But others are far less accessible. The Cosquer cave near Marseilles has its entrance fully 37 metres (120 feet) below present sea level and it was only discovered by a professional diver in 1985. The Cosquer cave entrance must have been well above sea level at the time when the artwork was done, so that Stone Age artists could get into it, and we know that sea level was indeed very low in 16,000 BC; in fact it was about 110 metres (360 feet) lower than it is today. The Cosquer cave is particularly interesting because it is full of stencils of handprints. The cave environment seems to favour the preservation of paintings and other remains. It was a great surprise to archaeologists to find the remains of a length of prehistoric rope, twisted by a right-handed person, in the Lascaux cave. There was also evidence, in the form of sockets for beams in the gallery walls, that wooden scaffolding had been put up in the cave to enable the artist to paint the images. Even so, an experiment by Michel Lorblanchet showed that an entire frieze of animals could be painted in just one hour.

The famous 'Venus' figurines date from about the same time or a little earlier. These have been found at about twenty-five sites scattered right across Europe from the Pyrenees to the Ukraine. They show a stylised, fleshy female form that may conceivably have been some ideal of womanhood or a celebration of human fertility. The art is conceptual rather than representational, and has more in common with twentieth-century Cubist art than with any art from the intervening centuries.

The simple, stylised drawings of animals discovered at Lascaux gave modern people an insight into the way people lived and the things that mattered to them at the time when they created them, 17,000 or more years ago. Like many other such discoveries, the Lascaux paintings enrich and extend us by putting us in touch not just with our remote ancestors but, in a sense, with ourselves as we were then. That reflection on where we have come from, and how we have travelled, is vitally important in telling us where we are and even we might be heading. The recovery of the past is one of the most important things we human beings do. No other species does it.

PLUTONIUM

(1940)

Plutonium was the first synthetic element to be produced on a large scale. It is an element with unusual chemical and metallurgical properties; one highly significant property is that it is fissionable. The way in which it was discovered and isolated is remarkable.

Enrico Fermi attempted to create transuranium elements. These are elements that do not exist in nature and have an atomic number that is greater than 92. Fermi's technique was to bombard uranium with neutrons. Fermi's initiative was taken up by others. In the spring of 1940, two scientists working at the University of California (Berkeley), Philip Abelson and Edward McMillan, exposed a natural uranium target to neutron bombardment. These neutrons were in turn produced by bombarding beryllium with deuterons accelerated in a cyclotron. The effect was the creation of a product that was in effect a new element, with the atomic number 93. They had discovered a brand-new element, the first transuranium element. It was found to have variant forms or isotopes. The stablest isotope was to be Pu-244. This has a very long half-life of eighty million years, which is long enough for it be found in very small quantities in nature.

The new element was named neptunium after the planet Neptune, because that was the planet that was immediately beyond Uranus. The discovery was followed by the isolation of the new element in 1944. The difference between discovery and isolation is a significant one. Discovery refers to the first proof that atoms of a new element exist. Isolation is the production or separation of a weighable amount of the new element in a pure form.

In 1940, three more Berkeley chemists, Glen Seaborg, Joseph Kennedy and Arthur Wahl, started looking for the next transuranium element, which would have an atomic number 94. They thought this would be a decay-product of the recently discovered neptunium. It was this element that would be named plutonium, after the planet beyond Neptune. The method they used, which involved oxidation, reduction and precipitation reactions, was to become the basis for the large-scale production of plutonium. During the course of these experiments, as different isotopes of the element were created, the three researchers learnt a lot about the nature of plutonium.

In the spring of 1941, another isotope of plutonium (Pu-239) was produced using neutrons generated by the Berkeley cyclotron. These were used on a uranium target surrounded by paraffin, which slowed the neutrons down and increased the chance that they would interact with the target. In March 1941, Seaborg and his colleagues subjected a sample of the Pu-239 isotope to irradiation with more neutrons from the cyclotron, and the sample appeared to undergo fission. The team then substituted a uranium sample as the target, produced fission again, but at only half the rate of the plutonium. This was a major discovery. It opened the possibility of using a controlled chain reaction to produce enough Pu-239 to fuel nuclear weapons. This awareness made the separation of plutonium and a thorough investigation of its chemistry a matter of urgency.

In the summer of 1942, the cyclotron method of producing plutonium was still yielding only tiny amounts of plutonium: not enough to weigh, not even enough to determine the physical and chemical properties of the new element properly. The first weighing of a compound containing plutonium came in September 1942, when less than 3 milligrams of PuO_2 was weighed. About a year later plutonium metal was produced, in silvery globules, but still only in small amounts. In the end, large-scale production of the isotope Pu-239 proved possible only with a controlled chain reaction of uranium, and this was achieved by Enrico Fermi and Leo Szilard – in Chicago.

Plutonium made a huge impact on the second half of the twentieth century as a fuel for nuclear weapons and nuclear power stations. The isotope Pu-238 has a fairly short half-life of eighty-eight years, and it emits a large quantity of thermal energy as it rapidly decays. It combines high energy radiation with low penetration, which means that it only needs minimal shielding for safety. These properties make it ideal for generating electricity without any direct maintenance at timescales close to a human lifetime. This makes it suitable for powering space probes. It has been especially useful for powering artificial heart pacemakers as there was no need for repeat surgery to replace batteries. For new pacemakers, plutonium has now been largely replaced by lithium-based primary cells, though there are still scores of plutonium-powered pacemakers implanted in living patients – and keeping them alive.

THE DEAD SEA SCROLLS

(1947)

From 1947 until 1979, ancient documents were discovered in a series of caves near the Wadi Qumran, close to the ancient settlement of Khirbet Qumran on the shore of the Dead Sea. These fragile documents consisted of religious writings, the earliest surviving copies of Biblical texts dating from the time of Christ. Because of their very early date, and the way in which some religious texts were later tampered with, edited to suit various revisionist views, the Dead Sea scrolls have enormous importance. They show the state of these religious texts as they stood before AD 100. One of the things they show is that beliefs and practices within Judaism were more diverse than had previously been thought.

The scroll caves were in a desert environment, and the sheer dryness of the air was a major factor in preserving the scrolls made of papyrus. It would not have been possible for papyrus documents to survive in the humidity of northern Europe.

The scrolls were discovered in eleven caves, all within a mile of the Qumran settlement site. None were found on the settlement site itself, but it is assumed (not necessarily correctly) that that is where they came from. The initial discovery was made by a Bedouin shepherd, Mohammed Ahmed el-Hamed, nicknamed 'The Wolf', in 1947. The story goes that Mohammed threw a stone into one of the caves in order to flush out one of his animals. When instead of hearing his stone hit the cave wall he heard the unexpected sound of a pot shattering, he went into the cave. There he found several ancient jars containing scrolls wrapped in linen. Dr John Trever interviewed a number of different men going by the name Mohammed 'The Wolf', each of whom gave a different version of events. In spite of this initial mystification over the discoverer and the exact circumstances of the discovery, the scrolls were found to exist, and they were taken to an antiquities dealer in Bethlehem, but he returned them when he was warned that they might have been stolen from a synagogue.

The scrolls then came into the hands of Khalil Shahin, a cobbler and antiques dealer. The Bedouin initially took only three scrolls from the cave, but it seems that they later went back for more, perhaps encouraged by Khalil Shahin, or Khalil Shahin went and took them himself. It was eventually agreed that the Bedouin would leave the scrolls with an impartial third party until they could be sold. The third party was George Isha'ya, a member of the Syrian Orthodox Church. He contacted a monastery in the hope of getting an appraisal of the nature of the texts. News of the discovery then reached Metropolitan Athanasius Yeshue Samuel, also called Mar Samuel. Mar Samuel examined the scrolls, sensed that they were very old and offered to buy them. He acquired four of them.

Then more scrolls appeared on the antiquities market. Professor Eleazar Sukenik, an archaeologist at Hebrew University, bought three: the *War Scroll, Thanksgiving Hymns* and an alternative version of the *Isaiah Scroll*. Professor Sukenik found out that Mar Samuel had acquired some scrolls and tried to buy them from him, but no agreement was reached. Then Dr John Trever of the American Schools of Oriental Research became interested. He compared the handwriting in the scrolls with that in the Nash Papyrus, the oldest known biblical manuscript then known, and saw that the writing was similar. Trever met Mar Samuel in 1948 and took photographs of the scrolls. These photographs have proved to be very valuable artefacts in themselves. Once the scrolls were removed from their linen wraps and their jars, and exposed to light, they started to deteriorate; the writing began to fade. Trever's photographs often show a much more legible text than is seen on the scrolls today.

By the end of 1948, many months after the first scrolls were dis-covered, the scholars were still unable to find the cave where they had been found. It was finally rediscovered in January 1949 by a United Nations observer.

In June 1954, the first batch of Dead Sea Scrolls was put on sale. They were advertised in the *Wall Street Journal* as 'The Four Dead Sea Scrolls. Biblical manuscripts dating back to at least 200 BC. This would be an ideal gift to an educational or religious institution by an individual or group.'

They were bought, at the Waldorf-Astoria Hotel in New York for $250,000. Mar Samuel did not do well out of this deal, as there were mistakes in the paperwork, and the US government creamed off most of the proceeds in tax.

Various lines of evidence have been used to date the scrolls – the style of the handwriting, the content of the texts, radiocarbon dating – and they show that they were not all written at the same time. They date from various times between about 200 BC and AD 100. The oldest of the documents is also the second largest of them, stretching to 6.7 metres (22 feet) in length. Radiocarbon dating puts it in the range 107 BC to 335 BC, which means that it is most likely to have been written around 200–225 BC. This very old document is known as the *Great Isaiah Scroll*. The only other Hebrew document to date from such an early period is the Nash Papyrus, which was found in Egypt and contains the Ten Commandments.

The *Temple Scroll*, which was found in Cave 11, was the longest scroll to be found. Its total surviving length is almost 8,2 metres (27 feet), and must originally have been longer. Over half of the text deals with the building of the Temple of Jerusalem. It is a sectarian text and was at one time believed, by Yigael Yaden, to be a version of the Torah written by the Essene sect. Another scholar, Hartmann Steggemann, takes a different view, that the scroll, which is clearly an important document, was nothing to do with the Essenes; its content was never once referred to in the writings of the Essenes.

Some of the scrolls were made of papyrus. Others were made of animal skin. The writing was done with quills and ink made from carbon black. Just one document was inscribed on thin copper sheets. The language used was Hebrew, in fact three different Hebrew dialects, classical Hebrew, Dead Sea Scroll Hebrew and proto-Tannaitic Hebrew. A few are written in Greek.

The texts in the scrolls include a commentary on the *Book of Habakkuk*, the *Manual of Discipline* and the *Damascus Document*. The Manual of Discipline provides a lot of information about the practices and beliefs of a sect, presumably the religious community at Qumran. The *Copper Scroll* list hidden caches of treasure, which are thought to have been Temple treasure hidden away prior to the destruction by the Romans. Naturally this list of treasure has attracted a lot of interest. The scroll refers to sixty-four separate underground hiding places scattered throughout Israel.

About one-third of the texts are fragments of the Hebrew Bible, fragments of every book except the *Books of Esther* and *Nehemiah*. About one-quarter of the texts are traditional Israelite religious texts not in the Bible, such as the *First Book of Enoch*, the *Book of Jubilees* and the *Testament of Levi*. Perhaps fifteen per cent of the texts have not been identified.

There were many problems in making the texts of the scrolls available for scholarly study. Some of the texts were published promptly. All of the writings found in the first cave were published between 1950 and 1956. The texts from eight more caves were published in 1963. Translations soon followed. But the finds from Cave 4 were not published quickly, and they amounted to almost half of the total texts. The international team given the responsibility for publishing these spent a great deal of energy defending their interpretations. The team and its leadership came in for some outspoken criticism for the long delay and for the arbitrary imposition of secrecy. Even after the team leader died in 1971, the team still refused to publish, determined to block the development of alternative theories about the scrolls. Eventually, the wall of secrecy was broken when seventeen of the documents were reconstructed from a concordance made in 1988 and which had fallen into the hands of 'outsiders', scholars who were not bound to secrecy. The hitherto secret documents were published in 1991. By chance, it seems, a complete set of photographs of the Cave 4 texts was published simultaneously in California. In the face of these exposures, the secrecy rule was given up. The complete texts of the Cave 4 texts were published in 1995, a publication date that might be seen as twenty-five years overdue.

The secrecy was due in part to a sense that the documents were of profound religious and historical importance. There is no doubt that they are, but their precise significance is still very unclear. Before their discovery, the oldest manuscript texts of the Hebrew Bible were from the ninth century; the Dead Sea Scrolls date from a thousand years earlier. One highly significant feature of the Dead Sea Scroll Bible texts is that most of them are the same as the later texts, which has been reassuring to both scholars and the faithful. Another major feature is the light thrown by the sectarian texts on variant forms of Judaism practised in the first centuries BC and AD.

An early theory about the scrolls, very widely held until the 1990s, is that they were the religious texts of the Essenes or possibly another sect that lived at Khirbet Qumran. The hypothesis was that the Essenes hid their sacred texts in the caves during the Jewish Revolt of AD 66; during the revolt they were massacred and therefore unable to retrieve their scrolls. In the *Community Rule* there is a description of an initiation ceremony which is strikingly similar to the account of an Essene initiation ceremony in Josephus. When Khirbet Qumran was excavated, two inkwells were found, suggesting that the scrolls were written there. Long tables were also found there, which might have been used for writing the scrolls.

But recently, differences between the texts and what is known of Essene teaching and way of life have emerged, so supporters of the theory have modified it. Instead of describing the Qumran community and the writers of the texts as Essenes, they describe them as 'Essene-like'.

Another theory is that the Qumran community was led by Zadokite priests or Sadducees. One document states purity laws that are identical to those attributed to Sadducees in rabbinic writings. There are also lists of festival dates in the scrolls, dates that follow the principles of the Sadducean calendar. Then, in 2000, it emerged that the date of the *Temple Scroll* was too early to be associated with the Essenes or the Sadducees, so neither of these theories suits the situation. The identification of several hundred different scribal hands at work on the scrolls might also seem to argue against their having been written within the small community at Qumran. On the other hand, the scrolls were being produced over a period of perhaps 200 years.

An alternative is that the scrolls came to Qumran from somewhere else. They may have come from various libraries in Jerusalem, including the Temple library. They may have been removed to the desert caves for safe-keeping at the time when the Romans were laying siege to Jerusalem in AD 68–70. That would account for the large number of scribal hands, the wide range in date of origin, and the wide range of conflicting religious ideas. This is exactly what you would expect in a long-established library. The hiding of the books would be a natural parallel to the systematic hiding of the Temple treasure which is specifically mentioned in the scrolls themselves. Growing numbers of leading scholars now support this theory, but the Qumran-Essene faction still has a lot of support and a sharp polarisation of views has developed.

When the scrolls were first found, Christians hardly dared to hope that writings actually dating from the lifetime of Jesus would throw light on the earliest days of Christianity. Perhaps Christian writings earlier than the Gospels would emerge, giving a more authentic account of the teachings of Jesus. Various people have tried to make a connection. Linking the scrolls with the Essene community, and linking that in turn with Qumran, opened the possibility that Jesus himself might have been an Essene, that he might have retreated to Qumran to study. This retreat into the desert beside the Dead Sea might have been the origin of the stories about Jesus in the wilderness. But as time has passed, there seems to be less and less to connect Jesus with the Essenes or with Qumran. Ironically, the new theory puts the origin of the scrolls in Jerusalem, where Jesus might well have seen and read them in the Temple library; his activities in Jerusalem are well documented. The new view of the Dead Sea Scrolls brings them much closer to the living Jesus, as these were among the very documents that he might have seen, handled and read as a student.

THE STEADY STATE
THEORY OF THE
UNIVERSE
(1948)

By the 1940s, the idea that the universe had begun with an explosion and was in a state of progressive expansion was widely accepted. Then in 1948 a rival view of the universe appeared, and with it a phase of lively debate among the physicists and astronomers. One of the leading exponents of the new idea was Fred Hoyle. As a young man during World War II, Hoyle had worked in the British Admiralty Signals Establishment. During that time he made friends with Hermann Bondi and Thomas Gold. The ideas that led on to the new view of the universe, the continuous creation theory, were born at that time, in conversations among the three men.

In 1948, their historic papers on continuous creation were published. Bondi and Gold published a joint paper, and Hoyle published a separate paper two months later. Bondi and Gold stressed the philosophical aspect of a perfect cosmological principle, one in which the universe would have a high degree of uniformity through both space and time. A major problem with the expanding universe theory was that it meant that either time was finite, its beginning marked by the initial explosion, or that there was some earlier universe. The view presented by Bondi and Gold either evaded or annihilated that problem (depending on your point of view) by asserting that the universe had always been the same; it had no beginning and would have no end. It had always been there and would always be there – time without end.

Fred Hoyle's 1948 paper had as its focus the continuous creation of the primordial hydrogen that would be necessary to maintain the steady state. His paper also put the theory into the context of general relativity. The two papers were thus complementary, though they were not really presented as part of a co-operative venture. It appears that Hoyle had earlier sent his paper to the editor of an American journal, who had rejected it. Only then had he sent it to the journal of the Royal Astronomical Society. So its publication just after the Bondi-Gold paper was coincidental.

More important, though, was the complete contradiction that now existed between the two major theories of the universe. The expanding universe theory carried with it the inescapable implication that the universe had had a specific beginning, billions of years ago. From 1948 until 1964, the supporters of the two theories battled it out with assertions and counter-assertions. Then, in 1964, the cosmic microwave background was discovered, and this was widely interpreted as the left-over radiation from the explosion that marked the creation of the universe. At last it seemed that there was incontrovertible proof that the expanding universe theory was true and that – therefore – the steady state theory was false.

Emotions ran high among the astronomers and physicists in the two camps. It was one of the bitterest scientific divisions of the twentieth century. Hoyle contemptuously referred to his enemies' theory as the Big Bang, a phrase which stuck; now everyone refers to it as that, though without contempt. Hoyle refused to accept the gradually mounting evidence that the universe did in fact start with a Big Bang and was expanding. In 1966, I attended a crowded lecture given by Fred Hoyle when he and his theory were seriously under siege. In it, Hoyle tried to reconcile the two views of the universe. He said there might have been a Big Bang and that the universe might have been expanding ever since that moment of creation. But in the expanding spaces between the separating galaxies, matter was condensing and new galaxies were continuously being formed. The universe might be expanding, yet also maintaining a constant density because of the parallel process of continuous creation. Big Bang and steady state could *both* be true. It was a clever but desperate argument. I wonder how many people in that huge lecture theatre audience in 1966 were persuaded by Hoyle's presentation.

Hoyle never really let go of his steady state theory, but went on finding fault with the expanding universe, which he derided as unscientific. Ultimately, the Big Bang had to be wrong because nothing can come out of nothing. And if the Big Bang happened once, why should it not happen again and again? The whole theory depended on belief in a one-off catastrophe. He also argued that the Big Bang theory was untestable and therefore should be regarded with suspicion.

In fact, there were some shortcomings in the expanding universe theory at that stage. There had been some miscalculations and the timescale for the history of the universe was far too short. The expanding universe also predicted a hot dense phase for the early universe, though at that time there was absolutely no observable evidence for this. Because of the timescale problem and the general lack of supporting evidence, it did appear that there were weaknesses in the expanding universe theory. That opened the door to an alternative model for the universe, which Fred Hoyle and his supporters were glad to supply.

The ramifications of this huge scientific controversy were enormous. The Big Bang carried with it religious overtones. It entailed a spectacular moment of creation, which allowed for the existence of a Creator-God, and made the theory popular with religious groups. But if the expanding universe theory allowed for the existence and participation of God, where did that leave Fred Hoyle and the other proponents of the steady state universe? They were made to appear Creation deniers and therefore Creator-God deniers.

There were problems that weakened the credibility of the expanding universe theory, but in time they were rectified. Recalculation gave the universe a longer history, and the microwave background radiation was discovered. Gradually, more and more pieces of evidence appeared in support of the expanding universe. Stephen Hawking commented that the fact that the microwave radiation had been found and that it was thought to be left over from the Big Bang, was 'the final nail in the coffin of the steady state theory'.

The steady state theory has few supporters today. Those few are mainly those who supported it from the start. Their main objections remain that nothing can be created out of nothing and that everything is made to depend on a single catastrophic event, an explosion which happened just once and has never happened since – and which is almost by definition incapable of scientific scrutiny. Belief in the Big Bang is an act of faith.

One of the main by-products of the steady state theory has been the goading that it gave to the expanding universe theorists. They were made to work much harder to find and present convincing evidence of their model of the universe. So, like many challenges to received wisdom, the theory had a very positive outcome on the development of science. The vehement arguments flung backwards and forwards during the dispute have left most scientists believing that the Big Bang theory is the best available description of the origin of the universe.

Fred Hoyle's idea of the existence of a C-field or Creation-field has taken on a life of its own within the expanding universe theory. This has negative pressure, enabling it to drive the steady expansion of the cosmos. In this way, it is similar to the inflation field that is now considered necessary to drive the inflation of the universe. The expansion of the universe, the flying apart of all the galaxies, is not the same as the scattering of fragments in a bomb blast. Instead, it is driven by the dynamic enlargement of the space between the galaxies – and this is the way forward towards an explanation for the acceleration in expansion noted by some scientists.

THE DECIPHERMENT OF LINEAR B

(1952)

The Mycenaeans of Bronze Age Greece and the earlier Minoans of Bronze Age Crete are famous for having been literate. At least some of them were literate, and they could write and read a syllabic script known to archaeologists by the uninspiring name Linear B. This ancient Aegean script had eighty-nine different signs. Sir Arthur Evans discovered the first clay tablets with Minoan 'hieroglyphics' at Knossos on Crete and published a tantalising selection of them in his huge book on Knossos, *The Palace of Minos*, though not enough to allow anyone else the chance of deciphering them. Evans clung to the hope that he could do that himself.

When Sir Arthur Evans died at an advanced age in 1941, he had got no further forward with the decipherment. He had found the first clay tablets back at the turn of the century and forty years on he had deciphered not one of them – not a single symbol. Once Evans was dead, other scholars might have had access to the inscriptions and systematic work on deciphering them could begin. In fact it was not until 1952, eleven years after Evans's death, and half a century after Evans discovered the first tablets, that they were actually published.

The American archaeologist Carl Blegen struck the Archive Room at Pylos on the mainland of Greece with his very first trench in 1939. There he found a huge cache of Linear B tablets. This large body of extra documents made the decipherment much easier.

The man who eventually deciphered Linear B was Michael Ventris, a young architect who developed an obsession with the untranslated tablets. He realised that some signs represented vowels, like *a*, and other signs represented vowels with consonants, like *pa*. The signs were written in horizontal lines from left to right, just like modern Western writing; we can tell this from the way all the lines on the clay tablets are aligned on the left side. Groups of signs were separated by a short bar, which implied that the sign groups were words. An early barrier to decipherment was the widespread belief that the Linear B language could not be Greek but had to be an earlier, Minoan, language. But there were some scholars who thought differently. They cleverly saw the frequency of Greek names in Homer as a sign that the Mycenaean (immediately post-Minoan) world Homer described was also a Greek-speaking world.

Michael Ventris, collaborating with the Cambridge University academic John Chadwick, guessed that some of the words on the Cretan tablets might be the names of Bronze Age towns on Crete. *Ko-no-so* might be Knossos, *A-mi-ni-so* Amnisos, and *Tu-ri-so* might be the nearby Minoan town of *Tylissos*. There were too many of these parallels to be a coincidence. It was even so quite remarkable – indeed a major discovery in itself – to find that tablets written in the 200 years before 1200 BC should refer to towns and villages by their modern names. It was a little like finding that a contemporary early Bronze Age inscription on one of the stones at Stonehenge read, 'This stone was raised at Stonehenge near Amesbury'. It implied an astonishing continuity of language and memory.

The hypothesis that the language of the tablets was Greek led to the emergence of more and more Greek words in the inscriptions. It was vindicated in 1953 when Carl Blegen studied some newly discovered tablets from Pylos. One of them had picture signs showing three-legged cauldrons. When Blegen substituted the syllables Ventris and Chadwick had proposed for the signs, he was astonished to see the word *ti-ri-po-de* appearing: the Greek word meaning 'tripods'.

After a great many exchanges of ideas – Ventris was very keen on circulating his ideas on neatly handwritten pamphlets – more and more Greek or near-Greek words emerged on the tablets. *Korwos* (boy) was very close to the later Greek word *kouros*. *Guasileus* (chief) was close to the later Greek word for king, *basileus*.

The decipherment of the tablets has enabled us to read the archives of the Minoans and Mycenaeans and gain a greater insight into the nature of the two civilisations. One very significant fact is that the Mycenaeans were Greeks, even though their civilisation ended in about 1200 BC and was followed by a 500-year-long dark age when there was no writing. The Greek language links the two together in a significant way. Homer wrote about the Trojan War in Greek. The Greeks at the time of the Trojan War, it turns out, also spoke and wrote in Greek. With the translation of Linear B, a door swings open on the world of Agamemnon and Achilles.

THE STRUCTURE
OF DNA
(1952)

From 1949 onwards, Francis Crick was researching into molecular biology at the Cavendish Laboratory. Two years after that he began working in collaboration with a young American biologist, James D. Watson, who was only twenty-three. Their great breakthrough came in 1953, when they constructed a molecular model of the extremely complex genetic material known as DNA (deoxyribonucleic acid). The molecular model was in the distinctive shape of a double helix. The new discovery was published in the scientific journal *Nature* in 1953. The one-page article opened modestly: 'We wish to suggest a structure for the salt of DNA. This structure has novel features that are of considerable biological interest.' It was a major understatement.

Watson and Crick went on to demonstrate that chromosomes consist of long helical strands of DNA containing the codified genetic material that determines how animal and human cells develop. These exciting new findings were confirmed by experiments by other scientists round the world.

Later Crick went on to research the nucleic acids, making far-reaching discoveries about the genetic code they contain. When Crick died in 2004, James Watson said, 'I will always remember Francis for his extraordinary focused intelligence. He treated me as though I were a member of his family. I always looked forward to being with him and speaking to him.'

Francis Crick was awarded the Nobel Prize for medicine and physiology in 1962, jointly with James Watson and Maurice Wilkins, his co-workers. James Watson returned to the USA, where he became director of the Cold Spring Biological Laboratories in New York.

The discovery of the structure of DNA and its significance was one of the great scientific breakthroughs of the second half of the twentieth century. It was a discovery with lots of ramifications. When it emerged that everyone has different DNA, the possibility of using it for identification presented itself. DNA has now become a major forensic tool. A criminal has now to leave only a few traces of human tissue at the scene of a crime, and he or she can be identified. This new technique has made it possible to solve some crimes that were committed decades ago and also, disturbingly, prove that some people serving very long prison sentences really did not commit the crimes for which they were convicted. At least DNA has ensured their release.

Family members have related (that is, similar) DNA, which means that DNA analysis can establish kinship links. This was how the remains of the last Tsar of Russia and his family were identified. This kinship feature can also help to resolve cases of disputed paternity. Since DNA can survive for a long time after death, it has also proved invaluable to historians, archaeologists and anthropologists in establishing kinship groups. DNA has created a whole sequence of new possibilities – including the prevention of genetically communicated disorders.

RAPID EYE MOVEMENT SLEEP

(1953)

Rapid eye movement (REM) sleep is a normal stage of sleep. It is characterised, as the name implies, by rapid movements of the eyes. This distinctive phase of sleep was discovered by Nathaniel Kleitman and Eugene Aserinsky at the University of Chicago at the beginning of the 1950s.

Distinct stages in sleep were discovered by monitoring volunteers, and observations showed that REM sleep typically occupies between twenty and twenty-five per cent of the total time spent asleep. It lasts in total up to two hours each night, but usually occurs in four or five separate phases which are shorter at the beginning of the night and longer towards the end.

The amount of time spent in REM sleep varies a lot according to age. Newly born children spend over eighty per cent of their sleeping time in rapid eye movement sleep. The per cent falls away with increasing age. The body behaves differently in a number of different ways during REM sleep. The release of certain neurotransmitters shuts down completely, which causes what is called REM atonia; this means that the motor neurons are not stimulated and the muscles of the body do not move. In some people, this REM atonia does not occur, and in that situation sufferers act out the movements that occur in their dreams. This is REM Behaviour Disorder. Another feature of REM sleep is irregularity of heart rate and breathing rate.

Rapid eye movement sleep was an intriguing discovery with a range of implications. REM sleep is physiologically different from other phases of sleep, which are described simply as non-REM sleep. There was a suspicion that this more active phase of sleeping was associated with dreaming, and it does appear that most of the dreams that we can vividly recall happen during REM sleep. The significance of REM sleep is still not fully understood and there are several theories about it. One is that memories are consolidated during REM sleep. Another is that it is especially important to brain development, in particular establishing mature neural connections. Studies show that deprivation of REM sleep early in life can lead to behavioural problems and permanent sleep disruption. This theory is supported by the pattern of decreasing REM sleep with age.

Another theory is the sentinel theory. Several different types of mammal were observed (rat, hedgehog, rabbit, monkey) while sleeping and their REM sleep phases ended in brief awakenings. This waking up does not happen in cats or people, but it is the case that people are more likely to wake up from REM sleep than from non-REM sleep. Frederic Snyder proposed in 1966 that this type of sleep is a kind of shallow sleep, activating the animal periodically so that it can scan its environment for potential predators and, if necessary, wake up to defend itself. This is in some ways an attractive hypothesis, but it is really not consistent with the muscle paralysis observed in REM sleep; if the body was being prepared to wake and take action, or take flight, more muscle activity would be expected, not less.

REM sleep is evidently both normal and essential to human beings, to mammals in general and also birds. Prolonged REM sleep deprivation leads to behavioural and physiological abnormalities. But the actual reason for it is still unknown.

ANTIPROTON
(1955)

A paper was published in November 1955 by four members of the Radiation Laboratory at Berkeley, California, announcing the existence of antiprotons. The four discoverers were Owen Chamberlain, Emilio Segrè, Clyde Wiegand and Thomas Ypsilantis. The antiproton they had discovered was a new subatomic particle. It was exactly like the proton, except that it had a negative instead of a positive electrical charge.

Some discoveries are made by chance, by scientists or voyagers stumbling on a new element or a new island. But the discovery of the antiproton was not one of those. It was the outcome of a systematic hunt that began as far back as 1928. It was in that year that the British physicist Paul Dirac developed a theory that described the behaviour of electrons. Dirac's equation was remarkable for its time, because it took account of both Albert Einstein's special theory and the effects of quantum physics, as put forward by Erwin Schrödinger and Werner Heisenberg. The mathematics of Dirac's equation worked, but no one took it very seriously because it allowed for particles of negative energy. At that time, it was generally considered that the energy of a particle could only be positive.

The attitudes of scientists shifted in 1932 when Carl Anderson, a young researcher at the California Institute of Technology, reported the observation of a positively charged electron, which he named the positron. Anderson was working on a project that he had inherited from his mentor, Robert Millikan. Dirac and Anderson were awarded Nobel Prizes in 1933 and 1936 for their discoveries. The proven existence of the positron, which is in effect the antimatter counterpart of the electron, suggested that an antimatter counterpart to the proton might also exist. These developments led to an expectation that such a subatomic particle existed and awaited discovery.

Dirac's theory proved to be very useful in explaining phenomena associated with electrons and positrons, so there was an expectation that it might also be successful in explaining protons. If that was so, the existence of an antimatter counterpart was (mathematically) required. So the search for this antimatter counterpart, the 'antiproton', got under way. It was a very long time before any real progress was made. Initially, there was no machine in existence that was capable of generating such a particle. The positron was discovered by probing cosmic rays with a cloud chamber, but this method was unlikely to work in the search for the antiproton.

In 1931, Ernest Lawrence had invented the cyclotron, a particle accelerator, but this was nowhere near powerful enough to produce antiprotons. The minimum amount of energy needed was about two billion electron volts and there was a better chance of getting a result if a beam of protons could be accelerated to three times that.

In 1955, a new machine was built at Berkeley, the Bevatron, a very powerful particle accelerator which would enable scientists to generate antiprotons; indeed it was built precisely to do this. It was capable of reaching 6.5 billion electron volts. Ernest Lawrence assembled a team to work at the Bevatron. Their task was to ensure that the machine reached the voltage required to produce an antiproton.

Creating an antiproton was now possible. One problem was going to be identifying the antiproton among the 40,000 other subatomic particles that would be generated. Another problem was the short lifespan of the antiproton. Within one-ten-millionth of a second of the antiproton's appearance, it comes into contact with a proton and both particles are annihilated. The likely velocity of an antiproton was calculated and a 'speed trap' was devised so that only particles travelling at the calculated speed would be identified. The moving particles were recorded on photographic plates, and the scientists expected that the annihilation event (of a silver or bromine atom in the photographic emulsion) would become visible on the plate as a star image.

These projections and speculations were turned into reality when the signature star image duly showed up in August 1955. The track of an antiproton could be seen travelling a short distance before meeting a proton; as these two particles were annihilated, nine new particles sprayed out from the point of collision, making the star. The antiproton had been discovered at last.

CROSSING
ANTARCTICA
(1957–58)

The idea of a Trans-Antarctic expedition originated with Ernest Shackleton. It was taken up again by Vivian Fuchs in 1949, when he was sheltering from bad weather. It occurred to Fuchs that with motorised transport he could cross the ice sheet more easily than the explorers of fifty years earlier, and that support by aircraft would also make such an expedition safer. Fuchs also had the additional idea of gathering significant scientific data on the crossing. In particular, he wanted to find out how thick the Antarctic ice sheet was.

The Commonwealth Trans-Antarctic Expedition of 1957–58 was the first attempt to cross the continent of Antarctica. It was under the overall leadership of Dr Vivian Fuchs and consisted of two teams. One was a British team led by Fuchs; the other was a New Zealand team led by Sir Edmund Hillary, setting off from the opposite side of Antarctica, and they met at the South Pole. Both teams used motorised vehicles for the journey. One task for the Hillary team was to set up food and fuel depots for use by the British team.

Fuchs described his team's journey to the South Pole under worsening weather conditions as 'one of the worst journeys in the world'. Fuchs somehow managed to maintain high morale and excellent discipline throughout. He had a very even temperament, showing neither frustration at delay nor elation at progress; every move was orderly and methodical, usually with Fuchs himself in the lead in his motorised Sno-Cat, *Rock n' Roll*.

The Hillary team arrived at the South Pole nearly three weeks before the Fuchs team. Fuchs had not intended Hillary to travel as far as the

Pole, and Hillary's decision to disobey Fuchs and press on to the Pole is controversial. Fuchs intended Hillary to wait for the main (British) crossing party and act as its guide for the rest of the journey. Afterwards, at a dinner held at the Royal Geographical Society, Fuchs said 'the great Antarctic row never existed at all'. But there had certainly been a clash of personalities between the two men, as was clear from the radio messages they exchanged – and they had been leaked to the press. Hillary gave Fuchs some high-handed advice to call a halt at the Pole and get the Americans to fly him out. If he did that, the New Zealanders could get back home before the Antarctic winter set in. Maybe the journey could be resumed the following season. But Fuchs had no funding arranged for that scenario and rejected Hillary's proposal out of hand; they would carry on as planned, and if necessary without the New Zealanders' help. To Hillary's credit, he gave in at once to this decisive leadership. He agreed to stick to Fuchs's original plan. As it turned out the second leg of the journey proved to be easier than the first. Fuchs's party left the Pole on 24 January 1958 and completed the crossing in ninety-nine days. It is a measure of Fuchs's planning and leadership skills that his original estimate had been 100 days.

A very important aspect of the expedition was a seismic survey. This entailed making soundings through the huge ice cap that covers most of the continent to find out how thick it was. The results of this survey were profoundly important in advancing understanding of both the ice sheet and the continent beneath it. The ice turns out to be very thick indeed, and in many places the solid rock of the continent is below sea level; it is at the South Pole. This means that instead of Antarctica being a single uninterrupted landmass it is an archipelago, an island group. There is one very large island, often known as East Antarctica, and a group of smaller islands, known as West Antarctica, beyond an area that without the ice would be shallow sea. A picture emerges of a continent not unlike Australasia, with one large island (Australia) and some smaller islands (Tasmania and the North and South Islands of New Zealand).

The seismic survey results also showed that the bedrock surface of the continent was very varied compared with the smooth plateaus of the ice surface. The rock was deeply furrowed by features that looked exactly like the U-shaped valleys that are seen in the Alps, Rockies and Himalayas. This discovery led on to the inevitable conclusion that it was the sliding motion of the ice sheet itself that had eroded these deep troughs. Scattered all over the surface of the ice sheet, often in lines, were small rocky knolls and crags. The seismic survey showed that these were actually the summits of mountains that were almost completely submerged by the ice, landforms known by the Inuit word *nunataks*.

Fuchs emerged as an outstanding polar expedition leader. On his return from the 1957–58 expedition he was immediately appointed director of the Antarctic Survey's scientific bureau. He had shown what a good leader he was in the year before the expedition. He had remained calm during the *Theron*'s dangerous passage through the icebound Weddell Sea in 1956, and had put his crew ashore efficiently and purposefully late in the season and under worsening weather conditions. These were conditions in which swift and decisive action was vital, and Fuchs proved very capable. His swiftness enable a team to build the foundations of a base for the expedition's main task in 1957–58, and he had to land the advance party and supplies quickly enough to enable the *Theron* to make her escape through the thickening ice as it closed in on them.

In a very real way, the Fuchs expedition opened Antarctica up to a whole string of discoveries. It enabled geographers and geologists to begin to study the processes of its formation and development. The seismic survey also provided a benchmark for later measurements which have been interpreted as indicating serious climate change.

RADIATION BELTS SURROUNDING THE EARTH

(1958)

The existence of a belt of radiation surrounding the Earth was first proposed by Immanuel Velikovsky, then later by Nicholas Christofilos. The reality of this radiation belt was proved in January 1958 by the *Explorer 1* mission, under the direction of James Van Allen of the University of Iowa. The radiation belt was then recorded and mapped in greater detail by subsequent probes and satellites: *Sputnik 3, Explorers 3* and *4, Pioneer 3* and *Luna 1.*

As more information was gathered about the phenomenon, scientists realised there was more than one radiation belt. The belt was found to consist of two main layers and they are named after its discoverer, Van Allen. The Van Allen belts consist of layers of energetic charged particles (or plasma) concentric with the Earth and held in position by the Earth's magnetic field. The Van Allen belts are associated with the polar auroras, the Northern and Southern Lights, which are caused by the charged particles fluorescing as they strike the upper atmosphere. Within the radiation belts, particles are able to penetrate layers of lead shielding one millimetre thick.

The belts extend from about 480 kilometres (300 miles) above the Earth's surface quite a long way out into space, out to about seven Earth radii. They are limited in latitude, extending roughly from the Arctic Circle to the Antarctic Circle. The polar regions are therefore left unprotected by the radiation belts, and this later provided an explanation for the (yet to be discovered, and indeed yet to develop) ozone holes in high latitudes. The Arctic and Antarctic regions are more vulnerable because they lack the protection of the radiation belts.

What Van Allen had discovered was a specific large-scale feature of the Earth. Subsequent exploration of other planets has revealed that they too have radiation belts around them, though the Sun does not.

The huge outer radiation belt is the one that extends about seven Earth radii out into space. It consists mainly of high-energy electrons and ions, and its population of particles fluctuates quite a lot as a result of geomagnetic storms, which in turn are triggered by variations in the Sun's behaviour. The inner Van Allen Belt extends from about 480 kilometres (300 miles) to 9,660 kilometres (6,000 miles) above the Earth's surface (from 0.1 up to 1.5 Earth radii) and contains a high concentration of energetic protons. The Earth's magnetic field is stronger here, which is why the belt has a higher density and higher energy level compared with the outer belt. Together, the radiation belts form an invisible cage girdling the Earth, absorbing and deflecting the solar wind and therefore protecting the Earth itself from excessive bombardment.

The Van Allen Belts can have various impacts on human activity. In 1962, a high-altitude nuclear explosion caused an amplification of the radiation belts and as a result of this a number of satellites, perhaps as many as one-third of them, went out of action. Geomagnetic storms acting through the radiation belts have sometimes damaged the electronic systems on spacecraft; the miniaturisation of these electronic systems has made them more vulnerable to these interferences and have to be turned off to protect them. The Hubble Space Telescope often had its sensors switched off when it was passing through areas of high-intensity radiation.

During the Apollo missions, astronauts had to pass through the Van Allen belts on the way to the Moon, and on the return journey too. Because of the speed of travel, they only spent brief periods in the radiation belts. The highest exposures were during *Apollo 14*, but it was felt that the levels of exposure to radiation were still safe. Another implication of the discovery is that the interplanetary environment outside the Van Allen belts is a good deal more hostile than that inside, because astronauts are exposed to more cosmic rays and the full effect of the solar wind. What the effect of prolonged exposure to these would be on a long space flight can only be guessed, but it may be that a manned voyage to Mars would be too dangerous to risk.

The Van Allen belts are believed to give the Earth some protection against the solar wind and they may even have a role in stabilising the Earth's magnetic poles.

THE FIRST PROBE
LANDS ON THE MOON
(1959)

In the late 1950s, the Cold War rivalry between the USA and the Soviet Union created a space race. In particular it was a race to the Moon. The Americans had little success with their initial probes, which were an attempt to establish a vehicle in orbit round the Moon. *Pioneer 1*, launched in October 1958, failed to reach a trajectory for the Moon and re-entered the Earth's atmosphere two months later. *Pioneer 2* was launched one month after *Pioneer 1* and that too failed to reach the Moon. *Pioneer 3* experienced a launch failure.

The Soviet endeavour was more successful. In January 1959, the Soviets launched a rocket at the Moon with simple aim of hitting it. In fact, the vehicle's trajectory took it past the Moon, but *Luna 1*'s fly-by was a major improvement on the Americans' track record. Then in March of that year the Americans launched *Pioneer 4*, which also achieved a fly-by, approaching within 59,500 kilometres (37,000 miles) of the Moon.

In the autumn of 1959, the Russians launched *Luna 2* from the Baikonur Cosmodrome in Kazakhstan, with the same object as *Luna 1*, to crash-land on the Moon's surface. This succeeded. After a flight lasting thirty-three hours, *Luna 2* landed on the Moon to the east of the Sea of Serenity near the Aristides and Archimedes craters. *Luna 2* was the first man-made object to strike the Moon's surface – and as a result its wreckage also became the first lunar litter. Just before impact, the craft sent back data confirming that the Moon had no magnetic field and no radiation belts. The Sputnik-like *Luna 2* had no propulsion system of its own, and it was guided along by the third stage of its booster rocket until the two (rocket and probe) separated shortly before the probe's impact; the rocket itself crashed onto the Moon about half an hour later.

The Russians capped this major success straight away with *Luna 3* the following month. *Luna 3* flew round the Moon, sending back to Earth the first photographs of the hitherto unseen far side of the Moon. The Moon turns on its axis in such a way that it always has the same side facing the Earth. The photographs sent back by *Luna 3* excited great interest because they revealed a huge tract of lunar landscape that had never been seen before.

The Soviet Luna programme was a two-pronged programme, to develop the technology for a manned probe to reach and land on the Moon, and to gather enough background data about the lunar environment to make this expedition possible. The Soviets were highly successful in these early stages, but the anticipated manned flights never materialised. Four Russian Luna probes reached the Moon before Neil Armstrong did, including the first soft landing on the Moon (*Luna 13*) but there was never a Russian manned flight to the Moon. The programme came to an end with *Luna 24* in 1976.

THE FIRST PERSON IN SPACE

(1961)

In 1961, the Soviet Union had another major success in the space race, beating the USA by getting the first man into space. Major Yuri Gagarin was launched from the Baikonur Cosmodrome in the spacecraft Vostok. Gagarin was launched into orbit round the Earth, travelling for over an hour and a half at more than 27,000 kilometres (17,000 miles) per hour. The flight ended with Gagarin landing at an undisclosed location.

This was major political success for the Soviet Union, and Gagarin was treated as a national hero. He was treated to a big reception in the Kremlin to celebrate his achievement. The Soviet leader Nikita Khrushchev sent the cosmonaut a message of congratulation from his holiday home on the Black Sea, 'The flight you have made opens up a new page in the history of mankind in its conquest of space.' He was right. It was a very significant step. Some people had been anxious that the trauma of space travel might be fatal to human beings. Gagarin's safe return from orbit showed that manned space flight really was possible.

The first manned flight into space was a major spur to the US space programme. President John F. Kennedy congratulated the Soviets on their achievement, adding that it would be some time before the Americans caught up with them in the field of rocket boosters. America's space programme was conspicuously lagging behind that of its rival. In that same year, 1961, President Kennedy called for massive funding to allow America's space programme to surge forward. In a speech to Congress, broadcast on radio and television, he asked for an additional 1,700 million dollars. The cash would be spent on achieving the goal of getting a man on the Moon. He went so far as to pledge that

America would land a man on the Moon – the first man on the Moon – by 1970 and return him safely to Earth. The plea for extra money was presented as 'this very urgent request', which shows how important the space race had become in the context of the Cold War. Americans, he said, had to 'work with the utmost speed and vigour' to advance their space programme.

The USA was not slow to catch up with the Soviet Union. Within weeks, an American astronaut, Alan Shepard, was sent into orbit.

The consequences of the first space flight for Yuri Gagarin were strange. He became an international icon, and as such he became too valuable a propaganda property to be risked on a future space mission – and the risks in those missions were still very great. The result was that he was banned from taking part in any future space flight. His death in a plane crash outside Moscow in 1968 is therefore rather difficult to explain. It may have been a simple accident, but some observers believe there were suspicious circumstances. All the parts of the crashed MiG-15UTI were collected and stored in sealed containers, and forensic examination of these fragments may explain the cause of the crash, but as recently as 2007 the Kremlin continued to veto any further investigation into Gagarin's death.

QUARKS
(1962)

A revolutionary new idea about atomic structure was that particles such as protons and neutrons were composite, that they were made up of combinations of even tinier particles – fundamental particles or quarks. The existence of these fundamental particles, the building blocks of matter, was proposed by Murray Gell-Mann. Following the statement of this hypothesis by Murray Gell-Mann of Caltech in 1962, scientists looked for evidence of the existence of these *sub*-subatomic particles. They looked for quarks in the showers of particles arriving from space, in the depths of the oceans and even in the stained glass of medieval cathedrals. They began to despair of finding them, and even Gell-Mann began to doubt whether they would ever be found, even if they existed.

Then the physicist William Fairbank, together with his colleagues at Stanford University, Arthur Hebard and George LaRue, carried out an experiment that appeared to demonstrate that quarks did exist. They used a version of the 'oil drop' experiment that was first used in 1910 by Robert Millikan to measure the charge on a single electron. Fairbank and his team used tiny spheres of niobium, a metal that becomes a superconductor when it is cooled close to absolute zero. When the niobium sphere is lifted in a strong magnetic field and stripped of its electrical charge, any charge that remains, even the charge of a single electron, can be detected.

The Stanford team detected positive and negative charges equal to one-third of an electron's normal charge. The result fitted precisely with the predicted charges for quarks, which the theoreticians declared would be either one-third or two-thirds of the charges measured in electrons. It was not absolutely certain, by any means, but it looked as if the Stanford physicists had verified the existence of particles smaller than electrons – quarks. And it looked as if Gell-Mann's theory about the structure of matter was true.

QUASARS
(1963)

Quasi-stellar objects, sometimes referred to as QSOs but far more often as quasars, are the most distant and the most luminous objects in the entire universe.

Quasars were discovered in 1963, thanks to the development of radio telescopes that were able to locate the sources of radio waves accurately. Cyril Hazard and his colleagues made observations of the radio source known as 3C273, and their calculations made the object a twelfth magnitude star-like object. 'Twelfth magnitude' is very faint; the object would need to be 250 times brighter than this to become visible. The higher the magnitude, the dimmer the star is. The Sun has an absolute magnitude (regardless of distance) of 4.8, Sirius 1.4. Normal stars like the Sun are not strong radio sources, which meant that objects like 3C273 must belong to some special category. Object 3C273 and other similar radio-source stars were called quasi-stellar radio sources, and this cumbersome phrase was soon shortened to quasars. Although the strong radio signal was an early identifying characteristic, it is now known that there are many more quasars that are not strong radio sources – possibly fifteen times as many.

Maarten Schmidt of Caltech used the 500-centimetre (200-inch) telescope at Mount Palomar to obtain the first spectrum from the newly discovered quasar. At first Schmidt could not make sense of the spectrum. After several months of scrutiny, he realised that the strong and broad emission lines in the star's spectrum were the familiar hydrogen-Balmer series – but red shifted by fifteen per cent. The red shift as such did not puzzle Schmidt, nor did the red shift by fifteen per cent, as it was already known that some galaxies were moving away from us at much higher speeds. What struck him was the relative brightness of 3C273 in relation to its distance. In spite of being far too faint to be visible to the human eye, it was one thousand times brighter than even a very luminous galaxy would appear to be at a distance of two billion light years. Two billion light years was the estimate of 3C273's distance from us, based on a red shift of 15.8 per cent.

It was not long before astronomers discovered more quasars, some with even higher red shift. These are quasars that are even further out in the universe and therefore moving away from us even faster because of the universe's expansion. The current record quasar, the quasar that is furthest away and moving away fastest, has a red shift that is defined as $z = 5.5$ (or 550 per cent). This corresponds to a velocity of 95 per cent of the speed of light. This quasar is about fourteen billion light years away from us; at speeds like these the distance is only an approximate estimate.

The quasars are releasing a tremendous amount of energy. Astronomers tried to find explanations for this, but they were hampered by the substantial variations in the quasars' brightness, even within periods as short as one week. One implication is that the object must be relatively small. In other words, if the quasar varies significantly in brightness over a period of one week than it must be smaller than a light-week in extent. This in turn carries an amazing implication – that a quasar can be brighter than a thousand galaxies, yet be no bigger than our solar system.

Another major mystery associated with quasars is the discovery that every few years a radio quasar erupts, hurling out huge blobs of radio-emitting plasma. This remarkable process is called superluminal motion, and the plasma blobs are able to move outwards at as much as ten times the speed of light. The eruption of plasma is therefore violating the special theory of relativity or, put another way, the phenomenon is giving us early indications that the theory of relativity is flawed. But scientists are extremely reluctant to allow this and seek other explanations for the observed eruptions, explanations that leave the theory of relativity intact.

The current explanation for the massive energy output from quasars, and their small size, is that they are associated with black holes. The theory is that material falling into a massive black hole is releasing gravitational energy. This ties in with the prevailing view among astronomers that there are commonly black holes at or near the centres of galaxies. Material falling into a black hole near the centre of a galaxy might release up to ten per cent of its energy in the form of gravitational potential energy transformed in various ways, for instance into X-rays and moving particles. Stars orbiting close to a quasar may first be inflated by the intense radiation field, then later tidally disrupted by the intense gravitational field. Finally, they may be spread into a swirling disc of material, the ultimate fate of which is to be swallowed by the central black hole. Scientists visualise quasars as depending on very large black holes; we have to imagine something with the mass of a hundred million Suns. They have calculated that the release of gravitational energy by a massive black hole on this scale devouring one star every year would power a typical quasar.

The 'star-like' feature that is a quasar turns out to be a really terrifying object, a huge star-eating black hole spitting out colossal amounts of energy – and from the farthest edge of the visible universe.

COSMIC MICROWAVE BACKGROUND RADIATION
(1965)

Until 1965 there were two rival theories of the universe, theories that were fundamentally contradictory. The expanding universe theory implicitly carried with it the notion of a specific beginning, a point in space and time when all the particles in the universe were in the same place, a point that was the beginning of both space and time. The steady state theory of the universe implied that the universe has always been the same and always will be, without beginning and without end. They were two diametrically opposed views, each with its supporters, who argued vehemently over the evidence.

Then in 1965 a major discovery was made that gave strong support for the expanding universe with a beginning in a big bang. Robert Wilson and Arno Penzias discovered cosmic microwave background spread right across the entire universe.

Cosmic microwave background radiation (CMBR or more often CMB) is a type of electromagnetic radiation. The spectrum of this radiation peaks at a frequency of 160 GHz, which corresponds with a wavelength of 1.9 mm.

An important part of the Wilson and Penzias discovery was that the microwave background is the residual glow from the Big Bang, the moment when the universe was created. This discovery, especially when combined with the earlier finding by Edwin Hubble that the galaxies are all rushing apart, strongly reinforced the Big Bang theory. The proponents of Big Bang theory (George Gamow, Ralph Alpher and

Robert Herman) predicted the existence of this radiation in 1948, and several scientists in the 1940s and 1950s made estimates of the very low temperature of the background radiation, varying between 2 and 28 degrees Kelvin; the universe had had a very long time to cool off. By 1960, the estimates of the temperature were very low.

Then in 1964–65 Arno Penzias and Robert Woodrow Wilson measured the temperature and discovered it was 2.725 degrees Kelvin. They were working at the Crawford Hill complex of Bell Telephone Laboratories in New Jersey; it was there that they built a Dicke radiometer to use for radio astronomy and used it in combination with a bizarre antenna that looked like an early flying machine to make their discovery. Penzias and Wilson were awarded the 1978 Nobel Prize in Physics.

It seems it was the Princeton research team (Robert Dicke, P. J. Peebles, P. G. Roll and D. T. Wilkinson) who contributed the interpretation that the radiation is a remnant of the Big Bang. When Dicke found out the use his rivals were making of a copy of his radiometer, he told his team, 'Boys – we've been scooped!'

According to the Big Bang theory, the early universe was composed of a hot plasma made up of photons, electrons and baryons. As the universe expanded and its density fell, collisions among particles became less frequent and so the temperature dropped. The cooling continued until it was possible for electrons to combine with protons to make hydrogen atoms. This happened when the universe was about 380,000 years old. After this, the photons scattered off the neutral atoms and started to travel freely through space, a process called decoupling. The photons have been cooling ever since. They have now cooled to 2.725 degrees Kelvin (or minus 270.4 degrees Celsius/minus 45.47 degrees Fahrenheit) and their temperature will continue to cool all the while the universe carries on expanding.

Later it was realised that the temperature measurement was specific to the astronomers' observational position near the edge of the Milky Way galaxy. If the measurement could be taken at other points in the universe, it would yield different readings. The cosmic background radiation is not uniform.

The radiation we are now measuring from the sky comes from a spherical surface that is called the surface of last scattering. This represents the distance from the Earth at which the decoupling event happened – 13.7 billion light-years. The light from that part of space is just reaching us on the Earth now. The Big Bang theory suggests that the cosmic background radiation fills all the space in the universe, and that most of the radiation energy in the universe resides in it.

PULSARS

(1967)

The long-standing dream of many astronomers (and non-astronomers too, for that matter) is to find evidence that there are intelligent life-forms elsewhere in the universe. Percival Lowell thought he had found evidence of an advanced civilisation on Mars when he mapped a network of canals that he saw through a telescope. With the advent of radio telescopes came the possibility that deliberately transmitted radio signals might be picked up from planets circling other stars. The discovery of pulsars seemed initially to be evidence of just this kind. As the name suggests, pulsars are stars that send out regularly pulsing radio waves.

The observed periods are short, from 8.5 seconds down to 1.5 milliseconds. The explanation for the regular and rhythmic transmission of signal is that the stars concerned, neutron stars, are highly magnetised and rotating. They send out a beam of electromagnetic radiation in the form of radio waves and the radiation is only observed here on the Earth when the beam is pointing in our direction. This is known as the lighthouse effect; the light shines all the time, but we only see the flash of light from the lighthouse at the moment when the continuously rotating beam of light is pointing towards us.

Neutron stars are extremely dense, and as a result their period of rotation is very regular, often as precisely regular as an atomic clock. In other ways neutron stars are more like our Sun, in that they have planets orbiting round them.

Discovering was not the same as understanding or explaining, though. Even after decades of research, there is still no agreed explanation for the way pulsars emit radiation.

The first pulsar was identified by Jocelyn Bell Burnell and Antony Hewish in July 1967. The feature that struck them most was the very regular pulse of the radio signal, which had the hallmark of an artificial signal, a signal transmitted by intelligent life. It seemed for a moment as if this might be the moment of contact with aliens in a remote corner of the universe, the 'little green men' of popular culture. Burnell and Hewish gave their first pulsar the identification number LGM-1: Little Green Men Number One. Later it was allocated a more serious number, CP 1919, and the idea that this was a radio beacon set up by an extra-terrestrial civilisation was relinquished. But in the first few weeks the proposition was seriously considered, and the scientists even considered suppressing the evidence in order not to unsettle or frighten people.

The idea that pulsars were rotating neutron stars was put forward independently by Thomas Gold and Franco Pacini in the year following the discovery. This was shortly afterwards proved to be correct by observation of a pulsar in the Crab nebula with a very short pulse period, thirty-three milliseconds. In 1964, Antony Hewish became the first astronomer to be awarded the Nobel Prize in physics. There was considerable controversy regarding this award, because Professor Hewish, Jocelyn Bell's PhD supervisor, was awarded the prize, while Bell herself, his student, was not, even though it was she who made the discovery.

In 1974, a pulsar was discovered orbiting another neutron star with an orbital period of only eight hours. Albert Einstein's theory of general relativity predicts that a system such as this ought to emit strong gravitational radiation and that the orbit should progressively contract as it loses orbital energy. Observation of this binary system, called PSR B1913+16, confirmed Einstein's prediction and gave the first evidence that gravitational waves exist.

The first planets to be discovered outside our own solar system were found orbiting a millisecond pulsar. It was Aleksander Wolszczan who made this momentous discovery in 1990. Astronomers had for a long time assumed that there were planets orbiting other stars, but suspected that they would be too small to detect. There are many other galaxies like ours, there are millions of other stars like our Sun, so it stands to reason that there must be hundreds of thousands of stars with planets circling them. It took until 1990 for astronomers to find one of them, but the crucial discovery proved beyond any doubt that other, extra-solar, planetary systems do exist. Statistically, it is very likely that some of these systems include planets with life forms developing on them. The hunt is on. It is in effect a discovery-in-waiting.

The early excitement about the discovery of pulsars generated speculation about the existence of Little Green Men far out in the universe. Ironically, it is unlikely that any form of life could survive in the intense radiation environment close to a pulsar; a pulsar is one of the *least* likely stars to have inhabited planets circling it.

AKROTIRI: THE BRONZE AGE TOWN ON SANTORINI

(1967)

The discovery of the Bronze Age town at Akrotiri was, like many other discoveries, a piecemeal affair. First a stone, then a wall, then another wall, then a room, and another room, and then a long gap before anything else happened. One of the problems with this discovery was that the settlement, or rather settlements, belonged to an ancient culture that was completely unknown in the first half of the nineteenth century. Interpretation was therefore very difficult in the early days.

NINETEENTH-CENTURY FINDS

The discovery of the Bronze Age town is dated to 1967, but there were several preludes to this historic moment, beginning 100 years before. In the nineteenth century, a realization dawned that the world described by Homer in the *Iliad* might be, at least partly, historically true, and that the Mycenaean civilisation of Agamemnon, Achilles and Nestor was a real culture. Schliemann demonstrated this at Troy and Mycenae. There was also a growing sense that an earlier Bronze Age civilisation might have preceded it.

It was the building of the Suez Canal starting in 1859 that first drew attention to Santorini as a possible location for this earlier civilization. Santorini is a little circlet of islands arranged in a ring round a huge circular bay. It is a gigantic ruined and flooded crater, wrecked during a cataclysmic eruption in the Bronze Age. The island group lies in the Aegean Sea due north of Crete and halfway between Greece and

413

Turkey. A peculiarity of the islands is that they are thickly coated in fine grey volcanic ash with layers of pumice. This was considered ideal for making cement for the harbour works at Port Said. A quarry was opened up in the cliffs at the southern tip of Therasia, the western island. Early on, the work of the quarrymen was impeded by large blocks of stone buried in the ash. The workmen knew at once from their shape and position that these belonged to a man-made wall.

From 1866, the site was excavated as an archaeological site, first by the owner, then by Ferdinand Fouqué, a vulcanologist who had come to Santorini to observe the spectacular volcanic eruption sequence happening out in the bay between 1866 and 1870. He was equally fascinated by the settlement that was emerging from under the ash on Therasia, and he established that the settlement had indeed been built before the ancient eruption of ash. At this stage, neither the Mycenaean nor the earlier Minoan civilisations had been recognised, so Fouqué had difficulty in making sense of what he was discovering. There were six rooms of a large house, with a walled paddock beside it and the remains of an old man caught and killed by the eruption. Fouqué also found traces of five more buildings across the quarry, so it looked as though there must have been a village on the site.

Fouqué gave up work on the quarry at the southern tip of Therasia because the site was too inaccessible, and switched his attention to Akrotiri, on the south coast of the large crescent-shaped main island, Thera. He found a site where stream erosion had exposed prehistoric remains at the bottom of a ravine. Fouqué wanted to excavate there, but the owner would not allow it. Fouqué's negotiations nevertheless did lead to two more Frenchmen, H. Mamet and H. Gorceix, being given formal permission to excavate, starting in 1870. As soon as they began digging at the bottom of the Akrotiri ravine they found walls preserved to a height of 1.8 metres (6 feet), a store room filled with painted vases, and a piece of pottery with ancient writing on it in an unknown script. They found exotic wall-paintings too, still attached to the walls. These were but a foretaste of what would be found a hundred years later. Nothing like these beautiful wall paintings would ever be found at the

Minoan sites awaiting discovery on Crete. Not even the great Labyrinth at Knossos would yield anything as complete or as well-preserved.

There was no doubt that the homes of wealthy, civilised and literate people had been discovered at Akrotiri, the citizens of some lost civilisation. This would be the moment where one might have expected the pace of excavation to quicken, the number of workmen to double, the investment and commitment to quadruple. Instead the excavation stopped and, apart from a small sample excavation in the next ravine to the east (by Robert Zahn), which again uncovered the remains of ancient houses, nothing further was done for a hundred years.

THE DISCOVERY OF THE MINOAN CIVILISATION ON CRETE

The Zahn dig took place in 1899. Evans's historic excavation at Knossos on the island of Crete began in the following year. It was Evans's discovery of the spectacular Minoan civilisation, and especially its remains at Knossos, that would make sense of the puzzling finds on Santorini. What emerged was that the powerful civilisation that had Knossos as its capital city had colonies or trading stations scattered throughout the Aegean. The Bronze Age town that had been glimpsed at Akrotiri on the south coast of Santorini was well-placed to be one of these wealthy trading posts. Evans knew he had found a great city once inhabited by, he believed, as many as 80,000 people, which was the powerhouse of a great ancient civilisation. He developed the idea, taken from ancient historians, that the Minoans had become rich on the back of a mighty sea empire. There were even Greek legends about King Minos, the King of Crete, and Athenian children taken in tribute, suggesting an oral tradition of a Bronze Age Cretan dynasty menacing and dominating the coastal cities of the Greek mainland.

It struck some scholars, even as early as 1900–10, that Evans's description of the Minoan civilisation on Crete was remarkably close to Plato's description of the evil empire of Atlantis. Evans himself never suggested this, but the Egyptologist James Blaikie did and, in 1909 and 1913, so did K. T. Frost.

As Evans's long career excavating Knossos drew to an end in the 1930s, another great figure in Aegean archaeology began to emerge – Spyridon Marinatos. From his discoveries he made an important link between the ancient destinies of Crete and Santorini, one that also had resonances in the Atlantis story. In 1932, Marinatos excavated a Minoan villa on the beach at Amnisos, now just a village on the north coast of Crete, but in the Bronze Age a thriving port serving Knossos.

SPYRIDON MARINATOS AT AMNISOS

According to his own account, Marinatos was prompted to go to Amnisos because of a reference in Strabo's *Geographica*: a mention that a harbour town and arsenal once existed there. Amnisos is much more famously mentioned in the *Odyssey* as the harbour town of Knossos, but perhaps Marinatos did not want to mention Homer and rouse suspicion that he was setting himself up as the heir of Schliemann. On the beach at Amnisos it is still possible to see, in a fenced enclosure, the huge squared blocks of stone marking the foundations of the villa that Marinatos excavated. Walking along the water's edge, it is also possible to see the lines of yet more well-built walls running out under the water; the north coast of Crete has sunk slightly since the Bronze Age, half-drowning the Minoan port.

What Marinatos found in his seaside villa at Amnisos was that some of the large foundation stones of the building had been pulled out of place as if by the dragging action of a large mass of water, the swash of a huge and powerful wave. He also found pumice and beach sand trapped inside the ruins. Marinatos published his finds in the Armageddon year of 1939; he proposed that the huge Bronze Age eruption on Santorini had sent tsunamis towards Crete, destroying not only the villa at Amnisos but the harbour town generally. It was part of a widespread catastrophe that brought the Minoan civilisation to an end.

Marinatos went on developing his eruption scenario in the 1950s, but he had done no further work to test it. The British archaeologist Glyn Daniel had commented in print in 1939 that what Marinatos's theory needed was 'additional support from excavations on selected sites'. That additional support came in 1967.

JAMES MAVOR AND THE VOYAGE TO ATLANTIS

In the 1960s, a new phase in the discovery of the Bronze Age town at Akrotiri began, in a rather surprising place. On the other side of the Atlantic, at the Woods Hole Oceanographic Institution, the young James Mavor developed an interest in pursuing the idea of the Minoan civilisation as the lost civilisation of Plato's Atlantis. He went to Athens to discuss the situation with Angelos Galanopoulos, a seismologist who agreed with Marinatos. It was Galanopoulos who made the important contribution of reconstructing Plato's story as a story of two islands. The larger (Crete) was the 'royal state', the smaller (Santorini) was the 'metropolis and religious centre'. In fact, this really reverses what the archaeology tells us – that Knossos on Crete was the capital and religious centre and Thera the outpost, the colonial possession. Galanopoulos got round this problem by assuming that the islands were switched round in the re-telling of the story, which may have been repeated orally many times before being written down by Plato's ancestor Solon.

In the summer of 1966, the Research Vessel *Chain* left Woods Hole for the Mediterranean, with Mavor on board. Mavor knew of Marinatos's interest in Santorini and of his ideas connecting Santorini and Crete. Mavor tried several times to communicate with Marinatos, but got no response until the expedition was over. Mavor's lively and engaging account in his excellent book *Voyage to Atlantis* makes me wonder whether his invitation to Marinatos to join in was couched in terms that Marinatos would easily have understood. He writes excitably of the *Chain* sailing to the Mediterranean, then of flying to Rome to meet the Pomerances of Great Neck before they departed for Crete to meet Nicolas Platon at the newly discovered temple at Zakro, then flying to Athens where he was diverted to Corinth to see the (unrelated) excavations there. How clear would this breathless itinerary or its purpose have been to Marinatos?

When the *Chain* arrived in the huge round bay on Santorini, serious data gathering started. Seismic profiling of the sea bed revealed layers of volcanic debris within the caldera (the huge crater centring on the bay), showing that the caldera had been created as much by collapse as by blowing out. The expedition and the data that it produced seemed to lead up several blind alleys. Galanopoulos left the expedition believing that land excavations could contribute little towards verifying the Atlantis theory. Buildings such as palaces or temples in the centre of the island of Santorini must have been totally destroyed when the caldera collapsed. Galanopoulos was right, yet Mavor clung to his vision of 'a prehistoric Pompeii . . . A city preserved under impervious ash would contain important artefacts that had perished at other Minoan sites – and perhaps Linear A tablets.' Mavor was right, but then the excavations undertaken in the nineteenth century by Fouqué, Mamet, Gorceix and Zahn had proved already that Minoan settlements were preserved in good order under the ash.

Marinatos had kept his distance, but wrote to Mavor in April 1967 to say that he, Marinatos, had been appointed director-general for any excavation in Santorini. The Greek Archaeological Service would put up two thousand US dollars; would Mavor put up a similar sum? Then came the right-wing military coup in Athens. As a staunch right-winger, Marinatos's fortunes changed rapidly with the colonels in power. He wrote again in May, 'the political situation here is excellent'. It was a point of view.

Marinatos finally travelled to Santorini with Mavor. In getting Marinatos to Santorini and in particular to Akrotiri, James Mavor made a contribution to archaeology that has been insufficiently recognised. Mavor knew that he was dealing with a complex, difficult man. But for the moment that was forgotten. The firm lead, the discovery of well-preserved prehistoric houses at Akrotiri, was the one Mavor followed. Unfortunately, neither the Fouqué house in the Akrotiri ravine nor the Zahn house in the Potamos ravine could be found again. Weathering, slope failure and vine growing had obliterated them. The lower parts of either ravine seemed likely to expose houses, but Marinatos was reluctant to dig at random. In 1967, a local man remembered the floor of a donkey cave collapsing, revealing what looked like a room underneath. Nearby a section of a field had subsided in a similar way, as if beneath the ash there were room-like cavities.

Marinatos found the donkey cave and made it the site of one of his first trenches. Mavor became uneasy about Marinatos, who seemed to be talking at cross purposes with the rest of the party. Mavor thought it was Marinatos' imperfect command of English, but Marinatos was exploiting this assumption to pursue his own ends. He had decided where to excavate, and he had decided to get rid of his North American friends too.

TREACHERY

The excavations began in 1967 at the donkey cave. There the seismograph had indicated an irregular rocky layer about 4 metres (14 feet) down. It was layer of spectacular finds. When the workers were only waist-deep the first Bronze Age pottery appeared. Marinatos showed only a passing interest in Mavor's new technology. 'Still the best archaeological tool is the shovel,' he said smugly. 'It works well and does not speak.' After an exhausting bout of seismic surveying elsewhere on the site, Mavor returned to find Marinatos looking into a pit. 'I do not need you any more,' said Marinatos. 'Not you or your friends. But do your tests anyway. Here we have found the walls of a house.' Marinatos at last showed his hand. The dig was his – and he would claim the discovery of the Bronze Age town.

Marinatos wanted Mavor's help in one further particular. He wanted a seismographic survey of the whole field. If it turned out that the Minoan land surface underneath the ash was fairly level, then it would be a plausible choice for site to build a city. This was the case. The gently sloping Bronze Age landscape was ideal for urban development. Mavor was keen to find and reopen Zahn's excavation, spending some time trying to rediscover the site, but Marinatos was not interested, sensibly deciding to limit his excavation to the one valley for the time being. In fact that is still the case. The Akrotiri excavation has enlarged since Marinatos' day, but not very much. Over the next century, perhaps, we can hope to see the excavation extending into the Potamos Valley, and the clearance of the ash in the ridge covering the town in between the two valleys.

By the second day of Marinatos's excavations a complete upper-storey room was revealed. Then he backfilled the site while he organised the expropriation of the site, which under the colonels was easy. Five days of feverish excavation followed Marinatos's return. He opened nine trenches scattered across the ravine, each producing fresh evidence of a Bronze Age town. Less than 90 centimetres (3 feet) down the workmen shouted, 'Wall plaster! Frescoes!' This was a building two or three storeys high with many of the internal walls still in place.

Spyridon Marinatos gave his own account of the excavation, illustrating his difficult relationship with the American team. He quarrelled with Emily Vermeule about 'the interpretation of certain important passages of the Bible'. What the disagreement was about is not worth pursuing but he was ready to escalate this conversation into a conflict and dignify it with publication. In his *Second Report on the Thera Excavations*, he makes no other mention of the Americans, who were undoubtedly there and helping, and who had contributed financially. Marinatos comes across as both boorish and unscrupulous.

He was now in no doubt about the importance of the site. He had found 'remnants of a grand city with numerous palaces and streets and signs of an old culture.' The explosive rift between Marinatos and the Americans was just round the corner; he was looking for an opportunity to ditch them. The summer of 1967 ended with Marinatos summoned back to Athens by the colonels; from there he sent Mavor a cutting of his press release. Mavor in turn publicised the 'Minoan Pompeii', truthfully describing it as 'one of the most startling archaeological events of this generation'. Marinatos was nettled by the publicity Mavor had trawled and reacted tetchily when interviewers pressed him to say that Akrotiri was Atlantis. He would say only that the 'palaces', as he mis-described the houses, could be as important as Knossos. Marinatos was sometimes ready publicly to admit that he thought Minoan Santorini was Atlantis, but in the television *Chronicle* interview he gave to Magnus Magnusson he was coy: 'It is not for archaeologists to say.' By this he implied that it was all right for others, media people like Magnus Magnusson for instance, to say it for them.

James Mavor has tried to make sense of the rift that developed in terms of misunderstanding, but the explanation is simpler. Marinatos was aware early on that he had stumbled on a very important site. He wanted it for himself and he did not want to share the glory with others, especially foreigners, and he wanted those foreigners off the site without delay. His only problem was finding a pretext, and a slight over the date of Mavor's press release was just sufficient. Had Marinatos wished to go on collaborating with Mavor – if indeed he had ever collaborated – a small matter like this would have been no barrier. The *New York Times* recognised the rift and gave details of Marinatos's accusation that the American team had made its results known to the public before he had made his official report to the Greek authorities. The newspaper noted the promotion of Marinatos to Inspector-General of Greek Antiquities.

Mavor retreated from the story of Minoan Santorini, bravely trying to come to terms with the treacherous way Marinatos had treated him. He paid tribute to Marinatos's ability, broader view and historical insight, but felt betrayed by him. It was James Mavor who brought Marinatos to the right place to rediscover, for the second time in a century, the great Minoan colony-town, the lost Atlantean city that had probably once been known as Therassos. A town of that name is recorded on a tablet at Knossos.

THE DEATH OF MARINATOS

Marinatos was supervising the excavation one day in 1974, characteristically standing on a wall top, when he overbalanced, fell backwards into Telchines Street, the Bronze Age city's main street, and was killed when he struck his head on a stone.

Since Marinatos' death and the fall of the colonels, the excavation of Akrotiri has slowed down. One reason for this slowing down is the discovery of whole suites of spectacular wall paintings, which give a wonderful insight into the ancient civilisation, and show how the Minoans viewed the world in around 1650 BC. But the wall paintings have to be removed for conservation, and that work has flooded the available facilities in Athens. There are doubtless many more houses waiting to be excavated, but they must wait until the conservation facilities can cope with the volume of work. There is a substantial building surviving three storeys high, fronting onto the East Square. Its exterior wall has been cleaned off and is in a good state of preservation. An upstairs window is still blind, blocked with ash, and you can see a vase standing on its window sill, half in and half out of the ash. It is a tantalising experience to look at that ash-filled building and speculate. What objects lie waiting to be discovered inside? Even more, what will its wall paintings show?

The wall paintings are perhaps the most significant discovery. They show us what people looked like, how they dressed, how they behaved during ceremonial occasions. There are boys and girls undergoing separate rituals that are rites of passage. They show, in one exceptionally beautiful fresco, what the goddess Therasia looked like. She is relaxing on her stepped throne, which looks very like a Minoan triple shrine, attended informally by her heraldic beasts, a monkey and a griffin. She accepts an offering from the monkey on one side while the griffin pleads for attention on the other. She was mentioned in the tablets at Knossos as She-from-Therassos. The Spring Fresco, which decorates an entire room, shows how the Minoans saw the natural landscape with its multi-coloured volcanic rocks, crocuses and mating swallows. Perhaps the most interesting fresco of all is a miniature fresco showing what a Minoan town looks like. The shape of the mountainous skyline in the background is identical to the skyline of Mavros Rachidhi to the west of the Akrotiri site, so there can be no doubt that the town in the fresco is Akrotiri itself. The fresco shows an isolated building up on the skyline, and if you climb to that point on the headland you can still see the remains there of a substantial stone building. Boats are shown between the town and the ridge, so we have confirmation of the existence of a harbour.

The Bronze Age town at Akrotiri is already giving us valuable information about the nature of the Minoan civilisation. Interpreting the complete frescoes from Akrotiri is also allowing us to make more sense of the much more fragmentary wall paintings at Knossos. So, after the long wait, we are now finding out much more about this exotic civilisation that flourished in the south-east corner of Europe 3,500 years ago.

THE FIRST PEOPLE SET FOOT ON THE MOON

(1969)

A man walked on the Moon for the first time on 21 July 1969. At 3.56 a.m. British Summer Time, the American astronaut Neil Armstrong stepped out of *Eagle*, the lunar module from *Apollo 11*, and cautiously descended a ladder onto the pale grey dusty surface of the Moon. As he placed the first human footprint into the Moon's fine dust he said, 'That's one small step for a man, one giant leap for mankind.' Shortly afterwards he was joined by his fellow astronaut Buzz Aldrin and the two of them experimented with moving about under the low gravity conditions. The historic moment was watched by hundreds of millions of people all over the world, on television. Armstrong was intrigued by the texture of the Moon dust under his feet. 'The surface is like a fine powder. It has a soft beauty all its own, like some desert of the Unites States.'

The Moon landing came as the climax of the *Apollo 11* mission, four days after blasting off from Cape Canaveral (or Cape Kennedy). After an uneventful flight, the Apollo went into orbit round the Moon. Armstrong and Aldrin transferred to the lunar module and started their descent to the Moon. There was a tense final moment, when without much fuel left they had to avoid a boulder-filled crater. The two astronauts stayed on the Moon for less than a day before lifting off to rendezvous with *Apollo 11*, still orbiting the Moon.

Five days later, scientists put the rocks collected on the Moon into quarantine for two months. For the moment frustrated geologists were only allowed to look at them through a window. The quarantine procedure was a precaution, in case there were organisms of any kind on the Moon that could infect plants or animals on the Earth. In fact, the rocks turned out to be sterile. They also, in due course, when dated, turned out to be very old. They were 4.5 billion years old, which is the date when the solar system was created. Rocks exposed at the surface of the Earth are much younger than this, because the Earth is more active planet and the surface rocks have been recycled many times. The Moon's surface shows every indication of being a very ancient landscape, little changed since its creation apart from the bombardment by meteorites.

Then came a strange moment, which with hindsight, seems like mass hysteria, a kind of psychological bushfire that swept through the USA. For some reason, millions of Americans were persuaded that they were watching a simulation staged in a film studio, or in fact some desert of the United States, to divert their attention away from the Vietnam War. Conspiracy theories multiplied. Millions more Americans, and others round the world, were more rationally concerned about the huge sum of money spent on the moonshot and the rest of the Apollo mission, believing that the money could have been spent more usefully, for instance in alleviating poverty, in funding health programmes, in aid for less economically developed countries. So, even as the event happened, people were reading a variety of different subtexts into it. Like many other such events, it was not just a dramatic and historic moment in itself, it carried with it a raft of political and cultural ramifications. Armstrong's landing on the Moon was in many ways a twentieth-century parallel to Columbus's fifteenth-century landing in the New World.

An important political aspect of the Moon landing was that it was a major blow in the Cold War. Americans had reached the Moon before the Russians. The Russians had been *beaten*. It was not actually said, but there was no need to say it.

The visit to the Moon was man's first step away from the Earth out into the solar system, and undoubtedly more symbolic than useful. The rock samples could as easily have been collected by a robot. Even so, the event marked a critical stage in man's interest in the cosmos. People speculated about journeys further afield and there was talk of a mission to Mars. The danger and the ever-increasing costs ruled that out, and subsequent missions have been undertaken by unmanned vehicles. Even the outer planets and their satellites have been flown past now, and the photographs taken in these encounters have been analysed in order to reconstruct the nature of the planets. The most striking feature that emerges from this data-gathering is the revelation of the planets' sheer diversity. Given their common origin, they are surprisingly different and individual. Another surprise, a spin-off from the Apollo moonshot itself, was the unexpected discovery of the jewel-like beauty of the Earth when seen from the Moon. No one had hitherto imagined how beautiful the Earth is: a simple enough idea, but never before thought of.

The *Apollo 11* mission to the Moon may have been a politically motivated stunt to show the Soviets that the USA was ahead, but it really did demonstrate the sophistication and precision that was possible in modern rocket science. Devices, whether manned or unmanned, could be sent scouting round the solar system to gather data and brought safely home again. It was very much the beginning of a new age in history, an age of reaching out into the cosmos.

TOLLUND MAN
(1970)

In the Silkeborg Museum on the Jutland peninsula in Denmark, the principal attraction, drawing visitors from all over the world, is the body of a long-dead man. He is called Tollund Man. The enormous fascination that this corpse exerts over people is explained by its great age and its unusual state of preservation. It was found in May 1950 in the Bjaeldskovdal bog 12 kilometres (7½ miles) west of Silkeborg. On 6 May, two men from the village of Tollund, Emil Højgård and his brother Viggo, were digging peat to burn in their stove when they accidentally disturbed the bog body.

The body was so well preserved at the time when it was discovered that its finders immediately called the police, thinking that this must be some recent murder victim. But the local police knew better. They remembered that ancient bodies had been discovered in this same bog in the past, in the 1920s and 1930s, and were ready to believe that this was another of them, as indeed it was.

Professor Glob, an archaeologist at Aarhus University, came to see the body and arrange for its removal to the National Museum in Copenhagen for scientific examination. The body was lying on its side, knees drawn up into a foetal position. The man wore a tight-fitting pointed leather cap with a leather thong tied under his chin. The astonishingly well-preserved face was relaxed and composed, as if sleeping. But round the man's throat was a plaited leather rope with its ends trailing down the back, showing that he had been garrotted. He had not died peacefully or naturally: he had been executed.

The body revealed some telling aspects of the man's lifestyle. He was between thirty and forty years old at the time of his death. There were two scars on his feet, which showed that for part of the year at any rate he must have walked barefoot, and from time to time accidentally cut his feet; but he also sometimes wore shoes. The red colour of his hair was a result of the body's immersion in the bog; he probably had brown hair in life. The contents of his stomach showed that for his last meal he had eaten a gruel containing thirty different kinds of seeds, including barley, knotgrass, linseed and camomile; it was an exclusively vegetarian meal.

The scientific investigation of Tollund Man included a radiocarbon date, which showed that he died in 350–400 BC, in the middle of the Iron Age. Why Tollund Man was strangled and then buried in the bog is still not known. He seems not to have been a criminal, as the body was evidently treated with respect. Those who were with him at his death closed his eyes and mouth; they also carried him to the peat bog and buried him there with care and some difficulty. The body was buried in the marsh a clear 50 metres (160 feet) away from firm ground; it was also buried 1.8 metres (6 feet) down in the peat. Many people have assumed from these details that he was offered as a human sacrifice to the gods.

It was a common practice in the Iron Age, and in the Bronze Age before, for people to deposit offerings in rivers, lakes, springs and bogs. Swords and shields have been recovered from the River Thames. The story about King Arthur's sword being returned to the Lady of the Lake as he lay dying has its roots in this belief system. The offering of a human sacrifice in a bog is in harmony with this. Ordinary deaths of ordinary people were followed by a cremation ritual. The fact that this body was not cremated but submerged in the bog shows that it was unusual. The way the body was dressed was also unusual. The man was wearing a leather cap and a leather belt, but was otherwise naked. This is reminiscent of the Cerne Giant, the chalk hill figure in Dorset in England, which is wearing a belt but is otherwise naked. The climate is such in Britain that people do not normally go about naked, so some special occasion or activity, some ceremony, is implied. The Cerne Giant evidently represents an Iron Age warrior, and it is known from Roman authors and artwork that warriors sometimes took their clothes off and fought naked.

There were also some clues to the special, ritual nature of the man's death in the stomach contents. The barley he had eaten between twelve and twenty-four hours before his death contained large quantities of ergot fungus, which is found on decomposing rye. Ergot induces hallucinations. This has led some researchers to argue that the food was intended to alter the victim's mental state. It is thought that ergotised barley may have been the source of the visions people had when they were initiated into the Eleusinian mysteries in the classical period, a few centuries after Tollund Man. The Roman historian Tacitus described rites of the goddess Nerthus, which were carried out in the region of which Jutland was a part. Human victims were sacrificed to Nerthus by drowning.

A by-product of the bog burial was the preservation of the body. The lack of oxygen in the bog slowed down the process of decomposition, and the acid in the bogs tanned the skin like leather. When the body was exposed to the air again, the process of decomposition resumed. In 1950, the technique of conservation was not very advanced, and a decision was made to preserve the head of Tollund Man, and a foot and a finger. The technique used was successful. In 1952, the head of Tollund Man was put on show when the Silkeborg Museum opened in its new premises, Silkeborg Manor.

Tollund Man was not the first body to be found in the bog. In 1938, about 50 metres (160 feet) from the place where Tollund Man would be found, another body was discovered. This was the body of a woman, Elling Woman. She had been strangled. We assume that she too was a sacrifice to the god of the bog. The two bog bodies form the centre of the Iron Age exhibition in the museum. Only the head of Tollund Man is original. For display purposes, the real head has been attached to a replica of the now-destroyed body.

Bog bodies in general and Tollund Man in particular are important to us as tangible, almost living links with the remote past. Skeletons have little in the way of individuality, nothing in the way of personality. But the bog bodies are real people with personalities. To look at the face of Tollund Man is like looking at the face of a sleeping father, someone we know, and who will shortly wake up, smile and speak to us. This is as close as we can get to communicating with a long-dead and pre-literate generation of our ancestors. Tollund Man was the inspiration for a poem by Seamus Heaney. In it he imagines that some day he will go to Aarhus and see the ancient bog body. He imagines that in the 'old man-killing parishes' of Denmark he will feel both unhappy and at home.

VALLES MARINERIS: CANYONS ON MARS

(1971)

One of the most spectacular features of the planet Mars is the network of canyons located just south of the Martian equator. It has been compared with the Grand Canyon, but it is on a much grander scale than that. If the canyon system were here on the Earth, it would stretch from one side of the United States to the other. At the centre of the system of valleys, which are about 80 kilometres (50 miles) wide, they merge to form a huge depression that is 640 kilometres (400 miles) wide. The canyons are very deep, in places 11 kilometres (7 miles) deep, which is seven times deeper than the Grand Canyon. There is nothing on this scale on the land surface on Earth; the nearest equivalent is the Rift Valley system that runs along the crest of the Mid-Atlantic Ridge, which unfortunately we cannot see because it is drowned under the waters of the Atlantic Ocean.

The system was visible through telescopes on the Earth, but its true scale and grandeur were only appreciated when the first close-up photographs were sent back by the space probe *Mariner 9* in 1971. That marks the effective discovery of the canyons, and it explains why the system was named the Mariner Valleys, or in Latin *Valles Marineris*.

The huge scale of the canyons started a debate about their origins. Mars had long been known to be a dry planet, so the presence of branching canyons prompted the thought – perhaps wishful thinking? – that once there had been huge volumes of water of Mars capable of eroding deep valleys. The canyons do indeed have some of the characteristics of river-eroded valleys: they have branches and they meander. But there are other aspects that seem to be impossible to explain in terms of running water. Some of the canyons are closed depressions, which means they cannot have been created by flowing water. There are localised features that were eroded by water and wind, but subsidence along fault lines is thought to have been the main process in creating this remarkable Martian landscape.

Astronomers, geologists and geomorphologists studied the *Mariner 9* pictures, and then the even higher-quality photographs sent back by the Viking orbiter. After close scrutiny of all the photographs sent back, it is now generally agreed that the canyon system has a complex history with several phases when different processes dominated. It began with the surface collapsing to form a series of deep basins. This faulting and subsidence was probably caused by the crust of Mars being domed and stretched in this area. Crustal tension is the cause of similar Rift Valley formation on the Earth. The basins then filled with water, forming lakes, and these became filled with layers of lake-bed deposits. The layering is interesting in itself, in that it implies cyclical changes in the hydrology, and perhaps these correspond to cyclical changes in climate such as we experience here on the Earth; in fact, cyclical climate change is the only available explanation. Most of the major climate changes on the Earth are caused by astronomical variations, such as the wobble of the Earth's axis, the slight wobble in the shape of the planet's orbit, and variations in solar radiation. It is easy to see that similar factors will lie behind cyclical changes in Martian climate too. Mars too displays orbital variations and is subject to the same solar variations as the Earth.

Then there was another phase of geological collapse as a result of tectonic activity, when the area was criss-crossed with faults and blocks of the Martian surface once again foundered. This made some of the earlier troughs wider and created connections between them. Subsidence along fault lines does happen on this large scale on the Earth too; the East African Rift Valley system is similar, a series of tensional rifts opening up across a dome.

Water still existed in the region at the time of this second phase of subsidence and the linking of the basins allowed this water to spill through from basin to basin and flow out at the eastern end of the system. The collapse of the blocks of Martian crust that sank created some very steep cliffs, and these became the focus of a series of huge landslides. Today, there is no longer any water on the surface, and all that moves along the canyons is dark sand, blown along by the wind and formed in places into large dunes.

There are very few impact craters inside the canyon system, which implies that it is not a very ancient land surface. It is also interesting that the fault scarps that form the sides of the canyons in places cut right across river channels, so they must have been formed later than at least one phase of river erosion on the planet. What we are building up is a picture of a landscape with a long, varied and complicated history. Those who study the development of landscapes on the Earth are very familiar with this. The Moon presents us with an ancient, dead landscape that has remained unchanged apart from a relentless peppering of impact craters for hundreds of millions of years. Mars is more like the Earth, with a surface that is geologically active and has also been subjected to a sequence of wind and water processes.

The Valles Marineris discovery is a classic example of one discovery leading on to many others. There was the exciting initial moment of discovery in 1971, when the Mariner photographs showed what the Martian landscape looks like. Then there was the twenty-year-long phase of analysis, discussion and debate that led to discoveries about the processes at work in the Martian landscape and atmosphere.

J/PSI PARTICLES
(1974)

The psi particle is a subatomic particle, a meson that consists of a charm quark and a charm anti-quark. It was discovered independently by two separate research teams, one headed by Professor Burton Richter at the Stanford Linear Accelerator Centre, the other headed by Professor Samuel Ting at the Brookhaven National Laboratory at the Massachusetts Institute of Technology. It was quite by chance that they found the same particle at the same time. They announced their independent discoveries on 11 November 1974.

This was an important discovery, as is witnessed by the rapid changes in high-energy physics that followed. Scientists working in this field refer to the changes happening at that time as 'the November Revolution'.

In 1976, Richter and Ting were jointly awarded the Nobel Prize in Physics for their discovery of psi particles.

In the 1960s, the first quark models of elementary particle physics were put forward by theoreticians. These models assumed that protons, neutrons and all other baryons are composed of the three different kinds of fractionally charged particles (quarks); the three different kinds were known as 'up', 'down' and 'strange'. The quark models were impressive in that they offered the possibility of an underlying order to what was seen as a 'zoo' of elementary particles, but they remained only theoretical. There was no proof that they existed.

Then, beginning in 1969, experiments revealed unexpected evidence that there were particles inside protons – and these might by quarks, perhaps. More experiments to find out the characteristics of these tiny particles suggested that these were in fact the quarks that the theorists had proposed. Then the characteristics of different kinds of quarks started to emerge. The research undertaken by the Richter and Ting teams was, ironically, not directed towards discovering more subatomic particles, but to explore new energy regimes. Ting and Richter, as independent discoverers of the particle, naturally gave it different names. Ting called it the 'J' particle and Richter called it the 'psi' particle. Scientists generally want to avoid favouring one discoverer over the other, so they tend to call the particle 'J/psi'.

The installations involved in this experimental work was formidable. The Brookhaven accelerator was a device about 180 metres (600 feet)in diameter. The Stanford Linear Accelerator Centre had a linear electron accelerator 3 kilometres (2 miles) long. There is a certain irony that scientists have to employ such colossal pieces of equipment in order to investigate the tiniest particles of matter. Richter's equipment included a carousel in which streams of electrons and positrons go round at high speeds in opposite directions. When head-on collisions happen, a motionless very heavy particle may be produced, and this in turn may turn into several other particles as it quickly disintegrates. The success of the Richter experiment depended on the collisions occurring at the right speed. The equipment allowed the speed to be adjusted finely, which was as well, because the new particle only appeared at one particular collision speed. When the speed was correctly set, the psi particle was produced, and it lasted, or 'lived', for a much longer period of time than expected.

The Ting experiment, an entirely separate initiative, depended for its success not on the speed of the collision but the direction.

Shortly after the new particle was discovered, it was confirmed by other teams working at Frascati in Italy and Hamburg in Germany. For centuries, both chemists and physicists had been working to find the smallest components of matter, the building blocks of the universe. First the smallest component known was the atom, then the smallest known was the atomic nucleus, then the smallest known was what became known as the elementary particle. Then it emerged that the elementary particles were made up of even smaller units, the quarks.

THE TERRACOTTA ARMY OF SHI HUANGDI

(1974)

The emperor Shi Huangdi, the founder of the Qin dynasty, was the first emperor of China; the name 'Shi Huangdi' literally means 'First Emperor'. He was born in 246 BC and ruled from 221 until his death in 210 BC. The great mound that covers his tomb has always been a conspicuous landmark outside the city of Xi'an (ancient Chang'an) in Shensi province, but it was only in 1974 that the first excavations, nearby, revealed some of the treasures in what is an enormous tomb complex on the scale of the pyramids of the ancient Egyptian pharaohs. Peasants digging a well found the first treasures, but it was not until the archaeological excavations began that the true scope and scale of the complex was appreciated.

The first professional archaeologist on the scene was Yuan Zhongyi. He still leads the excavations and directs the museum at the site. At first he believed that the excavation of the site would be over in a week. It was a major shock to discover the biggest chamber of the Terracotta Army, containing nearly 6,400 terracotta figures, all standing on a tiled floor. Excavating that first chamber took three years. Shortly after that excavation was finished the second and third chambers were discovered.

When the Chinese authorities first announced the discovery of the Terracotta Army in 1974, there were many people all round the world – from archaeologists to tourists – who wanted to come and see it. Considering the culture of the time, the Chinese were surprisingly open and accommodating about the great influx of foreigners, even organising tours to enable the visitors to watch the excavation in progress. At first the emerging army was protected from the elements by a makeshift tin roof, but now a large reinforced steel hangar has been raised over it. A museum was built next to the excavation to house the artefacts found all round the tomb site. The museum and the terracotta army attract two million visitors a year. Part of the fascination of the terracotta army is its sheer size. Part of it is the astonishingly beautiful detailing of the figures; the faces appear to be individual portraits. Although most of the original colour has weathered from the figures, they have an extraordinary hypnotic effect on those who see them, creating a sense of actually making contact with people from the Iron Age.

There is a reluctance in China to open up the tomb in its entirety, at least in the near future. This is probably in the best interests of thorough archaeological investigation and will allow finds to be properly conserved. But in recent years a team of archaeologists headed by Filippo Salviati made some new discoveries while opening up a further area of the emperor's tomb. Salviati found a life-sized model of a marsh complete with forty bronze sculptures of cranes, swans and geese.

Meanwhile, new discoveries are still being made about the Terracotta Army. It has been found that pollen included in two of the sculptures, a horse and a soldier, show that they were made in different kilns in different places; the horse was made close to the tomb while the warrior was made some distance away. The production of so many figures must have involved highly organized production on an industrial scale over a whole region.

The tomb was a major project, which the emperor began working on as soon as he ascended to his clan throne at the age of thirteen. The tomb became an expression of Qin Shi Huangdi's extraordinary ambition, not just for himself but for China. He ordered the building of a huge system of roads and canals. He connected various sections of the border walls of the kingdom into one continuous Great Wall, the forerunner of the present structure. He standardised systems of writing, weighing and measuring. He organised major hydrological works on the Yellow River to reduce the risk of flooding. He organised the administration of China into thirty-six separately governed commanderies. Each state had a military governor who was answerable to a civilian governor. But the civilian governor was assigned to a different command every few years – to avoid the risk of any individual building a local power base that could be a focus for insurrection. There was also an inspector in each commandery; it was his responsibility to inform the central government about the local implementation of centralised policies. The idea was to achieve delegation without fragmentation.

The First Emperor's achievement was enormous, but at great cost. Huge taxes were levied on a poor population; law was imposed tyrannically; strenuous efforts were made to destroy the teachings of Confucius. At the age of thirty-eight he styled himself First Emperor. His successor would be styled Second Emperor, and so on for ten thousand generations. The intention was that the imperial dynasty would rule China for that long, in other words for something like 250,000 years – an eternity of emperors.

The Terracotta Army was created life size and organised in strict battle formation, with bowmen and crouching crossbowmen at the front, more archers on the flanks, infantry, cavalry and chariotry in the centre and heavily armoured infantry bringing up the rear. The whole complex, including a palace, a cemetery and defensive walls, covered 10 square kilometres (4 square miles). It was in effect a capital city for the dead emperor to continue using in the afterlife, supplying all of his needs. The concept was similar to the provision for the Egyptian pharaohs, who took with them everything they needed for the afterlife. It took 700,000 slaves and prisoners of war thirty-six years to create the Qin emperor's city of the dead.

The imperial palace has not yet been unearthed, but legendary accounts describe it in terms that would make it an unparalleled archaeological discovery. It was said to contain rare jewels and a scale model of the emperor's earthly capital city, Chang'an. On the floor of the tomb was a stylised model or map of China itself, complete with its river systems; mercury flowed along the miniature river channels, simulating the flows of the Yangtze, the Yellow River and the other major rivers of China. It was said to contain a representation of the heavens, with clusters of stars represented by pearls. The entrance to the tomb was defended by mechanically operated crossbows that were designed to shoot down any mortal who tried to enter. The wonders of the tomb were described by the Chinese historian Sima Qian, who was writing only a few decades after the emperor's death, at a time when the work on the tomb had only just been completed. His description may be true, but it is more than a little disconcerting that it does not mention the Terracotta Army. It may be that Sima Qian was only allowed to find out a part of the truth about the burial complex.

How much of all this survives inside the burial mound can only be guessed, but much of it is likely to have been spoilt by groundwater and weathering. The burial chamber was cut into a water-bearing rock,which had to be waterproofed by lining the pit with a layer of bronze. A magnetometer survey of the mound shows that a large number of coins lie inside the tomb, which implies that the emperor's treasury was buried with him. Surveys of the soil have also shown high levels of mercury, which suggests that Sima Qian's description of rivers of mercury may have been true.

Exciting as the discovery of the Terracotta Army was, there is an expectation that still more exciting finds await eventual discovery in the tomb mound itself. Will the body of the First Emperor still be there? If so, it may be possible to find out through forensic examination whether he died in the manner that history has recorded. The emperor became increasingly paranoid after several attempts to assassinate him, and increasingly morbid. Indeed, the expenditure of time and effort on such a grand burial complex implies a strain of morbidity. He wanted to find an elixir of life, a potion that would enable him to live for ever. His scientists and doctors gave him mercury pills, which were supposed to make him immortal. Instead, they killed him.

One important result of the discovery of the Terracotta Army is that it has once again brought the name and the reign of the First Emperor to life. Everyone has heard of him now. The discovery in 1974 has given him the immortality he craved so much.

CHIRON
(1977)

Chiron is a strange object that circles the Sun between Saturn and Uranus. Discovered in 1977, it has the relatively large size of an asteroid, but in terms of its composition it is more like a comet. Chiron would make a very unusual comet as it is something like 50,000 times larger than the average comet, but it nevertheless has a distinctive 'coma', the nebulous aura that surrounds the nucleus of a comet. Because of its unusual in-between character, it was named after one of the centaurs, the creatures of ancient Greek mythology that were half-horse, half-man. Chiron himself was a kindly and civilised centaur, who was well disposed towards people, and who was the tutor of both Peleus and his son Achilles; he taught the boy Achilles to play the lyre.

Chiron's existence was not known until 1977, when it was discovered by Charles Kowal when he was examining photographs of the heavens. Once Chiron had been identified as a new and previously unrecognised object, earlier records were examined, and it was found that Chiron had been visible on photographs of the night sky taken as early as 1895, though no one had noticed it. The nebulous aura was not seen until 1988.

Chiron is about 400 kilometres (250 miles) across and it spins on its axis once every six hours. Its orbit round the Sun is strongly elliptical and unstable, and this is taken to show that Chiron got into its current orbit relatively recently, within the past million years. At its closest approach to the Sun it is 8.5 astronomical units from the Sun, which takes it inside the orbit of Saturn. At its furthest point out in the solar system it is nineteen astronomical units from the Sun, which takes it almost to the orbit of Uranus. An astronomical unit is the distance from the Earth to the Sun, 150 million kilometres (93 million miles). Chiron's wayward behaviour makes it look as if it is in some way 'mediating' between Saturn and Uranus, visiting first one planet and then the other.

This could perhaps imply that Chiron is likely one day to be captured by either Saturn or Uranus and become a moon orbiting one of those two planets. On the other hand, its orbit is tilted in relation to the orbits of Saturn and Uranus, which makes this interception fairly unlikely.

Astronomers believe that Chiron originally came from the Kuiper Belt, an extensive belt of asteroids out beyond the orbit of Neptune. One reason for believing that it has arrived in its present position fairly recently is the elliptical and unstable orbit. Over long periods the major planets have a way of shepherding the smaller objects with their gravitational fields and smoothing out such irregularities. Another reason for thinking Chiron is a new arrival is its coma and its comet-like tail. If Chiron had been circling the Sun at its present distance for a long time, the volatile elements that create the coma, such as methane and nitrogen, would have disappeared, evaporated off by the heat of the Sun. That would leave Chiron as a simple asteroid – if in an unusual place. Possibly Chiron was thrown inwards towards the Sun when it accidentally came under the gravitational influence of the planet Neptune.

As is often the way with such discoveries, once Chiron had been discovered, astronomers began to find more objects of the same type in the solar system. These half-asteroid, half-comet objects are sometimes referred to as 'centaurs'. Some astronomers treat Chiron as a planetoid or minor planet.

SATURN AND ITS RINGS
(1980)

Using the fairly primitive telescopes available in 1655, Christiaan Huygens saw what we now know as the *rings* of Saturn as a single solid and continuous disc. Over the centuries, as telescope technology has improved, more detail has become visible. Instead of one ring, it became clear that Saturn has several concentric rings. Then came the space probes of the late twentieth century.

The space probes *Voyager 1* and *Voyager 2* were launched from the Earth in 1977 on an epic voyage to explore the outer solar system. It took *Voyager 1* three years to reach Saturn, and it was found to be only 19 kilometres (12 miles) off-course when it got there. This was not the first time a man-made object had flown past Saturn, as *Pioneer 11* had done so a year earlier. Even before *Voyager* reached Saturn, startling new information was coming in about the ringed planet. For a start, it was found that Uranus had rings too, so Saturn was no longer the only ringed planet. Stephen O'Meara also observed dark radial features or spokes within the rings and noted them in a sketch. No one took any notice of this intriguing discovery until it was vividly confirmed by the photographs that were sent back by *Voyager 1* in 1980.

In 1978, Peter Goldreich and Scott Tremaine proposed that density waves are formed in Saturn's rings as a result of an interaction between the particles that make up the rings with Saturn's moons.

In 1979, *Pioneer 11* flew past Saturn. On its way it confirmed the existence of the E Ring. This is the outermost and therefore largest ring of Saturn. Goldreich and Tremaine came up with a theory to explain the grouping of the ring particles into distinct bands or rings. They proposed that tiny shepherd moons orbiting Saturn could be responsible for containing the ring particles in distinct rings and keeping them separate.

Voyager 1 was to send back a stream of data about the planet, including photographs. One discovery in 1980 was the existence of the F Ring and confirmation that there were indeed shepherd moons associated with it. As *Voyager 1* crossed the plane of the rings, passing literally right through them, it sent back data that enabled scientists to discover three new moons. One, called Teletso, was discovered by a team at the University of Arizona. Another, named Helene, was discovered by a team from the Pic du Midi Observatory. The third, Calypso, was discovered by D. Pascu, P. Seidelmann, W. Baum and D. Currie. Another discovery was that the peak brightness of the E Ring is reached in the orbit of the satellite called Enceladus, and this suggests that the moon itself may be the source of the particles that make up the E Ring.

Voyager 1 had passed Jupiter and was scheduled to pass other planets beyond Saturn. The Voyager project was possible only because the outer planets were arranged in a line at that time, something that only happens once every 175 years.

The visit to Saturn was a major technical achievement, showing that a mass of useful data could be sent back home to the Earth across a distance of 1.5 billion kilometres (950 million) miles. It marked a great leap forward in space exploration and discovery that was every bit as momentous as the Moon landing.

Voyager 1 passed within 124,000 kilometres (77,000 miles) of the surface of Saturn, and photographs taken from this distance showed bands of orange and yellow clouds striping Saturn's atmosphere, streaking along at alarming speeds of several hundred miles per hour. The clouds are thought to be made of frozen ammonia at a temperature of minus 170 degrees Celsius (minus 275 degrees Fahrenheit).

The mission was especially memorable for the images sent back of Saturn's rings. Until this moment the rings had only been observed through telescopes from the Earth. Now they became visible in much sharper detail, and they turned out to be more complex than had been thought. From the Earth just six broad bands are visible. The *Voyager* photographs reveal that these are made up of more than 100 distinct rings. Those interpreting the photographs were puzzled by what they saw. The new information if anything made the phenomenon of Saturn's rings more mysterious than ever.

Voyager 1 also sent back a scan of Saturn's largest moon, Titan, and revealed that there is a fifteenth moon. Titan is a very large object, larger than the planet Mercury, and large enough to have sufficient gravitational pull to hold onto an atmosphere. The data from Titan showed that its atmosphere is very similar to that of the Earth round about the time when life began to emerge around four billion years ago. This prompted the thought that maybe life exists on Titan.

Voyager 2 arrived in the neighbourhood of Saturn in August 1981 to gather yet more information. The G Ring was discovered and three new moons: Atlas, Prometheus and Pandora. Prometheus and Pandora were the first shepherd moons to be discovered. Some of Saturn's moons were found to follow the same orbit. The rings themselves were found to be composed of thousands of thin ringlets. Again in 1981, it was proposed that small moons or moonlets are embedded in the ring system. In 1981, Mark Showalter discovered the moonlet Pan in one of the gaps, the Encke Division, in 1990.

The outcome of the various probe missions to (and past) Saturn has been the accumulation of a huge new mass of information about the planet, it rings and its moons. Saturn has been found to have a surprisingly low density, less than that of water; this means that if an ocean large enough could be found, Saturn would float in it like a huge tennis ball. Saturn is now known to have over sixty moons. The visible rings start about 9,650 kilometres (6,000 miles) from the surface of Saturn and extend out into space about 55,000 kilometres (34,000 miles). They are made of boulders of ice and rock, each on average as big as an armchair, though some are no more than pebbles and others are as big as builders' skips. The rings form a huge structure overall, a disc about 240,000 kilometres (150,000 miles) across from edge to edge, yet only 90 metres (300 feet) thick. The ring system is divided into a large number of fine ringlets, like the grooves in a huge vinyl disc. Close examination shows that the fine ringlets are braided and irregular, and this may be further evidence for the shepherding effect of moonlets.

The scientists gained an enormous amount of new knowledge about Saturn, its rings and its moons. Ordinary people hearing about the project and seeing the images on television and in newspapers and magazines gained a real sense that the outer reaches of the solar system were no longer a no-go area about which nothing much more would ever be known. It may have been achieved robotically, but it was as if we had actually gone there. It was as if landfall had been made on the shore of another New World. We began to colonise it with our minds. The outer planets were, after all, a part of *our* solar system.

PLANETS ORBITING OTHER STARS

(1988)

We are very familiar with the planets orbiting our own Sun. They are close enough for us to be able to see them in the night sky. Sometimes we can see Mars or Jupiter with the naked eye, and Venus is often plainly visible as the Evening Star. But planets orbiting *other* stars are exceedingly difficult to find. This is partly because they are small and distant, and partly because they are not luminous; located very close to their host stars, any trace of them is drowned out by the light of their stars. Planets have only one-millionth of the brightness of their parent stars. They are only likely to be visible under exceptional circumstances: if they are in orbit a long way from the glare of their parent star, and if they are very large – even larger than Jupiter.

Certainly by the early eighteenth century, astronomers were reaching the conclusion that the Sun was just an ordinary star and speculating that if the Sun had a family of planets circling it, then so did many other stars. Isaac Newton wrote in 1713, 'If the fixed Stars are the centres of other similar systems, these, being formed according to a common design, must be all subject to the dominion of One.' By the middle of the nineteenth century, astronomers were actively searching for these distant planets. But how many stars had planets, and how typical our solar system would prove to be was completely unknown to them. Using the technology available to them, the nineteenth-century astronomers starting searching for extra-solar planets, but with little chance of finding them. This did not stop astronomers claiming that they had found them.

One of the earliest claimants was Captain Jacob of the Madras Observatory, who in 1855 reported orbital anomalies in the binary star 70 Ophiuchi. Jacob interpreted the anomalies as indicating that there was 'a planetary body' in that star system. Forty years later Thomas See of the University of Chicago and the US Naval Observatory reported on the same anomalies in the same star system. He said it proved that a 'dark body' existed in the system, one which orbited one of the twin stars every thirty-six years. Shortly afterwards, Forest Ray Moulton published a proof that a three-body system as described would not be stable, and therefore probably did not exist. In the 1950s and 1960s, claims were made for planets orbiting Barnard's Star. The present generation of astronomers is generally sceptical about those early reports of exoplanet detection.

With that history of false starts, the 1988 claim to have discovered an exoplanet was understandably couched in very cautious terms indeed. The Canadian astronomers Bruce Campbell, G. Walker and S. Yang made velocity observations of the star Gamma Cephei, which suggested that a planet is in orbit round it. Scepticism surrounded the publication of this claim, not least because the measurements were taken at the limits of instrumental capabilities at that time. In 1989, additional observations were published supporting the discovery Gamma Cephei's planet. Then material published in 1992 cast doubt on it. Then the application of new techniques in 2003 confirmed that the planet *does* exist. So 1988 did after all mark the indirect discovery of the first known exoplanet.

The modern generation of radio telescopes opened new possibilities and, through the 1990s, astronomers found evidence of the existence of more and more exoplanets. The first were confirmed in the 1990s. In 1992, the radio astronomers Aleksander Wolszczan and Dale Frail were able to announce that they had discovered planets orbiting a pulsar, PSR 1257+12. These pulsar planets may have been formed in an unusual way. They may be remnants of the supernova that produced the pulsar, or they may be the rocky cores of gas giants that survived the supernova and then spiralled back in towards their present orbits. However formed, this discovery is often cited as the first definitive detection of exoplanets. But the evidence was still indirect.

In October 1995, Didier Queloz and Michel Mayor of the University of Geneva announced that they had discovered an exoplanet that is in orbit round an ordinary star, 51 Pegasi. There was general surprise among astronomers at the specific type of planet Queloz and Mayor had discovered. It was a giant planet like Jupiter, yet orbiting fairly close to its parent star. Astronomers had thought in terms of gas giants like Saturn and Jupiter as cold planets, orbiting some distance from their stars; this was a hot giant. More discoveries of hot giants were to follow.

As many as twenty star systems are now known to have more than one planet, which makes it look increasingly likely that solar systems just like ours, with half a dozen major planets, are fairly common. In 1999, a multiple-planetary system was discovered, orbiting Upsilon Andromedae. It consists of at least three planets, all of which are like Jupiter. Early indications are that many systems have gas giants like Jupiter and Saturn. There are also indications that some of the systems have lots of comets. Infrared images show 'dust clouds' round stars that are very like the Kuiper Belt and Oort Clouds that girdle the solar system and are the sources of our (local) comets.

An interesting discovery was made in July 2003, using data from the Hubble Space Telescope. Steinn Sigurdsson and his team found the oldest known exoplanet. Our own solar system and all the planets in it were created about five billion years ago. The planet Sigurdsson discovered is the globular star cluster M4 in the constellation Scorpius, about 5,600 light-years from the earth. This is the only planet so far discovered to orbit a stellar binary (two stars circling one another); one star is a pulsar and the other a white dwarf. The planet is twice as massive as Jupiter and is thirteen billion years old: two-and-a-half times older than the Earth.

More exoplanets are being identified all the time. At the time of writing in 2008, 228 exoplanets are known to exist. Astronomers are tabulating and analysing their characteristics. One feature that is emerging is that the exoplanets orbiting close to their star have nearly circular orbits, while those orbit further out are subject to less tidal control by their stars and tend to have more eccentric orbits. The prevalence of circular orbits for planets in our solar system is already emerging as rather unusual. The fact that Jupiter, the giant planet, follows a circular orbit has an effect on the other planets. Jupiter shepherds the planets within its orbit, especially Mars and the Earth, into having more exactly circular orbits than they would otherwise have. This tendency towards circular orbits in our solar system is far more favourable to the evolution of life than a tendency towards eccentric orbits; it results in nearly uniform temperatures. Planets with strongly eccentric orbits must have climatic environments that vary too extremely to favour the development and maintenance of life.

Most of the exoplanets have been detected by various indirect means. Most of them are also giant planets, planets that are big enough to make some impact on their environment. The very first exoplanet to be seen, and photographed, is a planet orbiting a brown dwarf at a distance of 55 astronomical units. It was discovered and photographed using the Very Large Telescope in September 2006. The star is known only as 2M1207, and its planet is known as 2M1207b.

The rate at which exoplanets are being discovered implies that they must be very common. Astronomers are now estimating that at least ten per cent of Sun-like stars possess planets, and it may be a much higher percentage than that. The discovery that there are so many exoplanets has re-opened the possibility that some of them might support extra-terrestrial life. Several of the planets so far discovered do orbit their parent stars within the habitable zone, where it would be possible for recognisably Earth-like conditions to prevail. The planets that occupy the habitable zone are, to the astronomers' surprise, mainly giant planets that seem more like Jupiter than the Earth. In that case, it is more likely that it will be the larger moons of such planets that will shelter life.

Life is probably commonplace. But *detecting* life (unless the life forms have developed advanced civilisations) at interstellar distances is scarcely going to be possible with our current technology. It may become possible with as-yet-uninvented remote sensing techniques to look for life at these great distances, but that lies far into the future.

So far, all of the astronomical searching for exoplanets has been ground-based. Obviously there is a better chance of seeing the detail of distant planetary systems if the observing telescope is mounted on a satellite orbiting above the Earth's atmosphere. COROT, which was launched in 2006, is the only active space mission that is at the moment devoted to searching for exoplanets.

THE CHANGING LEVEL OF LAKE TANGANYIKA

(1989)

Lake Tanganyika is the second deepest lake in the world. It is 1,470 metres (4,800 feet) deep (only Lake Baikal in the Russian Federation is deeper). Lake Tanganyika's water level today stands at an altitude of 772 metres (2,532 feet) above sea level. In 1949 submerged valleys were discovered on the lake bed, leading down to depths of 550 metres (1,800 feet) below the lake's present day level. The existence of the valleys showed that the lake floor must once have been exposed, and that rivers once flowed across it.

The level of water in Lake Tanganyika fluctuates according to changes in the climate: that much is certain. In any environment, there is a significant relationship between precipitation and evaporation. If the rate of evaporation is well below the rate of precipitation, there will be a water surplus which will fill the rivers and lakes. If potential evaporation is well above the rate of precipitation, the environment becomes parched and arid, rivers dry up and lake levels fall. It has been known for a long time that in Africa the levels of lakes generally have risen and fallen as the climate has changed. But there has been considerable controversy about the amount of fluctuation in water level in Lake Tanganyika.

In 1989, some new evidence became available in the form of cores of lake-bed sediment. Because the sediment contains organic matter it was possible to radiocarbon date it. As a result, it has been possible to reconstruct the palaeohydrology of Lake Tanganyika over the last 40,000 years. The variations in lake level over the past 26,000 years correlate well with changes in the volume of ice in the world and the consequent changes in global sea level. It is perhaps to be expected that climate changes in the tropics would match the climate changes in middle and high latitudes. What was surprising about the data was that it showed that the fluctuations in Lake Tanganyika, a *southern* hemisphere lake, were in phase with those of African lakes to the *north* of the equator.

In the 1990s, more evidence became available in the form of fossils and more radiocarbon dates. In spite of the presence of the deeply submerged drowned valleys, the lake level has been remarkably stable over the last 3,000 years; that was not expected. From about 800 BC to AD 400, the lake basin was fairly dry, but that did not entail the lake level dropping noticeably. It was in about AD 550 that Lake Kivu began to empty into Lake Tanganyika, but this event was not accompanied by a major rise in the level of Lake Tanganyika. Some time between 1300 and 1600 the level of the lake rose. Then, between 1600 and 1900, it fell to its lowest level in the last 3,000 years. The picture is unclear, and often counter-intuitive.

On the long-time scale, it seems likely that very large climate changes are responsible for large changes in lake level, causing it to rise or fall by as much as 180 metres (600 feet). Short-term climate changes are responsible for small rises and falls of about 90 centimetres (3 feet). But there are other factors which are easy to overlook. For instance in the late nineteenth century Lake Tanganyika rose as much as 10 metres (35 feet) above its present level. It is tempting to try to relate that rise to some change in climate, such as a period of heavy rainfall, but it is known that it was entirely due to a log-jam on the River Lukuga, the lake's only outflow. When the dam broke, the level of the lake quickly returned to its present level, which is determined by the height of the bedrock sill at its exit.

THE MOONS OF NEPTUNE

(1989)

So far, only one spacecraft has visited the planet Neptune. The probe *Voyager 2* flew past it, collecting information and photographs as it went, in August 1989. The photographs revealed one very striking feature of the planet, which is its colour; it is a vivid, almost-purple blue.

The atmosphere of Neptune is mainly helium and hydrogen, with traces of methane. *Voyager 2* picked up details of Neptune's weather systems. The temperature at the cloud tops is minus 216 degrees Celsius (minus 357 degrees Fahrenheit), which is the lowest temperature known in the solar system. This contrasts with the temperature at the centre of Neptune's core, which is around 7,000 degrees Celsius (12,600 degrees Fahrenheit), about the same as the cores of other planets, and the same as the temperature of the Sun's surface. The planet has the fastest wind speeds seen anywhere in the solar system, measuring as high as 2,000 kilometres (1,300 miles) per hour. The wind speeds vary locally, and in particular according to whether they blow from east or west. It is the winds blowing in the opposite direction to the planet's rotation that tend to be the fastest winds.

Voyager 2 sent back to earth pictures of a Great Dark Spot in the cloud systems of its southern hemisphere, very like the Great Red Spot seen on Jupiter. The spot on Neptune is oval and 12,500 kilometres (7,800 miles) across. But the spot on Neptune is not such a long-lived feature as Jupiter's. When the Hubble Space Telescope was trained on Neptune in November 1994, the Great Dark Spot discovered in 1989 had gone. It had been replaced by another spot, a new storm, in the northern hemisphere. The huge elliptical features on Neptune and Jupiter are considered to be vast spiral storms of much the same type as the hurricanes we experience on the Earth. *Voyager 2* found a Small Dark Spot in 1989 too, a lesser cyclonic storm in the southern hemisphere. This was dark all over when first photographed, but as *Voyager* got closer to it, a bright centre emerged. Astronomers believe the spots are in effect huge holes in the cloud cover in the upper atmosphere. If so, they function like windows through to the lower atmosphere, the layer that on the Earth we call the troposphere.

Neptune seems to be a much livelier planet than Uranus in terms of its weather systems; *Voyager 2* flew past Uranus in 1986. The wind systems on the Earth are powered by the Sun. Neptune is too far from the Sun for it to have a sufficient input of energy to drive the winds, so it is assumed that it is heat from within the planet that drives them. It has generally been a surprise to find that the planets and moons of the outer solar system are as active and energetic as they are.

Because Neptune is so far from the Sun – thirty astronomical units, or thirty times further from the Sun than the Earth – it takes a very long time to pass round its orbit. As a result the Neptunian year is 165 Earth years long. Because of this, its seasons too are 165 times longer than Earth seasons. The result of these incredibly long seasons is that in recent years Neptune's south pole has become significantly warmer than the rest of the planet, because it has been tilted towards the Sun, not for months but for decades on end. The result is that the south pole is about ten degrees warmer than the rest of Neptune.

Voyager 2 made many discoveries about Neptune and its neighbourhood during its swift flight through in 1989. Between July and September, *Voyager* discovered six new moons orbiting Neptune. One of them was Proteus. This is an interesting body, as it is as large as a body of that density can be without being pulled into a ball shape by its own gravity. Proteus is irregular in shape, like many of the asteroids. It is the second of Neptune's moons in terms of its mass, though it has only one-quarter of the mass of Triton.

The four moons orbiting closest to Neptune are close enough to be within Neptune's rings. They are Naiad, Thalassa, Despina and Galatea.

The next moon, in distance out from the surface of Neptune, is Larissa, and this too was discovered by *Voyager 2* in 1989. The glut of new information about the Neptune system made astronomers focus on it more attentively, and as a result in 2002–03 five more moons were discovered – all of them relatively small and irregular in shape.

A curiosity of Neptune's very long orbit is that the planet has still yet to complete a full Neptunian year since it was discovered in 1846. It will not have made a complete circuit of the Sun until 12 July 2011.

OETZI THE ICEMAN

(1991)

The discovery of Oetzi the Iceman was one of those moments when modern people were excited, indeed almost overwhelmed, by the opportunity they were given to make contact with the remote past. The discoveries of the tomb of Tutankhamun, the Danish bog bodies and the Terracotta Army were similar moments.

On 19 September 1991, Erika and Helmut Simon from Nuremberg discovered a body high up above the snowline in the Alps. At first they and the rescue team who arrived shortly afterwards thought they had found the body of a mountaineer who had died there perhaps ten or twenty years earlier. The body was brown, hairless, emaciated and half-buried in the ice of the Similaun Glacier. The warmer weather of the late twentieth century had melted part of the glacier, exposing the corpse. The odds and ends scattered round the body suggested the remains of out-of-date rather than modern mountaineering equipment, so the authorities began to think in terms of a nineteenth-century mountaineering accident, then something much older. The copper axe found close to the body suggested that it might date from the Bronze Age. As the evidence was looked at, the body shifted from being ten years old to a hundred years old – to 3,000 or more years old.

The radiocarbon date showed that the body was even older than that. The man had died in 3300 BC. Bog bodies have been found dating from as much as 2,000 or 2,500 years ago. There are Egyptian mummies that are older, but nothing that old in the way of a well-preserved body has ever been found in Europe. 'Oetzi', as he has been called, is the only well-preserved prehistoric European ever to have been discovered. The death and preservation by freezing of the Iceman have given us unexpectedly detailed information about the way people lived and died in prehistory.

Tattered fragments of the Iceman's clothing survived. His underclothing consisted of a loincloth and belt. He was also wearing suspenders that held up leather leggings, very similar to the leggings worn by Native North Americans. A middle layer consisted of a tunic made of strips of animal skin carefully sewn together with twined animal sinews. Alternating strips of brown and black fur created a pattern of stripes. This tunic must have been magnificent when it was newly made, but at the time of Oetzi's death it was old and had been patched many times. The outer layer of clothing included leather shoes and a cloak about 90 centimetres (3 feet) long made of plaited grass, with seven or eight cross plaits holding the upper part together and a long fringe round the bottom: a sort of portable windbreak. Oetzi also wore a beehive-shaped fur hat.

Oetzi was aged thirty-five to forty, 160 centimetres (63 inches) tall, with wavy dark-brown hair. There were strange marks tattooed on his skin. They do not appear to be decorative. They may represent acupuncture points that were seen as appropriate to some medical problem he had. They may alternatively represent stages in his acquisition of adult status. In most societies, there are rites of passage marking an individual's arrival at new status – baptisms, confirmations, barmitzvahs, A Levels, graduations, weddings – and it may be that the overall pattern of tattoos represents a complete CV of his status in society, if only we could decipher it. It seems unlikely that we shall ever be able to find out what that status was, as we have no way at all of decoding the marks, although the fact that he owned the earliest known copper axe in Europe suggests that he may have held some high-status position. Or did he perhaps steal it?

The extreme thinness of the body was due to its drying out after death. The forensic experts at first assumed that Oetzi had been caught in a sudden storm, taken shelter in a rocky hollow beside the glacier and died there of hypothermia. It was only ten years later, when a set of X-rays was taken, that they realised they had overlooked something very significant. Embedded in the corpse's shoulder was a stone arrowhead. A fresh look at the corpse itself revealed that there was a fresh, unhealed cut in the skin at that point; there was also a corresponding tear or cut in his coat. Oetzi had been shot with an arrow shortly before he died. Further examination of his belongings now suggested that Oetzi had not only been fatally wounded and chased up into the mountains, but his killers had visited or revisited his body, moved it and strewn his belongings about. There are lots of theories about Oetzi's murder. Was it an execution, a punishment for some crime committed in the village down in the valley below? Or was Oetzi himself the victim of a crime, an undeserved attack by bandits?

The shaft of the fatal arrow had been removed, presumably by a well-meaning companion, to prevent any further aggravation of the wound. Oetzi had bruises on his hands, wrists and chest, suggesting he had been in a fight. One persuasive scenario is that Oetzi and a couple of companions got involved in a skirmish with a rival group of hunters. After being wounded, he may have been carried by his companions. Then, weakened by loss of blood, he neatly stacked his possessions against a rock and lay down to wait for death. His companions were either seen off or killed elsewhere. It may have been members of the rival group who found his body later and strewed his belongings about out of spite.

There was a parallel struggle for ownership of Oetzi's body 5,000 years later. The place where it was discovered was almost exactly on the border between Austria and Italy, which led to a fierce dispute over who should have the body. Clearly it was going to be a major tourist attraction when conserved and displayed. Helmut Simon, the man who discovered the body, returned to the Alps to celebrate his award of £50,000 in a court case over the rights to Oetzi. He decided to celebrate his win with another alpine hike, then he died when he fell 90 metres (300 feet) into a ravine. He had not signed the legal papers relating to the financial settlement, so neither he nor his widow got the £50,000.

The death of the Iceman was a personal disaster for him, but his accidental preservation through 5,000 years was an unexpected and unlikely bonus for us. It gives us a unique insight into the way people lived in the distant past. In some ways they were very like us, in others very different. And knowing about Oetzi somehow changes us a little. Our minds are extended by knowing more and more about the past, just as we learn an orientation to the world by listening to the experiences, beliefs and views of our parents and grandparents, we can adjust that orientation by referring to earlier generations. Through history and archaeology we can acquire some of the life experiences of those generations who have long gone before, and we are better equipped to evaluate our own situations.

THE KUIPER BELT

(1992)

Ever since Pluto was discovered in 1930, there was speculation among astronomers that other previously undetected small planets might exist in the outer solar system. The region beyond Neptune was a zone where it was anticipated that more bodies might yet be found, so the existence of the Kuiper Belt was a hypothesis astronomers had been discussing for decades before they actually found solid evidence for it. There were so many speculations and ideas about it that it is hard to say who was the first to propose it; naming a discoverer is equally difficult. It seems that the first astronomer to suggest that there was a population of planets and smaller bodies in the region beyond Neptune was Frederick Leonard. As soon as Pluto was discovered, Leonard reflected that Pluto was probably 'the first of a series of ultra-Neptunian bodies, the remaining members of which still await discovery but which are destined eventually to be detected.'

Then in 1943 Kenneth Edgeworth added an idea that was to define the Kuiper Belt. He suggested that in the region beyond Neptune the material in the cloud of debris at the time of the solar system's creation was too widely separated to condense into planets. Instead, the material would have condensed into a vast number of much smaller bodies. Edgeworth therefore proposed that the outer region of the solar system consisted of 'a very large number of comparatively small bodies'. He also proposed that from time to time some of these wandered outside this zone and visited the inner solar system as a comet. In fact Edgeworth contributed so many of the key characteristics of the Kuiper Belt that the zone is sometimes called the Edgeworth-Kuiper Belt.

Gerald Kuiper, after whom the belt is usually named, speculated in 1951 that the belt Edgeworth described had existed early on in the solar system's evolution. But he did not believe that the belt still existed today.

Like other astronomers of his time, Kuiper was under the impression that Pluto was about the size of the Earth and that a body of that size would clear a path round its orbit, just as the Earth itself has. A nebulous scatter of small objects would, he thought, have to exist much further out, towards the Oort cloud or right outside the solar system altogether. Kuiper himself, in other words, did not believe in the existence of the Kuiper Belt.

The hypothesis changed repeatedly in the decades following. In 1962, Al Cameron reverted to Edgeworth's theory that there is 'a tremendous mass of small material on the outskirts of the solar system'. Two years later Fred Whipple proposed the existence of a comet belt that might have a sufficient mass to cause the variations observed in the orbit of Uranus. Charles Kowal's 1977 discovery of Chiron led to speculation that it and other centaurs had arrived in their present orbits from some reservoir of bodies out beyond Neptune. Chiron was too unstable to have been its present position for very long, so it must have come from somewhere else. The discovery of Chiron therefore gave support to the idea that a Kuiper Belt existed.

Then support came from studies of comets. It had been realised that comets have finite life spans. When they approach the Sun, their surfaces sublimate off into space, so they are gradually burnt away. The fact that we are still seeing comets means that they must be continually replaced from somewhere. One source reservoir is the Oort cloud, the spherical swarm of comets that lies out beyond 50,000 astronomical units from the Sun, and hypothesised rather than discovered by Jan Oort in 1950. Probably the Oort cloud is the source of comets with a long return period, such as Hale-Bopp. These have orbits that take thousands of years to complete. But there are other comets with conspicuously shorter return periods, 200 years or less. By the 1970s, it was becoming clear that there was a distinct class of comets with a short return period and that these comets could not be coming from as far out as the Oort cloud. In 1980, Julio Fernandez proposed that they must be coming from a reservoir of comets 35–50 astronomical units from the Sun. Computer simulations run by Martin Duncan, Tom Quinn and

Scott Tremaine confirmed this line of thought; the short-period comets could not be coming from the Oort cloud, but must be coming from a source closer in. They also found that the long-period comets arrive in the inner solar system from any direction, which is consistent with a sphere-shaped Oort cloud, whereas the short-period comets arrive in the plane of the solar system. That would be consistent with a separate origin in a disc-shaped belt, although that disc is believed to be quite thick; in fact some astronomers have described the Kuiper Belt as being shaped like a doughnut. Because the phrase 'comet belt' and the name 'Kuiper' occurred in the opening sentence of Fernandez' paper, Tremaine referred to the belt as 'the Kuiper Belt' – and the name has stuck.

The astronomer David Jewitt became increasingly puzzled by 'the apparent emptiness of the outer solar system'. Using telescopes in Arizona and Chile, Jewitt and his graduate student Jane Luu scanned the sky searching for objects beyond Pluto. They used pairs of photographs and a blink comparator, the same method as Clyde Tombaugh and Charles Kowal. They were able to speed the blink comparator process up by using computer images to detect the differences between pairs of plates; this has since become standard practice. In 1988, Jewitt moved to Hawaii, where he was joined by Jane Luu. There they used the Mauna Kea telescope. It took five years years of searching, but in August 1992 they were able to announce the discovery of the first Kuiper Belt object. Six months later they found the second.

The Kuiper Belt as we now see it is a belt of asteroids in the region of the solar system that lies beyond the orbit of the planet Neptune. Neptune is 30 astronomical units from the Sun, and the belt extends from there out to 55 astronomical units. The (inner) asteroid belt has been known about for a long time simply because it is closer to the Earth and therefore easier to observe. The existence of the outer belt remained unknown until relatively recently, in spite of its enormous size and mass. It is twenty times wider than the asteroid belt and contains about 100 times as much rock debris and frozen material.

Like the asteroid belt, the Kuiper Belt consists of boulders orbiting the Sun, some of them large enough to be regarded as dwarf planets:

Pluto is among them. It consists of what are sometimes called planetesimals, which are fragments from the original protoplanetary disc that surrounded the Sun. They failed to coalesce into planets because they were simply too far apart. Instead they formed small bodies, all less than 3,200 kilometres (2,000 miles) across. The largest so-far-discovered trans-Neptunian objects are, in descending order of size, Eris, Pluto, 2005 FY9, 2003 EL61, Sedna, Orcus, Quaoar, Ixion and Varuna.

The Kuiper Belt is different from the inner asteroid belt in being in a much colder zone of the solar system and therefore contains a great deal of ice, made of frozen volatiles such as methane and ammonia as well as water. The Kuiper Belt was discovered in 1992. First, just a few objects in it were identified, but in the following ten years more than a thousand more were recognised. Astronomers believe that there are at least 70,000 objects over 120 kilometres (75 miles) across in the Kuiper Belt. They also believe that the Kuiper Belt is the home of most of the comets that have orbits that are shorter than 200 years long. The centaurs (mentioned earlier in the section on Chiron) are also thought to originate there. Centaurs are half-asteroid half-comet bodies orbiting among the gas giants. Many of these objects have elliptical rather than circular orbits.

The Kuiper Belt is emerging as a distinct and exotic region of the solar system, the habitat of a range of strange objects. It is also making the solar system look a more densely populated and more varied system than we thought it was. Another class of object that originates in the Kuiper Belt is the scattered discs. The dwarf planet Eris is one of these. They are bodies with very large orbits that take them out as far as 100 astronomical units from the Sun, or twice as far out as the outer edge of the Kuiper Belt.

Because the orbits of many of the Kuiper Belt objects are strongly elliptical, they cross the orbit of the planet Neptune. It may be that Triton was originally a Kuiper Belt object, circling the Sun on its own orbit, until it was captured by Neptune as it crossed its gravitational field. Triton now orbits Neptune as its satellite.

The discovery of the Kuiper Belt is part of a new look that astronomers are taking at the outer solar system. They speculate that there may be another pseudo-Kuiper Belt, which they are calling the Oort cloud, one thousand times further out and enveloping the solar system in a spherical nebula of small objects. In this phase of revision and uncertainty, all the objects in the Kuiper Belt and any other objects that may be circling the Sun even further out are referred to generally as Trans-Neptunian Objects, TNOs. The Kuiper Belt throws light on the way the solar system has evolved. Probably, the Kuiper Belt was originally much broader than it now is, but the Kuiper Belt objects that were further in were pushed out of the way by Saturn and Jupiter as they swept round their orbits. It is the lack of large planets (true planets) out beyond Neptune that has allowed this zone of small objects to accumulate and survive there. It is also thought that Uranus and Neptune switched places. As Neptune swung outwards into the Kuiper Belt it created major disturbances there, scattering a lot of Trans-Neptunian Objects into more eccentric orbits, in effect generating comets that would visit the inner solar system. The significance of the Kuiper Belt increased in 2006, when it was discovered by using the Hubble Space Telescope that at least nine stars other than our own Sun have Kuiper Belts round them. These distant Kuiper Belts were plainly visible to Hubble, even though families of full-sized planets circling the stars were not. But the presence of the Kuiper Belts implies that there might well be large planets within them.

In January 2006, the spacecraft *New Horizons* was launched with the specific mission to explore our own Kuiper Belt. It is scheduled to rendezvous with Pluto on 14 July 2015. After that it will go on to study another (yet to be selected) object in the Kuiper Belt.

LAKE VOSTOK
(1996)

Lake Vostock is the biggest of the lakes to be discovered underneath the Antarctic ice sheet. So far 150 of these subglacial lakes have been found. The discovery of lakes under the ice is profoundly significant because water lubricates the under side of the ice sheet and enables it to move faster and more easily. Middle latitude glaciers have for a long time been known to be 'warm-based', with meltwater under them that helps them to flow faster. It was until recently assumed that high-latitude 'cold-based' ice like the Antarctic ice sheet must move much more slowly, because it lacks this lubrication. But – unexpectedly – the Antarctic ice sheet is lubricated; it moves as fast as 1.8 metres (6 feet) a day where it crosses a lake. This means that the lakes are probably playing a previously unsuspected key role in delivering ice to the ocean.

Lake Vostok is in the middle of the large East Antarctic ice sheet. Although the lake itself is completely invisible because it is covered by a thick layer of ice, its position is clearly visible on satellite images because the surface of the ice over the lake is unusually smooth and level. It looks like a frozen lake, but it is not. The surface of the lake is 4,000 metres (13,000 feet) below the surface of the ice.

The lake was discovered in 1996 by British and Russian scientists who assembled a variety of data, including radar-imaging observations made from aircraft and radar measurements made from satellites. From all of this data they were able to infer the existence of the lake, though it has never been seen.

Lake Vostok is big, measuring 50 kilometres (30 miles) wide by 240 kilometres (150 miles) long. This makes it much the same size and shape as Lake Ontario. It is divided into two deep basins by a ridge. This makes it very similar to glacially eroded lake troughs elsewhere in the world, which are often made up of several deeply scooped rock basins. The lake is about 200metres (650 feet) deep over the ridge, 400 metres (1,300 feet) deep in the northern basin, 800 metres (2,600 feet) deep in the southern basin. There is an island in the middle of the lake. It is estimated that Lake Vostok contains as much as 5,400 cubic kilometres (1,300 cubic miles) of fresh water.

As we become increasingly aware of an increasingly polluted Earth, the unexpected discovery of this unspoilt lake comes as a pleasant surprise. Sealed underneath an ice sheet 3 kilometres (2 miles) thick, Lake Vostok's water must be the purest, cleanest, most uncontaminated on Earth. The lake's water is very old. It is thought to have a residence time of about a million years. Lake Ontario's water has an average residence time of six years, which is typical for open-air lakes of that size.

The lake is big enough for the Sun and Moon to exert a tidal pull on the lake water. The lake level duly rises and falls a centimetre or two. This small tidal shift is probably enough to generate a circulation within the lake, which would be necessary to support bacteria.

The air temperatures in Antarctica are very low, with summer temperatures hovering around zero and winter temperatures dropping to minus 60 degrees Celsius (minus 76 degrees Fahrenheit). In view of the climate, it is surprising that liquid water can exist in Antarctica at all. The reason it is there is the pressure exerted by the ice, which shifts the freezing point (downwards) in the same way that a pressure cooker shifts the boiling point (also downwards). There is also some geothermal heat from within the Earth, which helps to warm the bottom water in the lake. The ice sheet acts as an insulating blanket, shielding the lake from the cold air above it.

In 1998, an international research team based at Vostok Station produced one of the longest ice cores ever obtained. It was 3,623 metres (11,890 feet) long altogether. Samples of ice from near the lake surface have been dated, and they turn out to be 420,000 years old. This is taken to show that the lake has been sealed underneath the ice for at least 500,000 years, perhaps a million years. The research team had the self-discipline to stop drilling 90 metres (300 feet) above the boundary between the ice and the lake. This was to stop the lake from becoming contaminated by the 60 tons of aviation fuel the Russians poured down the borehole to stop it from freezing solid. One intriguing find from the ice, some of which is believed to have formed from lake water freezing onto the base of the ice sheet, is the presence of microbes. This suggests that the lake water supports life. The fact that the lake has been cut off from the outside world for such a long time in turn suggests that it may be a habitat where ancient bacteria may live, and that they may have characteristics which they developed half a million years ago, evolving differently from the microorganisms we are familiar with. The two lake basins may even have different ecologies.

The enormous weight of the ice sheet pressing down on the water contributes to a high concentration of oxygen, perhaps at levels fifty times higher than in normal freshwater lakes. Everyone is curious to know more about the mysteries of the lake, and there is an almost irresistible temptation to go on drilling down to see what the lake contains. Drilling into the lake would almost certainly contaminate it and therefore spoil whatever ecosystem has evolved there. The borehole would also release the pressure, and the lake could 'go off' like a gigantic ring-pulled can of beer; this could be very dangerous for the scientists working round the top of the borehole. This is one of those moments in history where the urge to press on into unknown territory has to be resisted. Here is a discovery for which we have to wait patiently.

In 2001, plans were initiated at the Jet Propulsion Laboratory to design and build a melter probe, nicknamed the cryobot. This is intended to burrow through the ice, unrolling a power and communications cable as it goes. When it reaches the lake, a small tethered submersible or hydrobot will swim off to search for life forms with a camera. Two more subglacial lakes were discovered in Antarctica in 2006. It may be that some of these lakes are interconnected by subglacial rivers. The movement of the ice sheet creates variable pressure on the different lakes, so water may suddenly be squirted powerfully from one lake to another.

One fascinating implication of the discovery of Lake Vostok is that its environment bears several close parallels to that discovered on Europa, one of the moons of Jupiter. If life exists in Lake Vostok, it probably also exists in the ice-sealed ocean of Europa. This development in Antarctica shows how discoveries in outer space and discoveries here on the Earth can be linked together – how new knowledge unexpectedly joins up with old, and in quite unexpected ways.

GAMMA RAY BURSTS
(1997)

Gamma ray bursts, often abbreviated by astronomers to GRBs, have until recently been a great mystery. About once every day the gamma ray sky lights up with a spectacular explosion. As late as 1996 no one knew what caused the explosions, where they were happening or even how far away they were. At NASA's Compton Gamma Ray Observatory, the two-dimensional position in the sky of each Gamma Ray Burst was recorded and mapped. The observatory was able to produce a 'star map' showing the apparent location of more than 800 of these explosions. Before the publication of this map, most astronomers imagined that most GRBs were taking place within our own Milky Way galaxy. But the map showed no evidence of this, no increase in density along the line of the Milky Way. The bursts were randomly spread across the sky. It began to look as if the Gamma Ray Bursts must be colossal bursts of energy from widely scattered locations outside our galaxy.

The question of the distance of the GRBs was a central subject of discussion among astronomers in 1995.

Then, in 1997, the thirty-year-long mystery was solved. The answer came from a range of different telescopes, some ground-based, others orbiting. The short-lived bursts of gamma ray photons are the most energetic form of light. They are associated, on the Earth, with nuclear explosions. It was as if the astronomers were watching some distant intergalactic nuclear war, using unbelievably powerful weapons.

A problem with observing the bursts is that they are 'fuzzy' – featureless and poorly resolved. This makes them difficult to locate. But then on 8 May 1997 an orbiting satellite picked up and precisely located a GRB, immediately relaying its position to astronomers manning ground-based telescopes. Within the hour, many of the world's most powerful telescopes were trained on the position of the latest GRB. They found there a faint and variable point of light which seemed to be connected with the gamma ray burst. This point of light had a red shift of 0.8, which is the distance scale of galaxies and quasars. If the light source and the GRB were connected then the GRB was coming from billions of light-years away.

So, some at least of the gamma ray bursts are linked with distant supernovae. This means that the gamma ray bursts mark the explosive deaths of very massive stars. The GRBs appear to be beacons that tell us about events occurring in the early universe.

THE TRASH ISLAND IN THE NORTH PACIFIC
(1997)

A huge floating island of rubbish has been discovered in the North Pacific Ocean. Charles Moore, an oceanographer, discovered the floating garbage while he was sailing home to California after taking part in a Los Angeles yacht race. Normally sailors avoid the large area within the North Pacific Gyre, simply because of the anticyclonic conditions and low wind speeds found there. But in spite of these deterrents Moore decided to take a short cut home across the largely unvisited North Pacific Gyre and it was there that he stumbled across the sea of waste. He was surprised to find himself surrounded, day after day, by enormous quantities of floating rubbish. Moore expected to see some land-originating garbage close to coasts, but here he was thousands of miles from land yet surrounded by garbage. 'Every time I came on deck there was trash floating by. How could we have fouled such a huge area? How could this go on for a week?'

Charles Moore inherited a fortune that his family had made in the oil industry. After this Pacific experience, which was for him a personal rite of passage, he sold his business interests to become an environmental activist, campaigning to urge consumers to use less disposable plastic.

There are some parallels between the newly discovered Trash Island and the much better known Sargasso Sea in the North Atlantic. Both oceans are dominated by a huge gyratory movement of water, which turns clockwise round a central area of relatively calm water. It is in this calm water that floating debris collects. The Sargasso Sea is about 3,200 kilometres (2,000 miles) long and 1,100 metres (700 miles) wide. In it is a great mass of floating seaweed. The Sargasso Sea was certainly known to

Portuguese sailors in the fifteenth century, and may even have been visited by mariners who had been blown seriously off-course in the Roman period. Rufus Festus Avienus, writing in the fourth century AD, described an area of the Atlantic as being covered with seaweed – a major feature of the Sargasso Sea.

In the Sargasso Sea, there is often a flat calm so, in the days of sail, ships were often stranded there. Even modern vessels can get their propellers snagged in the seaweed. The area has a reputation for being the 'graveyard of ships'. The combination of low wind speeds and lack of ocean currents leads to floating debris of every kind accumulating there.

The newly discovered Trash Island in the Pacific is similar in terms of location. It lies between Hawaii and California in the middle of the North Pacific, with strong ocean currents circulating right round it. It differs from the Sargasso Sea in one important respect: it is much larger.

In the nineteenth century, most of the floating debris in the Pacific was organic, consisting of material such as driftwood and wooden fittings from ships. This material eventually degraded and disintegrated. Today, much of the floating debris is plastic, which is used to make a wide range of items. Although some plastic is biodegradable, much of it is not. The rotation of the North Pacific water round the island helps rubbish from both California and Japan to accumulate. Some of the rubbish is thrown from ships and oil rigs, but a startling four-fifths of it originates on land. It includes footballs, kayaks, Lego blocks and carrier bags.

The Trash Island according to conservative estimates weighs three million tons, but some observers, including the discoverer of the Trash Island, the oceanographer Charles Moore, think it is now nearer 100 million tons. By 2008, the developing Trash Island appeared to have influenced the circulation of the ocean currents to the extent of developing into two patches, an Eastern Patch between Hawaii and North America and a Western Patch between Hawaii and Japan. The Eastern Patch retains the clockwise rotation of water round its circumference, which reflects the movement of water in the North Pacific Basin as a whole. The Western Patch has water rotating anti-clockwise round its circumference.

The Trash Island or Islands have been described as a plastic soup, and the rapid growth of the world's biggest rubbish dump gives cause for concern. The two islands put together now make a total area that is twice that of continental USA. The Western Patch almost reaches Japan. The Eastern Patch comes within 800 kilometres (500 miles) of California. Frequently the Eastern Patch encroaches on land areas in the Hawaiian Islands. When the Trash Island visits, its calling card is unmistakeable. It leaves a confetti of plastic covering the beaches. A proportion of modern plastic is degradable, but the non-degradable plastic is extremely durable. Some plastic objects fifty years old have been found floating in the Trash Island. Tiny plastic pellets, or nurdles, are the raw material of the plastics industry. Hundreds of millions of them are lost or spilt every year, and many of these find their way down drainage systems into the sea. Plastic is now thought to make up ninety per cent of all the rubbish floating in the oceans. A UN research programme came to the conclusion that on average a square mile of the ocean contains 46,000 pieces of floating plastic. The health risk, to marine life and ultimately to human beings, is enormous.

The Trash Island has gone undetected until very recently for two reasons. The North Pacific Gyre is a relatively unvisited part of the ocean. But much of the plastic debris floats just below the surface. And because much of the plastic is itself transparent when it is immersed in water it becomes invisible. The sea of rubbish as a whole is translucent and does not show up on satellite images.

CONVECTION CELLS
ON THE SUN
(1998)

In 1998, astronomers discovered something previously unnoticed about the surface of the Sun. Huge regions of its surface are rising, while other equally large areas are sinking. The English geologist and physicist Arthur Holmes hypothesised in the 1930s that this is happening in the interior of the Earth, and that these movements in the mantle are responsible for moving the Earth's crust not only up and down but sideways too. It was only to be expected that the Sun would have convection currents of the same type. The Sun's bubbling surface is at about 6,000 degrees Celsius (10,832 degrees Fahrenheit). As hot gas floats up to it, it cools, then descends to be heated up again.

The enormous upwellings and subsidences of gas in the Sun are on a scale that it is surprising they were not identified before. Much smaller rising and falling areas have been known about for a long time. These small convection cells are known as granules because of the granular texture they give to the Sun's surface. They consist of rising columns of superheated plasma at around 6,000 degrees Celsius (10,832 degrees Fahrenheit), and they are on average 1,200 kilometres (750 miles) in diameter. When the hot rising plasma reaches the surface it spreads sideways, cools and then sinks by way of the narrow spaces between the granules.

Astronomers have for thirty years been searching for evidence of rising and falling on a larger scale. First, they found evidence of convection cells the size of the Earth. The upwellings and subsidences discovered in 1998 are on an even larger scale, with each region measuring two or three times the size of Jupiter. The turbulent, chaotic-looking surface is apparently convecting on three different scales. A parallel might be the surface texture of a fast-flowing river in flood, which displays turbulence at several different scales, say 1 centimetre (⅖ inch), 20 centimetres (8 inches) and 1 metre (40 inches).

The new discovery is equivalent to mapping the pattern of major high- and low-pressure systems in the Earth's atmosphere. The Earth's pressure belts determine the direction of the wind, which always blows from high pressure areas to areas of low pressure, so mapping pressure belts is in effect tantamount to mapping the prevailing wind belts. In a similar way, mapping the broad pattern of upwelling and subsidence on the Sun's surface also maps the pattern of the turbulent lateral movements.

The gigantic convection cells on the Sun influence the location of sunspots, and sunspots eject streams of particles into space, some of which reach the Earth and influence weather patterns here. So the discovery of convection cells may have implications for changes in terrestrial weather, and also for predicting those changes.

The convection cells' discoverers believe that the cells may help to explain some of the remaining puzzles about the Sun's behaviour. It has long been known that the Sun rotates faster at its equator than it does at its poles. There is a possibility that the giant convection cells may help to explain this. It is one of those discoveries that is intriguing in itself, but may hold the keys to explaining a number of other phenomena in due course.

ANTARCTIC MELTING
(2001)

After the great research initiative given to it in the International Geophysical Year in the mid-1950s, investigation of the Antarctic ice sheet has continued under enormous momentum. New techniques are being applied all the time, and more and more detail has been emerging. One recent addition to this knowledge is about the movement of the ice, which can now be picked up remotely by satellite imaging. Very large areas of the ice sheet are moving very slowly indeed. There is only rapid movement where ice streams are leaving basins, passing between mountains, or moving over subglacial water.

Within the ice sheet there are great rivers of ice hundreds of miles long and which behave rather like valley glaciers. These convey ice from the interior towards the sea. The satellite measurements are also able to make fairly precise estimations of the altitude of the ice surface. Amid the many claims relating to global warming, the waning of the ice caps is always prominent, so some objective evidence of this is welcome – even if the warming itself is not. The satellite imaging shows that the average elevation of the Antarctic ice sheet was falling at a rate of just under 1 centimetre (⅘ inch), per year from 1992 to 1996. The accumulating evidence about the dynamics of the Antarctic ice sheet show that it can only have had a very small effect on global sea level: no more than 2 millimetres (¹/₁₀ inch), and those 2 millimetres could have been either a rise or a fall.

The twenty-first century prospects for Antarctica are unclear. The ice seems to be progressively thinning in West Antarctica, the area of the Ronne Ice Shelf, the Ross Ice Shelf and the lowland that connects them. This may lead to an ice surge, or the collapse of an ice shelf when large sections of the edge of the ice sheet that are currently grounded on bedrock float free. There is likely to be more melting of ice round the edge, where it is in contact with slightly warmer ocean water. That could cause more rapid waning of the ice sheet. On the other hand, the penetration of warmer air into Antarctica is likely to produce heavier snowfall there (as Captain Scott predicted a hundred years ago).

What the net effect of these changes will be is largely guesswork.

THE OSSUARY OF JAMES THE BROTHER OF JESUS

(2002)

The ossuary of James, a small chalk box made as a container for human bones, was discovered in Israel in 2002. It was brought to the notice of the public at a press conference co-hosted by the Biblical Archaeological Society and the Discovery Channel in October 2002. The Hebrew inscription on it ('Ya'akov bar Yoseph Achui Yeshua') identifies it as the ossuary belonging to 'James son of Joseph, Brother of Jesus'. The sensational nature of the inscription, together with its lack of provenance or pedigree, brought it under immediate suspicion. It seemed too good to be true. If it is authentic, it could be the first piece of archaeological evidence for the historical existence of Jesus. The Israel Antiquities Authority later declared it to be a modern forgery, but there are some scholars who believe that it is an authentic first-century artefact.

At the time of the announcement, the ossuary was owned by a well-known collector of antiquities, Oded Golan, an engineer living in Tel Aviv. He said that he had bought the ossuary decades before from an Arab antiquities dealer in the Old City of Jerusalem. He had had no idea of the inscription's significance.

There is good evidence to believe that the ossuary is a genuine artefact from the first century AD and several separate authorities have come to that conclusion. The Geological Survey of Israel commented that it was made of a chalk that was commonly used for constructing Jerusalem ossuaries, and dated it to the first century. The GSI also concluded that the ossuary showed no signs of being a fake; there are no modern tool marks on it, for instance, and the patina that showed its age appeared to be authentic. André Lemaire of the Sorbonne came to the same conclusion, going so far as to say that it was very possible that the ossuary had belonged to the James mentioned in the Bible as the brother of Jesus. Writing experts including Kyle McCarter and Joseph Fitzmyer dated the style of the inscription to the period 20 BC – AD 70. All these lines of evidence pointed towards authenticity.

The ossuary was to be displayed in the Royal Ontario Museum, but when it arrived in Toronto on 31 October 2002, the Canadian museum staff present were horrified to see that it had been packed in a cardboard box. When they unwrapped it with great apprehension the next day they found as they had feared that the ossuary was indeed damaged. There were several cracks, including one passing right through the inscription. The museum conservators repaired the cracks and in doing so discovered a new feature, a carved rosette on the side opposite the inscription.

The ossuary had its critics from the start. Robert Eisenman of California State University, Long Beach, who was a specialist in the biblical figure of James, thought the discovery was too good to be true.

The discovery of the James ossuary was followed a few months later, in January 2003, by the discovery of another, possibly connected, inscription known as the Jehoash inscription.

Then, on 18 June 2003, the Israeli Antiquities Authority published a damagingly negative report on the ossuary. In the IAA's view, the inscription was a modern addition. The ossuary and its patina might be genuinely old, but the inscription was recent and made to look old by the use of a chalk solution. The type of chalk used for the ossuary matched the type used in the first century for genuinely ancient ossuaries. Three coatings were identified in the ossuary's patina, but only the last coating covered the inscription and that was considered to be artificial. Different parts of the texts were carved in different styles, and they had been copied from a catalogue of Jewish ossuaries.

But the IAA's report has been contested. In 2005, after analysing the ossuary himself, Dr Wolfgang Krumbein declared that the IAA was wrong. The 2003 forgery claim was based on a series of mistakes, mistaken premises, prejudices, 'use of inappropriate methodology, mistaken geochemistry, reliance on unconfirmed data, disregard of information (such as the cleaning and preservation actions performed, and the use of a comparative isotope methodology despite the fact that the inscription fails to meet the conditions for such tests.' Krumbein went even further. He gave evidence that the patina in the inscription had been interfered with after the IAA's June 2003 declaration. Krumbein added that there was photographic evidence that the patina had been interfered with. 'The pictures further document recent (2005) addition of a reddish sticky or powdery and also rock staining material. These materials do not exist in photographic documents prior to 2005.'

These were implicitly very serious allegations. Someone had deliberately interfered with the surface of the artefact in 2003–05 in order to make the inscription look newly made. Krumbein concluded that the tests could not proved that the artefacts were genuine, but that the 'expert' witness evidence that they were forgeries was fatally flawed. It began to look as the forging of the inscription was itself forged.

So, the current situation is that some scholars strongly suspect that the inscription at least is a forgery, while other scholars are vigorously defending its authenticity.

The Jehoash inscription was found (it was said) at a construction site near the Temple Mount in Jerusalem, or in the Muslim cemetery. The inscription appears to describe repairs to the Temple by Jehoash, the son of King Ahaziah of Judah, and corresponded to the account given in the Second Book of Kings. The owner was another antiquities dealer, this time in Hebron. As with the James ossuary, the Geological Survey of Israel provided the authentication. This find had a different edge to it. The James ossuary was a problem to those who had a psychological problem with objective verification of a historical Jesus. The Jehoash inscription re-ignited the smouldering conflict between Muslims and the Israeli group called the Temple Mount Faithful. The Temple Mount Faithful claimed the find was a sign from God that the al-Aqsa Mosque on the Temple Mount must be demolished and the (Jewish) Temple rebuilt at once. In a politically dangerous situation like this, a neat solution would be to find evidence that the inscription is a fake. The situation became more complicated as two parallel controversies developed, surrounding the two unrelated artefacts. An Israeli historian had developed a theory that the two Books of Kings were based on public inscriptions, and put forward the view that a forger could have used his theory as a starting point. An expert in ancient handwriting from Hebrew University told the IAA and the police that he had met the owners of the stone, seen the inscription and knew that it contained a mix of Hebrew, Aramaic and Moabite letters. Another linguist, this time from Harvard, spotted spelling mistakes. Rumours of forgery multiplied, while the stone itself remained well out of sight.

In the Israeli press, there was a report that the IAA Theft Unit was concentrating on the possibility that the Jehoash inscription was being used as bait to attract a prominent wealthy collector in London. Then a link was found, by way of a private detective, to Oded Golan, the man who owned the James ossuary. This was where the stories of the two questionable artefacts converged. Oded Golan said that he himself did not own the Jehoash Inscription; the owner was a Palestinian dealer living under the Palestinian Authority. The investigation led on to the police searching Oded Golan's home, office and warehouse, and these searches produced among other things a photograph of Golan with the Jehoash Inscription. Golan was questioned again and then the police searched some rented storage space that Golan had not disclosed before. There they found scores of objects of doubtful authenticity, forged ancient seals and, damningly, inscriptions in various stages of manufacture along with tools and documents that would help in the making of forgeries. It was reported that under intensive questioning Golan promised to hand over the Jehoash inscription.

The IAA concluded in 2003 that the Jehoash inscription was fake. The stone was more typical of locations in Cyprus or somewhere further west (not Israel). The patina over the lettering was different from that on the back of the stone and it could be wiped away by hand.

The IAA may be on firmer ground in dismissing the Jehoash Inscription as a forgery, but it is still possible that the James ossuary is genuine, especially given Krumbein's observations, which indicate recent tampering. Several well-informed scholars believe the ossuary and its inscription may be genuine, and they are pressing for their examination by specialists from outside Israel.

Late in 2004, Golan and four other people were charged with running a forgery ring. It was alleged that they had the expertise to manufacture convincing fake antiquities, including an ivory pomegranate that had (until the court case) been generally accepted as the one proven relic of King Solomon's Temple. In February 2007, at Oded Golan's trial, the defence lawyer produced in evidence photographs that had been taken in Golan's home in 1976. The James ossuary can be seen in these photographs, resting on a shelf. The photographs are themselves genuine and untampered with. They provide significant evidence that the ossuary was not a forgery – at least not a forgery manufactured within the twenty-year-long period during which Golan was accused of running a forgery business. The photographs dating from 1976 show that the ossuary already existed then, and not only that but the inscription on it existed then too. If someone had forged an inscription saying 'James son of Joseph, Brother of Jesus' in the early 1970s, they would have been fully aware of the significance of what they were doing, and the implications of the potential value of the inscribed artefact to a collector or a museum. It is not credible that someone would have forged the ossuary and its inscription in the 1970s, or earlier, and then hoarded the object for thirty years.

There was another development in this strange story in 2007. In February of that year, James Cameron and Simcha Jacobovici held a news conference in New York to trail their television documentary *The Lost Tomb of Jesus*. This film outlines the discovery in 1980 of the Talpiot Tomb, which the film makers claim was Jesus's family tomb. It was to be premiered, appropriately, on the Discovery Channel. The film also includes the idea that the James ossuary originally came from the Talpiot Tomb.

The Talpiot tomb, the tomb the film makers claim as the tomb of Jesus, was found in the East Talpiot neighbourhood 5 kilometres (3 miles) south of the Old City of Jerusalem. It was found by chance when the site was being excavated for the foundations of a new apartment block. The building was completed in 1982 and the tomb has been preserved underneath it. Access to it is now by a flight of stairs leading down from the corner of Olei Hagardom and Avshalom Streets, though it is kept locked and it is not open to the public. The circle-within-a-V symbol over the tomb's door may be the 'Ascension eye' as in ancient Egyptian symbolism. Alternatively, it may be an ancient Hebrew symbol representing an eye peering through a doorway. The tomb contains six burial shafts and two arch-vaulted shelves where bodies were laid out. When the Talpiot Tomb was originally discovered there were ten ossuaries containing fragmentary human remains, of which one ossuary was subsequently lost. The film makers alleged that the tenth ossuary disappeared while it was being stored in a courtyard outside the Rockefeller Museum; they implied that the James ossuary was that missing tenth ossuary from the Talpiot Tomb.

The problem with this is the photographs used as evidence in the Golan trial, which show that the James ossuary was safely in Golan's home in 1976. If the James ossuary really came from the Talpiot Tomb, it must have been taken from it before the tomb's formal discovery in 1980.

Such things are not unknown. There is a beautiful gold and ivory statuette of a Minoan goddess known as the Boston goddess because it found its way into a Boston museum early in the twentieth century. Its provenance is unknown, but it was probably collected (or stolen) from a surface layer in the ruins of the East Wing of the Knossos Labyrinth, and removed and sold before the East Wing was excavated. The gold Ring of Minos, a spectacular object showing extraordinary religious scenes, was found on the surface at the spot where the Temple Tomb was later discovered. So it is possible for surface finds to disappear from archaeological sites, and for them to enter the antiquities market before the sites are formally excavated.

But the archaeologist who supervised the 1980 excavation of the tomb of Yeshua (the Talpiot Tomb), Professor Amos Kloner, has said that the ossuary that went missing from the tomb could not be the same as the one that turned up later as the James ossuary. The mysterious tenth ossuary, the one that disappeared, was completely unmarked, whereas the one that turned up in 2002 had the inscription 'James son of Joseph, Brother of Jesus' carved on the front and a rosette on the back. It was not the same object.

According to the documentary, forensic tests show that the patina on the James ossuary matches the patina found on the other ossuaries in the Talpiot Tomb, though this was later disputed by critics of the film.

The names on the ossuaries are the familiar names from the gospel story, names that have very special resonances for us today. The stone boxes are labeled Maria (Mary), Matia (Matthew), Mariamenou-Mara (Mary Magdalene?), Yeshua bar Yehosef (Jesus son of Joseph), Yose (the diminutive form of Joseph, therefore 'Joe') and Yehuda bar Yeshua (Judah son of Jesus). But scholars who are familiar with the history of the period know that these names were very common. Today, we sit up and take notice if we hear the names Jesus, Mary and Joseph. Jesus in particular has powerful resonances and associations – but in first century Jerusalem it was a common name, as was James. But the convergence of these names all in one place, one tomb, one family, was highly suggestive. The DNA of the material in the 'Jesus' ossuary did not match the DNA from the 'Mariamenou' ossuary. This was taken by the documentary makers to show that Mariamenou and Jesus were not blood relations, but that they were instead husband and wife; this Mariamenou was the Mary Magdalene whom others had also claimed was really the wife of Jesus.

It is a very tangled web of claims, counter-claims, exaggerations, deceptions. Yet there may be truth behind it. Take the names of the people buried together in the Talpiot Tomb. The names were common Jewish names of the first century, but the chances of those names all occurring within one family in a settlement as small as first century Jerusalem are very slight indeed. Jerusalem in the first century had a population of between 10,000 and 30,000; it was a town no bigger than present-day Glastonbury or Seaford. If we allow for the moment that the Talpiot Tomb really was the family tomb of Jesus, we can speculate that Jesus's brother James may for reasons unknown not have been buried with the rest of the family. It appears from the Bible texts that James died a long time after Jesus, a full thirty years later; perhaps by then the family tomb was full, or its location lost, or built over; perhaps there was some other reason why James was buried elsewhere. So the ossuary of James may never have been in the Talpiot Tomb in the first place.

No doubt new discoveries will be made as new techniques are found to examine the ossuary. This is one of those discoveries which is so loaded with political, religious, cultural agenda, and so charged with emotion that interpretation is always going to be very difficult.

THE BIG RIP THEORY
OF THE UNIVERSE

(2003)

By the end of the twentieth century, the Big Bang theory of the universe had won the contest over steady state; it had become the accepted consensus view of the way the universe worked. All that remained uncertain was whether the expansion of the universe might take its components so far apart from one another that they might remain apart, after the expansion came to a halt. The alternative was that when the expansion came to a halt the gravitational pull of all the fragments of matter would lead to an accelerating implosion. A third alternative had not really presented itself.

In 1998–2000, astronomers found unexpected evidence that the expansion of the universe is *not* slowing down. It is accelerating. Astronomical observation of bodies at the furthest edges of the universe shows that they are receding from us at increasing speeds. If these observations are accurate, it may mean that the universe will never cease expanding. As the receding galaxies accelerate towards and reach, perhaps even exceed, the speed of light, it will mean that we will no longer be able to see them.

This disturbing new finding has led to the development of a new theory of the universe, which is called the Big Rip. The pioneer of this theory is Robert Caldwell of Dartmouth University. He and his colleagues, Marc Kamionkowski and Nevin Weinberg, were discussing how a ball of matter might collapse under its own weight to create a galaxy. They were aware of dark energy and when they were altering the various factors in their computer models they found that if they factored in too much dark energy, it would stop the sphere from collapsing. Even more dark energy and it caused the sphere to explode. This did not prove that dark energy actually behaves in this way, but the exercise prompted a new line of thought. There is the possibility that gravity after all might not prevail: dark energy might prevail instead.

At the heart of the Big Rip model is the idea of a kind of unknown phantom energy that is causing the universe to expand, whether by pushing apart from within or – even more sinister – by suction from outside. This energy is not just overriding gravity, causing the galaxies to become further and further separated from each other, it will eventually cause the galaxies to expand and stars to explode. Even planets and individual atoms will be burst apart. When absolutely everything is ripped apart, the universe and time itself will end. Caldwell himself thinks the scenario is incredible, and it is one of the most horrific models for the universe ever conceived.

The fact that the energy, the motive power, for this process is completely unexplained and unknown does not mean that the theory can be discounted. Even if further evidence emerges that the Big Rip is really under way, we may still never find out what drives it. It is thought that a mysterious thing called dark energy, an anti-gravity force, may be driving the accelerating expansion.

If the rate of expansion continues to accelerate, it will override any compensating effect of gravity. Even the nuclear forces that bind matter together in the subatomic world will no longer be effective. Atoms will burst apart in just the same way as the outer universe.

If there is nothing to halt the acceleration, all the galaxies will recede from one another at the speed of light. That will mean that each galaxy will be left completely alone in a totally dark universe. We, in the Milky Way, would be unable to see any galaxies outside the Milky Way, whatever the power of our telescopes. That could happen within 100 billion years, even according to pre-Big Rip theory. According to Big Rip theory, the acceleration would happen at an accelerating rate.

By no means are all astronomers convinced by the Big Rip scenario. It would be surprising if they were. But Caldwell's scenario brings the projected end of the universe to a date perhaps as soon as 20 billion years into the future. By 19 billion years, we will know what is in store as all the other galaxies will have vanished from the sky. They will be rushing away from us at the speed of light. Sixty million years before the end of the universe the Milky Way galaxy (and presumably all the other by-now-invisible galaxies) will start to explode. Three months before the end of the universe, the solar system will inflate, the planets flying away from the Sun. An hour before the end, the Earth itself will explode. After that, in the last few hellish minutes, all the atoms will fly apart.

In order to turn dark energy into destructive phantom energy, Caldwell and his co-workers looked at the cosmological constant. This was a constant that Einstein called into play in his theory of general relativity. When Edwin Hubble discovered in the 1920s that the universe was expanding, Albert Einstein referred to the cosmological constant as his greatest mistake. But in recent years the constant has been revived by Caldwell and his colleagues, who use it in their theory, treating it as a variable. Other theoreticians are uneasy about tampering with the cosmological constant. Abraham Loeb, for instance, has said, 'If I had to place a bet, I would bet in favour of the standard cosmological constant.'

A problem with the Big Rip theory is that there is too little evidence to support it. Equations with variable constants in them can be made to prove anything. At the moment the theory simply stands as an awe-inspiring and terrifying prospect, but it is still only one of several possible alternative futures. Caldwell himself asks rhetorically, 'Who knows if it is right or wrong?' It is scarcely a winning argument.

MORE ABOUT THE
MOONS OF SATURN
(2005)

In 2005, the Cassini spacecraft launched by NASA continued to make exciting new discoveries about Saturn. Among other findings, Cassini discovered wandering moons, rubble-pile moons, and some new and clumpy rings of Saturn. The probe revealed that Saturn has a dynamic magnetosphere.

The movement of the small moons Atlas and Pan along their orbits within Saturn's rings causes density waves to pass through the rings. These waves enabled scientists to calculate the masses of the two moons. They have rather low masses, implying that they are very porous. This led on to the idea that they may be relatively loose structures, literally piles of rubble. In this they may be similar to the two moons Prometheus and Pandora, which shepherd Saturn's E ring.

Another moon of Saturn's was discovered, a tiny object only 5 kilometres (3 miles) across, which has been named Polydeuces. This moon acts as a companion (sometimes described as a 'Trojan') moon of the larger moon Dione. These Trojan moons are located in the same orbit as a larger moon, at gravitationally stable points just in front of or just behind the larger moon. Saturn is the only planet in the solar system to possess moons that are attended by smaller moons or, to put it differently, to possess small moons that are chaperoned by larger moons.

The images sent back to Earth by Cassini reveal several additional faint rings round Saturn. Some of these occupy what were previously thought to be gaps in the ring system, which has been found to be made of water ice. Several of the rings turn out to be kinked, a distortion which is probably to be explained by the presence of small shepherd moons.

Evidence was also found that Saturn has different winds at different altitudes. Something similar happens on the Earth where, in many places, high level winds perhaps 16 kilometres (10 miles) above the ground blow in the opposite direction to low-level winds. The Saturn images imply that convection is an important process within the Saturnian atmosphere and that energy is being transferred from Saturn's interior to drive the strong winds.

Abundant molecular oxygen was also detected. Scientists might once have been tempted to leap to the conclusion that this is evidence of the presence of life, but it is clear that there is no life on Saturn, so molecular oxygen can be generated without the aid of life forms. On the Earth, the abundance of molecular oxygen is uniquely connected to biological processes, yet on Saturn it cannot be. This may be a useful point to bear in mind during the long search for life on exoplanets; we should not get overexcited about the presence of oxygen.

PLUTO NOT A PLANET
(2006)

The gradual piecemeal increase in our knowledge of the solar system, and especially the outer solar system, was perhaps inevitably going to lead to a review of the way in which we view the system as a whole. In the nineteenth century, the solar system was a relatively simple and straightforward place, a void with the Sun at its centre and half a dozen planets orbiting round it.

The addition of Pluto to the list of planets in 1930 was a turning point. Many astronomers suspected that there were more planets or planetoids out there in the outer reaches of the solar system, and they started searching for them. In the 1940s, Edgeworth speculated that there was an entire belt of small objects, and eventually the Edgeworth-Kuiper Belt was discovered. Several objects close in size to Pluto were discovered, and Pluto was remeasured and found to be a very small planet indeed. By the 1990s, the time was right for a reappraisal of Pluto and the other small bodies in the solar system to decide exactly when a planet was not a planet after all.

In early 2006, there were still nine recognised planets. In order from the Sun they were Mercury, Venus, Earth, Mars, Jupiter, Saturn, Uranus, Neptune and Pluto. By August 2006, there were only eight. In between, the International Astronomical Union agreed a definition for planets, and also agreed that Pluto fails to match the definition. Instead, Pluto was put along with a number of other planetary bodies into a new category of 'dwarf planets'.

Pluto's career as a planet had lasted less than a century. In 1905, Percival Lowell started looking for Planet X, the missing planet beyond Neptune. He had in fact taken a photograph with Pluto showing on it, but he failed to notice or identify it before his death in 1916. Then in

1930 Clyde Tombaugh identified Pluto on a photographic plate and it suddenly acquired its exalted status as a full-blown planet. In 1978, James Christy discovered Pluto's moon, Charon, which seemed to confirm Pluto's planetary status. But then it emerged that Pluto is quite small; even Pluto and Charon together are smaller than our Moon. The recognition of the Kuiper Belt's existence in 1992 was the beginning of a sharp downhill slide in Pluto's status.

In 1999, the astronomers' debate about Pluto's status as a planet was publicised. The press represented this as the threatened demotion of Pluto. The IAU tried to calm the public outcry by saying that they merely wanted to number it – literally give it a number – alongside other Kuiper Belt objects. While this was going on, the composer Colin Matthews decided to compose an additional movement for Gustav Holst's famous orchestral suite *The Planets*. It was an odd moment to choose to do this. Pluto was discovered during Holst's lifetime; Holst lived on for another four years after the discovery was announced, composing new pieces during that time, yet he declined to write a piece for Pluto to add to his *Planets* suite. Now it looks as if Holst was right.

The situation was forced in a completely unexpected way. In January 2005, Michael Brown, a scientist at the California Institute of Technology, discovered a body which he thought might be a tenth planet. It was rocky and icy and it was to be called Xena. At this point, the International Astronomical Union realised that it would have to lay down a strict definition of a planet, so that it would be clearer as new bodies were discovered whether they qualified for planetary status or not. In October 2005, a search team using the Hubble Space Telescope found that Pluto has three moons. This did not qualify Pluto for planetary status, but improved its chances.

In April 2006, the Hubble Space Telescope observers discovered that Xena is slightly larger than Pluto. That meant that if Pluto was regarded as a planet, Xena must be regarded as a planet too. Clearly it was now time for the IAU to act. Within four months, the IAU had reached its decision. Xena was not a planet. Pluto was not a planet either. One of the deciding features the IAU insisted on was the effect that a planet has on its orbit. A planet has to have a sufficient gravitational field to be able to sweep clear its orbit and the immediate neighbourhood of that orbit. Pluto had demonstrably not done that because its orbit crosses over Neptune's.

THE HIGH ENERGY OF THE NORTHERN LIGHTS

(2007)

The fleet of THEMIS spacecraft launched by NASA in early 2007 made some important discoveries about some unusually spectacular displays of the Northern Lights that were called 'substorms'. One amazing and totally unexpected discovery is the existence of giant magnetic ropes that connect the upper atmosphere of the Earth to the Sun. Another is the occurrence of explosions out on the edges of the Earth's magnetic field.

The mission, led by Vassilis Angelopoulos at the University of California, Los Angeles, started producing results within a few weeks of launching. On 23 March 2007, a substorm of Northern Lights erupted across Canada and Alaska. There were strikingly vivid auroras flashing across the sky for over two hours. The substorm was photographed from the ground by a number of cameras set up at different locations. At the same time it was studied from above by the THEMIS satellites. The observers were startled to find that the auroras were flickering westwards very rapidly, twice as fast as they had thought possible. The auroras moved across 15 degrees of longitude, a whole time zone, in effect, in under a minute.

This was the most rigorous and comprehensive study ever made of a display of the Northern Lights. Scientists had been studying substorms for over a hundred years, yet most of what was being learned in March 2007 was completely new. A surprising feature of the substorm was its energy level. The total energy of the two-hour-long event is estimated to be 500,000 billion Joules. This is the energy level of an earthquake measuring 5.5 on the Richter Scale. What could be the source of the energy? The THEMIS satellites had an answer for this too – the Sun. Magnetic ropes were found to connect the Earth's upper atmosphere to the Sun. Solar wind particles flow towards the Earth and into the atmosphere along these ropes and it is the solar wind that supplies the energy for the auroras and geomagnetic storms. A magnetic rope is a plait of magnetic fields, twined in much the same way as a mariner's rope. Some spacecraft had detected evidence of the ropes before, but it needed the array of five THEMIS satellites to map their three-dimensional structure.

THEMIS picked up the first magnetic rope in May 2007. It was huge in scale, as wide as the Earth, and it was located about 64,000 kilometres (40,000 miles) above the Earth's surface, in the magnetopause. This is the boundary layer in the upper atmosphere where the solar wind collides with the Earth's magnetic field and interacts with it. The magnetic rope formed and then dissolved again after only a few minutes. But during that time it acted as a conduit for solar wind energy. Then other ropes formed. These quite bizarre events seemed to be quite a routine occurrence.

The THEMIS satellites also picked up some small explosions in the 'bow shock' area of the Earth's magnetic field. The bow shock is similar to the bow wave that forms at the front of a boat as it travels through the water. The point where the solar wind first bumps into the Earth's magnetic field is very similar to that, and when a knot of magnetism hits the bow shock there is an explosion. The explosions have the effect of heating up the solar wind particles to as high as ten million degrees and can stop the solar wind dead. This seems improbable, because the solar wind moves so fast – 1.6 million kilometres (1 million miles) an hour – but that is what appears to happen.

The THEMIS experiment was an extremely worthwhile one. An enormous amount was learned about auroras – an enormous amount that was both unexpected and exotic in character. The Earth turns out to be a much weirder place than we thought.

THE FIRST EARTH-LIKE PLANET OUTSIDE THE SOLAR SYSTEM
(2007)

Some Swiss astronomers were studying a star close to the brightest star in the constellation of Libra, a red dwarf called Gliese 581, when they noticed that it was wobbling. They were intrigued by this as they understood that there must be something massive though invisible fairly near it exerting a gravitational pull on it. The result of this was the discovery of a large planet, which they called Gliese 581-B. It was obviously too close to its star, subject to too much radiation and just far too hot for it to support any form of life. Then in 2007 the same team of astronomers noticed a second wobble in the star's movement, which implied the existence of a smaller planet further out. This was the cause of great excitement: the first Earth-like planet outside the solar system had been discovered. It is twenty light-years away from the Earth.

This smaller planet, Gliese 581-C, still had five times the mass of the Earth, which meant that it had strong gravity and therefore probably no mountains. Then the initial excitement waned as the implications of the planet's relative closeness to its star and the power of that star, a red dwarf about five times bigger than the Sun, dawned. This planet was almost certainly at the inner edge of the zone of habitability, probably too hostile to sustain life. It began to look as if 581-C was less like the Earth and more like Venus, the runaway-greenhouse planet of the solar system.

Then the Swiss team discovered yet another planet in the same red dwarf system, the third. This they called Gliese 581-D, and it was further out from its host star, probably on the outer edge of the

496

habitable zone. This means that it could be the equivalent of Mars. Frustratingly, too little information is currently available about C or D to be sure, and a much more detailed picture is needed; so far, for instance, nothing is known about the sort of atmosphere, if any, these planets have. If 581-D has an atmosphere containing greenhouse gases, for instance, this may warm it sufficiently to support liquid water and put it in what astronomers call 'the Goldilocks zone' of habitability.

It remains a possibility that a smaller planet orbits the red dwarf midway between C and D, just as the Earth orbits the Sun in the comfort zone between Venus and Mars. But it is an uncomfortable thought that if the Earth was circling just ten per cent closer to the Sun it too would be uninhabitable because it would not be able to retain liquid water.

The SETI project has been searching for intelligent life, and in effect for advanced civilisations, for fifty years now. Its array of antennae has been listening to the sky – and hearing nothing. But it may be simply that the antennae are trained on the wrong stars. The current Kepler project may move the process of searching into more productive territory. Kepler is a new spacecraft that has the specific mission of searching for stars that might have planets circling them. It is designed to detect the 'wink' of a star as one of its planets crosses in front of it. If Kepler can identify a list of stars that have suitable planets, then SETI could be deployed to focus on observing those. This would give a far better chance of finding Earth-like planets with intelligent life on them.

LIGHTNING ON JUPITER

(2007)

Stephen Hawking recently said, 'I think the years ahead will be a golden age of discovery.' The advent of radio telescopes, the Hubble Telescope and space probes has already produced a tsunami of new discoveries about the universe.

In February 2007, a NASA spacecraft named *New Horizons* called in on Jupiter on its way to Pluto. The NASA rocket scientists have discovered that by sending spacecraft through the gravitational fields of planets they can use those fields to add speed to their craft. The spacecraft is hurled like a slingshot on towards its next destination. *Voyager 1* gained extra velocity in this way from both Jupiter and Saturn slingshots. *New Horizons* had a velocity of 58,360 km/h (36,260 mph) in relation to the Earth on launching, ie after its last engine shut down. This was the highest Earth-relative velocity ever achieved by a spacecraft as it left the Earth. The craft has been accelerated to an astonishing 75,640 km/h (47,000 mph) relative to Jupiter (82,000 km/h–51,000 mph relative to the Sun) as a result of its Jupiter slingshot. The extra speed picked up will take three years off the spacecraft's journey to Pluto, which began in January 2006. It is possible to use a sequence of planets in this way to make a kind of high-speed interplanetary highway.

The visit to Jupiter was mainly designed as a fuel stop at a motorway service station. Even so, such visits are enormously expensive and it is an opportunity not to be missed to test out the instruments before reaching Pluto, and incidentally gather some more information about Jupiter.

The spacecraft carried out 700 observations, some of which

confirmed and amplified existing knowledge about Jupiter. But other observations resulted in new discoveries. One was the discovery of lightning in both of Jupiter's polar regions. Lightning is a phenomenon that had up to that moment only been seen on the Earth. Six flashes of lightning in the Jovian Arctic and seven in its Antarctic regions showed that this must be a regular feature of Jupiter's atmosphere. Given that on the Earth lightning is a phenomenon mainly of the warmer middle and low latitudes, these high-latitude lightning flashes were doubly significant. They imply that Jupiter's atmospheric circulation ensures the uniform distribution of heat round the planet, and also the existence of clouds of water vapour.

New Horizons was also able to make the first close-up observations of the Little Red Spot. The Great Red Spot on Jupiter is a well-known and long-lasting vortex in the atmosphere of Jupiter, a feature that has existed for hundreds of years. The Little Red Spot is a newcomer, a recently developed storm that appeared only a few years ago. Although it is called 'little' because it is half the size of the Great Red Spot, it is still seventy times bigger than the Earth and therefore in itself a major feature of the solar system.

New Horizons also passed Jupiter's satellite Io. This moon is volcanically active, and the spacecraft identified the eruption plumes from as many as eleven volcanoes. Some of them had been seen before, but three were new. One eruption plume rose to a height of 320 kilometres (200 miles) above its source, a volcano called Tvashtar. It was possible from these new observations to see how the ejected material, initially as transparent as steam, became visible as the plume cooled down. They were belching out huge volumes of material that travelled hundreds of millions of miles out into space, to be guided in large dense blobs along the tail of Jupiter's magnetic field. The surface of Io displayed over twenty major geological changes in the six years since it was photographed in 2001. The mission confirmed Io as the most active body in the entire solar system.

Very clear images of Jupiter's tenuous ring system were captured for the first time. Tiny moons, Metis and Adrastea, were circling close to the surface of Jupiter, and they were seen to be shepherding the material round the thin rings. The scientists examining the images looked for parent bodies that might have supplied material for the rings (as in Saturn's rings) but could not find any. They were left wondering if Jupiter's rings had evolved in a different way from Saturn's.

New Horizons has sped away from Jupiter, re-energised by its encounter. It has gone on at high speed, continuing on its way to the outer reaches of the solar system. It is due to rendezvous with Pluto and investigate the Kuiper Belt in July 2015. Then we can anticipate more exciting new images to be sent back to Earth and the analysis of those images to lead to more discoveries.

DEFORESTATION AS A CAUSE OF GLOBAL WARMING

(2007)

The rate of destruction of the tropical rainforests became a major cause of concern in the 1980s. Suddenly, environmentalists and the general public all over the world became aware that forests were being lost at such a fast rate that, in as little as one generation, there might be no rainforests left at all.

The causes of deforestation, which was under way by the 1960s, are well known. The rainforests are regions of fairly low-population density yet over-exploitation for timber, agricultural land, mineral resources, settlements and roads. Currently in Brazil 2 million hectares (5 million acres) of forest vanish each year and the figure is likely to increase. The felling for fuel is hard to criticise. In poor countries, firewood is the main, sometimes the only, source of fuel. Commercial logging is a major industry, and large areas are clear-felled to supply building timber and pulp for cardboard and paper consumption in the richer countries. An estimated fifty per cent of the world's timber and seventy-five per cent of the world's paper is consumed by fewer than one-quarter of its people, mainly those living in the United States, Europe and Japan.

The commercial logging that goes in tropical forests is simply unsustainable. The International Tropical Timber Organisation was set up specifically to regulate the international trade in rainforest timber and it stated in 1988 that in the world as a whole there was only a negligible amount of sustainable logging. Robert Repetto of the World Resources Institute has pointed to commercial logging as the biggest single agent of deforestation in the tropics. A similar view was expressed in the World Wide Fund for Nature's study, *Bad Harvest?*, published in 1996.

Some forest is cleared for local food production, but much is cleared for cattle ranching. The beef cattle are raised not for local consumption but for fast food consumed in the United States. It is said that every burger entails the clearance of 5 square metres (50 square feet) of forest – a very high cost. Powerful multinationals are now heavily involved in the commercial exploitation of the forest regions, whether for logging, oil and mineral extraction or power generation. The big hydroelectric power schemes have been responsible for drowning colossal areas of rainforest. These have a direct impact on clearing forest, but an even bigger indirect impact; they entail clearing swathes of forest for highways, railways and settlements.

There was increasing pessimism about the future of the rainforests as regional and global climate changed. The forest itself acted as a giant water reservoir, and clearing it has meant that less water has been retained in what used to be rainforest regions. Areas undergoing forest clearance therefore have a tendency to become desertified anyway. But the warmer conditions from 1980 onwards mean that cleared areas are drying out even faster and the smaller areas of forest that remain become more stressed, and less likely to survive. In other words, it was well known that global warming would have a detrimental effect on the forests.

In the 1980s, there were vigorous campaigns to halt or slow down the destruction of the forest. The powerful landmark television documentary *Decade of Destruction* by Adrian Cowell vividly highlighted some of these. Promises were made by the Brazilian government that things would change, but the rate of destruction has been maintained. The need to drive the national economy towards greater commercial production is powered by debt. In 1992, the Food and Agriculture Organisation (FAO) estimated that globally tropical forests were being lost at a rate of 17 million hectares (65,600 square miles) a year; the World Resources Institute estimate was over 194,250 square kilometres (75,000 square miles). One authority on tropical deforestation, Professor

Norman Myers, said in that same year, 1992, that 'the annual destruction rate seems set to accelerate yet further and could well double in another decade.' The global campaign to highlight the likely future problems associated with global warming has to a great extent overshadowed other environmental issues. Diatribes about climate change and its causes have swamped the concern many environmentalists once expressed for the rainforests. Indeed, many more modest and achievable environmental targets might have been met but for the overriding preoccupation – obsession, even – with man-made carbon dioxide as the cause of warming. There has been a determined effort on the part of politicians and the eco-warriors who supply them with their data and arguments to force people to change their lifestyles, to produce less carbon dioxide.

Then, in 2007, it was discovered that the deforestation programme in all its various forms has been responsible for generating huge volumes of carbon dioxide. The rainforests form an important cooling belt round the equator. Deforestation at its 2007 rate was releasing as much carbon dioxide into the atmosphere in just twenty-four hours as eight million people taking flights from London to New York. The Stern Report commented that deforestation is responsible for producing twenty-five per cent of the greenhouse gases believed (by the writers of the Stern Report) to be responsible for global warming. Transport and industry account for fourteen percent each. Aviation accounts for only three percent. This discovery led to the conclusion that halting deforestation in the tropical rainforests would be the simplest and most effective way of reducing carbon dioxide output. Whether reducing carbon dioxide would have any effect on temperature is another issue. The fact is that if politicians really believe that reduction of carbon dioxide emissions is the most important thing to do they should be turning their focus away from (relatively) harmless travellers and tackling the logging companies, to whom they continue to turn a blind eye.

For some reason, forests were left out of the original Kyoto protocols. They were also, inexplicably, left out of the carbon markets proposed in the most recent report of the International Panel on Climate Change.

Yet they were included in the Stern Report, where they were given major prominence as the best chance of reducing carbon emissions.

One environmentalist has commented, 'Tropical forests are the elephant in the living room of climate change.' Sir Nicholas Stern said that the destruction of the tropical forests during the four-year period 2008–11 alone is set to pump more carbon dioxide into the atmosphere than every flight in the history of aviation until at least 2025. Another recent environmental report has stated bleakly, 'If we lose the forests, we lose the fight against climate change.'

If conserving the rainforests is the best way of reducing carbon emissions, then countries like Brazil need to be given incentives to maintain them. The forests' role in reducing carbon dioxide emissions is only one reason for preserving them. They contain more than fifty per cent of the life on Earth, while covering less than seven per cent of the Earth's surface. They are responsible for generating most of the rainfall on the planet. They are home to 1.6 billion of the poorest people in the world, who depend on the forest for their livelihood.

There are lots of reasons for subsidising and conserving the rainforests. The governments of the rich countries continue to chase will-o'-the-wisp fantasy solutions to the carbon dioxide output problem, backing subsidies for biofuel, carbon capture schemes, and even nuclear power stations. It is as if they are insisting on backing the wrong horse – even when Stern and other recent reports have told them the name of the certain winner in the race.

THE ALTAR OF ZEUS ON MOUNT LYKAION
(2008)

This book ends with a discovery that may seem small in scale compared with some others that are much grander in scope, such as America, evolution, relativity or the Big Bang. But it stands here as representing the many piecemeal discoveries that happen all the time, the discoveries that are too small to make newspaper headlines and yet add significant new pieces of knowledge. In this case, the discovery adds a small piece to the jigsaw of religious beliefs and practices in ancient Greece. It is useful extra information in itself, and carries all sorts of implications; like other discoveries it is a link in a chain, a step in a long staircase, a polyp in a coral reef.

Nearly 2,000 years ago, in the second century AD, the Greek traveller Pausanias visited Mount Lykaion in southern Greece. From the mountain's summit 1,370 metres (4,500 feet) above sea level, he had a breathtaking panoramic view across Arcadia, the heart of the Peloponnese. In his famous guidebook, *Description of Greece*, Pausanias described what he saw there.

On the highest point of the mountain is a mound of earth forming an altar of Zeus Lykaios, and from it the Peloponnesos can be seen. Before the altar on the east stand two pillars, on which there were of old gilded eagles. On this altar they sacrifice in secret to Lykaion Zeus. I was reluctant to pry into the details of the sacrifice; let them be as they are and as they were from the beginning.

A joint Greek-American team of archaeologists investigated the summit of Mount Lykaion in 2004–08, and found evidence confirming

505

that what Pausanias described was true. The site had been investigated before, though not for a hundred years. K. Kontopoulos excavated there in 1897, and K. Kourouniotes in 1902. Between them they discovered that the mound described by Pausanias was indeed a large mound of blackened earth. Its surface was 30 metres (100 feet) in diameter and it stood about 1.5 metres (5 feet) high. The earth altar contained burnt stones, lots of animal bones (belonging to cows and pigs), tiny pieces of pottery dating from the fourth and fifth centuries BC, clay figures, a clay figure of a bird and two small bronze tripods. To the east of the altar they found two stone bases, which were probably the bases for the pillars Pausanias described as supports for the gilded eagles.

There was a great deal of debris that represented the remains of burnt offerings left by worshippers. Among the fragments of offerings were found miniature vases, bronze tripods and rings, an iron spit, iron blades and even silver coins. Large numbers of animal bones were found among the altar debris, so we know for certain that animals were sacrificed to Zeus on Mount Lykaion. Several ancient writers say that human sacrifices took place too. Pausanias seemed anxious not to discuss what went on there, which suggests that he may have known people were being sacrificed, but so far there is no archaeological evidence of this.

One of the most surprising discoveries the archaeologists made was that the worship of Zeus had been going on at the summit of Mount Lykaion for a very long time – from long before the time of classical Greece. Pausanias described the altar of Zeus as consisting of a mound of earth. What the archaeologists found was a huge flattened cone of ash from the pyres of sacrifice, located on the top of the southern peak.

Pottery fragments found at the site showed that dedications were being made at the ash altar as much as 5,000 years ago. The ancient Greeks worshipped Zeus, but they had inherited their god from an earlier pantheon, that of the Minoans, who are known to have worshipped Zeus in the Bronze Age. The Minoans worshipped many other gods too, and its seems that the most powerful of them was Poseidon; Zeus became the most important god later. They also worshipped a range of goddesses, the most powerful of whom was known as Potnia, The Lady.

The archaeologists found a seal made of rock crystal, also Minoan in date, which was deposited on the altar in about 1500 BC. On it was carved the head of a bull, one of the most powerful symbols of the Minoan belief system. The bull was one of the manifestations of the god Poseidon; the bull was the focus of the bull-leaping ceremonies at the Minoan temples. The presence of a Minoan seal on an Arcadian altar shows that there was a link between the people living in Arcadia in 1500 BC and the Minoans, who were the Bronze Age people of Crete. The precise relationship between the dazzlingly innovative Minoan civilisation on Crete and the people of mainland Greece is not known, but the mainlanders were great admirers of the flourishing civilisation on Crete. They copied many aspects of Minoan art, architecture, religion and culture – and were shortly to take over for themselves the Minoan commercial empire, with its lucrative trading operation spreading all over the Aegean.

The Minoans developed a religious cult that focused on mountain tops, where they built peak sanctuaries. There is a fine peak sanctuary on the summit of Mount Juktas, not far to the south of the Minoan city of Knossos. The Mount Juktas sanctuary was discovered and excavated by Arthur Evans, the official discoverer of Knossos, in 1909. There in 2100 BC the Minoans built a triple shrine overlooking a precipice, performed animal sacrifices on a large rectangular altar, burnt the remains on pyres, and swept the ashes down into a jagged crevice in the bare rock. Though in ruins and off the tourist route, it is a place with a marvellous presence, a melodramatic place where even now it seems possible to reach out to the gods.

In time, the powerful priestesses who were based in imposing temples down in the cities brought the rural cults into their own sphere, probably in order to enhance their own power. In the temples they even simulated the peak sanctuaries. In the Labyrinth at Knossos they created a special shrine with wall paintings representing the mountain scenery, and for the priestess they installed a throne carved into the stylized shape of a mountain peak.

This 'urbanised' version of the peak sanctuary cult came later, from about 1650 BC, and after that it looks as if the alfresco cult, with its mountain top ceremonies, gradually died out. But it was widespread, evidently practised on other mountain tops in Crete and elsewhere in the Aegean region. Probably the most significant discovery was that of the peak sanctuary on Mount Petsophas on the eastern coast of Crete, perched on a dizzy precipice above the Minoan town of Palaikastro. Petsophas was discovered and thoroughly explored by J. L. Myres in 1902. His very detailed published description of Petsophas was an important benchmark against which later discoveries might be measured. An archaeological discovery without proper publication is in a sense not really a discovery at all. A discovery must be communicated, shared, to be worthy of the name.

From the evidence archaeologists are now finding on Mount Lykaion, it looks as if the peak sanctuary cult was in full swing in mainland Greece even from the earliest days of the Minoan cult. This is a very surprising discovery indeed.

The idea of worshipping gods on mountain tops was a persistent and widespread one in antiquity. The mountain tops were literally nearer to Heaven. They were also obvious places to set up altars to try to control the forces of nature and propitiate the gods of the weather, and many of the early gods were weather gods. In the *Iliad*, written down for the first time perhaps in 700 BC, Homer frequently refers to Zeus as a cloud-gathering storm god and his home was believed to be on a mountain top, a place of storm clouds, lightning and thunderbolts, Mount Olympus.

Solomon was king of the Israelites at the time when the first temple was built in the city of Jerusalem in around 930 BC. A sequence of events seems to have taken place there that was similar to what had already happened in Minoan Crete 700 years earlier. Solomon extended his power over the Israelite high places, as they were called in the Hebrew scriptures: the peak sanctuaries out in the rural areas. It is easy to imagine a similar process happening all over the Eastern Mediterranean region. As urbanisation got under way, political power was increasingly centralised in the towns. It was quite natural for religious power, the power of the priesthood, to become centralised in the towns too.

Greek mythology contains two traditional birthplaces for Zeus. One was Mount Lykaion in Arcadia. The other was the yawning cave high up on Mount Dikte in Crete. The Diktaian Cave has been described as the Bethlehem of the pre-Christians. The goddess Rhea was said to have given birth to Zeus in the cave. Another tradition had King Minos trekking up to the cave every nine years to meet Zeus. Perhaps the Zeus cult was imported intact to the Greek mainland, complete with the tradition that Zeus was born 'right here'. The summit of Mount Lykaion was certainly used as a focus for worship, as a sacred place, for over 3,000 years.

Below the altar, which represents the accumulated remains of 500 years' worth of sacrifices to Zeus, stretching across a mountain meadow is a hippodrome, an ancient stadium with ancillary buildings. This complex of buildings and running track was designed to accommodate an ancient athletic festival in honour of Zeus and served all Arcadia and attracted pilgrims from all over Greece. This fundamentally religious festival rivalled the similar festival of athletics that was held at Olympia, and formed the model for the modern (but completely secular) Olympic games. The Lykaion festival began in about 700 BC.

The festival games were no longer held at Mount Lykaion in the time of Pausanias, showing that the sanctuary of Zeus was by then already in decline. The Sanctuary of Zeus at Olympia has been very well known since antiquity. It seems strange that this other Sanctuary of Zeus, only 35 kilometres (22 miles) away on Mount Lykaion, should have been so neglected and – but for Pausanias – forgotten. But a lot of knowledge is forgotten and has to be rediscovered. There had been no archaeological excavation at Mount Lykaion for a century before this recent 2004–08 project. The excavations have been a great success and are to continue.

The long-term plan is to create a Mount Lykaion archaeological park to protect the site and the landscape round it; probably it will have a visitor centre. Perhaps then Mount Lykaion will become as well known as the Sanctuary of Zeus at Olympia. There are perhaps thousands of archaeological sites round the world that could be of great interest to informed visitors and general tourists – if only money and effort were invested in drawing people's attention to them.

People's lives can be greatly enriched by having their attention drawn to what is there to be seen in the world around them. This is a process that has been especially successful in the world of wildlife. The media, and committed television documentary makers like Sir David Attenborough and Adrian Cowell in particular, have enormously expanded people's awareness of discoveries about the living environment, and the many controversial conservation issues that surround it. But this has not been done, except fitfully, experimentally and generally unsatisfactorily for discoveries about the landscape. Nor has it been done at all satisfactorily for discoveries about the remains of the past, either in the media or in the landscape itself.

I live in Sussex, which can be taken as a representative English county. Back in the sixth century, Sussex was an autonomous Saxon kingdom, the pioneer kingdom of the South Saxons, founded by the earliest colonists who fled from the European mainland coast when their homes were threatened by the rising sea. Sussex was the focus of an important Bronze Age kingdom too, from 2000 BC until 1500 BC. In the central area of the South Downs, there is a cluster of princely graves containing exotic grave goods; and right at the centre of this cluster of rich graves was a spectacularly rich royal burial in an oak coffin beneath Hove Barrow, a giant barrow that was built for a Bronze Age king of Sussex - and destroyed in 1857.

Sussex had its own rich culture before the Bronze Age too, in the new Stone Age. One by one the cult places of that period, 4000–2500 BC, have been discovered and excavated, mainly by local people and many of them amateur archaeologists. There were six large ditched and banked ceremonial enclosures. Two of them were fortified, one in the western Downs (at The Trundle) and one in the eastern Downs (at Whitehawk on Brighton racecourse). Sixteen oval and long barrows have been discovered, arranged in two clusters, one near The Trundle and one to the east of Whitehawk, between Brighton and Beachy Head. There are three clusters of flint mines, one in the midst of the eastern long barrow group, one in the western long barrow group and one in the middle, to the north of Worthing.

From this pattern of discoveries, we can tell that there were highly organised Stone Age communities under way here, every bit as interesting as the contemporary communities who were busy building Stonehenge and Avebury in the chalklands to the west, and yet there is nothing in the landscape to guide people to these places, not even the discreetest information board, not even a pamphlet available from the local tourist offices, to tell people what they might see or what it might mean.

And this is only a tiny example of what is happening – or rather not happening. Discoveries have been made all over Britain that are not publicised, not assimilated into contemporary culture. The result is a communal lack of appreciation of the past and a consequent separation from it and a vandalising of its relics. It was incomprehension that led to the levelling and total destruction of the Hove Barrow for housing development in the nineteenth century. It was the same lack of appreciation that led to the destruction for gravel extraction of the Earls Barton and Irthlingborough Barrows in Northamptonshire in the twentieth century.

As James the Just said, quoting his brother, 'They know not what they do.'

Discovery is without meaning unless it is communicated, unless it is shared. It is nothing unless it adds to communal knowledge. And far, far too much of what is discovered, whether by explorers, scientists, astronomers, archaeologists or any of the other specialist researchers, is kept within the confines of the academic journals of their respective disciplines. In an earlier section, we explored the tragic story of the discovery of the cause of childbed fever by Ignaz Semmelweis. His discovery was ignored. He became so frustrated by rejection that he became depressed and then descended into clinical insanity. He died in 1865, drowning in a profound sense of failure, beaten to death by the guards at his asylum. Yet four years before he died he wrote a book about his findings, and that book was read by Joseph Lister. Lister took Ignaz Semmelweis's discovery and made it into an event that was more than epoch-making, it was civilisation-changing – the introduction of antiseptic surgery.

Writing down and publishing the discovery made all the difference. The message is the simple and fundamental message of Hector, the teacher in Alan Bennett's play *The History Boys*: 'Pass it on.'

Pass it on.